THE CAMBRIDGE COMPANIC
NINETEENTH-CENTURY THOUGHT

The nineteenth century was seemingly a period of great progress. Huge advancements and achievements were made in science, technology and industry that transformed life and work alike. But a growing pride in modernity and innovation was tainted by a sense of the loss of the past and the multiple threats that novelty posed. *The Cambridge Companion to Nineteenth-Century Thought* provides an impressive survey of the period's major ideas and trends. Leading scholars explore some of the most influential concepts and debates within philosophy, history, political thought, economics, religion and the social sciences, as well as feminism and imperialism. Some of these debates continued into the following century and many still remain relevant in the present day. This Companion is an excellent tool for readers seeking to understand the genesis of modern discourse across a range of humanities and social science subjects.

GREGORY CLAEYS is Professor of the History of Political Thought in the Department of History at Royal Holloway, University of London. He is a specialist in nineteenth-century radicalism and socialism.

A complete list of books in the series is at the back of this book.

THE CAMBRIDGE
COMPANION TO

NINETEENTH-
CENTURY THOUGHT

EDITED BY
GREGORY CLAEYS
Royal Holloway, University of London

CAMBRIDGE
UNIVERSITY PRESS

CAMBRIDGE
UNIVERSITY PRESS

University Printing House, Cambridge CB2 8BS, United Kingdom

One Liberty Plaza, 20th Floor, New York, NY 10006, USA

477 Williamstown Road, Port Melbourne, VIC 3207, Australia

314–321, 3rd Floor, Plot 3, Splendor Forum, Jasola District Centre,
New Delhi – 110025, India

79 Anson Road, #06-04/06, Singapore 079906

Cambridge University Press is part of the University of Cambridge.

It furthers the University's mission by disseminating knowledge in the pursuit of
education, learning, and research at the highest international levels of excellence.

www.cambridge.org
Information on this title: www.cambridge.org/9781107042858
DOI: 10.1017/9781107337541

© Cambridge University Press 2019

First published 2019

Printed in the United Kingdom by TJ International Ltd. Padstow Cornwall

A catalogue record for this publication is available from the British Library.

Library of Congress Cataloging-in-Publication Data
Names: Claeys, Gregory, editor.
Title: The Cambridge companion to nineteenth-century thought /
edited by Gregory Claeys, Royal Holloway, University of London.
Description: Cambridge, United Kingdom; New York, NY: Cambridge
University Press, 2019. | Series: Cambridge companions to literature |
Includes bibliographical references and index.
Identifiers: LCCN 2019000695 | ISBN 9781107042858 (hardback) |
ISBN 9781107696143 (paperback)
Subjects: LCSH: Civilization, Modern – 19th century. | Intellectual life – History –
19th century. | BISAC: LITERARY CRITICISM / European / English, Irish, Scottish, Welsh.
Classification: LCC CB417.C36 2019 | DDC 909.81–dc23
LC record available at https://lccn.loc.gov/2019000695

ISBN 978-1-107-04285-8 Hardback
ISBN 978-1-107-69614-3 Paperback

CONTENTS

CONTENTS

ADAM BUDD is Lecturer in British History at the University of Edinburgh and Senior Fellow of the Higher Education Academy. He is the editor of *The Modern Historiography Reader: Western Sources* (2009) and author of numerous studies in eighteenth-century culture. His documentary study of authorship, editing and bookselling during the Scottish Enlightenment is forthcoming.

GREGORY CLAEYS is Professor of the History of Political Thought at Royal Holloway, University of London. He is the author of *Machinery, Money and the Millennium: From Moral Economy to Socialism* (1987), *Citizens and Saints: Politics and Anti-Politics in Early British Socialism* (Cambridge University Press, 1989), *Thomas Paine: Social and Political Thought* (1989), *The French Revolution Debate in Britain* (2007), *Imperial Sceptics: British Critics of Empire, 1850–1920* (Cambridge University Press, 2010), *Searching for Utopia: The History of an Idea* (2011; German, Spanish, Portuguese, Japanese editions), *Mill and Paternalism* (Cambridge University Press, 2013), *Dystopia: A Natural History* (2016) and *Marx and Marxism* (2018). He has edited *The Cambridge Companion to Utopian Literature* (Cambridge University Press, 2010), *The Cambridge History of Nineteenth-Century Political Thought* (with Gareth Stedman Jones, Cambridge University Press, 2011) and some fifty volumes of primary sources and criticism.

MIKE GANE is Professor Emeritus in the School of Social Sciences, Loughborough University, UK. He has degrees from Leicester University (BA Sociology) and the LSE (PhD Sociology). His main focus of research has concerned the origins and development of social theory with monograph studies of Comte, Durkheim and Mauss, Foucault and Baudrillard. He is currently interested in researching the legacy of the 1960s to subsequent social theory, particularly in the context of the evolution of neoliberalism and globalisation.

WENDY HAYDEN is Associate Professor of English at Hunter College, City University of New York (CUNY), where she directs first-year composition and teaches classes in history of rhetoric, gender and rhetoric, and composition theory and practice. Her book, *Evolutionary Rhetoric: Sex, Science, and Free Love in*

Nineteenth-Century Feminism, was published in 2013. She has published articles in *College Composition and Communication* (CCC), *The Journal of Academic Librarianship*, *Rhetoric Review* and *Rhetoric Society Quarterly*, as well as several book chapters. Her research interests include nineteenth-century feminist rhetoric, rhetorics of sexual literacy, composition and information literacy pedagogy and archival research and digital scholarship in undergraduate research.

SAREE MAKDISI is Professor of English and Comparative Literature at the University of California, Los Angeles. His most recent books are *Reading William Blake* (Cambridge University Press, 2015), *Making England Western: Occidentalism, Race and Imperial Culture* (2014) and *Palestine Inside Out: An Everyday Occupation* (2008).

ROGER SMITH is Reader Emeritus in History of Science, Lancaster University, UK, Honorary Fellow of the Institute of Philosophy of the Russian Academy of Sciences, Moscow and an independent scholar. He has written and taught on intellectual history, especially of psychology and the human sciences. Most recently, he is the author of *Free Will and the Human Sciences in Britain, 1870–1910* (2013), *Between Mind and Brain: A History of Psychology* (2013) and *The Sixth Sense of the Avant-Garde: Dance, Kinaesthesia and the Arts in Revolutionary Russia* (with Irina Sirotkina, 2017). He is currently publishing an intellectual history of the sense of movement.

KEITH TRIBE is Senior Research Fellow at the University of Tartu as well as an independent scholar and translator with a background in history and the social sciences. Among his recent publications are *The Economy of the Word* (2015), *The Contradictions of Capital in the Twenty-First Century* (edited with Pat Hudson, 2016) and *The History of Economics: A Course for Students and Teachers* (with Roger E. Backhouse, 2017). His new translation of Schiller's *Aesthetic Education of Man* was published in 2016 and his new translation of Max Weber, *Economy and Society*, Part I is to be published in 2019.

NORMAN VANCE is Emeritus Professor of English Literature and Intellectual History at the University of Sussex and Visiting Professor at Ulster University. His research has focused on the interplay of literature, society and religious thought particularly in nineteenth-century Britain and Ireland. His publications include *The Sinews of the Spirit: The Ideal of Victorian Christian Manliness* (1985, repr. 2009), *Irish Literature Since 1800* (2002) and *Bible and Novel: Narrative Authority and the Death of God* (2013). He edited *The Oxford History of Classical Reception 1790–1880* (with Jennifer Wallace, 2015). He has served as a peer reviewer for the Irish Research Council and the UK Arts and Humanities Research Council and is a former trustee of the English Association.

GEORGIOS VAROUXAKIS is Professor of the History of Political Thought at Queen Mary University of London, and Co-director of the Centre for the Study of the History of Political Thought. He works on the history of political thought (British, French and American, nineteenth and twentieth centuries), with particular emphasis on political thought on nationalism, patriotism and cosmopolitanism, intellectual history of ideas of 'the West' and ideas of 'Europe' and political thought on international relations and imperialism. His books include *Liberty Abroad: J. S. Mill on International Relations* (2013), *Mill on Nationality* (2002), *Victorian Political Thought on France and the French* (2002) and *Contemporary France: An Introduction to French Politics and Society* (with David Howarth, 2003).

NORBERT WASZEK is Professor of German (History of Ideas) at the University of Paris VIII. He was educated in Germany (MA Bochum 1978), in Scotland (MLitt. Stirling 1980) and at Cambridge (PhD Christ's College 1984), then submitted his professorial thesis (Habilitation) at the Sorbonne (Paris I, 1998). His books include *Man's Social Nature: A Topic of the Scottish Enlightenment in Its Historical Setting* (1986) and *The Scottish Enlightenment and Hegel's Account of Civil Society* (1988).

JOHN E. WILSON is Professor Emeritus of Church History at Pittsburgh Theological Seminary. From 1972 until 1984 he was an ordained minister in the Reformed Church of Switzerland. He holds the Habilitation in Theology (theol. habil.) from the University of Basel. He is the author of *Schelling und Nietzsche* (1996), *Schellings Mythologie* (1993), *Introduction to Modern Theology, Trajectories in the German Tradition* (2007) and *Der christliche Overbeck* (2017).

ACKNOWLEDGEMENTS

Thanks go to all the contributors for their hard work in bringing this volume together, and at the Press, to Bethany Thomas, Tim Mason and Linda Bree for their assistance throughout the commissioning and production process.

CHRONOLOGY

I

GREGORY CLAEYS

Introduction

There is one great fact, characteristic of this our nineteenth century, a fact that no party dares deny. On the one hand, there have started into life industrial and scientific forces, which no epoch of the former human history had ever suspected. On the other hand, there exist symptoms of decay, far surpassing the horrors recorded of the latter times of the Roman Empire. In our days, everything seems pregnant with its contrary. Machinery, gifted with the wonderful power of shortening and fructifying human labour, we behold starving and overworking it. The new-fangled sources of wealth, by some strange weird spell, are turned into sources of want. The victories of art seem bought by the loss of character. At the same pace that mankind masters nature, man seems to become enslaved to other men or to his own infamy. Even the pure light of science seems unable to shine but on the dark background of ignorance. All our invention and progress seem to result in endowing material forces with intellectual life, and in stultifying human life into a material force. This antagonism between modern industry and science on the one hand, modern misery and dissolution on the other hand; this antagonism between the productive powers and the social relations of our epoch is a fact, palpable, overwhelming, and not to be controverted.[1]

No judgement on an epoch stands forever. Karl Marx's prophecy that 'the emancipation of the Proletarian' was 'the secret of the nineteenth century' has come and gone without being realised, a mighty effort notwithstanding. His sense of the extraordinariness of the times, however, and of the juxtaposition of exultant promise and alarming decay, remain with us. Every epoch is unique, and few resist flattery in proclaiming the superiority of their collective selves. The nineteenth century was the most optimistic period in humanity's voyage, and it rarely failed to proclaim its triumphs, and to exult in its marvels. Its shortfalls were less often acknowledged.

Yet we must concede some of this immodesty. Three features of the period are outstanding among many. First, humanity moved in immense numbers into cities, leaving behind the rural existence and the dust of 10,000 harvests that had defined the lives of most since time immemorial. For most the pace of life increased dramatically, and a sense of secular historical time displaced an attitude towards nature and cosmos in a space now defined by bewildering novelty and an ever-multiplying volume and increasing intensity of stimulae. Humanity's outlook and identity now became increasingly and fundamentally urban. By the century's end, many embraced the Babel-like glass and concrete skyscraper, modernity reaching up to conquer the heavens, as the embodiment of the era's aspirations. Second, unparalleled innovations and marvellous achievements in science and technology transformed work and life alike. Third, the desire for liberty, for collective control, for independence from oppression and exploitation, extended itself from individuals to class, gender, nation and race, in an increasingly conscious and universal effort to encompass all humanity (see Chapter 2 by Georgios Varouxakis, which treats this in the context of the growth of a variety of liberalisms). The slave trade and then slavery were virtually abolished by the time Lincoln emancipated American blacks in 1861 and the Tsar Russian serfs in 1863. From 1848 onwards, in particular, European nations began to demand their independence from the servitude of great empires, and to proclaim the desirability of unity based on the identifying group bonds of nation, language and ethnicity. But nations, too, had many excluded 'others' – gypsies, criminals, minorities of all types – as Saree Makdisi's contribution in Chapter 11 shows us. Gradually non-whites began to claim rights formerly jealously guarded by propertied white males, rebelling in colonies and empires and gaining increasing recognition as legitimate claimants. Slowly, across this period, too, the female half of humanity forced its claims to recognition and dignity. By the century's end the 'subjection of women', as John Stuart Mill and Harriet Taylor Mill termed it, was widely assailed. Women attained the vote for the first time in several nations, and began to emerge from confinement in 'separate spheres', as Wendy Hayden shows in Chapter 10. These challenges to the arrogance of established order in the name of 'emancipation' and 'liberation' constituted the 'spirit of the age' for many.

These were monumental achievements for a species habituated to and seemingly dependent on servitude. In each of these features, and most of all in their combination, the epoch offered or at least suggested the alluring promise of emancipation and of a world defined by universal rights and the universal recognition of human dignity. The long nineteenth century (1789–1914/17/18) was thus an era in which, at least in Europe and the Americas, Christian ideas of Providence were succeeded by a concept of 'progress' that seemingly promised opulence, greater personal autonomy, the extension of life, the conquest of disease and the prospect of happiness for the many. This induced and was driven by a feeling of secular utopianism in which the old heaven now seemed nearly transplanted to the new earth, and the future sacred timeless space became an imminent secular euchronia, or good time.

Science and technology took pride of place in underpinning this ideal: for most, the good time meant good things in abundance. After the steam engine and railway came, by the century's end, the telegraph and telephone, radio and the cinema, refrigeration, radiation, the internal combustion engine, the aeroplane, automatic weapons and countless other inventions. The Baconian promise of mastering nature was now seemingly fulfilled. To attain legitimacy, an approach to any subject now had to be 'scientific'. Optimism suffused the age as the old, the traditional, the irrational and obscure, cherished and time-worn custom, seemed everywhere challenged by the new and the radical. Youth itself seemed to exemplify progress. From now on every generation began to define itself by its distance from, rather than its proximity to, its parents and ancestors. Cults and movements of reform sprang up to brand these claims, with names like Young Germany, Young Italy and the Young Hegelians. Novelty itself became commendable, as 'old' as such came to seem primitive and suited only to humanity's infancy and immaturity. In politics new opinions were increasingly democratic opinions, as the majority began to claim its sovereignty. As the eighteenth century receded, the principles of the Enlightenment and the American and French revolutions now seemed destined to conquer the monsters of kingly despotism and priestly superstition. The power of public opinion, and of the emerging press, seemed to prove the primacy of profane over sacred knowledge. Everywhere reason seemed to be on the march, defining humanity's final coming of age.

Much of this optimism now appears illusory. As Marx indicated at mid-century, such a powerful sense of promise and hope could not but prove delusional and did not last. The early warning signs were clear and ominous: progress had winners and losers. The former few indeed, it seemed, only prospered at the expense of the latter many. In 1798 Thomas Robert Malthus' *Essay on Population* already warned of an inevitable 'surplus population' of the poor. In the first great work of economic analysis of the epoch, *On the Principles of Political Economy and Taxation* (1817), David Ricardo took this to mean subsistence wages for the working classes were permanent: the poor were doomed to remain poor. But the rich seemed equally destined to become richer. Examining the concentration of wealth that the capitalist mode of production promoted, and that was accelerated by every economic crisis, Karl Marx assumed class struggle to result inevitably, and deduced from this the inevitability of a proletarian revolution that would usher in an ideal communist society of peace and plenty. Meanwhile conditions of work in the new 'manufactories' were much more arduous and hazardous than traditional agricultural labour. Already by 1820 doctors in the factory districts pointed to crippling disabilities and reduced life expectancy among those tending the new machines. The narrower division of labour, increasingly reducing work to single repetitive tasks, did indeed produce the 'mental mutilation' of which Adam Smith had warned. Outside work the situation was not much better. Observers of the degradation of the new urban slums echoed the gloom and despair that hung over them. Even to the newly triumphant bourgeoisie, the commercial and industrial middle classes, modern urban life, which loosened the traditional bonds of authority, implied some disorientation, loss, alienation and anxiety. The limits of consumerism and maximised stimulation for amusement were already evident, though they were still far from reached. Their comforts were also threatened by the growing claims of the dispossessed. The revolution of 1789 seemingly revealed a rising tide of expectations of greater social equality and more universal prosperity. To landowners and the well-to-do the subsequent revolutions of 1830, 1848 and 1871 threatened still more disruption to come. By 1918 most of the great European monarchies had been replaced by republics. To some intellectuals, like Friedrich Nietzsche, however, democracy meant little more than mob rule, and reversion to an atavistic, primitive type of humanity. Resistance to the claims of equality had been present from early on in the nineteenth century, however. The defence of genius, or the culture of the few, sometimes identified with classical Greece, more often with the aristocracy, attempted to counterbalance the onslaught of mediocrity, with ultimately very mixed results.

Everywhere, thus, modernity seemed to herald strife and conflict between old and new, and rich and poor. My introductory chapter here suggests that by the time the century's most influential text – Charles Darwin's *On the Origin of Species* (1859) – appeared, it seemed obvious that the price of progress, a process in the coming decades that would be increasingly conceived as the 'survival of the fittest', might well be very high indeed for those – whole classes and races – who were now deemed 'unfit' for this brave new modern world. Here humanity was defined by biological science. It was indeed 'evolving', but whether the gain outweighed the pain was a moot point, and the destination remained unclear. Darwin expressed, however, one crucial limit to what remains for us the dominant liberal paradigm, defined by ideals of toleration and the extension of rights. What good were wistful 'rights' proclamations when nature's course was far more certain? How indeed could any morality but the right of the strong prevail? And the strong now were the wealthy, especially the commercial classes. Their god was money. 'Our people have no ideals now that are worthy of consideration', lamented Mark Twain in 1906, the 'Christianity we have always been so proud of' now being replaced by 'a shell, a sham, a hypocrisy'.[2]

To those who saw the losses entailed by these processes as outweighing the gains, the dark clouds of cultural pessimism began gathering well before the celebratory decadence of the *fin de siècle* epoch arrived. The worst forebodings were fulfilled with the colossal slaughter of the First World War. Yet then the Bolshevik Revolution of 1917 proclaimed another starting point for humanity, promising a universally inclusive vision of industrial prosperity, peace and brotherhood in which empires would be renounced and Enlightenment extended even further beyond its hitherto established boundaries. To its critics in turn, however, Bolshevism represented an age of proletarian masses in which the gentlemanly values that defined civility would erode in the face of the incessantly vulgar egalitarianism of the many, as a manifestly public desire physically to exterminate the old aristocracy and the new bourgeoisie alike became increasingly apparent. Bolshevism's cosmopolitanism had an uphill struggle, too. Against the scenario that the many would inherit the earth, embracing one another as brothers and sisters, was pitted nationalist fantasies in which particular peoples became the chosen few. Many countries, notably the young United States, regarded themselves as providentially inheriting the earth for their benefit. Britons often assumed their mighty empire proved the same point. So did France. In continental Europe, Houston Stewart Chamberlain announced the 'Germanic peoples' had entered on the stage of history in *The Foundations of the Nineteenth Century* (1910), in fulfilment of their Teutonic destiny, an ideal to which Hegel and even to some degree Marx subscribed (Norbert Waszek details the former's enduring influence on the period in Chapter 4). But this was to be achieved, like everything else, only through 'struggle'.

By 1914 this struggle was symbolised, perhaps more than anything else, by the Maxim or automatic 'machine' gun, which made imperial conquest so much easier, but that boomeranged with devastating effect upon its European inventors when the Great War commenced. Now the fantasy of remaking the world was transformed into the reality of destroying it. The cataclysm of 1914–18 came all the more as a surprise given the sense of authoritative rational discovery and conquest that extended equally across the globe and across all fields of human knowledge in the preceding century. Collectively the chapters in this volume demonstrate how rapid and persuasive was the transfer of authority from traditional sources to the new. Theology gave ground steadily to the onward march of the natural and social sciences, which made strong claims respecting objectivity and predictability and thus their own epistemological supremacy (see John E. Wilson's account in Chapter 3 of the trajectories of theological criticism). History offered itself as a master science increasingly focused on evidence and the interpretation of empirical fact, as Adam Budd shows us in Chapter 6. Political economy even more successfully proclaimed itself in command of the interpretation of the laws of social nature, though its proclamation of the inevitability and superiority of 'capitalism', as Keith Tribe indicates in Chapter 7, was hardly uncontested. And, as Mike Gane demonstrates in Chapter 5, the social sciences were not long in following suit in assuming some of the authority of the natural sciences. Theology lingered longer on the fringes of this debate, and sometimes at the centre, than sceptics imagined it would. Its defeat in several key areas, most notably in the debates over Darwinian evolutionism, offered new justifications for oppression, conquest and even the extermination of less 'efficient' or 'fit' peoples, as the moral demands of Christian mercy gave way to scientific imperatives (but in the early modern era Christianity had marched hand in hand with imperial conquest everywhere). Where the conquest of knowledge promised slow, gradual improvement, here its results heralded, once again, intolerance, struggle and bloodshed in the name of 'progress'.

The chapters in this volume attest to the fact, then, that ambiguity haunted the nineteenth century virtually from the outset. A growing pride in modernity was mixed with the sense of loss of much of the past, and the multiple threats that novelty posed. The erosion of older forms of identity – rural, local, religious – was made up for in part by new ones, both larger (nationalism, imperialism) and smaller (the individual self). Pride of place is often given to the later modern 'invention' (which was really only a redefinition) of the self. Writers like Samuel Butler (in *Erewhon*, 1872) made clear that humanity had begun to act consciously like the machines that were its notional slaves, commencing a servitude that threatened a very uncertain future. Humanity's growing sense of individual identity swelled with and yet was also alarmed by the 'discoveries' of the unconscious and, with eyes somewhat averted, sexuality, with Freud, as Roger Smith indicates in Chapter 8. Its sense of group identity expanded with the proclamation of 'rights' of individuals and groups alike; and with new feelings of the collective, whether the madding crowd of Le Bon or the proletariat of Marx, of the nation and of the empire. After political economy and history, psychology too now put forward its claim to be considered a master science. In biography, autobiography and literature (as Norman Vance indicates in Chapter 12), the celebration of self embraced the feeling of uniqueness, the new sense of the public space, the confessional mode of personal unfolding and the cult of celebrity. The claim of superior, civilised individuality made it easier for nations to encompass vast territories of empires and colonies as conquests extended the European idea globally under the common racist pretence that non-whites would welcome it. New nations, especially the United States, could affect an innocence and virtue that the older palpably lacked. Millions embraced the new America as a beacon of hope and equality when Europe itself seemed to flag. All the leading nations imagined themselves superior to the rest, and smiled upon by God, even as slaughter in the trenches commenced. But America in particular came to embody the promise of well-being for the many. Here individuals sought happiness with a fervency their ancestors would have marvelled at. Here, and increasingly everywhere else, they found it (when they found it), by and large, through trafficking in commodities, through acquiring and using things. The utopia of modernity would ultimately come to be defined as much by this process of acquisition, possession and consumption as the desire for equality. The consequences were exhilarating but upsetting. Though the spell of modernity is now largely broken, it is a combination we have learned to live with.

NOTES

1 Karl Marx and Frederick Engels, *Collected Works*, 50 vols. (London: Lawrence & Wishart, 1975–2005), vol. 14, pp. 655–6.
2 Mark Twain, *Autobiography of Mark Twain*, 3 vols. (Berkeley: University of California Press, 2010–15), vol. 1, p. 462.

2

GEORGIOS VAROUXAKIS

State and Individual in Political Thought

Liberalism and democracy are wrongly seen as inseparable by many people today – despite the alarming evidence provided by some governments that are democratically elected yet behave in strikingly illiberal ways. But liberalism and democracy are neither necessarily interchangeable nor allied, either conceptually or historically. The playground on which the relationship was forged and first tested was nineteenth-century politics and thought in Europe and America. It was also in the nineteenth century that the diverse meanings of the two terms were debated and established. For there was neither one 'liberalism' nor one meaning of 'democracy'. Far from it – we are dealing with 'essentially contested concepts' here. The dramatic escalation of events and succession of regimes during the French Revolution, ending up with the usurpation of power by Napoleon Bonaparte – before he was defeated by the united European great powers – meant that a new world had dawned, or so it seemed to many. Several political systems had been tried and failed within a couple of decades, but that only whetted thinkers' appetite for reflection on the reasons for the failures and for proposals for doing (or failing!) better next time.

Having said the above about the French Revolution, it is important to avoid Eurocentrism as much as possible and remember that the story of democracy and of thinking about democracy in the modern world was a quintessentially transatlantic affair. Apart from the brief and controversial experiments in France during a phase of the French Revolution, it was the United States of America that provided the world with the unprecedented experiment of an extended republic whose government was based on elections on an extended franchise (the voting systems of the different states varied, but they were based on a far wider electoral base than was the case in, say, Britain in the first half of the nineteenth century). And though the American authors of the *Federalist Papers* (1788) had tried hard to dissociate the new American constitution they were defending from 'democracy' (by which they meant what we understand as direct democracy on the

8

Athenian model) and to call their proposed regime 'a republic', by the first decades of the nineteenth century the American system was widely called a 'democracy'. Thus when a French aristocrat went to America to study the future of Europe, he called the resulting book *De la démocratie en Amérique* (*Democracy in America* (1835, 1840).[1] And thanks both to the French aristocrat's reflections and to other travellers' reports and comments, it was the American experiment that was the main testing ground for debates on democracy in Britain as well as elsewhere in Europe.[2]

The *Federalist Papers* were not the only manifestation of American political thought that combined theoretical reflection with immediate (and indeed urgent) practical aims. American nineteenth-century political thought remained very close to day-to-day political action, perhaps due to the fact that the American political system was closer to democracy than any other at the time and thus until well after the American Civil War (1861–5) most of the political thought work was produced by people who were at the same time major political actors.[3] Meanwhile, it is also useful to remember that, in nineteenth-century America, '[i]n the realm of ideas the renaissance was largely dominated by old-world thought'.[4] Thus, though America was increasingly important, both as a producer of ideas and as a playground for political experiments, space limitations here mean that we can only focus on some major European thinkers and currents, characteristic of broader movements and influential far beyond the Old Continent.

A major factor that needs to be stressed is the memory of the French Revolution and the overwhelming sense displayed by most political thinkers in the early and mid-nineteenth century that they had to find a new equilibrium following the upheavals of the period 1789–1815. France was bound to feel the tectonic movements more directly and inevitably most French thinkers were very busy thinking about a new dispensation.[5] But others in the rest of Europe could not be unaffected either. The enormity of the cataclysm that had hit Europe in the previous decades led several of the early nineteenth-century thinkers to search for a synthesis that would overcome the competing forces that had clashed in the past, by combining them. Hegel is the best-known of these thinkers seeking a synthesis (but far from the only one). Thus Hegel's political philosophy in *Philosophie des Rechts* (1821) was 'a grand synthesis of all the conflicting traditions of the late eighteenth and early nineteenth centuries. Its theory of the state wedded liberalism with communitarianism; its doctrine of right fused historicism, rationalism and voluntarism; its vision of ideal government united aristocracy, monarchy and democracy; and its politics strove for the middle ground between left and right, progress and reaction.' In other words 'Hegel saw himself as the chief synthesiser, as the last mediator, of his age. All the conflicts between opposing standpoints would finally be resolved – their truths preserved and their errors cancelled – in a single coherent system.' And the attraction of Hegel's political philosophy lay 'in its syncretic designs, in its capacity to accommodate all standpoints; any critique of the system, it seemed, came from a standpoint whose claims had already been settled within it'.[6] But the aspiration to combine the opposing currents of the time in a new synthesis was also the ambition of thinkers as diverse as Saint-Simon, Auguste Comte, John Stuart Mill and many others. Some of these attempts at synthesis were more 'liberal' than others, meanwhile (Comte cannot be called 'liberal' by any stretch of the term's meaning).

It is not easy to define or describe 'liberalism' in the nineteenth century. The variety of theories calling themselves 'liberal' and seen by later historians as 'liberal' is bewildering. But a felicitous way of grasping some of the versions and nuances is proposed by H. S. Jones, who argues that one can define liberalism's limits through a set of oppositions. One of the oppositions Jones draws attention to is that formulated by Pierre Rosanvallon between British and French ideas of liberty. French ideas of liberty are not compatible with English liberalism according to Rosanvallon. The two traditions are characterised by competing solutions to the problem of the relationship between power and freedom. The British liberal solution was to pursue freedom through the limitation of power by establishing checks and balances as well as guarantes of individual securities or rights. The solution preferred by most French liberals was the rational control of power, not its limitation[7] (it is noteworthy that a similar distinction had been proposed by John Stuart Mill in the nineteenth century to describe what he saw as crucial differences in the 'national characters' of the French and the English respectively[8]). As Jones correctly notes, the antithesis Rosanvallon proposed is valid, but only to the extent that it describes the dominant strain of liberalism in each of the two countries; but it is important to remember, Jones stresses, that the antithesis occurs also within each of these countries (and that the Anglophiles from Montesquieu onwards were closer to the 'English' version than to the dominant French, while, on the other hand, someone like Jeremy Bentham fitted better a 'French-style rationalist' type than the tradition of English liberalism as described by Rosanvallon).[9]

Meanwhile, Rosanvallon himself, in another essay, although he distinguishes between 'economic liberalism', 'political liberalism' and 'moral liberalism', nevertheless argues that it can be legitimate to speak of 'liberalism in the singular', and to see liberalism as 'a single prospect of emancipation at work' provided one accepts that liberalism is not a doctrine, but rather that *liberalism is a culture. From this comes both its unity and contradictions*'. Thus 'Liberalism is the culture at work in the modern world that since the beginning of the seventeenth century has been attempting to win emancipation from both royal and religious authority ... Its unity is that of a *problematic field*, a work to accomplish, a sum of aspirations.' According to Rosanvallon, '[t]he intellectual history of liberalism finds the unity of its object in [the] search for an alternative to inherited relations of power and dependence'.[10]

So who were the liberals, what did they stand for and what did they make of democracy? Given the diversity and polysemy we have just referred to, the best way to answer that question is to focus on the main contributions of some selected seminal thinkers. One of the most influential thinkers who reflected on the relationship between democracy and liberty was Alexis de Tocqueville (1805–59). Born to a Norman aristocratic family that had paid a high price for its royalism at the hands of the Terror during the French Revolution, Tocqueville was an unlikely champion of the irreversible march of democracy. And yet, he did argue that the advent of 'democracy' was a providential fact of history and that instead of resisting it, those who worried about some of its possible effects ought to work towards guiding it away from those dangerous consequences rather than attempt to resist its coming. The latter enterprise would be futile, he insisted. As John Stuart Mill put it in a review of Tocqueville's classic book, *Democracy in America*, Tocqueville's claim was that the march of democracy was like a river. Attempting to stop or reverse the course would be as futile as attempting to turn back the flow of a river. But one could always divert the flow of a river to avoid flooding particular cities or areas one wanted to protect. That was quite a felicitous metaphor for what Tocqueville had set out to do.

It is important to clarify that by 'democracy' Tocqueville meant at least two different things. Scholars have identified many different meanings of the term in Tocqueville's long book, but they all boil down to two major senses in which 'democracy' was used, one political and another social. In the political sense Tocqueville used 'democracy' to describe a representative political system based on an extensive franchise – a meaning more or less similar to what democracy means today, except that today the franchise is expected to be universal, whereas in the nineteenth century, restrictions of gender (men only), property qualifications (only those who paid a certain minimum of taxes having the vote) and minimum educational qualifications (only those who could read and write, for example, being allowed to vote), etc. were acceptable and highly recommended by most liberals. The other sense in which Tocqueville used 'democracy' is more complex. It meant a social state (or 'state of society') in which the most prevalent characteristic and value was 'equality of conditions'. Equality of conditions did not mean equality of wealth. It meant equality of status. There had been, Tocqueville explained, a slow but steadily advancing equalisation of conditions in the Christian world over the previous seven centuries. From a feudal world where the aristocrats could not conceive of the serfs who worked for them as belonging to the same species as themselves, there had been a gradual process whereby people were coming to be more and more equal in front of the law and in terms of status and respect. That process had many drawbacks and dangers, according to Tocqueville, and a high price was to be paid in terms of individual greatness, taste and other values thriving in an aristocratic state of society. But it was also more just, and therefore preferable. So he did not want to advocate any attempts to stem the advent of the democratic state of society (a thing that would be impossible in any case), but rather to warn of the implications and recommend ways in which its worst repercussions could be averted. Tocqueville identified some particularly insidious dangers. He argued that in a democratic state of society, such as America was, the principle of equality became the dominant principle or value and permeated every aspect of society. One of the results of that was that each person's reason was considered to be as good as another's, and any authority was undermined. Given that societies needed some authority, ultimately, however, the only authority left in a democratic state of society was the authority of numbers. Once a majority emerged on an issue, people immediately accepted that the majority must be right, and even those who took a different view started internalising the majority opinion.

The other dangerous tendency Tocqueville identified was that people in a democratic state of society would tend to withdraw from any public or collective affairs and concentrate on their individual and family concerns and mainly on their own material advancement. He emphasised that in America he noticed that people were restless and unhappy in the midst of their relative prosperity. He attributed that to the fact that, in a democratic social state, where equality of conditions reigns, the race is open to all, and therefore, those who fail in the race feel they have only themselves to blame (unlike what would be the case in a status-bound aristocratic society, where people's fate was determined by the social positions or status they inherited from birth). Those factors made for a pervasive individualism in democratic societies. Both of the drawbacks Tocqueville identified had very dangerous political implications, he thought. The elevation of the authority of numbers to the role he described meant that there was a serious danger of the 'tyranny of the majority', of majorities crushing everyone and everything that did not agree with them each time. That was a lethal danger for what Tocqueville valued more than anything else: liberty – a 'sacred' thing in his eyes. The individualist tendency to isolation and neglect of any collective or public concern would lead to the atomisation of society and therefore to the impotence of individuals in front of an ever more powerful governing power at the centre. Ever-increasing centralisation was going to be the result. The main danger that followed from all the above was what Tocqueville called a 'soft despotism'. The government and its agents would usurp more and more powers, they would undertake to do more and more for society and individuals, meanwhile individuals would be pleased to be left alone to their money-making pursuits and to have more and more things done for them by the state. Thus this new form of despotism would not be cruel, it would not torture people on the wheel and the like, but would rather be insidious and soft, paralysing their will to freedom, individuality and difference and leaving them more and more impotent in the face of an all-powerful central power.

Interestingly, Tocqueville also saw some potential signs of hope for the future within the American society that he studied for clues to the future of democracy. He thought that some of the dangers inherent in a demo-cratic state of society might be offset by some of the effects of democracy in the political sense, at least as the latter worked in the United States. Thus freedom of the press, the existence of political parties, the federal nature of the American constitution and, most importantly, habits and institutions of local self-government and voluntary associations in America gave him hope that such substitutes for older 'intermediary bodies' might be able to resist the omnipotence of the central government and preserve freedom in a demo-cratic society.[11] Tocqueville's great anxiety was that most of these habits that he identified as positive and hopeful in America were absent from France and were more likely to be incidental to the circumstances and origin of the 'Anglo-Americans' than inherent in the democratic state of society. Hence his deep anxiety about the future of liberty in a socially democratic France.

Another thinker who had deeply reflected on the sociological preconditions of political regimes and institutions – and had significantly influenced Tocqueville – was the French historian and politician François Guizot (1787–1874). Guizot was for a long time neglected but has now been recognised by historians to have exerted a considerable influence on nineteenth-century liberal thought globally. During the last years of the Bourbon restoration (1815–30) Guizot, a member of the liberal opposition to the regime, gave a series of particularly influential lectures at the Sorbonne. In the published version of some of those lectures, in his *History of Civilization in Europe* (first published in French in 1828), Guizot argued that there was a dis-tinctive feature unique to modern European civilisation, which made for its 'particular physiognomy.' All civilisations that had preceded that of modern Europe, 'in Asia or elsewhere, including even Greek and Roman civiliza-tion', struck one with 'the unity which pervades them. They seem to have emanated from a single fact, from a single idea; one might say that society has attached itself to a solitary dominant principle, which has determined its institutions, its customs, its creeds, in one word, all its developments.'[12] As a result of the exclusive or over-preponderant dominance of *one* principle or power, those earlier civilisations had either become extinct or – hardly better – had stagnated at some point in their history. Guizot adduced the examples of Egypt and India as cases where the eventual exclusive preponderance of one principle or class had led to stagnation, and that of Greece as a case where the preponderance of one principle, the 'democratic principle', had led, after a most rapid and wonderful development, to the exhaustion and dissolution of society. In contrast, the civilisation of modern Europe had been displaying 'continuous' and 'steadily progressive' growth for the previous fifteen centuries. The reason was the existence in Europe, since the fall of the Roman Empire, of a continuous struggle between different forces, ideas, principles, values, groups, with each trying to prevail and take exclusive hold of society but none of them ever succeeding in doing so. According to Guizot, it had been that diversity and continuous struggle that had kept European civilisation 'steadily progressive' throughout fifteen centuries.

This was a powerful and influential idea that was used by Guizot (a member of the Protestant minority in France) and by many other nineteenth-century thinkers in defence of diversity and against uniformity. One of those who made the most of that idea was the British liberal thinker John Stuart Mill (1806–73). Mill found this idea in Guizot's *Histoire de la Civilisation en Europe* and adopted it enthusiastically. From some time in the early 1830s when he read that work, Mill started (consistently and repeatedly) to emphasise the paramount importance of diversity, struggle and the need for the keeping up of an 'organised antagonism' in society if progressiveness were to be preserved and stagnation to be avoided. Formulations of this idea can be found in a great number of Mill's published works and correspondence.[13] Guizot's message on the importance of diversity and the lethal danger imminent in the over-preponderance of any power, group or idea was also crucial for Tocqueville, Matthew Arnold, Walter Bagehot, Peter Chaadaev, Lord Acton and many other nineteenth-century thinkers.[14]

But though they would agree on the principle of diversity – or, as Mill was to call it, 'organised antagonism' – not all of these liberal thinkers agreed on the institutional implications of that principle. Thus, Guizot was notoriously known for his insistence on a restricted franchise. On the other hand, Mill, while admiring Guizot as a historian, was vociferously critical of Guizot's refusal (in his capacity as a politician) to widen the franchise during the July monarchy (we will see more on Mill's proposed alternative to most mainstream liberals' reluctance to accept universal suffrage shortly). And several other distinctions between different kinds of liberalism have been identified.[15]

One of the issues the French Revolution had accentuated and that the nineteenth century had to face was that of where sovereignty lies. A distinctive answer to the problems raised by the question of sovereignty was formulated by the French group of thinkers collectively known as the Doctrinaires, and particularly by François Guizot, in the shape of the idea of 'the sovereignty of reason' (the idea is obviously related to Guizot's historical argument about the causes of progressiveness discussed above). Guizot made clear in the 1820s that he did not believe 'either in divine right or in popular sovereignty, as they are almost always understood'. He saw in them 'only usurpations of power'. He believed, rather, 'in the sovereignty of reason, justice, and law. There is the legitimate authority for which the world is looking; for reason, truth, and justice are nowhere complete and infallible. No man, no assembly of men, possesses them or can possess them without gaps and limits.' In other words, for Guizot, there could be by definition no legitimate absolute power and there could be no rightful sovereign on earth. But, as Pierre Rosanvallon explains, in contrast to Benjamin Constant, Guizot did 'not at all ground this denial of worldly sovereignty on the principle of the inviolability of the rights of the individual, but rather begins with the assumption of the fallibility of all human power, to the extent that it is always different from reason'.[16] The question to be asked then, is, 'But how is this reason to be found *in* the world? How to reconcile the presence and absence of sovereign reason as a practical matter?' According to Rosanvallon, 'The theory of the sovereignty of reason resolves this question by turning sociologically to a theory of *capacities*: no one can pretend to possess reason, but certain individuals turn out to be more capable than others of recognizing and following it.' As a result,

> the object of the representative system changes its nature. It no longer involves a complex arithmetic of interest and wills. Rather, it is a matter of 'gathering and concentrating all the reason that exists scattered in the world', or 'extract[ing] whatever of reason, justice, or truth exists in society in order to apply it to the practical requirements of government'.[17]

According to Guizot, 'What we call *representation* ... is not an arithmetical machine employed to collect and count individual wills, but a natural process by which public reason, which alone has a right to govern society, may be extracted from the bosom of society itself.'[18] Thus, Rosanvallon argues, for Guizot, the theory of limited suffrage based on property and capacity was 'rooted in this conception of representation'. It was 'understood as an alternative to universal suffrage and not as the first step, prudentially limited, on the road towards it. In Guizot's system, the middle classes have thus consecrated for them a function that transcends their class, in the economic sense of the term: they are instituted as agents of the realization of the universal.'[19]

The notion of 'capacities' highlighted by Rosanvallon as a criterion of who should vote and elect the representatives represents another cluster of complex questions and nuances central to the relationship between democracy and liberalism in the nineteenth century. For not all liberals agreed on what constituted proof of capacity to vote and thus participate in the election of representatives. Guizot made himself infamous by responding to demands for extension of the suffrage to more than the approximately 200,000 men who had the vote in July monarchy France by saying: 'enrichissez-vous par le travail et par l'épargne'.[20] In other words, to the complaint that only those who had a high income were allowed to vote, Guizot was replying: make yourselves rich, so you can meet the existing threshold (the statement did no justice to Guizot's complex thinking on 'capacities' and certainly did his reputation no good at all). But capacity for voting did not have to depend on income necessarily. A complex answer to that question was provided by a man whose liberal credentials are rarely disputed, John Stuart Mill.

Mill was, for most historians, the paradigmatic nineteenth-century liberal. Besides being the author of the closest liberalism comes to an equivalent of a bible, the essay *On Liberty* (1859), Mill became a Member of Parliament for the Liberal Party between 1865 and 1868. And his activism as a journalist, campaigner and intellectual on behalf of several liberal causes is notorious. The essay *On Liberty* has very often been misunderstood as a defence of, as it were, 'doing as one likes'. That is a misreading. Mill was adamant that the principle he was proposing to establish was badly needed exactly because 'in consequence of this absence of rule or principle, one side is at present as often wrong as the other; the interference of government is, with about equal frequency, improperly invoked and improperly condemned'. In other words, he was going to argue for interference in many cases where it was absent, besides also arguing for refraining from interference in cases where it was invoked by his contemporaries. The 'one very simple principle' that Mill proposed in the essay was not that simple. But he spent the rest of the essay explaining its implications and applications and defending it eloquently and passionately. That principle is,

> that the sole end for which mankind are warranted, individually or collectively, in interfering with the liberty of action of any of their number, is self-protection. That the only purpose for which power can be rightfully exercised

over any member of a civilized community, against his will, is to prevent harm to others. His own good, either physical or moral, is not a sufficient warrant. He cannot rightfully be compelled to do or forbear because it will be better for him to do so, because it will make him happier, because, in the opinions of others, to do so would be wise, or even right. These are good reasons for remonstrating with him, or reasoning with him, or persuading him, or entreating him, but not for compelling him, or visiting him with any evil in case he do otherwise. To justify that, the conduct from which it is desirable to deter him, must be calculated to produce evil to some one else. The only part of the conduct of any one, for which he is amenable to society, is that which concerns others. In the part which merely concerns himself, his independence is, of right, absolute. Over himself, over his own body and mind, the individual is sovereign.[21]

Arguably it is the last two sentences that have misled many to mistake *On Liberty* for a text advocating 'doing as one likes'. But attentive readers will find many arguments in the book that were far from preaching that message.[22]

In his 1861 book *Considerations on Representative Government*, Mill prescribed particular institutional arrangements that would make representative democracy make the most of itself. His criterion of the goodness of a form of government was 'the degree in which it tends to increase the sum of good qualities in the governed, collectively and individually; since, besides that their well-being is the sole object of government, their good qualities supply the moving force which works the machinery'. This meant that the other criterion of the merit of a government was the quality of 'the machinery itself', in other words the degree to which it was fit 'to take advantage of the amount of good qualities which may at any time exist, and make them instrumental to the right purposes'.[23] It was this attempt to combine the developmental aspects of a political regime (the degree to which it improved the collective or 'national' character of the people) with its practical merits in making the most of the people who were to be governed at each stage of their development that was the main focus of Mill's arguments in *Considerations*.

The first of the above two aims was why Mill strongly criticised the common saying that if only a good despot could be found, 'despotic monarchy' would be the best form of government. Mill maintained that this was 'a radical and most pernicious misconception of what good government is'. Even if the hypothetical good monarch were all-seeing and superhuman in the amount of work and energy they put into the job, the result would be calamitous in terms of its effects on the whole population they ruled. The inevitable result from such rule would be the population's utter passivity and ignorance. Moreover, besides their intelligence, the people's moral capacities would also be 'equally stunted'. For '[w]herever the sphere of action of human beings is artificially circumscribed, their sentiments are narrowed and dwarfed in the same proportion'. Thus, 'Let a person have nothing to do for his country, and he will not care for it'.[24]

According to Mill, ideally the best form of government was

> that in which the sovereignty, or supreme controlling power in the last resort, is vested in the entire aggregate of the community; every citizen not only having a voice in the exercise of that ultimate sovereignty, but being, at least occasionally, called on to take an actual part in the government, by the personal discharge of some public function, local or general.[25]

A 'completely popular government' was best, Mill had argued, for 'the excellence of a political constitution'. It was both 'more favourable to present good government and promotes a better and higher form of national character, than any other polity whatsoever'. Its superiority with regard to 'present well-being' rested upon two principles. The first was, 'that the rights and interests of every or any person are only secure from being disregarded, when the person interested is himself able, and habitually disposed, to stand up for them'. The second principle was, 'that the general prosperity attains a greater height, and is more widely diffused, in proportion to the amount and variety of the personal energies enlisted in promoting it'.[26]

But exercising sovereignty does not mean 'governing' and it is important to remember Mill's definition of it as 'supreme controlling power in the last resort'. Thus, in chapter v ('Of the Proper Functions of Representative Bodies') he stressed that it was necessary to bear in mind the distinction between the 'idea or essence' of representative government and 'the particular forms in which the idea has been clothed by accidental historical developments, or by the notions current at some particular period'. According to Mill, the 'meaning' of representative government is, 'that the whole people, or some numerous portion of them, exercise through deputies periodically elected by themselves, the ultimate controlling power, which, in every constitution, must reside somewhere. This ultimate power they must possess in all its completeness. They must be the masters, whenever they please, of all the operations of government.' This having been said, however, he went on to argue that there is 'a radical distinction between controlling the business of government, and actually doing it'. For '[t]he same person or body may be able to control everything, but cannot possibly do everything; and in many cases its control over everything will be more perfect, the less it personally attempts to do'.[27]

Thus, Mill discarded as completely misplaced the usual complaints of critics of representative assemblies as mere talking shops. It was exactly talking that was the job of such assemblies, 'when the subject of talk is the great public interests of the country, and every sentence of it represents the opinion of some important body of persons in the nation, or of an individual in whom some such body have reposed their confidence'. On the other hand, '*doing*, as the result of discussion', was the task 'not of a miscellaneous body, but of individuals specially trained to it'. That is why Mill advocated specialised legislative commissions charged with formulating the details of legislation and putting their legislative proposals in front of the elected assembly for approval or rejection. The job of the representative assembly was 'to see that those individuals are honestly and intelligently chosen, and to interfere no further with them, except by unlimited latitude of suggestion and criticism, and by applying or withholding the final seal of national assent'. It was, Mill thought, the very fact that most unfitted such numerous assemblies of representatives for 'a Council of Legislation', which qualified them the more for their proper office: 'namely, that they are not a selection of the greatest political minds in the country, from whose opinions little could with certainty be inferred concerning those of the nation, but are, when properly constituted, a fair sample of every grade of intellect among the people which is at all entitled to a voice in public affairs'. Their part was

> to indicate wants, to be an organ for popular demands, and a place of adverse discussion for all opinions relating to public matters, both great and small; and, along with this, to check by criticism, and eventually by withdrawing their support, those high public officers who really conduct the public business, or who appoint those by whom it is conducted.[28]

Given his avowed fear of the over-preponderance of any one class and his concomitant desire to see the power of numbers counterbalanced in some way, and given how most other nineteenth-century liberals proposed to avert that danger, one could have expected Mill to have recommended restrictions to the franchise. But this was not his way of resolving such problems. Instead, in chapter VII of *Considerations* ('Of True and False Democracy; Representation of All, and Representation of the Majority Only') Mill rejected the argument that the way to avert the dangers of democracy was to limit the democratic character of representation. He argued that two very different ideas are usually confused under the name 'democracy': 'The pure idea of democracy', on the one hand, 'according to its definition, is the government of the whole people by the whole people, equally represented.' On the other hand, democracy 'as commonly conceived and hitherto practised', was 'the government of the whole people by a mere majority of the people, exclusively represented'. The former was synonymous with the equality of all citizens. The latter was 'a government of privilege', favouring the numerical majority, who were the only ones with any say. This was 'the inevitable consequence of the manner in which the votes are now taken, to the complete disfranchisement of minorities'.[29]

There was one simple way of achieving real and equal democratic representation for all citizens, and Thomas Hare had shown how this could work in practice.[30] Real equality of representation would only be obtained when 'any set of electors amounting to the average number of a constituency, wherever in the country they happen to reside, have the power of combining with one another to return a representative'.[31] A system of personal (proportional) representation such as that proposed by Thomas Hare would enable people who had distinguished themselves 'by their writings, or their exertions in some field of public usefulness' and thus made themselves known and admired by even small numbers of people in most districts in the country, to be elected to parliament as soon as they attained the number of the quota required for each seat in parliament. According to Mill, 'In no other way which it seems possible to suggest, would Parliament be so certain of containing the very *élite* of the country'.[32]

It was of paramount importance to solve this problem. For Mill believed that the 'natural tendency of representative government, as of modern civilization, is towards collective mediocrity'. However, this was not the end of the discussion: 'But though the superior intellects and characters will necessarily be outnumbered, it makes a great difference whether or not they are heard.' In the 'false democracy' that gave representation only to the local majorities in each constituency, the voice of 'the instructed minority' would almost certainly not be represented in the representative assembly.[33] If, on the other hand, Hare's system were adopted, the champions of unpopular doctrines would get a hearing in the nation's supreme tribune, and thus there would be 'a fair comparison of their intellectual strength, in the presence of the country'. That would give people a chance to find out 'whether the opinion which prevailed by counting votes, would also prevail if the votes were weighed as well as counted'.[34]

Coming to the crux of the matter, Mill highlighted the urgency of 'the function of antagonism' that he had been tirelessly stressing since he read Guizot: 'This portion of the Assembly would also be the appropriate organ of a great social function, for which there is no provision in any existing democracy, but which in no government can remain permanently unfulfilled without condemning that government to infallible degeneracy and decay. This may be called *the function of Antagonism*' (emphasis added).

In every government there was some power that was stronger than all the rest and that power tended perpetually 'to become the sole power'. Half-intentionally and half-unconsciously, the strongest power was 'ever striving to make all other things bend to itself; and is not content while there is anything which makes permanent head against it, any influence not in agreement with its spirit'. Yet, if it succeeded in 'suppressing all rival influences, and moulding everything after its own model, improvement, in that country, is at an end, and decline commences'. For, as Mill went on, '[h]uman improvement is a product of many factors, and no power ever yet constituted among mankind includes them all: even the most beneficent power only contains in itself some of the requisites of good, and the remainder, if progress is to continue, must be derived from some other source'. In words unmistakably reminiscent of Guizot's second lecture on civilisation in Europe, Mill declared: 'No community has ever long continued progressive, but while a conflict was going on between the strongest power in the community and some rival power; between the spiritual and temporal authorities; the military or territorial and the industrious classes; the king and the people; the orthodox, and religious reformers.' And 'When the victory on either side was so complete as to put an end to the strife, and no other conflict took its place, first stagnation followed, then decay.' Mill conceded that the ascendancy of the numerical majority was 'less unjust, and on the whole less mischievous, than many others', but stressed that it was nevertheless attended

> with the very same kind of dangers, and even more certainly; for when the government is in the hands of One or a Few, the Many are always existent as a rival power, which may not be strong enough ever to control the other, but whose opinion and sentiment are a moral, and even a social, support to all who ... are opposed to any of the tendencies of the ruling authority.

The tyranny of the majority posed a much graver danger though:

> But when the Democracy is supreme, there is no One or Few strong enough for dissentient opinions and injured or menaced interests to lean upon. The great difficulty of democratic government has hitherto seemed to be, how to provide, in a democratic society, what circumstances have provided hitherto in all the societies which have maintained themselves ahead of others – a social support, a *point d'appui*, for individual resistance to the tendencies of the ruling power; a protection, a rallying point, for opinions and interests which the ascendant public opinion views with disfavour. For want of such a *point d'appui*, the older societies, and all but a few modern ones, either fell into dissolution or became stationary (which means slow deterioration) through the exclusive predominance of a part only of the conditions of social and mental well-being.[35]

Now, it was exactly this great need that 'the system of Personal Representation' was designed to supply. The only quarter where one could look for 'a supplement, or completing corrective, to the instincts of a democratic majority', was 'the instructed minority'. But, in the way representative democracy operated up to then (in the US for example), that minority had 'no organ: Mr. Hare's system provides one. The representatives who would be returned to Parliament by the aggregate of minorities, would afford that organ in its greatest perfection.' What was more, the way Hare's model of representation would allow the instructed few to be represented in Parliament meant that they would not be offensive and hence resented: 'A separate organization of the instructed classes, even if practicable, would be invidious, and could only escape from being offensive by being totally without influence.' Things would be different under the plan Mill was recommending:

> But if the *élite* of these classes formed part of the Parliament, by the same title as any other of its members – by representing the same number of citizens, the same numerical fraction of the national will – their presence could give umbrage to nobody, while they would be in a position of highest vantage, both for making their opinions and counsels heard on all important subjects, and for taking an active part in public business. Their abilities would probably draw to them more than their numerical share of the actual administration of government; as the Athenians did not confide responsible public functions to Cleon or Hyperbolus ... but Nicias, and Theramenes, and Alcibiades, were in constant employment both at home and abroad, though known to sympathise more with oligarchy than with democracy. The instructed minority would, in the actual voting, count only for their numbers, but as a moral power they would count for much more, in virtue of their knowledge, and of the influence it would give them over the rest.

As a result, a democratic people 'would in this way be provided with what in any other way it would almost certainly miss – leaders of a higher grade of intellect and character than itself. Modern democracy would have its occasional Pericles, and its habitual group of superior and guiding minds'.[36]

But while he insisted on the need to have the instructed elite represented with a voice in parliament, Mill simultaneously insisted on giving the vote to – almost – all citizens, for a number of reasons. He gave great emphasis to the education of the intelligence and of the sentiments of citizens as one of the main benefits of free government. For people whose occupations provide few if any intellectual stimuli (such as manual labourers) the exercise of political franchises provided 'a potent instrument of mental development'. Distant and complicated interests were brought to the attention of everyone if they had a say in political affair and their circle of moral concern expanded to include their fellow citizens.[37]

But independently of this argument, Mill also adduced an argument based on justice: It would be 'a personal injustice to withhold from any one, unless for the prevention of greater evils, the ordinary privilege of having his voice reckoned in the disposal of affairs in which he has the same interest as other people.' If one was 'compelled to pay, if he may be compelled to fight, if he is required implicitly to obey, he should be legally entitled to be told what for; to have his consent asked, and his opinion counted at its worth, though not more than its worth'. For 'Every one is degraded, whether aware of it or not, when other people, without consulting him, take upon themselves unlimited power to regulate his destiny.'[38]

There would be some exceptions, but they were 'required by positive reasons, which do not conflict with this principle, and which, though an evil in themselves, are only to be got rid of by the cessation of the state of things which requires them'. He thus stipulated a minimum requirement of intellectual aptitude in asking for voters to be able to 'read, write and perform the common operations of arithmetic'. But he hastened to clarify that it was a demand of justice 'that the means of attaining these elementary acquirements should be within the reach of every person'.[39] Another requirement Mill stipulated was the payment of taxes. Allowing people who did not pay any taxes at all to vote would separate the power of control from 'the interest in its beneficial exercise'. People should not be allowed to put their hands into other people's pockets 'for any purpose which they think fit to call a public one'. He also stressed that the receipt of parish relief should disqualify the recipient from the franchise. Mill emphasised that all the exclusions he proposed were not in their nature permanent. 'In the long run ... we might expect that all, except that (it is to be hoped) progressively diminishing class, the recipients of parish relief, would be in possession of votes, so that the suffrage would be, with that slight abatement, universal.'[40]

However, 'though every one ought to have a voice – that every one should have an equal voice is a totally different proposition'. Thus Mill asked further: 'When two persons who have a joint interest in any business, differ in opinion, does justice require that both opinions should be held of exactly equal value?' If,

> with equal virtue, one is superior to the other in knowledge and intelligence – or if with equal intelligence, one excels the other on virtue – the opinion, the judgment, of the higher moral and intellectual being, is worth more than that of the inferior: and if the institutions of the country virtually assert that they are of the same value, they assert a thing which is not.[41]

Mill admitted that the difficulty was that of ascertaining which of the two people in question was the wiser or the better man, and therefore hastened to explain that this was impossible to do so in the case of individuals.[42] But he asserted that, 'taking men in bodies and in numbers, it can be done with a certain approach to accuracy'.[43] In a statement consistent with the main message of *On Liberty*, Mill clarified further that: 'There would be no pretence for applying this doctrine to any case which could with reason be considered as one of individual and private right. In an affair which concerns only one of two persons, that one is entitled to follow his own opinion, however much wiser the other may be than himself.' But things had to be different, according to Mill, when it came to 'things which equally concern them both; where, if the more ignorant does not yield his share of the matter to the guidance of the wiser man, the wiser man must resign his to that of the more ignorant'. In such cases, 'Which of these modes of getting over the difficulty is most for the interest of both, and most conformable to the general fitness of things? If it be deemed unjust that either should have to give way, which injustice is greatest? That the better judgment should give way to the worse, or the worse to the better?'[44]

Now, 'national affairs are exactly such a joint concern'. All should have a vote, but some should have more than one vote, if they could prove some kind of intellectual superiority and expertise, that would allow them to have opinions that ought to be weighed more than those of others. Mill offered a number of examples and possible ways of ascertaining such superiority in individuals and ways in which 'plural voting' might work in practice. Few of his proposals have incurred as much criticism and ridicule as this. And yet, he had been clear from the beginning that he did not feel too strongly about the details, but only about the principle. He was aware that all those suggestions he had made were

> open to much discussion in the detail, and to objections which it is of no use to anticipate. The time is not come for giving to such plans a practical shape, nor should I wish to be bound by the particular proposals which I have made. But it is to me evident, that in this direction lies the true ideal of representative government; and that to work towards it, by the best practical contrivances which can be found, is the path of real political improvement.[45]

But it was the principle that was very important for Mill.

Mill's example is important, both because of his status as the iconic liberal and because of the complexity of his attitude towards democracy. He is often seen as sceptical about democracy. Yes, by the standards of his own time he was seen as an extreme democrat by most. His reservations about the way democracy was practised in his time (giving whichever group passed as the majority the whole say) do not make him a reluctant democrat but a real democrat, in his eyes. His case demonstrates that there are very different versions of democracy, and, he would insist, some are much better than others.

But there were other, highly influential nineteenth-century thinkers who opposed both democracy and liberalism outright and sought to resolve the problems of the post-revolutionary era in very different ways. Some are less known today than their prominence and influence in the nineteenth century would warrant. A nineteenth-century thinker whose ambitions were comparable to those of Hegel, and who has often been compared to Hegel, was Auguste Comte (1798–1857). He is interesting for our purposes here as he elaborated a meticulous system that constituted one of the main challenges to liberalism and democracy in the nineteenth century. Comte is not usually included in histories of political thought. He is mainly seen as a philosopher who made important contributions to the history and philosophy of science and as the founder (or precursor) of sociology. Yet Comte himself envisaged his work as primarily *political*, as a project for social and political reorganisation after the cataclysm of the French Revolution and then Napoleon's rule.[46] He regarded his scientific and epistemological work as a digression that would reinforce the 'scientific' basis of his political project. Comte's life and work have been usually interpreted as having been dramatically divided into two phases. The first phase, according to this reading, was seen as dedicated to his epistemological search for the history and the classification of the sciences. Comte's main work of that period was the six-volume *Cours de Philosophie Positive*, published between 1830 and 1842.[47] The second phase is understood to have been preoccupied by his development of his political project accompanied by his elaborate enunciation of the 'Religion of Humanity'. The major work of that phase was the *Système de Politique Positive*, published in four volumes between 1851 and 1854.[48] The division of Comte's life and work into the two periods goes together with a usually more or less positive and admiring evaluation of his work produced during the first phase, accompanied by the judgement that the second phase saw Comte's mental decline. This is how one of the first proponents of the two-Comtes thesis, John Stuart Mill, concluded his summary exposition of the absurdities the *later* Comte had come up with in his essay *Auguste Comte and Positivism* (1865): 'Others may laugh, but we could far rather weep at this melancholy decadence of a great intellect.'[49] The majority of Comte specialists today discard the sharp division of Comte's career into two distinct phases. Instead they stress the continuity of his preoccupations and the fact that Comte had already formulated his plans and ambitions for the political and social reorganisation of European society from his early writings of the 1820s (the so-called *opuscules de jeunesse*).

According to the founder of positivism, 'the fundamental problem' was that 'of reconciling Order and Progress'. But all other schools of thought of his time were utterly incapable of achieving such a reconciliation. There were, in his time, 'no opinions which possess more than the purely negative value of checking, and that very imperfectly, the error opposite to their own'.[50] According to Comte, 'Positivism, and Positivism alone, can disentangle and terminate this anomalous position'. The principle upon which it depended was: 'As long as Progress tends towards anarchy, so long will Order continue to be retrograde.'[51] In a move similar to that of Hegel discussed at the beginning of this chapter, Comte placed himself between what he presented as two extreme parties. On the one hand, there were the supporters of eighteenth-century and revolutionary principles that had completed their work of undermining the Ancien Régime with the French Revolution and now had no reason for being. Their continuation led only to destructiveness of any principle of order and hence to anarchy. On the other hand, there was the reactionary or retrograde party that went to the other extreme out of fear of the anarchical tendencies of their opponents and wanted to undo everything the French Revolution had done and stood for. It was obvious to Comte that both were wrong.[52] His own motto was 'Order and Progress'. He insisted that progress was only the development of order and that neither order nor progress were possible without each other. What he called the 'metaphysical politics' of the seventeenth and eighteenth centuries had been a purely negative political philosophy, necessary for overthrowing the old order, the *Ancien Régime*. But having achieved that goal, that negative philosophy, focused on the 'rights' of individuals, popular sovereignty and other such demands, was unable to contribute anything to the necessary reorganisation of society. The principles of metaphysical politics were purely *critical* principles. But what was needed then, in the nineteenth century, were *organic* principles (the similarity with the thought of his former master Henri Saint-Simon was evident in this distinction between critical and organic epochs, as in much else). Already in what he kept referring to as his 'fundamental *opuscule*' of the early 1820s Comte had stressed that the advocates of critical, negative, metaphysical eighteenth-century political philosophy needed to understand 'that weapons of war cannot, by a strange metamorphosis, suddenly become building instruments'.[53]

Comte's solution to the problem he identified was radical. He proposed a complete reorganisation of advanced European societies on the basis of his 'scientific' elaboration of sociological rules. Around the middle of the 1840s he also invented a new religion that would reinforce the social bonds, the Religion of Humanity. The political project that Comte developed in his later years was, as Mill put it later, 'liberticide'. Comte thought democratic representation a useless distraction and considered ideas such as rights and liberty as remnants of the 'metaphysical' stage of human development that the 'positive' era had to dispense with. As a major part of his new arrangements, Comte envisaged a separation of spiritual from secular power. The secular power would manage the industry and economy and would be headed by capitalists. But it would operate on a small scale: the secular states (Comte sometimes called them republics, or cities) would be around the size of Belgium, Ireland or Tuscany. Meanwhile, however, the spiritual authority, based in Paris and headed by Comte himself (and after his death by his successor) would oversee the spiritual, educational and moral edification of people in the entire 'Western Republic', which Comte envisaged to include the whole of Western Europe as well as settler colonies such as the Americas, Australia and New Zealand. Measures such as the stipulation that 150 books selected by Comte would be the only ones allowed to be read did not do much to increase the project's popularity with liberals, either in Comte's time or in ours. Comte created a utopia that he thought was based on scientific edifices and on a sound philosophy of history, thanks to which the analysis of the past provided clear guidance for the future. The derision his projects attract today should not obscure the fact that they had many followers in the nineteenth century. (British followers such as Frederic Harrison could be taken as liberals in some sense, and yet Harrison considered himself a disciple of Comte. The novelist George Eliot was a staunch admirer of Comte and expressed great admiration even for his later, political work, the *System of Positive Polity*; Comte's global reach from South America to Bengal was astonishing).[54] In the century of gigantic system builders, Comte's was one of the most daring systems, but not out of place.

NOTES

1 Alexis de Tocqueville, *Democracy in America*. Historical-Critical Edition, Bilingual Edition, 4 vols, ed. Eduardo Nolla, trans. James T. Schleifer (Indianapolis, IN: Liberty Fund, 2010).

2 On Britain see Elza Dzelzainis and Ruth Livesey, eds., *The American Experiment and the Idea of Democracy in British Culture, 1776–1914* (Farnham: Ashgate, 2013); Robert Saunders, *Democracy and the Vote in British Politics, 1848–1867: The Making of the Second Reform Act* (Farnham: Ashgate, 2011), pp. 142–59; Frank Prochaska, *Eminent Victorians and American Democracy* (Oxford: Oxford University Press, 2012); David P. Crook, *American Democracy in English Politics. 1815–1850* (Oxford: Clarendon Press, 1965); G. D. Lillibridge, *Beacon of Freedom: The Impact of American Democracy upon*

Great Britain 1830–1870 [1955] (New York: Perpetua, 1961). On France see the classic study: René Rémond, *Les États Unis devant l'Opinion Française 1815–1852*, 2 vols. (Paris, 1962). On Italy see Axel Körner, *America in Italy: The United States in the Political Thought and Imagination of the Risorgimento, 1763–1865* (Princeton, NJ: Princeton University Press, 2017).

3 See James Young, 'American Political Thought from Jeffersonian Republicanism to Progressivism', in *The Cambridge History of Nineteenth-Century Political Thought*, eds. Gareth Stedman Jones and Gregory Claeys (Cambridge: Cambridge University Press, 2011), pp. 374–408, at p. 374.

4 Vernon L. Parrington, *The Romantic Revolution in America 1800–1860* [vol. II of *Main Currents in American Thought*] (New York: Harvest, Brace & Company, 1954), pp. 310–11.

5 See, for example, Jack Hayward, *After the French Revolution: Six Critics of Democracy and Nationalism* (New York: Harvester Wheatsheaf, 1991); Pierre Rosanvallon, 'François Guizot and the Sovereignty of Reason', in *Democracy Past and Future*, ed. Samuel Moyn (New York: Columbia University Press, 2006), pp. 117–26.

6 Fredrick C. Beiser, 'Hegel and Hegelianism', in *The Cambridge History of Nineteenth-Century Political Thought*, eds. Gareth Stedman Jones and Gregory Claeys (Cambridge: Cambridge University Press, 2011), pp. 110–46, at pp. 110–11.

7 Pierre Rosanvallon, 'Political Rationalism and Democracy in France', in Rosanvallon, *Democracy Past and Future*, pp. 127–43.

8 See Georgios Varouxakis, *Mill on Nationality* (London: Routledge, 2002), pp. 71–4.

9 H. S. Jones, 'Las variedades del liberalismo europeo en el siglo XIX: perspectivas británicas y francesas', in *Liberalismo y Poder: Latinoamérica en el siglo XIX*, eds. Iván Jaksić and Eduardo Posada Carbó (Chile: Fondo de Cultura Económica, 2011), pp. 43–61.

10 Pierre Rosanvallon, 'The Market, Liberalism, and Anti-liberalism', in Rosanvallon, *Democracy Past and Future*, pp. 147–59, at pp. 153–6.

11 The ideas of intermediary bodies as barriers to despotism went back to Charles-Louis de Secondat, Baron de La Brède et de Montesquieu, *The Spirit of the Laws*, ed. and trans. A. M. Cohler, B. C. Miller and H. S. Stone (Cambridge: Cambridge University Press, 1989).

12 François Guizot, *The History of Civilization in Europe*, trans. W. Hazlitt, ed. L. Siedentop (London: Penguin, 1997), pp. 27–8.

13 See Georgios Varouxakis, 'Guizot's Historical Works and J. S. Mill's Reception of Tocqueville', *History of Political Thought* 20 (1999), 292–312.

14 On Guizot's impact on Russian thought see Catherine Evtuhov, 'Guizot in Russia', in *The Cultural Gradient: The Transmission of Ideas in Europe 1789–1991*, eds. Iván Jaksić and Eduardo Posada Carbó (Lanham, MD: Rowman & Littlefield, 2003), pp. 55–72. On Guizot's thought and importance see the classic study: Pierre Rosanvallon, *Le Moment Guizot* (Paris: Gallimard, 1985).

15 See, for instance, Larry Siedentop, 'Two Liberal Traditions', in *The Idea of Freedom: Essays in Honour of Isaiah Berlin*, ed. Alan Ryan (Oxford: Oxford University Press, 1979), pp. 153–74.

16 Rosanvallon, 'Guizot and the Sovereignty of Reason', p. 123.

17 François Guizot, *The History of the Origins of Representative Government*, ed. Aurelian Craiutu, trans. Andrew R. Scoble (Indianapolis, IN: Liberty Fund, 2001), p. 55. See also Rosanvallon, 'Guizot and the Sovereignty of Reason', p. 125. As Rosanvallon commented, 'Guizot's originality, in fact, chiefly resides in the way he sociologically instrumentalized the concept of the sovereignty of reason. If no one can pretend to own reason, then it is impossible, he says, to escape the need for a theory of its *mediation*. It is here that the theme of capacities, which is at the heart of the Doctrinaires' problematic, is born.'

18 Guizot, *History of the Origins*, pp. 295–6.

19 Rosanvallon, "Guizot and the Sovereignty of Reason', pp. 125–6. On the political thought of Guizot and the other *Doctrinaires* see also Aurelian Craiutu, *Liberalism Under Siege: The Political Thought of the French Doctrinaires* (Lanham, MD: Lexington Books, 2003); Lucien Jaume, *L'individu effacé, ou le paradoxe du libéralisme français* (Paris: Fayard, 1997); and Jeremy Jennings, *Revolution and the Republic: A History of Political Thought in France Since the Eighteenth Century* (Oxford: Oxford University Press, 2011).

20 'Enrich yourselves through work and thrift'.

21 John Stuart Mill, *The Collected Works of John Stuart Mill*, eds. F. E. L. Priestley and John M. Robson, 33 vols. (Toronto, ON and London: University of Toronto Press, 1963–91), vol. XXVII, pp. 223–4 [referred to hereafter in this chapter as CW].

22 See, for example, Gregory Claeys, *Mill and Paternalism* (Cambridge: Cambridge University Press, 2013).

23 Mill, CW, vol. XIX, pp. 390–1.

24 Ibid., pp. 399–401.

25 Ibid., pp. 403–4.

26 Ibid., p. 404.

27 Ibid., p. 423.

28 Ibid., pp. 432–3.

29 Ibid., p. 448.

30 On Thomas Hare's scheme see: F. D. Parsons, *Thomas Hare and Political Representation in Victorian Britain* (Basingstoke: Palgrave Macmillan, 2009).

31 Mill, CW, vol. XIX, p. 453.

32 Ibid., p. 456.

33 Ibid., p. 457.

34 Ibid., p. 458.

35 Ibid., pp. 458–9.

36 Ibid., pp. 459–60.

37 Ibid., pp. 467–9.

38 Ibid., pp. 469–70.

39 Ibid., p. 470.

40 Ibid., pp. 473–4.

41 Ibid., p. 473.

42 See also Mill, *A System of Logic*, CW, vol. VIII, pp. 847–8.

43 Mill, CW, vol. XIX, p. 473.

44 Ibid., pp. 473–4.

45 Ibid., p. 475.

46 According to one of the most prominent contemporary Comte scholars, 'contrary to what is usually thought, Comte's positivism is not a philosophy of

science but a political philosophy. Or, if one prefers, Comte's positivism is a remarkable philosophy that doesn't separate philosophy of science from political philosophy.' Michel Bourdeau, 'Auguste Comte', *Stanford Encyclopedia of Philosophy*, [2008] 2014, http://plato.stanford.edu/entries/comte.

47 Auguste Comte, *Cours de Philosophie Positive*, 2 vols., ed. Jean-Paul Enthoven (Paris: Hermann, 1975). The original six volumes were published in 1830, 1835, 1838, 1839, 1841 and 1842 respectively.

48 Auguste Comte, *Système de Politique Positive*, 4 vols., 5th edn (Paris: Carilian-Gœury and V. Dalmont, Société positiviste, 1929) [first published in 4 vols., 1851–4]. For an English translation see Auguste Comte, *System of Positive Policy: Or Treatise on Sociology, Instituting the Religion of Humanity*, 4 vols. (London: Longmans, Green & Co., 1875–7).

49 Mill, *CW*, vol. x, p. 367.

50 Comte, *System (Engl.)*, vol. 1, p. 56.

51 Ibid., pp. 57–8.

52 See Frédéric Brahami, 'Sortir du cercle: Auguste Comte, la critique et les rétrogrades', *Archives de Philosophie* 70 (2007), 41–55.

53 Auguste Comte, 'Plan of the Scientific Work Necessary for the Reorganization of Society' (1822/1824), in Auguste Comte, *Early Political Writings*, ed. and trans. H. S. Jones (Cambridge: Cambridge University Press, 1998), p. 57.

54 See Mary Pickering, 'Conclusion: The Legacy of Auguste Comte', in *Love, Order, and Progress: The Science, Philosophy, and Politics of Auguste Comte*, eds. Michel Bourdeau, Mary Pickering and Warren Schmaus (Pittsburgh, PA: University of Pittsburgh Press, 2018); T. R. Wright, *The Religion of Humanity: The Impact of Comtean Positivism on Victorian Britain* (Cambridge: Cambridge University Press, 1986); Gregory Claeys, *Imperial Sceptics: British Critics of Empire 1850–1920* (Cambridge: Cambridge University Press, 2010).

3

JOHN E. WILSON

Remaking Theology: Orthodoxies and Their Critics

In the nineteenth century Roman Catholic orthodoxy (right belief) was defined by Scripture (the Bible), Catholic tradition, and, since 1870, the magisterium of the papal office. Eastern Orthodox Christianity was also characterised by the authority of Scripture and tradition, but it was only gradually affected by the conflicts that are the subject matter of this chapter. In Protestantism, for which Scripture was the ultimate authority, orthodoxy was defined by early Christian creeds (shared with Catholic tradition) and by confessions of the Reformation period.[1] All these traditions held certain basic doctrines in common: God's creation of the world, revelation, the divinity of Christ and the doctrine of the Trinity, but each had its distinguishing complexity, and all had long since developed erudite dogmatics and scriptural studies. The Enlightenment of the previous century had raised questions and doubts about these orthodoxies but had not seriously jeopardised their standing in the respective churches, societies and governments.

With the exception of France, all European nations entered the nineteenth century with church establishments instituted by law. Orthodoxy gave the religious basis for the union of church and state and with it the requirement of obedience to God. In France establishment had been abolished by the Revolution but was soon to be reinstated. All established churches were embedded in social structures that were centuries old. They typically involved a wealthy, landed upper class, a middle class of professionals and a lower class of farmers and labourers. Priests or ministers were responsible for public worship and the moral education of the population. Everything had changed by the end of the century. Disruption of the social structure, caused by political and industrial revolutions and the progress of democracy, disrupted establishment. This, together with rapid progress in the natural, historical and social sciences, democratic religious movements and new innovative theologies, disrupted orthodoxy. Both establishment and orthodoxy survived the century, but with severely weakened social and political significance.

In the four representative nations considered here, Britain, France, Germany and the United States, an important sign of democratic progress was the elimination of religious tests that restricted civil freedoms (mainly participation in government) for non-established religious groups. In France they were eliminated by the Revolution. Restrictions for Roman Catholics were lifted in Protestant Britain in the third decade of the nineteenth century. In Germany both Catholicism and Protestantism had for a century and a half enjoyed the benefits of establishment. Civil restrictions on Jews were lifted in Britain and Germany in the second half of the nineteenth century. In the United States religious tests and church establishment by law had been prohibited at the federal or national level by the Constitution. For a time legal establishment survived in individual states, but eventually all the states adopted the federal law. However, former legally established churches long remained cultural establishments. In the most settled areas, particularly New England, the clergy of the dominant Protestant churches were supported by the politically and economically dominant upper class, so that there is a certain parallel between these churches and the Church of England. The Roman Catholic Church and American Jewish religious organisations were to show a similar pattern of cultural establishment. Through immigration Roman Catholicism became by mid-century the single largest religious group in the United States, but it participated only in a minor way in the theological conflicts that characterised Protestantism.

Political disestablishment in the United States presented obvious challenges to Protestant orthodoxy's dominant position in the culture. No change was more significant than freedom of the press, especially as it stood in connection with the Enlightenment's liberation of reason. As literacy increased and printed works became more plentiful and affordable, individualist free thought could be found in all classes. Unitarianism, named for its rejection of the doctrine of the Trinity because the doctrine was considered irrational, emerged in the United States as in Britain at the end of the eighteenth century. Deism, the Enlightenment's religion of reason, continued into the first half of the nineteenth century. In the previous century American Deists – including a number of the Founding Fathers of the Constitution – usually kept their religious views among themselves, not wishing to stir controversy and valuing the churches as the means of moral education. This was possible until the end of the century, when Thomas Paine's *The Age of Reason* (1793/4) sparked widespread outrage. Paine attacked not only the established churches but Christianity itself. In the early nineteenth century the book spurred free-thinking political agitation, particularly in England.

A more effective criticism of establishment and its orthodoxy came from developments in popular religion, especially in America. It is perhaps explainable by historical influences that in the nineteenth century the main points of religious belief in John Locke's *Reasonableness of Christianity* (1695) coincided in the nineteenth century with typical religious beliefs of American Protestant common folk. Locke had argued that the Church of England should limit its concept of essential Christian belief to basic facts or 'fundamentals' easily understood by common labourers with little or no time for literary pursuits. These facts were that the creator had given humanity reason and the law, but because of human frailty or sin the creator also gave the Messiah or Christ, whose divine origin was evidenced by his miracles, to bring the message of forgiveness and renewal of the law and to promise eternal life to those who in believing did the best they could to live moral lives. And as Locke argued, these facts were in conformity with human reason.[2] Locke had also written, in his *Letter Concerning Toleration* (1689), that a church should be a voluntary association, not a political establishment. If one adds the force of emotional spiritual experience, one has the common elements of popular Protestant religious culture in the United States in the nineteenth century. Its beginning is marked by the 'Second Great Awakening' initiated in the year 1800 on the western frontier in Kentucky. The earlier 'Great Awakening' of the 1740s in Britain and the American colonies had occurred mainly under the leadership of university-educated theologians within the established churches, and most held a doctrine of election by grace. In the 'Second Great Awakening' a minor revolution occurred. Freedom from traditional authorities, free will, common sense reason and born-again spirituality – all emphasising the central role of the individual – became the rule, while at the same time conformity to a pattern of biblical literalism was equally prominent. Knowledge of the Bible and little else qualified for pastoral leadership, and populist leaders excoriated the 'knowing better' of the eastern religious establishment.[3] Yet the Awakening soon occurred in the east as well. It focused preaching on the moral responsibility of every person to make a free will choice for God, right living and eternal life instead of personal pleasure and hell to follow.

The Awakening often ignored settled churches to found independent congregations among the poor and disaffected, with good and problematic effects. Such democratic forms of popular religion, habitually disdainful of higher education, easily engendered demagoguery, irrationality and credulity, but they also evoked new dreams and visions, political and social as well as religious. Quickening ferment lay in the Awakening for black churches. Biblical themes and stories, particularly the story of God's liberation of the Hebrew slaves in Egypt, were an enduring spiritual inspiration. Native Americans only peripherally benefited. In spite of notable exceptions they and their lands were mainly treated as objects of colonial empire-building, the so-called Manifest Destiny of national expansion to the Pacific Ocean. The injustices of European and American racism and colonialism – usually justified by some form of natural law – would not be effectively confronted until late in the following century. Religious orthodoxies were partly to blame for this omission: they focused typically on dogma and personal morality, having a long tradition of leaving larger ethical issues to the Christian state.

Towards the end of the century a new cultural establishment with a simplified form of orthodoxy emerged, largely from the Awakening tradition, which cut across the differences among Protestant churches to form a united front against the 'modernism' of Darwinism and biblical criticism: Fundamentalism. Socially, it was, as were all establishments, conservative and nationalist. The 'fundamentals' were essential facts of belief, a feature similar to the simplicity of beliefs in the Second Great Awakening. A typical list included the authenticity of the miracles of the New Testament, the virgin birth of Christ, his bodily resurrection and return at the end time and the inerrancy of Scripture. Yet Fundamentalism was also modern. It unquestioningly accepted technological progress, and its facts-oriented interpretation of the Bible often reflected modern scientific method. Like the Awakening Fundamentalism – or Evangelicalism, as it soon preferred to be called – it emphasised 'born-again' religious experience. It was not limited to America but characterised much free-church belief in Britain as well. Revivalism was the popular means of communication. In America Dwight L. Moody (1837–99) was its most important exemplar. In Britain the Baptist preacher Charles Spurgeon (1834–92) preached to thousands in his London Metropolitan Tabernacle. Through foreign missions Evangelicalism became a world Christian movement.

Liberal theology came to prominence through the influence of the universities. It was known not only for its appropriation of Darwinism and biblical criticism but also for its advocacy of progressive social programs. Serious theological conflicts between fundamentalists or evangelicals and liberals characterised Protestantism both in Britain and the United States. At the end of the century in Britain an uneasy compromise was reached, but with no real resolution, and there was still substantial opposition to the new sciences among evangelicals. In the United States no compromise was reached; fundamentalist-liberal conflicts lasted well into the following century. Another area of conflict was the position of women. As leaders of reform movements and women's suffrage they were often called radicals and heretical violators of women's place in the biblical order of creation. And yet in the churches' foreign missions women advanced to leadership positions and continued to do so in the following century.

During the nineteenth century, political and social upheaval had a profound effect on the life of the churches, especially in France. The French Revolution began with the 'Declaration of the Rights of Man' in 1789, but then launched the Terror, and not only disestablished but dissolved the Roman Catholic Church and its priesthood. Then it attempted to establish a religion of nature, which failed. Prior to the Revolution the hierarchy of the Church had been closely involved in aristocratic France's autocratic and repressive system of government, and many hated the Church for it. Yet in large areas particularly of rural France the people remained devoted to Catholicism, and soon priests who fled France during the Terror began to return. Napoleon was not religious but became convinced that the state needed the Church to support morality. In 1802 a concordat between France and the papacy re-established the Church, placing the state in ultimate control, including the policing of worship; normal duties and services were left to the Church. Catholicism in France had previously been known for its spirit of independence from Rome, but the result of the Revolution and Napoleon's patronising was a Church that drew ever nearer to Rome.

In the decades following the Napoleonic Wars church establishments were shaken by workers' protest movements, such as Chartism in Britain, and by the rise of socialism and its progressive ideas. The immediate causes were the rapid progress of industrialisation and the ever-increasing mass of poor labourers and persons without work. Communitarian enterprises, involving communities of owners and workers, were not at first irreligious and often benefited from the financial support of wealthy religious philanthropists. But socialist ideas were usually directed against religious orthodoxy and establishment. In France a famous early social reformer, Claude Henri, Comte de St. Simon (1760–1825), was an aristocrat who renounced his title. Near the end of his life he wrote *Le Nouveau Christianisme* (The New Christianity), in which he spoke of the divine origin of Christianity and the proof of this in its ethics, but also of its having obscured its social mission by preoccupation with mysteries and observances. He advocated turning over the authority of clergy to scientists, whose knowledge could lead towards a better and more just future. A similar strain of Christian socialism can be traced through the century in France. Later the widely influential 'positivism' of Auguste Comte (1794–1859) held that true knowledge in all possible fields was determined only by science. He conceived social and intellectual history in three stages: the theological stage of belief in God; the metaphysical stage of abstract ideas about universal reason; and the age of empirical science. In the age of science the 'Religion of Humanity' replaces belief in God, and under the guidance of the new science of sociology life is to be made just and humane for all.[4]

In Britain and for a time in the United States Robert Owen (1771–1858) worked to establish industrially productive communities that lived and worked under healthy conditions, with a just distribution of income and schools and free-time activities for all. He distrusted the religion of the churches and in his later years rejected it because it was not socially progressive. According to Karl Marx (1818–83), who resided in London from 1849 until his death, humanity was defined in the modern world by its market value. The working poor had the least value, but bore the burden of those with real value, the wealthy. The capitalist system – including the religion that supported it and that it supported – estranged everyone from true humanity, rich as well as poor. 'The criticism of religion', he wrote, 'ends with the teaching that man is the highest being for man, hence with the categorical imperative to overthrow all relations in which man is a debased, enslaved, forsaken, despicable being'. Religion was the revolution's most seductive opponent: it was 'the opium of the people'.[5]

Like establishments elsewhere the Church of England was slow to respond to social change. It had long supported the SPCK (Society for the Promotion of Christian Knowledge), whose focus was the schooling of poor children in the cities, but reach and effect were limited. Some British novelists and lay members of the Church – famously Charles Dickens (1812–70) – contributed significantly to movements to right social ills. The most notable attempt by an individual of the Church was led by the theologian Fredrick Denison Maurice (1805–72). He supported workers' rights and was a founder of several institutions for the education of labouring men and women. He became involved in the cooperative movement, in which workers banded together to produce goods and share proceeds, although most of these ventures failed. Theologically he saw social division as inhibiting the worship of God, for he understood God as the ground of unity among all human beings.[6] A similar thought motivated the work of William Booth (1829–1912), founder of the Salvation Army (1878). For Booth, while the Holy Spirit of God united, different orthodox doctrines among the churches divided. Hence doctrines such as the Eucharist or Lord's Supper were excluded. Booth's widely read work, *In Darkest England and the Way Out* (London, 1890), gave a vivid account of misery in the slums, but then at the end proposed the solution of resettling Britain's poor in supposedly unoccupied areas of the world – an odd twist to British colonialism. For all social classes, poor and rich alike, church unity was best represented by the popularity of the music and poetry of the hymns.

Priests and ministers had always been involved in pastoral care among the poor, but only in the second half of the century were specialised establishment-supported church organisations created to provide material aid. By the end of the century all the churches in Europe, Britain and the United States were involved in such charitable missions. A new theology, the 'social gospel', had emerged earlier among liberal Protestant theologians in the United States, soon with counterparts in Britain and Germany. It commonly understood the purpose of Christianity as primarily directed to the poor and culturally disadvantaged, and it spoke idealistically of realising the Christian hope of the Kingdom of God. With proposals such as the redistribution of wealth it met stiff resistance. In 1891 Pope Leo XIII issued the encyclical *Rerum Novarum* (On the Rights and Duties of Capital and Labour). It was an important statement in support of justice for labourers, but it made no radical proposals and did not disturb Catholic orthodoxy.

A famous work published in 1802 in France, François-René Chateaubriand's *Genié du christianisme* (The Genius of Christianity) celebrated the beauty and greatness of Catholicism and presaged the full restoration of the Church after Napoleon. Beginning with the July Revolution of 1830, however, and continuing throughout the century, the Catholic Church in France was subject to the highly unsettling effect of alternating periods of revolution and restoration. The Church elsewhere was also faced with disruptive controversy. By mid-century the pope in Rome was under pressure from the political power and liberal thought of the movement to unite Italy. In reaction to this and other modernist influences, in 1864 Pope Pius IX issued a 'Syllabus of Modern Errors' that Catholics must reject, including freedom of religion, toleration of Protestantism by the state, the separation of schools from the Church, the separation of Church and state and the idea that the pope 'can and ought to reconcile himself with progress, with liberalism, and with modern civilization'.[7] The Syllabus was preceded in 1854 by the proclamation of the dogma of the Immaculate Conception of the Virgin Mary. In 1858 a widely publicised miracle, the appearance and words of Mary at Lourdes in France ('I am the Immaculate Conception'), renewed a Catholic tradition of miracles in support of dogma. Modern appearances of Mary had begun with instances in 1830 and in 1840 in Paris, and again in 1846 near the French village of Sallete. In 1870 the First Vatican Council proclaimed the dogma of papal infallibility, effective when the pope announces that he is making an infallible statement of Catholic belief. It was evidently a response to the threat of liberal innovations, but it has been invoked only once, in the declaration of the dogma of the Assumption of Mary into Heaven in 1950. Its important effect was indirect: it secured the infallibility of Catholic doctrine with the pope as its guardian. A number of theologians considered the dogma theologically unsound and conflicts also arose among liberal Catholic laity, especially in Germany. Most who had scruples eventually set them aside and remained in the Church, but a significant minority separated to form the Old Catholic Church. The Roman Catholic Church maintained its anti-modernist course for the rest of the nineteenth and most of the twentieth century. It also remained characterised by its ancient ethnic-national diversity. (Protestantism, if less diverse, was no less ethnic and national). As in American Fundamentalism, Catholic anti-modernism did not include opposition to the technological advances of industrial society.

One cannot mention the appearances of Mary without taking note of popular Catholic piety. It was this, certainly not alone but more than anything else, that carried the anti-modernist Church. If the pious among the people are generally not visible to the eye of the historian, there are exceptions, as in the case of the women and at times children who witnessed the appearances of Mary. But no exception is more striking than the short life of a secluded nun, Thérèse of Lisieux (1873–97), visible through the posthumous publication of her spiritual autobiography: *L'histoire d'une âme* (The Story of a Soul). It was widely read in France and was of significant influence in the Church. In 1925 she was declared a saint.

In the eighteenth century both Protestant and Catholic orthodoxy had been influenced by the rationalist methods of Enlightenment thought, as evidenced by the theological works of the period. A notable and influential feature of Protestant orthodoxy in Britain was the attempt to demonstrate the authenticity of biblical writings and to find evidences of God in nature. The rational method of these studies would become a bridge to the biblical criticism and endeavours of Christians in natural science in the nineteenth century. Nathaniel Lardner's *Credibility of the Gospel History* was first published in 1727 and later republished with additional volumes. The most important work in natural theology was William Paley's *Natural Theology*, published in 1802, which found evidence for God's existence in the design of nature. In the early nineteenth century both works, but especially Paley's, were common textbooks in theological education in Britain and the United States.

Throughout the nineteenth century rationalist philosophy in its secular forms of scepticism, agnosticism and atheism gained steadily in popularity. Among the most notable new schools of thought was Utilitarianism, founded by the atheist British philosopher Jeremy Bentham (1748–1832), who gave it its characteristic feature: happiness for the individual and for the greatest number of people. In the eighteenth century both Christian and secular thought had often made happiness an ideal, so in this sense Bentham's philosophy was not new. Other challenges to Christianity emerged from the scientific study of world religions. Through the mediation of world trade, colonialism and Christian missions, knowledge of other religions became a potent element in academic scholarship. Societies of interested persons were formed for the purpose of increasing information and exploring participation in non-Christian religious thought and practice. In France Eugène Burnouf (1801–52) and later Ernest Renan (1823–92) published works on oriental religion and languages. In Germany Arthur Schopenhauer (1788–1860) argued for Buddhism as an alternative to Christianity. In Britain Max Müller (1823–1900), author of several works on the ancient language and religion of India, was an influential advocate of the study of comparative religions. The first significant work in comparative religions by a theologian in the Church of England was F. D. Maurice's *The Religions of the World and their Relation to Christianity* (1847). In the United States the first was by the Unitarian minister James Freeman Clarke (1810–88): *Ten Great Religions: An Essay in Comparative Religions* (1871). Both were influenced by the unorthodox religious thought that understood all religions as expressions of human beings' inborn relationship to God, a theory rooted ultimately in Platonism but given modern form by the German theologian Friedrich Schleiermacher and by the English poet-theologian Samuel Taylor Coleridge (see below).

In facing the intellectual challenges of the nineteenth century, Protestant theology in the universities of Britain and Germany concentrated increasingly on moral and aesthetic reason, both of which avoided the problem of scientific proof. In both the German philosopher, Immanuel Kant (1724–1804), had considerable influence. Drawing on the scepticism of David Hume (1711–76), Kant demonstrated that 'pure' reason was limited in its reach. For example, it cannot arrive at a first cause of the world because it can never arrive at an end of the regression of conditions and causes. But a proof was possible for the 'practical' or moral reason: the existence of the moral law in the mind of all human beings necessarily involved the existence of God for its completion. An influential Kantian philosopher, Johann Gottlieb Fichte (1762–1814), made the universal 'moral world order' the equivalent of Christianity's Kingdom of God. Kant also opened a philosophical door to Romanticism: in the experience of beauty and of the sublime or awesome, rational thought is overwhelmed by a host of thoughts and feelings, experiences that became the basis of a new aesthetic philosophy. The German poet-philosopher Johann Wolfgang von Goethe (1749–1832), in his drama *Faust*, drew the reader into the dark, irrational and evil side of human experience – a feature of much Romantic literature of the nineteenth century and one that, together with other explorations of human experience, challenged social convention as well as orthodoxy's moral teaching. The seemingly odd couple of empirical science and Romantic feeling and mystery (soon including occult Spiritism) existed together throughout the century.

Renewed interest in the mystical in the Christian tradition was a characteristic of several forms of Catholic and Protestant theology in the nineteenth century. The most famous was the 'Oxford Movement' in the Church of England, documented by the publication *Tracts of the Times* (1835–41). In the first half of the century Oxford University was particularly conservative in its theology, and it was conservative thought that brought forth 'Tractarianism', as the Oxford Movement was also called. It returned theologically and spiritually to ancient and medieval Catholicism. While the Oxford Movement opposed modern secular rationalism, it affirmed, besides the mysticism of ancient tradition, traditional Catholic scholastic reason. Its major figure, John Henry Newman, was to develop a moral proof of the existence of God similar to that of Kant, namely that since moral truths in one's conscience lead one to act against egotistic interests, God must exist as their cause. In a certain sense the Oxford Movement culminated in Newman's conversion to Roman Catholicism in 1845. Most in the Movement remained in the Church of England, but largely because of Newman's conversion and that of many of his sympathisers 'Tractarianism' met a cold reception by most bishops. Nevertheless its effect on the theology of the Church of England was lasting, especially by the interest it fostered in Anglican history and tradition. Generally speaking, history was of great interest in the cultures of the time, and by the end of the century all major universities were involved in the publication of historical texts.

The publication of the *Origin of Species* (1859) by Charles Darwin (1809–82) had been preceded by various works based on the increasing knowledge of organic and inorganic natural history. These had provoked controversy with evidence that neither the kind of creation described in the Bible nor the span of time since creation suggested by it could be true history. Early in the nineteenth century a French professor at the Museum of Natural History at Paris, Jean Baptist Lamarck (1774–1829), had theorised that God created nature with the power of life and gave it certain laws, then left natural processes to evolve. Nature produced a series of beings beginning with simple forms and progressing to higher complex forms that culminate in human beings. Changes in the environment caused new behaviour that became instinctive and was passed on by inheritance. This was the first scientific theory of the evolution of life forms, but since according to Lamarck God knew and willed what the evolutionary result would be, it was also theory about God's design of creation.[8] But Lamarck's theory was controversial, especially since God was not, as in the biblical book of Genesis, directly involved in creating the different forms of nature. In his book *The Vestiges of the Natural History of Creation*, first published in London in

1844, Robert Chambers used concepts of evolution from Lamarck, spoke of creation by God and, like Lamarck, contradicted the biblical account of creation. But scientists found its applications of scientific method frequently inaccurate or fanciful. Its real importance was as a popular work that prepared the way for Darwin. Another important predecessor was Louis Agassiz (1807–73), since 1847 professor at Harvard. Agassiz researched and classified phenomena empirically but attributed species to direct creation by God. Darwin's theory of evolution had no need of God; nothing beyond nature, natural history and natural law (all as simply given) was required. In his later work, *The Descent of Man* (1871), which shows the influence of Auguste Comte's stages of intellectual history, Darwin argues that religion and the idea of God as the highest good developed through the social instinct, which itself evolved from the recognition that groups were stronger in the struggle for existence than individuals. Nevertheless it was Darwin's theory that human beings descend from primates that got the most attention.

In the churches Darwinism could be ignored when it remained distant, as in rural areas and among the poor, or when one for whatever reason chose to ignore it. But it was not distant for theology in the universities and among educated ministers or wherever it became controversial among the laity. It could be rejected outright or mediated with creation by God, which meant combining Darwin's theory of natural selection with some form of created design. Agassiz's position was accepted as compatible with the Biblical account of creation and was advocated for example by the prominent Princeton theologian Charles Hodge (1797–1878). Asa Gray (1810–88), another Harvard professor, a friend of Darwin and a popular source for liberal theologians, is a prominent example of a mediator of Darwinian evolution with created design.

The advantage of Darwin's understanding of evolution was that conclusions did not exceed the evidence. This was what made them, or promised to make them, irrefutable. Darwin had been impressed by Paley's arguments from design in *Natural Theology* (see above), particularly by what Paley said about the design of the eye, which Paley frequently discusses in the work. To refute Paley required a better explanation, which Darwin gave with the theory of natural selection.[9] No creator was required, much as in the previous century David Hume had reasoned that one does not need a creator to explain the existence of the universe. But natural selection was not only about such evolutionary accomplishments. Often it involved intense competition, and some interpretations emphasised the 'tooth and claw' fight for survival. Arthur Schopenhauer's earlier philosophy of a godless, aimless, irrational will that underlies and drives all reality made Darwinism appear particularly dark. 'History and experience', he wrote, show us 'unspeakable misery wherever we look and whatever avenue we explore'.[10]

The British Utilitarian philosopher John Stuart Mill (1806–73) was also impressed with the argument from design about the eye, and he went so far as to state: 'I think it must be allowed that, in the present state of our knowledge, the adaptations in Nature afford a large balance of probability in favour of creation by intelligence.'[11] But Mill was equally impressed by misery and the cruel side of nature. According to Mill, if God is omnipotent, then God must will misery. And if God is good, then God cannot be omnipotent. Religion is, however, useful for those who hope that it may be true, and in the past it has lifted the human spirit for the moral good of humanity. For the 'rational sceptic' (Mill himself) 'it remains a possibility that Christ actually was what he supposed himself to be – not God, for he never made the smallest pretension to that character ... but a man charged with a special, express, and unique commission from God to lead mankind to truth and virtue'. In any case religion's moral influences 'are well worth preserving'. For the rational sceptic these moral impressions do not amount to what can be properly called a religion, but they are 'excellently fitted to aid and fortify that real, though purely human, religion which sometimes calls itself the Religion of Humanity' (compare Comte above). In making the moral good the rule of our life 'we may be cooperating with the unseen Being to whom we owe all that is enjoyable in life'. This idea admits 'the feeling of helping God – of requiting the good he has given by a voluntary cooperation which he, not being omnipotent, really needs, and by which a somewhat nearer approach may be made to the fulfillment of his purposes'.[12]

A German theologian some years younger than Mill, Albrecht Ritschl (1822–89), had a similar understanding of the relationship between nature and morality. In his essay 'Christian Perfection' Ritschl reasons that human beings are part of nature, delivered to 'all possible evils' of nature and human society, and may be crushed by the 'machine of the world'. In order to live in freedom one must be lifted spiritually 'above the world'. The means to this spiritual lifting is God's revelation in Christ, who reconciles the sinner to God.[13] The basic element is the same as in Mill: the conflict between nature and the moral good. According to Ritschl's chief work, *The Christian Doctrine of Justification and Reconciliation* (published in 1874, the same year as Mill's essays on religion), Immanuel Kant's practical or moral reason gives a 'spiritual' proof of God in contrast to proofs related to natural science, and the laws of the spirit or the moral life are different from those of nature that science investigates. Ritschl reasons that the creator must have created nature for the purpose of its subjection to spiritual, moral truth, and it is to this truth that the Christian is converted in reconciliation with God. The similarity to Mill extends to Ritschl's use of the otherwise Utilitarian concepts of pleasure and pain: the pain of suffering under the dominion of nature and the world; the pleasure of spiritual dominion over the world.[14] On the basis of his premise that Christ's 'unique worth lies in the manner in which he mastered his spiritual powers', Ritschl argues that there is no compelling reason to believe his birth was miraculous. Furthermore the work of Christ is not his sacrificial death for the forgiveness of sins, as in traditional orthodoxy, but his demonstration and enabling of the moral victory of spirit over nature.[15] Ritschl's histories, always a central part of his work and notable in the acceptance of biblical criticism, interpreted the course of Christianity in accord with his central ideas. At the end of the century 'Ritschlianism' was not only the most prominent theology in Protestant Germany, but it was also rapidly gaining in popularity in the universities and seminaries of Britain and the United States.

With his positioning of anthropology at the centre of theology and the understanding of Jesus, Ritschl stood in a tradition of liberal theology in Germany that began decades earlier with Friedrich Schleiermacher (1768–1834), a major figure in Romanticism. He is often called the most important theologian of the century because of the extensive influence of the new foundation he gave religious thought, which he developed partly in recognition of Kant's limitation of reason (see above). Schleiermacher published his seminal work in 1799: *On Religion: Speeches to its Cultured Despisers*. The 'cultured despisers' were those among Schleiermacher's friends who considered orthodox Christianity antiquated and irrational. Schleiermacher agreed that orthodox doctrine was unconvincing. The reason was that it had lost the ground from which it first arose and should still arise, namely what Schleiermacher called, in German, 'Gefühl', feeling. He meant feeling of a unique kind. Its focal point is the moment of feeling-perception prior to the objectification that occurs in scientific observation. Immediate experience, of a flower, for example, is a moment of undivided unity with what is experienced. Only secondarily does experience divide into consciousness of the self as subject against an object that the self can know and investigate.[16] Through reflection on pre-objective experience and the language and psychology of religion, Schleiermacher concludes that, while God cannot be objectively known, God communicates meaningfully with all persons through the immediacy of feeling. The most meaningful of these communications are the world religions, and the highest recipient of religious meaning is Jesus, whose teaching of love is religion's perfect expression. But Schleiermacher emphasises the freedom of every person for such reception, assuming one is open to it. In his later work, *The Christian Faith*, Schleiermacher makes 'the feeling of utter dependence' on God the basis of a new interpretation of Christian doctrine, one that should not conflict with science because the relationship from which it arises is not objective. Only secondarily, in reflection, is it made objective. Since Schleiermacher defined the relationship to God by feeling, he could say that belief in objective miracles was not necessary for faith, although he did not argue against them. Jesus was the one great miracle: a purely human being for whom God was immediately present in feeling, a presence that made him the incarnation of God and the teacher of truth. The proof was the believer's experience, as she or he was drawn into Jesus' personal relationship with God.

Schleiermacher's theology was hardly orthodox, although his intent was to reform Christian orthodoxy for modern life and thought. His influence extended, however, into orthodox theology itself. An orthodox theologian only needed to select what was helpful and ignore or reject the rest. For example, a theologian could take from Schleiermacher the loving, community-building work of the Holy Spirit in terms of a psychology of feeling and incorporate it into orthodox belief. With similar modification Schleiermacher's influence can be found in Catholic thought.

Jacob Friedrich Fries (1773–1842) was a German philosopher influenced by Schleiermacher, Kant and Plato. He agreed with Kant that the 'understanding' is limited by the bounds of physical sense to the comprehension of phenomena. His concept of reason is, however, Platonic: it is related to the transcendent reality of God beyond the reach of the understanding, and through it human beings receive ethical and religious ideas. In the early twentieth century, Fries' thought was represented by Rudolf Otto (1869–1937), who published his well-known work, *The Idea of the Holy*, in 1917. In Britain the early mediator of German philosophy, Samuel Taylor Coleridge (1772–1834), conceived the relationship between understanding and reason in essentially the same way as Fries, although he never mentions Fries. He refers only to sources in the English Platonist tradition. Coleridge's influence extended to America through William Ellery Channing (1780–1842), who became the major theologian of Unitarianism on both sides of the Atlantic, and through Channing's student, Ralph Waldo Emerson (1803–82). In his 'Divinity School Address' delivered at Harvard in 1838, Emerson defines understanding and reason as does Coleridge, and the communications of reason are 'sacred oracles of truth'.[17] But whereas reason for Coleridge had Christian truth as its highest form, Emerson's reason is an example of genial Romantic free thought, ever evolving in speculation about transcendent reality and the meaning of life.

Schleiermacher's colleague at the University of Berlin, the philosopher G. W. F. Hegel (1770–1831), was also of significant influence on theology and religious thought. Like Schleiermacher he reflected on the unity of the human subject and the object of its perception, but he rejected Schleiermacher's theory of pre-objective feeling as having no real content. He also rejected Fries' concept of reason as irrational and disagreed with Kant's thesis that reason cannot know God. His interest lay in the rational philosophical analysis of objective thought as the identity of knower and what is known. Essentially they are not two, but one, in two modes of being. This involved not only objects of perception, but all things humanly meaningful: science, culture, religion and human history, which had now progressed to philosophical recognition of the identity of subjective and objective in all reality. The life of history is 'Spirit', which Hegel develops in his first major work, *The Phenomenology of Spirit* (1807). Primitive humanity had to cope with a hostile environment, an alienation of self and world that it had to master or overcome through arduous work. Historical process involved ascending levels of alienation and their overcoming. In belief in the God-human, Christ, human beings first became aware of their oneness or identity with God as the ultimate reconciliation of self and reality. But this was not yet knowledge of absolute identity, mainly because in Christian belief God stands apart from and above the human believer, a remnant of alienation. The deficiency is philosophically overcome in the 'absolute idea' of Spirit's knowledge of its identity with itself, the knowledge of the unity of all in all. The absolute Idea becomes the foundation for the expectation that current and future alienations in the complexities of human life may be overcome.

The broad acceptance of Hegelianism in Germany opened a way for understanding Darwinism before Darwin, and Darwinism was less controversial in Germany than in the United States or Britain. But soon Hegelianism gained in popularity among philosophers and liberal theologians also in these countries. After Hegel's death two opposing interpretations of religion emerged among his students, both with a basis in his writings. In his later lectures on the philosophy of religion the God of Christianity is real and the meaning of identity or Spirit is expressed by God's encompassing love, so that Christian faith and philosophy seem but two sides of the same coin. In other works, however, faith and religion are lower, limited forms of thought, which are lifted to the Absolute only by philosophy. Among the right wing of Hegel's interpreters were theologians who found in Hegel a new way of interpreting Christianity. For the left wing, religion was not only inferior but also detrimental to philosophical truth. This was especially true for the radical 'Young Hegelians'. According to Ludwig Feuerbach (1804–72) the history of Spirit was simply the history of human beings; God was an ideal fantasy. Love was for Feuerbach 'The Essence of Christianity', as his book of 1841 is titled. Love was so much a need in human life that human beings, above all in their misery, projected the ideal of love into an imaginary heaven with an imaginary holy family of Father, Son and an idealised mother in the Virgin Mary. Individual immortality was also an imagined projection into this heaven. What humanity needed was loving communities organised to overcome alienation. For Karl Marx, the beginning of the communist revolution lay in Feuerbach's criticism: 'the criticism of religion is the premise of all criticism'. 'Man makes religion – this is what humanity must now understand.'[18]

Another left-wing Hegelian, David Friedrich Strauss (1808–74), made theological history with his publication of 1835, *The Life of Jesus Critically Examined*. In the extensive main part of the work Strauss developed the earlier formulated thesis that the gospels of the New Testament were written following a period of oral tradition. Strauss' important addition was that oral tradition transformed a human Jesus into a mythical, idealised God-man and miracle worker. No intent to lie was involved, but only a telling about Jesus and his deeds that increasingly took on fantastic forms. Jesus' miracles were not true history; neither were the Christmas and Easter stories. Practically the entirety of the gospels was 'myth'. Moreover one knows empirically that no human being can be perfect as Jesus was supposed to have been. In the conclusion Strauss writes that historical and philosophical criticism can only alienate the educated church minister from traditional faith, but honesty requires criticism. Strauss recommends that the minister accommodate himself to the faith of the people he serves while endeavouring to raise their awareness to a more truthful, philosophical understanding. In another work published in 1840–1, *Die christliche Glaubenslehre* (The Christian Doctrine of Faith), Strauss 'dissolves' the doctrines of traditional orthodoxy into their historical origins; they belong to the past. In a later work he writes that the religion of Christ must now be transformed into the 'Religion of Humanity', the concept Comte had formulated (see above). In his last work, published in 1871, *Der alte und der neue Glaube* (The Old and the New Faith), he contrasts the antiquated 'old faith' of Christianity with the 'new faith' of the Darwinian world view and modern secular culture.

Closely associated with Strauss were the Hegelian historians Ferdinand Christian Baur (1792–1860) and his 'Tübingen School' of critical New Testament scholars. Baur's important work was in New Testament literary criticism, in which he and his school made advances in understanding the composition of New Testament writings, advances that became major signposts for later scholarship. Strauss and Baur had not initiated historical criticism of the Bible, but their work and controversial conclusions spurred its development as nothing had done before. Criticism of the Bible and early Christianity now came to the centre of theological attention in Europe, Britain and the United States. Not only theologians but also and increasingly academic secularists contributed scholarly work to the effort. The most notable was Ernest Renan's *Histoire des origines du christianisme* (History of the Origins of Christianity), whose first volume, *Vie de Jésus* (Life of Jesus), published in Paris in 1863, was especially widely read.

Conservative German reaction to Strauss was sharp. In the church newspaper he edited, the orthodox theologian E. W. Hengstenberg (1802–69) called Strauss' *Life of Jesus* the 'beast from the abyss' in the New Testament's Book of Revelation, chapter 11.[19] In his commentary on Revelation 20:1–3, Hengstenberg interpreted the 1,000 years of the suppression of Satan as beginning with the coronation of Charlemagne in the year 800, therefore ending approximately in 1800, which means with Napoleon and his wars against European political and religious establishments.[20] Hengstenberg's reaction to Strauss and modernity was very much like anti-modernism in Roman Catholicism and American Fundamentalism. In general, however, the response of theologians was moderate, in recognition that issues raised by Strauss needed to be addressed by their own scholarly work. The publication in Britain of *Essays and Reviews* in 1860 and of *Lux Mundi* in 1889 were significant events in the recognition of critical scholarship among orthodox theologians of the Church of England. At the same time, caution was raised against the potential of criticism for mere destruction and the consequences for religious and social institutions.

As noted above, the last quarter of the nineteenth century saw the rise of the popularity of Ritschlianism, an influential school of German theologians who recognised Albrecht Ritschl as their most formative influence. At the core of Ritschlianism was the demonstration that theology could avoid the problem of miracles that Strauss and modern science posed by focusing on the higher truth of spiritual life. In this effort none exceeded the work of Adolf Harnack (1851–1930), Professor of Theology in Berlin and by far the most famous of the school. Well known in Britain and the United States, he was twice offered a chair in theology at Harvard. For Harnack, Jesus was a full human being whose teaching was a mixture of inherited Jewish thought and the entirely original product of his own uniquely personal relationship to God (an influence of Schleiermacher). In his best-known work, *What is Christianity?* first published in 1900, Harnack summarises the originality of Jesus' teaching under three headings: the Kingdom of God and its coming in personal spiritual life; the fatherhood of God and the infinite value of the human soul; and the higher righteousness and the commandment to love. As in Ritschl, an essential benefit of Jesus' teaching is spiritual elevation above 'the tyranny of matter' and spiritual 'dominion over the world'.[21] The immortality of the soul in its infinite value, not the bodily resurrection of Jesus, belonged to the essence of Christianity. According to

Harnack's history, as Christianity entered the Greco-Roman world it left the Jewish aspects of Jesus' teaching behind and adopted instead Greek and Latin forms: Platonic metaphysics and Stoic ethics. But the core teaching of Jesus, the product of his unique relationship to God, was kept as the essence of Christian teaching, and so it has remained throughout the course of Christian history. Each new culture has contributed its own historical forms and discarded others, but the essence has remained. The influence of D. F. Strauss is visible in the impermanence of doctrines other than the essence of Jesus' teaching.

Ernst Troeltsch (1865–1923), who received his schooling under Ritschlian teachers, explored the historical evidence for how the progress of science modifies religion and how religious values do or do not influence social ethics. His first major work was published in 1902: *The Absoluteness of Christianity and the History of Religions*. He argues that all religions are subject to historical relativity (time and place), but that they are also revelations of an 'Absolute' that transcends the relativities of history. Christianity may claim absoluteness only in one sense, namely as a religion of personal redemption that purifies from guilt and pride – an 'idea' that, even if Christianity were extinguished, must reappear in history. Troeltsch sees a tendency to ethical convergence of religions that suggests a universal goal towards which they are moving. In another work he coins the term 'religious apriori' for a disposition of the human mind through which it is connected with the absolute 'divine life'.[22] One recognises the influence of Schleiermacher and Fries. In a time of world-encompassing Christian missions, Troeltsch spoke of the inseparable connection of Christianity and Western culture in these missions. He advocated a community of world religions based on mutual respect and understanding.[23]

William James (1842–1910), Professor of Philosophy at Harvard, argued in his *Varieties of Religious Experience* (1902) that religion is 'feeling' and has nothing to do with science or the understanding. Its primary forms are those of the great religious figures of history, whose teachings demonstrate significant moral similarities. As a pragmatist he judged religion, like John Stuart Mill, by its benefits or effects. For James these are morality, love of others and a sense of security. In the 'sub-consciousness' a higher self is operative that, similar to Troeltsch's 'religious apriori', connects the mind with a mysterious all-encompassing reality that transcends all conceptions of it. This mystery must be real, James argues, because it produces the benefits of religion. Both Troeltsch and James were to have significant influence on liberal theology in the twentieth century.

At the end of the nineteenth century all religious orthodoxies were in a defensive position towards modern culture, but they were still a significant force in church and society, especially in Roman Catholicism and American Fundamentalism. Liberal Protestant theology, for its part, confidently led the way in the rapidly developing field of biblical criticism and in meeting the challenges of Darwinism. But it rested on theologically uncertain ground. Liberal theology's foundational concepts were subject to fluctuation, particularly as basic ideas in philosophy changed. Theologies like Adolf Harnack's that reduced Christianity to a core of practicable general concepts could make an actual revelation superfluous and a church unnecessary. For the time being, however, liberal theology was in ascendency. Orthodox theology would not find new and positive sources of energy until after the First World War, for example in the work of a Danish theologian almost completely overlooked in the nineteenth century, Søren Kierkegaard (1813–55). But whether theologians and churches were orthodox or liberal, by the end of the century indifference towards the churches was growing and in the cities was a serious problem. Competition and opposition in the form of atheist or agnostic secularism, new philosophies, eastern religions and Spiritism had increased. The social and economic condition of the industrial poor had steadily worsened. With some notable exceptions an ethical blind eye was turned to the injustices of colonialism, racism and increasingly anti-Semitism. Especially, but not only, in central Europe chauvinistic nationalism religiously venerated the nation and its military power, often incorporating the nation's Christian heritage, whether Catholic or Protestant, and claiming the will of God. Few recognised the signs of the catastrophe that loomed on the near horizon.

NOTES

1 See H. Bettenson and C. Maunder, eds., *Documents of the Christian Churches* (Oxford: Oxford University Press, 2011).

2 J. Locke, *The Reasonableness of Christianity, with A Discourse of Miracles and Part of a Third Letter Concerning Toleration*, ed. I. T. Ramsey (Palo Alto, CA: Stanford University Press, 1958), pp. 10–11, 55–63, 75f.

3 N. O. Hatch, *The Democratization of American Christianity* (New Haven, CT: Yale University Press, 1989), pp. 170–9.

4 A. Comte, *The Positive Philosophy* (Cambridge: Cambridge University Press, 2009), Book VI.

5 Karl Marx and Frederick Engels, *Collected Works* (New York: International Publishers, 1975), vol. 3, pp. 175–6, 182.

6 J. Morris, *F. D. Maurice and the Crisis of Christian Authority* (Oxford: Oxford University Press, 2005), p. 146.

7 *The Encyclical Letter of Pope Pius IX and the Syllabus of Modern Errors, Dated Dec. 8, 1864* (Catholic Church, n.d., n.p.).

8 A. S. Packard, *Lamarck, the Founder of Evolution* (New York: Longmans, Green & Co., 1901), pp. 376–8.

9   P. Barrett and R. Freeman, eds., *The Works of Charles Darwin*, vol. 16: *The Origin of Species, 1876* (London: Pickering & Chatto, 1988), pp. 151–4.

10   A. Schopenhauer, *The World as Will and Representation* (New York: Dover, 1958), vol. 1, p. 323.

11   J. S. Mill, *Nature, Religion, and Theism* (London: Longmans, Green & Co., 1874), pp. 171–5.

12   Ibid, pp. 37–43, 255–6.

13   A. Ritschl, *Christliche Vollkommenheit, Theologie und Metaphysik* (Göttingen: Vandenhoeck & Ruprecht, 1902), p. 19. My translation.

14   A. Ritschl, *The Christian Doctrine of Justification and Reconciliation*, H. R. Mackintosch and A. B. Macaulay, eds. (Edinburgh: T & T Clark, 1900), pp. 205, 628–9.

15   Ibid, pp. 332–3, 456–7, 477–84.

16   F. Schleiermacher, *On Religion* (Cambridge: Cambridge University Press, 1988), pp. 31–2.

17   D. Robinson, ed., *The Spiritual Emerson* (Boston, MA: Beacon Press, 2003), pp. 67–70.

18   Marx and Engels, *Collected Works*, vol. 3, pp. 175–6.

19   As reported by Strauss in *Die Halben und die Ganzen* [The Halves and the Wholes] (Berlin: Franz Duncker, 1865), p. 67.

20   E. W. Hengstenberg, *The Revelation of St. John* (New York: R. Carter, 1852–3), vol. 2, pp. 334–5.

21   A. Harnack, *What Is Christianity?* [1900] (Minneapolis, MN: Fortress Press, 2011), pp. 150, 271.

22   E. Troeltsch, *The Absoluteness of Christianity* (Louisville, KY: Westminster John Knox, 2005), pp. 98–106; E. Troeltsch, *Religion in History* (Minneapolis, MN: Fortress Press, 1991), pp. 33–45.

23   E. Troeltsch, 'Mission in der modernen Welt', in *Gesammelte Schriften*, vol. 2 (Tübingen: Mohr Siebeck, 1913), pp. 791–804.

4

NORBERT WASZEK

Philosophy in the Wake of Hegel[*]

1831 and After

When Hegel died in late 1831, suddenly and unexpectedly, he still reigned, widely acclaimed, over philosophy – and not just in many German-speaking territories. The thought of people inspired by Hegel's ideas continued to evolve for a long time, from Finland to Naples, from Russia and Poland to France and further afield. However, there was also some awareness that a peak had been attained and limits reached. 'Our philosophical revolution has come to an end. Its great circle was closed by Hegel', wrote Heinrich Heine in his *On the History of Religion and Philosophy in Germany* (1835),[1] and with this he might well have been echoing Eduard Gans, who ended his 1831 obituary on his teacher and friend Hegel by saying that, 'Hegel leaves many ingenious disciples, but no successor; for philosophy has, for the time being, completed its circle.'[2]

For all of that, not even Heine and Gans, who might be considered among the earliest on the wing of sometime disciples more divergent from Hegel, so-called Left Hegelians,[3] really questioned that 'Hegelian philosophy', as John Edward Toews put it, 'had embodied the truth'.[4] A bridgehead had been attained, a current state of learning there was no going back on or from. The work of the pathfinder or pioneer had been done, leaving not a wake so much as a track, which, though liable in large part to disappear, due to improvements and further advances the pioneering made possible, raises important questions about the history and methods and foundations of the human sciences.

This chapter attempts to show how some of Hegel's disciples contributed to changing the contours of philosophy: they developed new academic disciplines out of Hegel's *Encyclopaedia of Philosophical Sciences* that soon

[*] Thanks to the Director of the Centre of Classical German Philosophy at the Ruhr University Bochum/Germany, Birgit Sandkaulen, for comments on an earlier version of this chapter.

emancipated themselves from the metaphysical fetters by which they were previously confined. But to describe the transition as one from metaphysics to empiricism would oversimplify the issue at stake.

David Friedrich Strauss,[5] who would soon revolutionise Protestant theology with his seminal *The Life of Jesus* (1835–6),[6] came to Berlin in 1831 with the principal purpose of listening to Hegel's lectures. He was able to hear only a few before Hegel's death, but this dramatic loss moved him to stay steadfast in his intention to deepen his knowledge of Hegel's philosophy. He wrote to an old friend: 'Hegel has died, but has not died out here.'[7] By 'here' he meant the intellectual and institutional milieu within which Hegel's philosophy was continued by a 'school' of devoted students, also called a 'circle of friends',[8] some of them professors already in Hegel's lifetime. It is hardly surprising that after Hegel's death Strauss attended the lectures of three professors who had been close to Hegel, Philipp Konrad Marheineke, Leopold von Henning and Karl Ludwig Michelet, as well as those of Friedrich Schleiermacher.[9] A little later, Strauss took an active part in the debates and events often described as that process of division between 'young and old', or 'left and right' Hegelianism, nowadays taken as warrant to speak of the original existence of a 'school'.

Leaving for a little later details on how that Hegelian 'school' emerged, developed and divided, it should be underlined from the start quite why Hegel's philosophy was especially liable, in contrast with others, to become a 'school'. This is intimately related to Hegel's wide conception of philosophy, his well-known integration into an encyclopaedic system quite a number of different fields of study already, or soon to become, distinct academic disciplines. As the full title of the relevant book suggests – *Encyclopaedia of the Philosophical Sciences in Basic Outline* – Hegel sought a systematic account of all 'philosophical sciences'. Given the overwhelming richness of material he could of course do so only in 'outline' even what one translator emphasised as just '*basic* outline'.[10] Hegel's disciples thus had the opportunity (burden, some might say) of spelling out consequences of Hegel's 'outline' for whichever respective disciplines within which each was becoming (or aspired to be) a specialist. As early as 1844, in his seminal biography of Hegel, Karl Rosenkranz already articulated the thesis that Hegel's school had emerged almost naturally, as a matter of course, out of the philosopher's encyclopaedic system. As a member of the inner circle of Hegel's 'friends' and followers (though never formally a 'student' of Hegel in the strict sense), Rosenkranz was obviously well informed and personally acquainted with most scholars he mentioned. As we shall see, his thesis might even be read as a reflection on his own work and its development. Rosenkranz's discussion of why

Hegel's philosophy was particularly liable to create a 'school' climaxes in a passage that warrants quotation in full:

> Finally, the encyclopaedic universality [of Hegel's philosophy] offered gateways to all particular directions in scientific research. Even when the disciple renounced any intention to modify any principle [of Hegel's system], the option remained open to him to prove himself in the speculative assessment and penetration of a particular subject matter, to render service to its development and thus to foster philosophy itself. The theologian, jurist, natural scientist, linguist, political scientist, historian, aesthetician, all will be called upon to active cooperation in the great work. The master needed journeymen, and the journeymen had the prospect of becoming masters in their [respective] disciplines. This animated assiduity – [to be found] in Marheineke, Gans, Hotho, Michelet … [and Rosenkranz lists another dozen] – launched itself on the different sciences with a lust for conquest, and caused in them substantial transformations that are far from completed.[11]

We can examine this thesis first with the help of significant examples, from three different and complementary disciplines – history of law, art history and the history of literature, associated with prominent Hegelians: Gans, Hotho and Rosenkranz himself – before looking at what Hegel refers to as 'one of the sciences which originated in the modern age' – political economy, in its relationship to philosophy (cf. the emblematic §189 of his *Elements of the Philosophy of Right*)[12] – concluding with Lorenz Stein that something can be added as regards the emergence of sociology out of German Idealism, what Herbert Marcuse called 'the emancipation of sociology from philosophy'.[13]

Hegel's School

The existence in his lifetime of a Hegelian 'school', when Hegel was at Berlin, is beyond doubt. An account of its formation and development could include a lengthy list of former students, friends and followers[14] already transmitting Hegel's thought to the next generation, and often using Hegel's manuals. Another indicator of the existence of a 'school', published defences of its founding figure, can be seen as early as the 1833 foreword (by Gans) to the first posthumous edition of Hegel's *Philosophy of Right*. Until almost the end of the nineteenth century, disciples of Hegel continued to publish texts in an apologetic or critical vein: when the master was attacked, his former students and friends were ready to reply.[15] Other documents confirming the lively existence of a 'school' that had emerged out of Hegel's philosophy include the *Yearbook for Scientific Criticism* (*Jahrbücher für wissenschaftliche Kritik*), for over twenty years the leading Hegelian review, and generally remaining close to the philosopher's intentions and convictions.[16] The first complete edition of Hegel's works,[17] edited by a 'circle of friends of the deceased',[18] is also very relevant. This not only republished the philosopher's printed books, it created a new corpus by editing the vast cycles of previously unreleased lectures. These lectures presented disciples with difficult tasks, managed differently according not only to the capacities respective to different editors, but with the condition as well as quality of the bodies of material they had to work with. Together the editions of Hegel's completed books and the posthumous compilations or editions of other material fulfilled a double function for Hegel's school. They were brought and stood together by the need to work together, with greater unity and mutual cohesion as Hegel's disciples; and methods of communication were established presenting more clearly to the outside the presence and image of the school.

This is not, however, the end of the story for the edition of Hegel's 'works' by his 'circle of friends', especially granted our concern here with what emerged, formed or was developed from within Hegel's encyclopaedic outline. Keen to build upon Hegel's systematic labours, disciples when they transformed Hegel's lectures into books were tempted to exaggerate, canonise and maybe even enclose as a *system* what was systematic but not set hard in their master's teaching. Whereas recent editions of student notes on Hegel's lectures[19] show him experimenting with material and over the years changed not just details but the very structure of presentation, at least some of the editors of the first collected works smoothed out differences and tensions, giving a semblance of closed and rigid system of a kind that Hegel never advocated. The prime case to explore these difficulties is Heinrich G. Hotho's edition of Hegel's *Aesthetics*.[20] On the one hand, his edition is an admirable achievement, transforming *disjecta membra poetae* (Hegel's own lecture notes, in disorder and overcharged with later additions; notes from a variety of former students who attended the lectures in different years) into a well-written, organised and successful book.[21] On the other hand, and more recently, Hotho's work has come under some fire, not only for liberties taken with the material at his disposal, but for burying in the text changes arbitrarily introduced, and modifications of his own devising.[22] The issue need not be settled here; in the end, it might be a question of perspective: while some readers appreciate a well-written book, without the niceties of a critical apparatus, others want to know what the philosopher said exactly in one year or the other.

While there were of course dissensions between Hegel's disciples before 1831, Hegel in person had some charisma and an ability to settle disputes or effect reconciliations well before antagonisms were generated. The cohesion of his school might even have been reinforced during the period of shock and grief at his sudden death, when feelings of gratitude were fresh and strong and united 'friends' to continue collective work on the *Yearbooks* and the first edition of collected works. A little later, the inevitable ensued. Hegel was no longer there to bridge conflicts and the school's unity was undermined.

It has been a commonplace of the history of ideas that a 'split' or 'dissolution' of the Hegelian school ensued, whether twofold (right/old and left/young) or threefold (criticism-prone left; preserving and defensive centre; accommodating and conservative right).[23] The left/centre/right terminology, from the seating arrangement in the French Assembly since 1789, came from David F. Strauss, originally with an irony some of his readers missed.[24] It is no accident that it was in his discussions of Christology that Strauss elaborated this distinction, for questions related to religion played a leading role in the debates of the 1830s, although not with a huge precedence over political (in particular constitutional questions) and social issues.

Eduard Gans, the Law of Inheritance

Among disciplines emergent from Hegel's encyclopaedic system, the first, chronologically speaking, was in Eduard Gans'[25] *The Law of Inheritance in World Historical Development*.[26] Gans' study had begun to appear as early as 1824, when Hegel was still around to comment upon the enterprise. Within the universal history of civil law, Gans considered the law of inheritance as a special development, by no means the side issue it might seem to some at first glance, but of vital social importance because of its intrinsic connections. Whereas laws of inheritance (plainly) concern the passing on of property, rights and obligations upon the death of an individual, Gans conceived their academic study as necessarily a part of philosophy.[27] Since he made no secret of his adherence to 'the last, profound and up to date configuration of philosophy … Hegel's system',[28] Gans in the realisation of his project untiringly scrutinised Indian, Chinese, Jewish and Islamic laws of inheritance, before turning to Greece and Rome. Not averse to the provocation of the historical school of law and its uncontested leader, von Savigny, Gans had larger reasons to challenge Savigny's privileging a single tradition with his *History of Roman Law in the Middle Ages*.[29]

In his *Lectures on the Philosophy of World History*[30] Hegel followed a similar course through much the same civilisations attended to by Gans. When he mentions Gans' recent publication in a letter, he not only seems proud of his disciple's success; commenting on it, he states explicitly that Gans had based his study in the history of law on his own lectures on world history.[31] This is how Hegel wished his disciples to make productive use, each in his own discipline, of the appropriate outline provided in his *Encyclopedia*.

Gans was not the only student who, in the spirit of Hegel, turned to a specialised treatment of a legal subject. Karl Ludwig Michelet, at the time another doctoral student, relates in his autobiography how Hegel orientated him towards a law subject for his thesis.[32] Unlike Michelet, however, who later turned to other fields,[33] Gans remained a professor of law (he even advanced to the office of Dean of the Law Faculty in 1831). More important for the present chapter, he became a pioneer of *comparative law in a universal perspective*. It is no exaggeration to say that, building on the mere intentions or the programmatic statements of such forerunners as Montesquieu, the elder Feuerbach and his Heidelberg teacher Thibaut,[34] Gans really created that discipline and executed its programme in an exemplary manner with his *Law of Inheritance*. In this achievement, his debt to Hegel cannot be doubted. He declared it often enough and with gratitude. It was almost inevitable, nevertheless, that this enterprise also led Gans beyond Hegel. On the one hand, the very richness of the historical material induced Gans, as he put it himself, gradually to stray from the systematic structure of Hegel's philosophy.[35] On the other hand, Gans liberated his new discipline from Hegel's exclusive retrospect – 'the owl of Minerva begins its flight only with the onset of dusk'[36] – and opened it to the future.[37]

Hotho's Philosophical History of Art

There is no surprise in Hotho's[38] ambition to match Gans' achievements in the history of law with his own efforts towards a philosophical history of art. The two men were in close contact, and indeed friends.[39] Belated in appearance and fragmentary in form the final fruits of Hotho's work perhaps were, but the intentions of the discipline he embraced and cultivated are still clearly outlined in his earlier contributions to the above mentioned *Yearbook*.[40] In one of his first articles, commenting on a recent inquiry into justice in its world-historical development,[41] Hotho considers the relation of Hegel's School to the specific task of furthering new disciplines: 'While Descartes, Spinoza, Kant and Fichte required confessors [*Bekenner*], but no disciples who were [at the same time] collaborators, it belongs to the principle of contemporary philosophy [meaning Hegel's philosophy] that, considering the breadth and variety of the subjects to be conquered, it cannot accomplish itself without the help of diversely talented collaborators.'[42]

According to Hotho, the disciples turned to Hegel's philosophy when they sought principles that could assist in their new elaboration of particular fields. In that perspective it was characteristic of Hotho to privilege Hegel's late Berlin *Encyclopedia* over the earlier *Phenomenology*, calling the latter outdated, of 'a time, the interests and claims of which lie behind us'. Hotho's own enterprise of a Hegelian history of art was elaborated at a period when a so-called Berlin School of art history, with authors like Aloys Hirt and Carl Friedrich von Rumohr, was fashionable. Hotho built upon their work in a concern for descriptive precision and accurate chronology, but called them 'spirited [*geistvolle*] empiricists'. His own concern was for a furtherance of Hegel's philosophy by way of critical development, and against subordination of works of art under the categories of a stringent system – a dogmatic procedure that might or might not be called pseudo-Hegelian. His work here was no abandonment of a project of a world-historical and philosophical history of art, as he made plain in another review for the *Yearbooks*:

> The drive towards a treatment of history that is at once world-historical and philosophical is beginning at last to extend itself to the history of art ... The author of these pages holds the opinion that the history of art, which has hitherto flourished in its empirical direction, has not only to be dealt with philosophically, but has to be integrated and carried through as a part within the science of beauty and art.[43]

While this sounds indeed Hegelian, Hotho cannot be called a mere epigone, a humdrum or parroting follower, given the important revaluation of Greek and Roman art and reconsideration of Northern and Christian art within his project. Throughout his own life Hegel remained under what E. M. Butler referred to polemically in a famous book as 'the tyranny of Greece over Germany',[44] and guilty of neglect or disparagement of contemporary art. Hotho too had something of a habit of denigrating contemporary artworks, but did not maintain the view of Greek culture as ultimate standard. It was for him only one epoch (among others); each epoch, Hotho insists, has its own value. Hence his dedication of so much time and energy in later life working on Christian painting.[45]

Rosenkranz' History of Literature

Karl Rosenkranz' efforts towards a history of literature, elaborated in various studies starting in 1830, may here serve as the third example, culminating in the first fundamental study of Diderot in German and a string of late publications.[46] He can also be considered a pioneer, beside J. F. Herbart, his predecessor at Königsberg in Kant's former chair, of a systematic philosophy of education.[47] His two earliest studies (the first from 1830, when Hegel was still alive) give a good idea of Rosenkranz' perspective and intentions. Although Hegel is not explicitly mentioned in the 1830 text – beside its concentration on poetry of the Middle Ages, this might account for the book's warm welcome from Ludwig Tieck and other authors of the Romantic movement[48] – Rosenkranz in his preface already stresses his desire to provide 'a history of poetry from the philosophical point of view'.[49] Reflecting on those years, Rosenkranz in his autobiographical writings makes more explicit the Hegelian connotation of his enterprise, its principal perspective the pursuit of the 'history of consciousness and how it reflected in the poetic productions of the Middle Ages'.[50] As if the allusion to the 'history of consciousness' was not clear enough, he added a little later that he was at the time completely under the spell (*Befangenheit*) of Hegel's *Phenomenology*. While it was from there, notably the chapter on the 'religion of art', rather than from Hegel's lectures on aesthetics, that Rosenkranz took his leading principles,[51] he defends himself against charges of a narrow-minded pseudo-Hegelian scholasticism. Not for him subjection of empirical material to an already completed system.[52] His criticism of the *Phenomenology* as 'one-sided and insufficient' with regard to the Middle Ages was followed up with an attempt to 'complete and perfect' its treatment.[53] His *Handbook* of 1832/33 is world-historical in its scope (from the oriental world, via Greek and Roman antiquity, towards modern European poetry) with a strong Hegelian flavour and now explicit references to Hegel.[54]

Rosenkranz also went beyond Hegel in trying to unite the aesthetic classifications, e.g. according to the forms of poetry (epic, lyric and didactic), with a closer attention to individual works of poetry, and handling an astounding wealth of material. It was probably this quality of his work that allowed his emancipation of the discipline of the history of literature from the Hegelian system. He also reinforced the Hegelian perspective on the development of literature, notably with a conspectus at the end of his third and final volume[55] – a provision decided on as a result of exchanges between Rosenkranz and Hotho.[56] The creation of disciplines out of Hegel's encyclopaedic system was a co-operative enterprise. Looking back on his *Handbook* in his autobiography, Rosenkranz was well entitled to the proud claim that his history of poetry was the 'first completely realized effort in the field, written according to aesthetic principles and with a world-historical perspective'.[57]

Political Economy: A Science that Originated in the Modern Age

The case of political economy is more intricate but probably also of greater importance. As indicated above (cf. note 12), Hegel himself had celebrated the discipline as one that 'does credit to thought', its recent emergence associated with the three names of Adam Smith, Jean-Baptiste Say, David Ricardo – all still regarded as its founding fathers. In this new science the quality that Hegel most appreciated was that 'it finds the laws underlying a mass of contingent occurrences'. Comparing this science with that of astronomy, Hegel spelled out the distinct achievement of political economy: 'it bears a resemblance to the planetary system, which presents only irregular movements to the eye, yet whose laws can nevertheless be recognized'.[58] The use Hegel made of the discoveries of the political economists, whom he had thus acknowledged his indebtedness in his 'system of needs' (§§ 189–208) and in further sections of his account of 'civil society', too, has often attracted keen interest. This has continued from a famous passage of Karl Marx's preface to his *A Contribution to the Critique of Political Economy* (1859),[59] through twentieth-century Hegel scholarship.[60]

While that subsequent history is beyond this chapter's scope, it should be made clear that Hegel's disciples were fully aware of this integration of political economy into his system. In his preface to his 1833 edition of Hegel's *Philosophy of Right*, Gans explains that even the science of political economy 'is given its due place in the treatment of "civil society"'.[61] In his own lectures, published some years ago now,[62] Gans went further along the same lines by complementing Hegel's hints to eminent economists with a fuller, tripartite outline of economic doctrine: (1) Jean-Baptiste Colbert's 'mercantile system'; (2) the 'physiocratic system' exemplified by François Quesnay; (3) the 'now dominant' and 'only true' 'industrial system',[63] founded by Adam Smith and further elaborated by Ricardo and Say. Gans explicitly professes the later system and considers it capable of 'infinite perfection'.[64] In some later lecture courses Gans appears to have integrated German authors on economic theory into the third category, notably Karl Heinrich Rau (1792–1870)[65] – according to Friedrich Engels, one of the rare German economists who Marx had really studied (his main focus was on the 'great French and English [authors]').[66] Gans also made a few passing remarks on Saint-Simonian theories in that context,[67] a subject dealt with in an earlier part of his lectures and in other texts.[68]

Important here is that Gans clearly saw the need to say more on the new science of political economy, hence his outline of different stages of economic thought. He also acknowledges that a whole new terminology had been coined by the new discipline.[69] Unlike with his own project on the universal history of the law of succession, he did not, however, think it necessary to separate the discipline of political economy from Hegel's 'system of needs': the fundamental opening section of the larger part of Hegel's system, entitled 'civil society', presented in Hegel's *Philosophy of Right* and, even more succinctly, in the corresponding paragraphs of his *Encyclopedia* (§§523–8).

In contrast, Hegel himself, after having published his *Philosophy of Right* (1820/1821[70]), appears to have had second thoughts on the matter. This becomes evident in his later *Lectures on the History of Philosophy*,[71] where he deals in various places with the changing contours of philosophy. Already in the context of his treatment of Plato, Hegel says that 'the word philosophy has had different meanings at different times' and among the eccentric examples he uses to illustrate his point are 'the English who call philosophy what we call experimental physics and chemistry'.[72] When he later mentions Newton, he comes back to the different scope attributed to philosophy in different countries:

> Mathematics and physics are called by ['the English'] Newtonian philosophy. Also in most recent times this expression is still in use. Observations are being made on political economy, on the course of wealth; the political economy of Adam Smith has gained fame in England. Such general principles as the liberalization of trade are there called maxims of philosophy, are called philosophy.[73]

Hegel goes on to give an example for this use of the term 'philosophy' from an 1825 speech by George Canning,[74] an example Hegel had found when reading *The Morning Chronicle*.[75] In passages quoted, Hegel is already excluding implicitly such uses of the term 'philosophy' and at least one set of students' notes on his 1825/6 lectures says explicitly, 'everything that is derived from general principles is called philosophical. We intend to exclude all these aspects from the focus of our treatment.'[76] Thus, it is only coherent that Hegel, when treating of Scottish philosophy in his lectures,[77] applies this exclusion: he does not present Smith's economic ideas, but mentions him in the context of other authors (Francis Hutcheson, Adam Ferguson, Dugald Stewart) writing on moral subjects, saying 'in this sense the economist Adam Smith is a philosopher too',[78] obviously an allusion to Smith's *Theory of Moral Sentiments* (1759), though no definite proof of his firsthand knowledge of the text. Hegel appears to have been aware that Smith (like Hutcheson and Ferguson) developed his economic ideas while in a university chair of moral philosophy (at Glasgow in his case) and conceived these ideas initially as branches of that discipline. Of course, Smith subsequently did much to emancipate the modern discipline of economics (just like Ferguson for sociology). Hegel, on the other hand, is writing from the other side of the divide, seeking a philosophical synthesis *after* these sciences had emerged. Political economy, like any other science, is providing him with material for his philosophical enterprise, but can in itself no longer be considered part of 'philosophy'.

Lorenz Stein: First German Sociology

The case of Lorenz Stein is fascinating.[79] Herbert Marcuse in his study *Reason and Revolution*, written in exile in the United States, devotes around fifteen pages to Stein, the fourth and final section of a chapter on the transitional figures (next to Stein stand the utopian socialist Claude Henri de Saint-Simon, Auguste Comte, the French father of sociology and, curiously, the in most respects extremely conservative Friedrich Julius Stahl[80]) responsible for the rise of social theory.[81] Marcuse goes as far as to refer to the long introduction to Stein's *History of the Social Movement in France*[82] entitled the 'concept of society', as 'the first German sociology'.[83] The claim that Stein was the very first German sociologist might have been, indeed has been contested,[84] but Stein is certainly *one* of the crucial authors who, as transitional, belong to Marcuse's category. Marcuse understands 'sociology' to designate 'a special science, with a [specific] subject matter, conceptual framework, and method of its own' and he adds a little later that sociology 'sets itself up as a realm apart … with a province and truth of its own'.[85] The process of 'emancipation' of sociology as a 'special science' implied for Marcuse an 'anti-philosophical bent of sociology'.[86] Sociology had to separate itself from other fields of study too, e.g. economics, in order to gain recognition as an autonomous discipline. But 'above all', says Marcuse, sociology had to sever itself 'from any connection with philosophy'.[87] The 'above all', which Marcuse does not fully explain, probably refers to the privileged position, even dominance, which idealist systems had acquired in the German-speaking territories after Kant. In its struggle for 'emancipation', sociology had to throw philosophy overboard (especially any idealist 'speculation', taken in the general pejorative and not in the specifically Hegelian sense). While for several of the founding fathers of the discipline, and for Comte in particular, it may thus be true that 'sociology was patterned on the natural sciences',[88] the case is more complicated for Stein.

Without Stein's vital French experience,[89] the events during his Paris stay (October 1841 to March 1843), his reading of early socialist literature and personal exchanges with Victor Considerant, Louis Blanc, Etienne Cabet and others, he would not have become the thinker as he is now known. While Marcuse does not belittle the French impact,[90] first of all Stein's Hegelian heritage remained stronger than Marcuse believed.[91] Certainly Marcuse's appreciation is wanting of how the two currents of thought, Hegelian and French, intertwined in Stein's conceptions. Where the question becomes tricky and the interaction needs precise determination, Marcuse contents himself with the vague inadequate image of a Hegelian skeleton in the clothes of contemporary French social critics.[92]

Even without room here to analyse in detail Stein's indebtedness to Hegel, biographically or systematically,[93] we can identify misunderstandings in the common view that Stein gradually withdrew from Hegel's philosophy to turn to empirical evidence.[94] It might, however, be said that with Stein's *History* the impact of Hegel *increases*. While in Stein's earlier text, *Der Socialismus und Kommunismus des heutigen Frankreichs*,[95] the organising principle was the idea of equality, Stein in the *History* abandons this,[96] puts stronger emphasis on the social conditions in which the idea gains its meaning[97] and finally replaces it with the Hegelian idea of the development of freedom – '[w]orld history is the progress of the consciousness of freedom'.[98]

If the basic idea of Stein's sociology is 'the antagonism between state and society', as Marcuse clearly sees it,[99] the distinction between the two entities goes back to Hegel's *Philosophy of Right*, in which these figure as the second and third elements of 'ethical life', the third and final parts of Hegel's book. The precise shapes and definitions that Stein gives to society and state are largely taken from Hegel, even in their terminology, e.g. the 'system of needs'[100] and in the definition of the concept of state as 'the actuality [or 'realisation'; according to the different translations] of the ethical idea'.[101]

If the concept or idea of the state is incompatible with a lack of freedom, the abstract idea still requires for its realisation a 'constitution which addresses itself to every citizen and guarantees liberty to the individual'.[102] Since these individuals 'are all members of society; and it is society which determines their individual positions',[103] the full realisation of freedom depends upon social conditions. Society thus 'becomes the true fountainhead of liberty and dependence'.[104] From this stems the necessity of the new discipline of sociology, in order to analyse modern society, a task that implies for Stein, once again very Hegelian, the study of the history of society.

The history of French society had been such as to establish an antagonism between capitalists and proletarians, which Stein diagnosed quite bluntly – in his diagnosis, unlike his discussion of possible remedies, he was not far removed from Marx.[105] Since the proletarian was unable to acquire capital and thus deprived of social mobility, he could not develop his personality. In his apology for private property, Stein emphasises the intimate relationship between private ownership and personal freedom, and remains close to Hegel's ideas on the subject.[106] Society is in principle free because founded on private ownership, but can degenerate into a system of dependence: drawing this lesson from his study of French conditions, Stein formulates it in general terms. Freedom can result only from social emancipation, a mere political revolution is not enough.[107] That is why Stein's 'sociology' extends to the practical task of creating the social conditions that alone can overcome the dependency of underprivileged classes, their 'acquisition of material and intellectual goods',[108] in other words Stein's two capital Bs, *Besitz* and *Bildung*, property and education/culture. Stein awards this task of 'elevation of the lower classes', that is, the overcoming of their dependence, to an enlightened administration.[109] In fact, one might say that Stein here is operating *two* new disciplines, sociology and the science of administration.[110] The two are related like diagnosis and cure in medicine.

Who, though, could have the authority to induce an administration to take the recommended direction, if due to mutual antagonisms within, the polity had sunk to a tension between polarised classes? Stein's answer has often been found wanting, his opting for 'a kingship of social reform'[111] often mocked, looked down upon as an out-of-time apology for a model or even restoration of monarchy. Yet Stein was not naïve, nor can his views simply be filed away as yet another conservatism. There are respects in which Stein's option might usefully be compared with that of Bettina von Arnim (née Brentano; 1785–1859) in her almost contemporary *This Book Belongs to the King*, and her subsequent but then still unpublished project of a 'book on the poor' (*Armenbuch*). Bettina also appealed to the King of Prussia to alleviate the sufferings of the poor.[112] Stein, though, was no romantic. More seriously, he appears to have had in mind Benjamin Constant's notion of 'neutral power' (*pouvoir neutre*).[113] However that may be, Stein is by now recognised as a founding father of the social state,[114] which he could not have become without Hegel.

NOTES

1 Heinrich Heine, *On the History of Religion and Philosophy in Germany* (published as three articles in the French *Revue des Deux Mondes* in 1834, and as a book in 1835). Now in the critical edition, *DHA = Düsseldorfer Heine Ausgabe*, 16 vols, ed. Manfred Winfuhr (Hamburg: Hoffmann & Campe, 1973–97), here vol. 8/1, p. 115. The English translation is Ritchie Robertson's from: *The Harz Journey and Selected Prose* (Harmondsworth: Penguin, 2006), here p. 289.

2 Eduard Gans, 'Nekrolog [of Hegel]', in *Allgemeine Preußische Staatszeitung*, no. 333 (1 December 1831) 1752 (unless otherwise indicated, translations of German sources are my own).

3 The claim that Young Hegelianism began already with Heine's *History* … can be found in Gerhard Höhn, *Heine-Handbuch. Zeit – Person – Werk*, 3rd edn (Stuttgart abd Weimar: Metzler, 2004), p. 350. For Gans, see N. Waszek, 'War Eduard Gans (1797–1839) der erste Links- oder Junghegelianer?', in *Die linken Hegelianer. Studien zum Verhältnis von Religion und Politik im Vormärz*, eds. Michael Quante and Amir Mohseni (Paderborn: Fink, 2015), pp. 29–51, though arriving at a nuanced conclusion.

4   John Edward Toews, *Hegelianism: The Path Toward Dialectical Humanism,
    1805–1841* (Cambridge: Cambridge University Press, 1980), p. 5.

5   Cf. N. Waszek, 'David Friedrich Strauss in 1848: An Analysis of His
    "Theologicopolitical Speeches"', in *The 1848 Revolutions and European
    Political Thought*, eds. Douglas Moggach and Gareth Stedman Jones (Cambridge,
    Cambridge University Press, 2018), pp. 236–53.

6   D. F. Strauss, *Das Leben Jesu, kritisch bearbeitet*, 2 vols (Tübingen: Osiander,
    1835–1836); English edition: *The Life of Jesus, Critically Examined*; translated
    from the fourth German edition [by Marian Evans, better known as George
    Eliot] (London: Chapman Brothers, 1846).

7   D. F. Strauss, 'Letter to Christian Märklin' (1807–49), dated 15 November, 1831,
    in *Ausgewählte Briefe von David Friedrich Strauss*, ed. Eduard Zeller (Bonn: Emil
    Strauss, 1895), p. 8: 'hier ist Hegel zwar gestorben, aber nicht ausgestorben' (the
    German is given in order to keep the pun 'sterben' versus 'aussterben').

8   A group of the philosopher's friends and former students who constituted them-
    selves as an 'association' or 'society' in order to prepare a complete edition of
    Hegel's works, lectures and other manuscripts on behalf and to the benefit
    of Hegel's family (the editors worked on a voluntary basis, leaving the royalties
    to Hegel's widow and children).

9   As Strauss reports in the same letter to Märklin; Strauss, *Briefe* (1895), p. 9 f.

10 Cf. G. W. F. Hegel: *Encyclopedia of the Philosophical Sciences in Outline, and
    Critical Writings*, trans. A. V. Miller, Steven A. Taubeneck and Diana I. Behler, ed.
    Ernst Behler (New York: Continuum, 1990); *Encyclopedia of the Philosophical
    Sciences in Basic Outline*, trans. and eds. Klaus Brinkmann and Daniel O.
    Dahlstrom (Cambridge: Cambridge University Press, 2010).

11 Karl Rosenkranz, *Georg Wilhelm Friedrich Hegels Leben* (Berlin: Duncker &
    Humblot, 1844), p. 381 f.

12 Hegel, *Elements of the Philosophy of Right* [henceforth Hegel, *Philosophy of
    Right*] ed. Allen W. Wood; trans. H. B. Nisbet (Cambridge: Cambridge University
    Press, 1991), p. 227.

13 Herbert Marcuse, *Reason and Revolution: Hegel and the Rise of Social Theory*
    [1941], 2nd edn, with supplementary chapter (New York: Humanities Press,
    1954), p. 375.

14 Eduard Gans, Leopold von Henning, Hermann Friedrich Wilhelm Hinrichs,
    Heinrich Gustav Hotho, Philipp Konrad Marheineke, Karl-Ludwig Michelet,
    Karl Rosenkranz, Wilhelm Vatke. In what follows, three of them (Gans, Hotho
    and Rosenkranz) will be commented on in some detail.

15 Among the numerous examples, cf. Rosenkranz's pamphlet against Rudolf
    Haym, which even bears the term 'apology' in its title: K. Rosenkranz, *Apologie
    Hegels gegen Dr. R. Haym* (Berlin: Duncker & Humblot, 1858); see also the
    eulogy for Hegel's birth centenary: C. L. Michelet, *Hegel, der unwiderlegte
    Weltphilosoph: eine Jubelschrift* (Leipzig: Duncker & Humblot, 1870).

16 Cf. *Die 'Jahrbücher für wissenschaftliche Kritik': Hegels Berliner Gegenakademie*,
    ed. Christoph Jamme (Stuttgart-Bad Cannstatt: Frommann-Holzboog, 1994).

17 *Georg Wilhelm Friedrich Hegel's Werke*, Vollständige Ausgabe durch einen Verein
    von Freunden des Verewigten, 18 vols. (Berlin: Duncker & Humblot, 1832–45).

18 According to the volumes themselves and to the contract with the publisher, the
    'circle of friends' consisted of Philipp Marheineke, Johannes Schulze, Eduard

Gans, Leopold von Henning, Heinrich Gustav Hotho, Carl Ludwig Michelet and Friedrich Förster. Later, other editors were associated: Ludwig Boumann, Hegel's son Karl, Karl Rosenkranz and Bruno Bauer. For further details see: Christoph Jamme, 'Editionspolitik. Zur "Freundesvereinsausgabe" der Werke G. W. F. Hegels', *Zeitschrift für Philosophische Forschung* 38 (1984), 83–99.

19 The critical edition of student notes on Hegel's lectures began with Hegel, *Vorlesungen über Rechtsphilosophie 1818–1831*, 4 vols, ed. Karl-Heinz Ilting (Stuttgart-Bad Cannstatt: Frommann-Holzboog, 1973–4). Many other lectures have since been edited in the series: Hegel, *Vorlesungen. Ausgewählte Nachschriften und Manuskripte* [different vol. eds.], 17 vols. (Hamburg: Meiner, 1983–2007).

20 *Georg Wilhelm Friedrich Hegel's Vorlesungen über die Aesthetik*, 3 vols, ed. H. G. Hotho (Berlin: Duncker & Humblot, 1835–8) [= vol. 10.1–3 of the *Werke*; see above, note 17].

21 The numerous translations of Hotho's edition (into French, Italian, Russian, etc.) confirm Sir Malcolm Knox' verdict: 'Hotho did his work brilliantly'; Hegel, *Aesthetics: Lectures on Fine Art*, ed. and trans. T. M. Knox. (Oxford: Clarendon Press, 1975), vol. 1, p. vi.

22 Cf. Annemarie Gethmann-Siefert, 'H.G. Hotho, Kunst als Bildungserlebnis und Kunsthistorie in systematischer Absicht – oder die entpolitisierte Version der ästhetischen Erziehung des Menschengeschlechts', in *Kunsterfahrung und Kulturpolitik im Berlin Hegels* [Hegel-Studien Beiheft 22], eds. A. Gethmann-Siefert and Otto Pöggeler (Bonn: Bouvier, 1983), pp. 229–62.

23 Cf. Toews, *Hegelianism*, pp. 203–54; in greater detail: Henning Ottmann, *Hegel im Spiegel der Interpretationen* (= vol. 1 of *Individuum und Gemeinschaft bei Hegel*) (Berlin and Boston: de Gruyter, 1977).

24 D. F. Strauss, *Streitschriften zur Vertheidigung meiner Schrift über das Leben Jesu und zur Charakteristik der gegenwärtigen Theologie*, Heft 3 (Tübingen: Osiander, 1837), p. 95 (for the first evocation of the threefold division), the whole chapter 'Verschiedene Richtungen innerhalb der Hegelschen Schule in Betreff der Christologie' for its explication, pp. 95–126.

25 Cf. N. Waszek, 'Eduard Gans on Poverty and on the Constitutional Debate', in Douglas Moggach, ed., *The New Hegelians: Politics and Philosophy in the Hegelian School* (Cambridge: Cambridge University Press, 2006), pp. 24–49.

26 Eduard Gans, *Das Erbrecht in weltgeschichtlicher Entwicklung: Eine Abhandlung der Universalrechtsgeschichte* [four volumes published in Gans' lifetime; two more were projected when Gans died suddenly in 1839] (4 vols.: I: Berlin: Maurer, 1824; II: Berlin: Maurer, 1825; III: Stuttgart & Tübingen: Cotta, 1829; IV: Stuttgart & Tübingen: Cotta, 1835).

27 Gans, *Das Erbrecht in weltgeschichtlicher Entwicklung*, vol. 1, p. xxix: 'Als Wissenschaft ist sie [i.e. die Rechtswissenschaft] nothwendig ein Teil der Philosophie'. Gans' phrase corresponds exactly to Hegel's own formula 'The science of right is *a part of philosophy*'. Hegel, *Philosophy of Right*, p. 26, § 2.

28 Gans, *Das Erbrecht in weltgeschichtlicher Entwicklung*, vol. 1, p. xxxix.

29 Friedrich Carl von Savigny, *Geschichte des römischen Rechts im Mittelalter*, 6 vols. (Heidelberg: Mohr, 1815–31). By the time Gans began his *History of the Law of Inheritance*, the first three volumes of Savigny's book were available. An

English translation exists of vol. 1: *The History of the Roman Law During the Middle Ages*, trans. E. Cathcart (Edinburgh: A. Black, 1829).

30 Cf. the older edition of the introduction only – G. W. F. Hegel, *Lectures on the Philosophy of World History: Introduction: Reason in History*, trans. H. B. Nisbet, with an introduction by Duncan Forbes (Cambridge: Cambridge University Press, 1975) – with the recent edition of the 1822/3 lectures: *Lectures on the Philosophy of World History: Manuscripts of the Introduction and the Lectures of 1822–3*, ed. and trans. Robert F. Brown and Peter C. Hodgson, with the assistance of William G. Guess (Oxford: Oxford University Press, 2011).

31 G. W. F. Hegel, 'Letter to Karl J.H. Windischmann' (1775–1839), dated 11 April 1824, in *Hegel: The Letters*, trans. Clark Butler and Christiane Seiler, with commentary by Clark Butler (Bloomington: Indiana University Press, 1984), p. 565; cf. Hegel's enthusiasm about Gans' nomination in a letter to Cousin, 5 April 1826: 'Gans has been named Professor of Law at our university, which has caused me much satisfaction in every respect'. *Hegel: The Letters*, p. 638.

32 K. L. Michelet, *Wahrheit aus meinem Leben* (Berlin: Nicolai, 1884), p. 76: 'From your specialty [Michelet had completed his law studies in 1822], Hegel said to me, you ought to take the topic [of your thesis]. He even suggested the precise subject to me … and this is how I came to write on *De doli et culpae in iure criminali notionibus*' (Berlin: Petsch, 1824).

33 Notably to ancient philosophy and to Aristotle in particular. That he edited Hegel's *Lectures on the History of Philosophy – Hegel's Vorlesungen über die Geschichte der Philosophie*, 3 vols, ed. K. L. Michelet (Berlin: Duncker & Humblot, 1833–6) [*Werke*, vol. 13–15; cf. note 16] – belongs to the same context.

34 Gans quotes Montesquieu, P. J. A. Feuerbach and A. F. J. Thibaut regularly. Thibaut followed the career of his former student with a sympathetic interest and Feuerbach, in a note published shortly before his death in 1833, went as far as to say that he expected from Gans what he could not realise in his lifetime; *Anselms von Feuerbach kleine Schriften vermischten Inhalts* (Nürnberg: Otto, 1833), p. 165.

35 In an autobiographical note he wrote in early 1835 (published in: *Hallische Jahrbücher für deutsche Wissenschaft und Kunst*, vol. 3, 1840), p. 902.

36 Hegel, *Philosophy of Right*, p. 23.

37 Cf. Hans-Christian Lucas, '"Dieses Zukünftige wollen wir mit Ehrfurcht begrüßen": Bemerkungen zur Historisierung und Liberalisierung von Hegels Rechts- und Staatsbegriff durch Eduard Gans', in *Eduard Gans (1797–1839): politischer Professor zwischen Restauration und Vormärz*, eds. R. Blänkner, G. Göhler and N. Waszek (Leipzig: Leipziger Universitäts-Verlag, 2002), pp. 105–36.

38 Cf. Elisabeth Ziemer, *Heinrich Gustav Hotho (1802–1873): ein Berliner Kunsthistoriker, Kunstkritiker und Philosoph* (Berlin: Reimer, 1994).

39 In 1825 they travelled to Paris together. Their six months there was a formative period for both. On their way back to Berlin, they stopped over in Stuttgart – where they met the famous publisher, Cotta, and arranged for both of them to contribute to periodicals belonging to his empire – and then in Weimar, where they were received by Goethe. Both left accounts of their travel and stay: Heinrich Gustav Hotho, *Vorstudien für Leben und Kunst* (Stuttgart: Cotta,

1835), for his stay in Paris, see pp. 177–222; Eduard Gans, 'Paris im Jahre 1825', in *Rückblicke auf Personen und Zustände* (Berlin: Veit, 1836), pp. 1–47.

40   Among his later works: *Geschichte der deutschen und niederländischen Malerei*, 2 vols. (Berlin: Simion, 1842–3); *Die Malerschule Huberts van Eyck nebst deutschen Vorgängern und Zeitgenossen*, 2 vols. [uncompleted] (Berlin: Veit & Co., 1855–8); *Geschichte der christlichen Malerei in ihrem Entwicklungsgang dargestellt*, 3 vols. [uncompleted] (Stuttgart: [s.n.], 1867–72). His ten contributions to the *Yearbooks* span the years 1827 to 1833; see Ziemer, *Heinrich Gustav Hotho*, p. 372.

41   By a certain J[ohann] Saling, *Die Gerechtigkeit in ihrer geistgeschichtlichen Entwickelung* (Berlin: C. F. Plahn, 1827); cf. Hotho's review of the book in *Jahrbücher für wissenschaftliche Kritik* 31–4 (August 1828), 251–65.

42   Hotho in *Jahrbücher* 31–4 (August 1828) 252.

43   Hotho, 'Review of Amadeus Wendt, Über die Hauptperioden der schönen Kunst oder die Kunst im Laufe der Weltgeschichte. Leipzig: Barth, 1831', in *Jahrbücher* 113 (December 1832), 902.

44   Eliza M. Butler, *The Tyranny of Greece Over Germany: A Study of the Influence Exercised by Greek Art and Poetry Over the Great German Writers of the 18th, 19th and 20th Centuries* (Cambridge: Cambridge University Press, 1935).

45   Cf. Hotho, *Geschichte der christlichen*.

46   Karl Rosenkranz, *Geschichte der deutschen Poesie im Mittelalter* (Halle: Anton & Gelbcke, 1830); *Handbuch einer allgemeinen Geschichte der Poesie*, 3 vols. [I: *Geschichte der orientalischen und der antiken Poesie*; II: *Geschichte der neueren Lateinischen, der Französischen und Italienischen Poesie*; III: *Geschichte der Spanischen, Portugiesischen, Englischen, Skandinavischen, Niederländischen, Deutschen und Slawischen Poesie*] (Halle: Eduard Anton, 1832–3); *Goethe und seine Werke* (Königsberg: Bornträger, 1847, 2nd edn 1856); *Die Poesie und ihre Geschichte: eine Entwicklung der poetischen Ideale der Völker* (Königsberg: Bornträger, 1855); *Diderot's Leben und Werke*, 2 vols. (Leipzig: Brockhaus, 1866); *Neue Studien*, 4 vols. (Leipzig: Koschny, 1875–8).

47   K. Rosenkranz, *Die Pädagogik als System. Ein Grundriß* (Königsberg: Bornträger, 1848 – new edition with an introduction by Michael Winkler. Jena: Paideia, 2008). The text was translated into English as early as 1872 – *Pedagogics as a System*, trans. Anna C. Brackett (St. Louis, MO: Studley, 1872) – and is still reprinted.

48   As Rosenkranz relates in his autobiographical work: *Von Magdeburg bis Königsberg* (Berlin: Heimann, 1873), p. 426 f.

49   Rosenkranz, *Geschichte der deutschen Poesie im Mittelalter* (1830), p. vi.

50   Rosenkranz, *Von Magdeburg bis Königsberg*, p. 424.

51   Ibid., p. 424 and cf. Rosenkranz, *Hegel: Sendschreiben an den Hofrath und Professor Carl Friedrich Bachmann in Jena* (Königsberg: Unzer, 1834), pp. 122 f.

52   Rosenkranz, *Geschichte der deutschen Poesie im Mittelalter* (1830), p. viii: 'Von einem vor der Durchforschung des Gegebenen bereits fertigen System, dessen Formeln ich vielleicht nur mit besonderem Stoff von Außen her angefüllt hätte weiß ich nichts.'

53   Rosenkranz, *Von Magdeburg bis Königsberg*, p. 424.

54   E.g. Rosenkranz, *Handbuch* (1832), vol. I, p. 160, 234; vol. II, p. 228; vol. III: pp. iii f.

55   Rosenkranz, *Handbuch*, vol. III, pp. 397–434.

56 As Rosenkranz himself underlined in his *Handbuch*, vol. III, p. xi; cf. Ziemer, *Heinrich Gustav Hotho*, pp. 184 f.

57 Rosenkranz, *Von Magdeburg bis Königsberg*, p. 475 f: 'ein Werk, welches der erste vollständig durchgeführte Versuch auf diesem Felde nach festen ästhetischen Prinzipien und mit weltgeschichtlichem Sinn geschrieben war'.

58 Hegel, *Philosophy of Right*, p. 227 f, § 189 and addition.

59 Karl Marx, *A Contribution to the Critique of Political Economy* [1859], ed. with an introduction by Maurice Dobb [1970, 2nd edn 1977] (Toronto, ON: General Books, 2012), p. 11: 'the material conditions of life, which are summed up by Hegel after the fashion of the English and French of the eighteenth century under the name of "civil society"; the anatomy of that civil society is to be sought in political economy.'

60 Georg Lukács, *The Young Hegel: Studies in the Relations Between Dialectics and Economics* [1948], trans. Rodney Livingstone (London: Merlin Press, 1975); Manfred Riedel, *Between Tradition and Revolution: The Hegelian Transformation of Political Philosophy* [1969], trans. Walter Wright (Cambridge: Cambridge University Press, 1984); N. Waszek, *The Scottish Enlightenment and Hegel's Account of 'Civil Society'* (Dordrecht: Kluwer, 1988).

61 Eduard Gans, 'Preface', in Hegel, *Grundlinien der Philosophie des Rechts*, 2nd edn, ed. E. Gans (Berlin: Duncker & Humblot, 1833), pp. v–xvii, here p. viii. English trans. in Michael H. Hoffheimer, *Eduard Gans and the Hegelian Philosophy of Law* (Dordrecht: Kluwer, 1995), pp. 87–92, here p. 88.

62 There are now three editions of Gans' lectures on natural law and the universal history of law, a course he repeated frequently and enlarged constantly from the late 1820s almost to his death in 1839: E. Gans, *Philosophische Schriften*, ed. Horst Schröder (Berlin: Aufbau, 1971), here p. 108 ff; *Naturrecht und Universalrechtsgeschichte*, ed. Manfred Riedel (Stuttgart: Klett-Cotta, 1981), here p. 82 ff; *Naturrecht und Universalrechtsgeschichte: Vorlesungen nach G. W. F. Hegel*, ed. Johann Braun (Tübingen: Mohr-Siebeck, 2005), here pp. 164–6.

63 Gans, *Naturrecht und Universalrechtsgeschichte* (2005), p. 165.

64 Gans, *Naturrecht und Universalrechtsgeschichte* (1981), p. 84: 'Wir bekennen uns zum Industriesystem von Adam Smith'; Gans, *Naturrecht und Universalrechtsgeschichte* (2005), p. 166: das 'Industriesystem [ist] einer unendlichen Vervollkommnung fähig'.

65 Gans, *Naturrecht und Universalrechtsgeschichte* (2005), p. 165.

66 Cf. Engels' Preface to the second volume of *Capital* (1885); *Marx-Engels-Werke*, vol. 24 (1963), p. 14 – English trans. by I. Lasker (Moscow: Progress Publishers, 1956), p. 6: 'Marx began his economic studies in Paris, in 1843, starting with the great Englishmen and Frenchmen. Of German economists he knew only Rau and List, and he did not want any more of them.'

67 Gans, *Naturrecht und Universalrechtsgeschichte* (2005), p. 166.

68 Cf. Gans, *Naturrecht und Universalrechtsgeschichte* (1981), pp. 51 f; Gans *Naturrecht und Universalrechtsgeschichte* (2005), pp. 58–63. For Gans' most detailed account of Saint-Simon and his school, see his text on Paris in 1830, in *Rückblicke auf Personen und Zustände* [1836], ed. with an introduction and notes by N. Waszek (Stuttgart-Bad Cannstatt: Frommann-Holzboog, 1995), pp. 91–102; cf. N. Waszek, 'Eduard Gans on Poverty', pp. 24–49, esp. pp. 35–41.

69 Gans, *Naturrecht und Universalrechtsgeschichte* (2005), p. 166.

70 The front page of his book shows '1821', but the book was already available in late 1820.

71 Cf. the old edition by K. L. Michelet, *Vorlesungen über die Geschichte der Philosophie*, 3 vols. (Berlin: Duncker und Humblot, 1833–6) [Werke, vols. 13–15]; reprinted in the widely available *Theorie Werkausgabe* [*TWA*], 20 vols., eds. Eva Moldenhauer and Karl Markus Michel (Frankfurt/Main: Suhrkamp, 1969–71), vols. 18–20, which mixes the lectures of different years, with the new edition – *Vorlesungen über die Geschichte der Philosophie*, 4 vols., eds. Pierre Garniron and Walter Jaeschke (Hamburg: Meiner, 1986–96) [Hegel, *Vorlesungen*, vols. 6–9] – based mainly on students' notes from the 1825/26 course.

72 Hegel, *TWA*, vol. 19, p. 34.

73 Hegel, *Vorlesungen*, vol. 9, pp. 127 f.

74 George Canning (1770–1827), at the time (1822–7) Secretary of State for Foreign Affairs and Leader of the House of Commons under the Earl of Liverpool as Prime Minister. Canning's speech was reported as follows: 'a period has lately commenced when Ministers have had in their power to apply to the state of the country the just maxims of profound philosophy'.

75 That Hegel read the relevant article – *The Morning Chronicle*, 14 February 1825, p. 3 – is proven by his surviving excerpt, first published in Hegel, *Berliner Schriften 1818–1831*, ed. Johannes Hoffmeister (Hamburg: Meiner, 1956), p. 701; cf. Michael J. Petry, 'Hegel and "The Morning Chronicle"', in *Hegel-Studien* 11 (1976), 11–80, here 31 f.

76 These notes are to be found in the Polish Academy of Science at Cracow, MS, no. 57, p. 15. The identity of the student is not firmly established, but the name of 'Helcel' is generally attributed to them.

77 Hegel, *TWA*, vol. 20, pp. 281–6; Hegel, *Vorlesungen*, vol. 9, pp. 144–8.

78 Hegel, *TWA*, vol. 20, p. 285: 'Auch der Staatsökonom Adam Smith ist in diesem Sinne Philosoph.'

79 Among the rare English studies of Lorenz Stein is Diana Siclovan, '1848 and German Socialism', in *The 1848 Revolutions and European Political Thought*, pp. 254–75.

80 Cf. John F. Toews, 'The Immanent Genesis and Transcendent Goal of Law: Savigny, Stahl and the Ideology of the Christian German State', in *American Journal of Comparative Law* 37 (1989), 139–69.

81 Marcuse, *Reason and Revolution*, pp. 374–88.

82 Lorenz Stein, *Geschichte der sozialen Bewegung in Frankreich von 1789 bis auf unsere Tage* [1850]: German edition by Gottfried Salomon, 3 vols. (Munich: Drei Masken, 1921, reprinted: Hildesheim: Georg Olms, 1959); The so-called English edition is unfortunately a 'condensed' version, omitting more than half of the original, which alone can be cited below. *The History of the Social Movement in France, 1789–1850*, intro., ed. and trans. Kaethe Mengelberg (Totowa, NJ: Bedminster Press, 1964).

83 Marcuse, *Reason and Revolution*, p. 375.

84 Cf. for example, Lutz Geldsetzer, 'Zur Frage des Beginns der deutschen Soziologie', *Kölner Zeitschrift für Soziologie und Sozialpsychologie* 15 (1963), 529–41.

85 Marcuse, *Reason and Revolution*, p. 375.

86 Ibid., p. 376.

87 Ibid., p. 375.

88 Ibid., p. 376.

89 Cf. my article: 'Lorenz von Steins Frankreicherfahrung im Spannungsfeld von Idealismus und Soziologie', in *Lorenz von Stein und der Sozialstaat*, ed. Stefan Koslowski (Baden-Baden: Nomos, 2014), pp. 64–82.

90 Marcuse, *Reason and Revolution*, p. 379: Stein 'paid close attention to French social critics and theorists of the period'.

91 Ibid., p. 382: 'Despite the retention of Hegelian terminology, Stein succumbs to the positivist, affirmative tendencies of early sociology.'

92 Ibid., p. 381: 'Stein clothes the skeleton conception that he took over from Hegel with the material got from the French critical analysis of modern society.'

93 For further details on this see my presentation of the French edition of Stein's theoretical introduction to his *History of the Social Movement in France*: Stein, *Le concept de société*, trans. Marc Béghin, with an introduction and bibliography by N. Waszek (Grenoble: ELLUG, 2002), pp. 9–61.

94 For a more intelligent version of that perspective, see Stefan Koslowski, *Die Geburt des Sozialstaats aus dem Geist des deutschen Idealismus: Person und Gemeinschaft bei Lorenz von Stein* (Weinheim: VCH, Acta Humaniora, 1989); cf. my review in: *Politische Vierteljahresschrift*, 37 (1996), pp. 378–84.

95 L. Stein, *Der Socialismus und Kommunismus des heutigen Frankreichs* (Leipzig: Otto Wigand, 1842).

96 Stein, *The History of the Social Movement in France*, p. 78: 'the original moving force in the revolution is not the idea of equality'.

97 The new title, *History of the Social Movement in France*, was not chosen by accident.

98 Hegel, *Lectures on the Philosophy of World History* (1975), p. 54.

99 Marcuse, *Reason and Revolution*, p. 381.

100 While the German original – Stein, *Geschichte der sozialen Bewegung in Frankreich* (1959), vol. 1, p. 29 – uses Hegel's expression 'System der Bedürfnisse' (cf. § 189 f. of *The Philosophy of Right*) the English edition: *History of the Social Movement in France* (1964), p. 50, misses the parallel and translates rather freely: 'set in motion through human needs'.

101 Stein, *Geschichte* (1959), vol. 1, p. 46: 'die Wirklichkeit der sittlichen Idee' (cf. § 257 of Hegel, *Philosophy of Right*) – English edition: *History* (1964), p. 56.

102 Stein, *Geschichte* (1959), vol. 1, p. 37 – English edition: *History* (1964), p. 52.

103 Stein, *Geschichte* (1959), vol. 1, p. 50 f – English edition: *History* (1964), p. 58.

104 Stein, *Geschichte* (1959), vol. 1, p. 52 – English edition: *History* (1964), p. 58.

105 There exists a rich literature on the relationship of Marx and Stein, from the late nineteen century onwards; cf. for example, Franz Mehring, 'Stein, Hess und Marx', *Neue Zeit* xv, no. 2 (1897), 379–82; Herbert Uhl, *Lorenz von Stein und Karl Marx: zur Grundlegung von Gesellschaftsanalyse und politischer Theorie 1842–1850* (Tübingen: University Press, 1977).

106 For an excellent analysis of Hegel's views on the matter, see Joachim Ritter's 'Person and Property in Hegel's Philosophy of Right (§§34–81)', in *Hegel on Ethics and Politics*, eds. Robert B. Pippin and Otfried Höffe (Cambridge: Cambridge University Press, 2004), pp. 101–23.

107 Stein, *Geschichte* (1959), vol. I, p. 81 – English edition: *History* (1964), p. 70.

108 Stein, *Geschichte* (1959), vol. III, p. 104: 'Die Freiheit ist erst eine wirkliche in dem, der die Bedingungen derselben, die materiellen und geistigen Güter als die Voraussetzungen der Selbstbestimmung, besitzt.'

109 Stein, *Geschichte* (1959), vol. I, p. 48 (Stein's own italics): 'in der Verwaltung wird ... die *Hebung der niederen Klassen* zum wesentlichen Gegenstand'. The term 'elevation' (*Hebung*) is reminiscent of Hegel's *Aufhebung* in the three-fold sense of suppressing (latin: *negare*), preserving (*conservare*) and elevating (*levare*).

110 When Stein – after being fired from the University of Kiel, when the 1848 rising of the duchies of Schleswig and Holstein against Denmark had failed – finally settled in Vienna, he undertook to write a multivolume science of adminis-tration: *Die Verwaltungslehre*, 7 vols. (Stuttgart: Cotta, 1865–8; 2nd edn in 10 vols. 1869–84).

111 Stein, *Geschichte* (1959), vol. III, p. 41: 'ein Königtum der sozialen Reform'.

112 [Bettina von Arnim], *Dies Buch gehört dem König*, 2 vols. ([Berlin]: Schroeder, 1843); the critical edition provides a wealth of notes and explanations: *Politische Schriften*, eds. Wolfgang Bunzel, Ulrike Landfester, Walter Schmitz and Sibylle von Steinsdorff (Frankfurt/Main: Deutscher Klassiker-Verlag, 1995).

113 While appreciating the July monarchy, Stein says that it did not 'succeed in fully incarnating the neutral power of which Benjamin Constant had spoken'. Stein, *Geschichte* (1959), vol. II, p. 51.

114 Cf. Karl-Hermann Kästner, 'From the Social Question to the Social state' (trans. Keith Tribe), *Economy and Society* 10 (1981), 7–26.

5

MIKE GANE

The Origins of the Social Sciences

Many of those who lived through the turbulent period sparked off by the revolution in Paris in 1789 such as Jeremy Bentham (1748–1832) in England, Georg Wilhelm Friedrich Hegel (1770–1831) in Germany and Madame de Staël (1766–1817) in France, concurred in their different ways that what was at work was the action of human reason, in a progressive direction – that had been subverted by reaction – and that the new century would renew the progress promised by the initial event. There was a widespread sense that the revolution had missed its opportunity for lack of knowledge of what it could and should have achieved and that its basic work of social construction was unfinished. The question became: what kind of social science would facilitate and guide this progression, and to what end? And then, given a continuation of general enlightenment, what kind of political leadership would take up and apply it? And in any case what had subverted the revolution? What had it nevertheless produced? The years 1789–1815, from the point of view of 1815 might have seemed to have been a movement from monarchy to restored monarchy in France through a period of violent, terrorist aberration. What did this signify other than a complete breakdown of normal society?

In order to give some sort of justification to what had happened in this period there was recourse to mythology (certainly focused on the ideals of the revolution as well as the institutions that survived), but almost immediately also recourse to new forms of social science as a complement to myth. In this perspective the end of the revolutionary wars in France in 1815 marked the period of the return of the many exiles of all shades of opinion, and thus somewhat idealised nostalgia for the old regime as well as a sense that there had been movement towards a better, more just future. In fact the revolution as it had developed into a war on a European and world dimension had set off a chain of events that ignited movements for national unity in Germany and Italy. It also became a model in itself of social progression interpreted as part of a tradition that would be developed in the communist movement since, once interpreted as a period in which the feudal aristocracy gave way to an emergent bourgeoisie, there would be another step, another revolution but to a higher stage of human society. The revolution of 1789 in this interpretation was not an aberration but an event that was part of the normal development of human progress through defined stages marked by revolutionary upheavals. Yet, in this kind of interpretation, another variant was possible: Bonapartism itself could be a model; in other words the modernisation of the means of warfare and its unifying effects could be used in combination with conservative, even reactionary, restorations of quasi-feudal hierarchies to further social progress. There was therefore not one model emanating from the French Revolution and counter-revolution but several. In this chapter the origins of sociology in France, Britain and Germany are examined in this context with reference to the writings of Auguste Comte, Hebert Spencer, Emile Durkheim and Max Weber.

Comte and a New Science of the Social

Auguste Comte was born on 19 January 1798, at Montpellier in the south of France. Educated first at the newly created Lycée at Montpellier he then entered as a prodigy the Polytechnique in Paris at the age of 16. It was still run under military discipline. In 1816, under the restored monarchy, the Polytechnique was closed down after student unrest. In 1817 Comte became secretary to Henri de Saint-Simon (1760–1825) with whom he spent about seven formative years until he branched out on his own account in 1824, a year before Saint-Simon's death. Comte's main source of income was as a teacher of mathematics and an examiner. In the years 1819–28 he wrote a number of essays on politics and social theory, in which he outlined an ambitious programme of work, and that indeed he spent the rest of his life trying to complete.[1] The first of the tasks was to establish a theory of the way the sciences had developed so as to understand the logic of their emergence and the common methodological features of the system that the sciences were in the process of formation. The old religious certainties no longer had the authority to legitimise political power faced with this pro-gression of scientifically demonstrated knowledge.

In the first period of Comte's life, his work up to 1842 is best understood as an attempt to transform the doctrine of Saint-Simon by drawing on the models and ideas of the sciences that dominated Paris from 1800 to 1830, and developing the new scientific idiom of sociology. In the second period of his writings to his death in 1857 he developed ideas that he had already initiated with Saint-Simon, now worked up in a religious idiom appropriate to the new context of revived social Catholicism in France. Comte was hostile to all the regimes of his period, to absolute monarchy, constitutional monarchy, a Parliamentary Republic, Bonapartism and Communism – certain in the belief that the final revolution was imminent. This could be achieved through the joint action of the modern proletariat, a new scientific priesthood and the affective influence of women. Saint-Simon, in search of funds, appealed to Napoleon directly to allow him to develop schemes appropriate to a modernising programme. Comte appealed in the 1850s to Napoleon III in a similar style. Comte never tired of describing his objective as one of searching for a way to end the Western Revolution.[2]

Comte's aim was to show that the transition between theology and the social order to come was not simply one of the linear advance of reason in the abstract. He rejected the idea that any culture or society could pass directly from a theological polity to a scientific one. The problem of the intermediate stage was crucial – and here there was great complexity. The problem was a pivotal one since Comte presents his orders of the 'twofold movement' – the movement of positivity (science and industry), and the continuous decline of theology – in relation to an end state. His analyses were to be falsifiable demonstrations of laws, not the revealed truths of a religious prophet. Comte's claim, therefore, is that his innovation in the human sciences introduces into historical logic a new way of thinking about European history: the facts of this history are marshalled according to the intervention of a scientific conjecture. The wager that Comte makes here is to introduce the law of the development of human cognition (growth of science and rational cultures), as a general law of European history (emergence of a society ruled by science). It was not just each individual mind, but all human social organisation that has been and will be determined by this cognitive cultural logic (positivism) either directly or indirectly.

After a brief flirtation, around 1816, with liberal democracy, Comte set positivism against the liberals and he argued the importation of the British parliamentary system could only be a transitory phenomenon (it was for him simply an inversion of the divine right of monarchs). His depiction of the metaphysical culture and polity included its predominant egoism, its culture of human rights and equality, bourgeois notions of liberty, even probability mathematics. Comte, as early as 1825–6, identified *homo economicus* of the economists as a metaphysical illusion; in his early writings the essential theses on the primacy of social theory over political economy were already in place. Comte's initial fame, however, rested on the *Cours de Philosophie Positive* (translated and condensed by Harriet Martineau as *A Positive Philosophy*), which appeared in six volumes between 1830 and 1842 (the first two lectures had appeared previously in a revue in 1829).[3] The lectures deal with the sciences in a strict order. This monumental piece of work, a course of sixty lectures aiming to be a summation of scientific knowledge, was very carefully ordered so that the last sections, which give birth to 'sociology', draw strength from the logic of the system of knowledge and completes it. Comte places himself within the system of sciences, intervenes in them, judges them, identifies where knowledge seems to be blocked or irrationally organised. The first sciences deal with the most general phenomena, the later ones more concrete and complex ones. There is a hierarchy of laws that are dependent on each other. This is not simply a 'sociology of knowledge' though that is involved, but an attempt to begin the governance of the sciences. Comte was able to draw on his prodigious memory (from a young age he was able to perform memory feats, for example to recall several hundred lines after one hearing, and to repeat backwards a page of words he had read once), for this vast canvass, and the final section of *A Positive Philosophy* on 'sociology' includes a detailed account of European history from the Renaissance employing what he called the historical method.

Comte's work, then, is organised in terms of one basic law (the law of the three states) and a consideration of the way in which each science establishes a specific contribution to scientific methodology. Comparing and organising the sciences into a system, as yet incomplete, Comte uses lessons from one science to develop another, pushing the system to greater and greater integration. In effect his sociology is a logical extension of biology – itself newly established from about 1800. The sociologist can learn from the mode of intervention of medical science: it treats pathology, it establishes a model therapeutics. His view was that the system of the sciences would be completed within a short period of time and French society could be organised around it. As such France could take the lead in the movement to the final stage of human progress. To theorise this he had to construct a comparative history specifying the unique route that France was to take as it approached the threshold of the final transition. He was wildly mistaken on this conjecture, for not only was he living in a period of great scientific vitality and turbulence, this progression did not suddenly cease. His advice that certain forms of scientific enquiry that were beyond human utility should not be continued was, fortunately, disregarded. The revolutions kept coming, not least the Darwinian revolution that occurred within a couple of years of Comte's death.

After he had completed his massive founding work, he entered a period of personal and intellectual crisis. He separated from his wife Caroline Massin within days of completing his six-volume work. He gathered around him some leading intellectuals and organised a society of positivist thinkers who worked with him to establish a political programme, and this was active in the revolution of 1848 in France. But by then, Comte had gone through a traumatic unfulfilled affair with Clotilde de Vaux who had died suddenly in 1846. As an effect of these crises, emotional and political, Comte undertook to rewrite the whole of his system. But the central question remained: what kind of governing agency should be created to establish the final, third state of social evolution? In his second set of writings from the mid 1840s Comte reframed his analyses as a religion, the Religion of Humanity. This divided his followers as many, notably Emile Littré (1801–81) and J. S. Mill (1806–73), refused to go down that path. Comte himself argued that this was no fundamental break in his thinking, such a development was a logical and foreseen development of his ideas. The culmination of his second set of writings is the *Système de Politique Positive* (System of Positive Polity) (1851–4), which is, as its subtitle announces, a *Treatise on Sociology, Instituting the Religion of Humanity.* This second set of reflections is set in what he called the 'subjective' mode of a religious discourse incorporating the element of emotion in the history of humanity and giving a new role to women. It is dedicated to Clotilde de Vaux, whose appearance in Comte's life he said had been inspirational. He transformed her into a saint, worshipped at a shrine he made in her honour and wanted her to be remembered as the indispensable co-constructor of the new religion.

It was from that moment that Comte's reputation as 'slightly mad' began: the moment that he began to identify himself at the head of the vast theoretical and religious cult to save humanity. In the subjective mode Comte's imagination was set to work to design an elaborate utopia. New alliances would come into being within the frame of a secularised Catholic church, a cult organised around his writings for a universal system of education, the birth of a new priesthood and new sacred trinity (Space, the Earth, Humanity). As in the mediaeval period the highest sacred spiritual authority of the new priesthood, the Pontiff, would oversee the profane, temporal powers on the basis of their mastery of scientific knowledge; a renewed system of chivalry combined with the figure of the Virgin replaced by Saint Clotilde would introduce a new era of gender relations. A period of proletarian dictatorship, however, would be necessary in the stages leading to the final polity. A new positive calendar that Comte drew up in the 1840s dates modern time from 1789, thus rejecting both the new calendar of the French Revolution (1792–1805), and Napoleon's return to the Gregorian calendar after 1805 – Comte did not reject the revolution but wanted to lead it in a new direction. 'Humanity' could be the object of a new religion, replacing the worship of the Supreme Being installed during the revolution. The reign of the new religion he thought would begin definitively in 1855.

This astonishing readiness to risk becoming the object of derision, the mixture of profundity and superficiality, allows us to see Comte's deep allegiances to the Catholic tradition while at the same time providing a relentless critique of Catholic and Deistic doctrines. His synthetic Religion of Humanity appears as an eclectic concoction (he included the image of Clotilde de Vaux within the pantheon) more or less designed to alienate all other religious traditions – so that when the Religion of Humanity was taken up, as in the United States, there was an immediate temptation to reorganise it so as to align it with Protestant values. In Britain the religion split into rival sectarian camps. In France the positivist camp was divided between Littré and those following the earlier writings and Laffitte who continued the religious writings. Comte actually thought the greatest conversions to the new religion would be within Islam and that the final centre of world religion would be in Istanbul not Paris. However bizarre these ideas might seem it is important to remember that the Saint-Simonians who inspired Comte in his youth also believed that mass conversions of this kind, even the conversion of a culture from one language to another, could be achieved rapidly and smoothly and that a female messiah would appear in the East to lead the world out of chaos. Comte himself, though ridiculed by it, was an outrider of the Saint-Simonian messianic school, not an isolated 'mad' philosopher. He did not take his own important conception of continuity and tradition seriously enough, and even in his own time doubts were expressed as to whether he had the slightest idea of what constituted a social structure so alienated was he from contemporary life (he proudly announced that to realise 'cerebral hygiene' he had stopped reading any other literature other than purely scientific papers). Modernity for Comte was a constantly changing kaleidoscope of reason and unreason, completely comprehensible as the effective metamorphosis of theological into metaphysical forms: either by inversion (the false revolution) or by the force of reason (the rise of Deism and post-theological religion). He had to show, via his new science of sociology, that his Religion of Humanity was not a secular metamorphosis of Christian belief, but the logical development of the progression of the positive and industrial movement.

Crucial in this new theorising were two fundamentally new concepts: altruism and sociocracy, both coined by Comte. The basic problem of Western culture was the dominance of egoism, actually encouraged by the Catholic Church and the new metaphysical polity. He invented the word altruism as a counter to such egoism; and an orientation towards altruism in ethics would eventually triumph with the new Religion of Humanity. But in order for this to be a stable solution he vigorously rejected both aristocratic, theocratic and democratic structures, which in post-revolutionary France were aggravating formations. He contrasted them with what he called 'sociocracy' – where transmission of social status was achieved not by birth or election, but by appointment and adoption. A new patrician stratum would be formed on the basis of wealth and industrial expertise, and this would be transmitted in a new caste-like formation that guaranteed its stable continuity. Wealth would be even more concentrated in this society, and inequalities would become pronounced. But the newly formed proletariat, subject to the rigours of positivist education, would learn submission and resignation. The period of the dictatorship of the proletariat would eliminate the bourgeoisie but only to entrench the proletariat itself at the bottom of the status hierarchy. In this expressly utopian scenario, the new positivist priesthood, ruled by an absolute Pontiff, would counsel the industrial patriciate with the support of a newly formed matriarchy in the family. One of the key utopian elements in this vision was the evolution of virgin mothers, a new evolution towards parthenogenesis. The sexual drive itself would be effective in the sphere of morals on condition it was sublimated. J. S. Mill commented at length on these ideas and concluded that Comte aimed to establish a new kind of despotism, one that went much further than the classic models in controlling the intimate details of an individual's life.

What obsessed Comte were the problems that the 'metaphysical' stage – that between the theological and the positive in social progression – posed for social theory. Comte's analyses do not fit comfortably alongside classical or neoclassical economics; they reject almost all of their fundamental assumptions as liberal theorists such as Herbert Spencer were well aware. Comte's ideas were not aligned to support Social Darwinism, feminism or imperialism either. But they did play an important role, surprisingly, in the later evolution of social liberalism; and the Comtists were alongside the Marxists in setting up the International Workingman's Association and in the Paris Commune, 1871, largely because Comte sought the support of the proletariat for his projects. Doctrinally the Comtists were against the independent creation of cooperatives, and in favour of state intervention in organising production. Durkheim's later recognition of Comte as a theorist of the division of labour appears to acknowledge a contribution to economic thought – yet Durkheim did not follow this up, and developed themes around law and sanction rather than production. It was Herbert Spencer, not Comte, who placed the category of industrial society centre stage in the sociological analysis of modernity.

Spencer and the Reaction Against the Positive Polity

Writers surveying social thought of the nineteenth century just at the period of the First World War, such as Ernest Barker and Bertrand Russell, confirmed that the figure most in vogue during the late Victorian and Edwardian epoch was Herbert Spencer (1820–1903). Curiously influential on the development of sociology elsewhere in the world he made no lasting impact on the development of sociology in Britain, for his influence suddenly waned after 1918. This history should not obscure the fact that sociology was very much a mid-nineteenth-century product after its coinage and elaboration by Comte and then others in the 1840s. Although much of the language of this sociology was first developed by Comte, Spencer claimed in the 1860s the sociological terminology was in all essentials his invention. By the 1960s, however, it was widely held that there was no classical sociology in Britain such was the total eclipse of Spencer's social thought. Recent new assessments have attempted with some success to establish the centrality of his classical liberal contribution to sociology as a discipline.[4]

Spencer took up the political economy associated with the name of Adam Smith from the mid-eighteenth century with its concepts of division of labour, specialisation and national wealth in a perspective of an economy driven by natural laws, and gave this problematic a new home. The new conceptual matrix, already organised around the theme of evolution, was the selective process of elimination, or, as Spencer famously expressed it, the 'survival of the fittest'. As a first approximation it would be possible to say that Spencerian sociology was simply a form of Social Darwinism, and as such combined scientism, biology, economics, sociology and positivism. Yet the twist that Spencer gave to the older physiocratic and utilitarian doctrines was actually of a different character, since his thought was critical of the late Victorian celebration of imperialism, and social and eugenic engineering.[5] His main ideas were worked out in mid-century around the theme of individuation and the vitality of the natural community beyond the state. Population pressure would be eased since individuation itself would divert energy away from reproduction. In contrast to the social logic of Comte's theory, social evolution, he argued, leads to a society in which the state will become dramatically reduced in size and function. Spencer wrote in support of a common thematic of mid-nineteenth century theory – the hoped-for withering away of the state, a latent anarchism that retained a vision of the individual liberated from state oppression. This did not prevent him from inventing a 'euthanasia machine' for executing the worst criminals.[6]

Readings of Spencer now tend to emphasise his formation in the tradition of dissenting non-conformist Protestantism. A basic thematic of individual independence is retained throughout his intellectual career, even if this seems at first sight to be at variance with a project for a sociology giving precedence to the social. Spencer wanted to show that the development and progression of individual liberty within a non-governed community was a truth that could be scientifically demonstrated, not simply revealed within a religious tradition. Thus he had recourse to a secularised theory of science and scientific development that paralleled step by step that of Comte. Although both Comte and Spencer gave phrenology a place in their theories, it was only Spencer that developed an individual psychology (though the individual possessed no free will) – Comte had no space between the biological and the social for the individual self was a metaphysical illusion. Spencer, on the other hand, held that the individual was an essential reality whose emancipation was dependent on the withdrawal of the state from all but the essential function of sanctioning a minimal legal framework of individual life. It is the vitality of the individual's self-determination, not the activity of the state, which has been the creative force in history and society: the encroachment of the state into education, economics, health, family, even the postal service and the money supply, was an aberration. Unlike the physiocrats of the eighteenth century, Spencer was not supportive of enlightened despots but favoured democratic forms as the least-worst option. His sociology contrasted peaceful industrial democratic forms against governments devoted to war. Governments and public administrations in general, however, tend to be inefficient in comparison with private organisations, thus growth of the state leads not just to a curtailment of liberty of the individual but also a considerable increase in legalism and bureaucratic incompetence.

But, like Comte, Spencer entered a period of great intellectual crisis. As the various expansions of public authorities and their administrations took place in the latter part of the nineteenth century in an imperial context, Spencer was forced into a more and more defensive position. Imperial authority was destructive of native cultures, and state socialism was destructive of local cultures.[7] Altruism through the state was destructive of genuine natural altruism that arises spontaneously in any society. State development beyond a minimum that could be defined precisely leads to a deformation of natural creative evolution itself and to a series of perverse effects. From very early on Spencer wrote on poverty relief and the Poor Laws, and was consistently opposed to any state intervention: things should work out naturally, without incompetently organised public altruism. State interventions requiring extensive progressive taxation would lead only to distortions of economic life and its providential functioning; and social life would be subject to the continued influence of the weakest and dependent, on those who would otherwise not survive by the natural laws of evolution or those failing to learn how to adjust and adapt to them. His reactions to late Victorian developments included a revision of his ideas on social and gender equality: this should never be engineered legally. Spencer was more of a libertarian, individualist, anarchic free-market sociologist, than an apologist for a Victorian ethics of social improvement. The new sociology he developed from the 1880s was very specifically redesigned as a critique of the directions of organised capitalism and as a defence of the utopian idealisation of the society that had existed around the mid-century with the emblematic victory of the movement for a world open to free trade. This sociology had first emerged and seemed perfectly attuned to the world after the revolutionary Napoleonic Wars and before the new tensions that developed in nation states after 1880. Spencerian sociology was radical and critical (because it went well beyond utilitarianism). The virtual anarchic utopia he espoused survived in a strand of economic thought that was regarded as somewhat eccentric until it made its dramatic reappearance in a novel form of neo-liberalism a century later.

So how did this critical ideology work as a science? Spencer presented his writings on sociology as part of a series he called 'synthetic philosophy' (1860–92). A rather dramatic clearing of paths was announced with the declaration that all theology would be put to one side: God's realm was simply unknowable. Spencer was not an atheist but an agnostic (this very term invented by T. H. Huxley (1825–95) was occasioned by this debate.) Huxley, sometimes referred to as Darwin's 'bulldog' worked tirelessly to spread the gospel of biological evolution. And by 1880 his crusade had made considerable gains with the general public and indeed opened up the universities to the importance of laboratory science. Spencer laboured on with the general project alone: philosophical principles, biology, psychology, sociology and then ethics. God's laws had become nature's laws. Additional volumes appeared at regular intervals but studies on astronomy and geology planned for the series were never completed. The space-time universe of literal biblical Christianity, however, had been undone; in its place, according to Spencer, was one basic two-state law. This law at the heart of his evolutionary synthetic philosophy held that every domain passes from a condition of homogeneity to one of heterogeneity.

The volumes on the new science of sociology were thus part of 'A System of Synthetic Philosophy' – the omnibus title for his philosophy (which had its 'first principles'), and then multiple volumes on biology, psychology, sociology and ethics. Volume 1 on sociology was almost 900 pages; it went through a number of editions. Further volumes concerned 'ceremonial institutions' and 'political institutions' (together in volume 2) and 'ecclesiastical institutions', 'professional institutions' and 'industrial institutions' (together as volume 3).[8] The major difference with the equally monumental works of Comte, also conceived overall as a work of philosophy, was that Comte had invented the discipline of 'sociology' as well as coining 'positivism' for its methodology and the word 'altruism' (and thus had invented the opposition egoism-altruism so fundamental to Spencer's thought) as a step towards scientific ethics. Spencer's logic was exactly the same and involved therefore a complete rewriting of the sociology and ethics in an almost identical project and taking almost twice as long to realise. The basic materials were different, and the sociological argument was reorganised, yet sociology again came to recognise the importance of altruism. But Comte and Spencer reached diametrically opposite conclusions. This of course provoked head-on clashes between the Comteans and Spencer himself and this came to a head in 1885.[9]

Spencer's basic programme then was a new positivism: the identification of the specific stages of social evolution read through the vision of a philosophical logic of the general law of evolution – from homogeneity to heterogeneity in each sphere – the logic of the part was that of the whole. Spencer simply omitted Comte's long trudge through mathematics, physics and chemistry. Taking a short cut, he took biology as the science providing the models for living organisms, as demanded by Comte. This led Spencer to a sociology of structures, functions, systems and processes of differentiation, integration of different levels of the development of life and creative evolution through selection (survival or elimination). But if Spencer did not simply chart a linear evolution since there could be regression, the central obsession of his analyses was the search for the line of evolutionary progression – progress always went, repetitively, from the homogeneous to the heterogeneous. The hierarchy of developmental levels were the backdrop for his key analyses. The pattern of stages was both a complex outcome and a development of a cross-cutting feature: the dynamics of variation between what he called martial versus industrial social activity. Earlier societies tended to be more militaristic, later ones more industrial, yet at each stage a society could be drawn into militarism. Thus it was a simple matter to define where social development was leading from the 1880s, since he had identified Bismarckian state-socialism as essentially connected with militarism, as was late Victorian imperialism. Relentlessly his work became a prolonged and sustained protest against the lurch of society into more and more violent, hierarchical, state-led and anti-liberal forms. His ideal was the slow development of a civil society within the spontaneous creation of the web of private contracts: the intimate connection of unregulated small-scale capitalism and individual freedom with its natural and unsentimental processes of natural selection. It should be noted that this ideal did not imply, he insisted, the elimination of the uncivilised by the civilised by militaristic imperialists.[10] Selective elimination did not work through force as such, though evidently in terms of the development of means of warfare this effect on populations was at work. Specific ethical and moral virtues were produced in such conflict, he admitted, and this had been an essential moment of progressive evolution. Essentially, however, the basic features of civilisation, around the central value of the individual being, were produced through industry, exchange, market competition, personal trust and honesty, outside of the state: distortions of the market through taxation and even political party competition would eventually wither away as militarism declined towards a zero point.

Spencer's volumes on scientific ethics emerge at the end of the century in a sociology against the grain of big organised capital and imperial expansion. His position became defensive, and conservative, reorienting its radical utopianism. He refused to back any state intervention even if its objectives were to protect the individual. His politics did not seek to transform society by violent revolution in order to bring it to a new level of complexity – this would happen naturally. It advocated disarmament and he opposed what he saw as the 're-barbarisation' of society (a significant acknowledgement of the new classification – savagery, barbarism, civilisation). Whereas Comte outlined a utopia in which a new priesthood would exercise sacred surveillance over profane industrialism, Spencer indicated a quite different utopia; he drew this vision from his theoretical analysis of evolution, in which priestly authority, which had already almost completely vanished among the Dissenters, would entirely disappear. But would this happen? Spencer's verdict was that the condition that could make this happen, the arrival of the free post-industrial society, would not be fulfilled during an epoch threatening both militarism and a system of production and distribution under state control.

Even though Spencer's sociology was dressed up in the jargon of evolutionary theory and philosophy it is important to examine the way it was constructed. He had written volumes on biology and psychology before moving to sociology, and it is important to note the limits he placed on the principle of selection that he called the 'survival of the fittest' since he argued that it did not apply to the whole range of societies studied in his works. He was not an advocate of 'Social Darwinism'. At the higher end of social evolution, such natural selection no longer applied when population pressure had been eliminated. His basic evolutionary scheme was a structured procession, starting with simplest tribes, these became compounded by incorporation and fusion – and then doubly and trebly 'compounded' as their complexity produced differentiation and integration into political and other institutions. Explaining this process Spencer illustrated the movement of differentiation in separate spheres (domestic, ecclesiastical, professional, ceremonial, political, religious and industrial). And to the opposition martial (dominated by war) versus industrial society (dominated by work) he added without much elaboration a third type: aesthetic – the highest type (dominated by 'life'). Spencer's view was that industrial formations were organised around contract, and if this required at first the discipline of work the value system of 'equal freedom' for all would generate the move to a society in which work discipline would eventually give way. His analysis of the professions indicated that they would be the bearers of this new increasingly secular utopia.[11]

But why did Spencer need to invent a titanic metaphysical system with sociology at the heart of it? It could be said that he started with some basic propositions about politics and society and he simply dressed up these ideas in the rhetoric of scientific formulae. More generously it could be said that he had certain general ideas in mind and systematically explored them, drawing out their metaphysical implications. But why should he need sociology as such if, as is well known, his conclusions, to support individual freedom against the growth of socialism, mass democracy and imperialism, were already in place? Why would he need, over a period of labour of over forty years, to trail through all previous social types in order to show that individual life and freedom needed to be defended? An early formulation perhaps provides an answer: 'I look upon despotisms, aristocracies, priestcrafts, and all the other evils that afflict humanity, as the necessary agents for the training of the human mind' he wrote in a letter of 1843. He suggested that 'every people must pass through the various phases between absolutism and democracy before they are fitted to become *permanently* free' and he added 'if a nation liberates itself by physical force, and attains the goal without passing through these moral ordeals, I do not think its freedom will be lasting'.[12] Thus social evolution works through stages, and the evolution has a telos: sociology would be the guide through to this future, and indeed, it is in itself part of this very process and its continuation from generation to generation through an appropriate educational practice.

What he wanted to demonstrate was that there was a law of evolution and that this applied equally to social development as a natural phenomenon. Ignorance of this by legislators could only lead to erroneous and misguided efforts, requiring constant corrections and rectifications. His view was that there had been a 'marvellous organisation which has been growing up for thousands of years without government help … without the design of any one'. Yet legislators 'cannot believe that society will be bettered by natural agencies.' His conception of the role of sociology was that it defines the natural line of social evolution: any legislative proposal should be questioned as to how 'it falls within the lines of this evolution, and what would be the effects of running counter to the normal course of things'. Spencer laments that 'not only is no such question ever entertained, but the one who raised it would be laughed down in any popular assembly, and smiled at as a dreamer in the House of Commons'.[13] It is not as if he suggested that the roll back of the state would liberate a pure individual. Only a society that has been through the struggle, the 'moral ordeal' can produce an individual who can be permanently free. His writings on education and justice can be read in this light: a free society must educate its citizens in freedom, for freedom.[14]

These writings on education had wide take-up in the nineteenth century – they were written 1854–9 and widely disseminated. They work on the proposition that individuals should be encouraged to learn from their own mistakes and discover the world for themselves. Harsh punishment and brutality (which, he notes, are prevalent in the great public schools) do immense damage. But schools should be free from state control; reform should come through persuasion. The basic objective is to establish a society in which the rule of equal freedom is respected and developed. His writings on ethics and justice work out further dimensions of equal freedom in social life. To do this he developed Comte's opposition between egoistic conduct (privileging self-interest) and altruism. One would expect that he might support Adam Smith's view that the self-interest of profit-making benefits others indirectly through the famous action of the hidden hand (a natural harmony that could well be the mysterious result of divine law). In fact he takes a different route. The evolutionary progression to the highest form of civilisation passes not by the hidden hand of God in the market but by the egoism that can be found within the pleasure of pure altruism – for in advanced altruism there is a benefice for the self.

At this point instead of eliminating altruism, Spencer envisages a coalescence of egoism into the altruism of the gift.[15] It was to the great surprise of an audience at a banquet in New York held in his honour in 1882, when he said they were working too hard. It was not what was expected of the prophet of the survival of the fittest in the struggle for existence. The individual would give altruistically, but should not intervene to save another person from the negative consequences of an action – this was essential if the natural process of the reality principle was to be maintained, and genuine learning from mistakes was essential. It was sociology, not political economy, which would deliver the ultimate and complete philosophical and scientific legitimation of social progression. Marx and Engels distinguished the utopian from the scientific theorists, but clearly Comte and Spencer were both scientific and utopian. Spencer met Comte in October 1856 in Paris. A brief discussion took place largely it seems about each other's health: Comte advised Spencer to get married.[16]

It is interesting to turn to the American take-up of this debate on sociology. In fact Comte's work was transplanted to the antebellum south, not only in the first English translation of Comte's lectures on mathematics, but also in the strange use of sociology in the 1850s by George Fitzhugh (1806–81) to justify the institution of slavery against the market.[17] In the so-called Gilded Age (1870–1900) many intellectuals were attracted to the modernity of positivism and sociology found its way into the American higher education colleges, for the Comteans and the Spencerians had their own disciples there developing their ideas in vigorous debate. W. G. Sumner (1840–1910), who had studied at Oxford in the 1860s, taught courses in sociology at Yale from 1872. There was sociology at Kansas University from 1890, at Chicago from 1892 and at Columbia from 1894. L. F. Ward (1841–1913), the leading American Comtean, eventually taught at Brown University. Sumner also read Herbert Spencer and argued that government intervention would always fail against what he called 'social folkways'. Lester Ward attempted to combine Comte with Spencer, and developed at great length an up-to-date version of the system of scientific knowledge, and argued that scientific government would be able to intervene successfully to overcome social pathologies in introducing 'sociocracy'. It was the Comteans who gave key intellectual support and legitimation to government interventions in the so-called Progressive Era (1900–20).

There were other major thinkers in America working their way out of the Comte–Spencer matrix. William James developed a psychology out of Spencer's initial studies and a philosophy of pragmatism, while Thorstein Veblen (1857–1929) developed an original institutional economics that combined Comte, Spencer and Marx. The America of 1900 was of course the crucial site of the industrial revolutions associated with mass industrial automobile production, but also of the bicycle and the first aircraft. Veblen identified an important new stage he calls the machine process as the continuous application of science to industry. Alongside and dominating machine industry, he argued, was a new pecuniary business culture of finance capital. This, he suggested, was fundamentally a continuation of aristocratic militarism, a renewed barbarian culture that could be analysed as notions of deception and cunning as developed by Lester Ward. A new leisure class had developed with a pre-modern culture of conspicuous consumption, and was at war not only within itself but also with the genuinely workmanlike culture of industry (itself in the process of deskilling). Veblen also identified elements of modern consumerism in which status and display predominated, features he saw as continuing barbarian ceremonies.

Durkheim and Weber: Sociology After the Heroic Age

Both Emile Durkheim (1858–1917) and Max Weber (1864–1920) in Europe went through an early period in which they explicitly espoused, for a short time, the Darwinian idea of selection by elimination, Durkheim in his doctoral thesis published in 1893 and Weber in his inaugural lecture of 1895. The sociological traditions in France and Germany produced different continuations, however. In France, Durkheim's case was very much in line with Comte's (and Spencer's) project that would lead to a scientific ethics. In Germany, in Weber's case, this ideal was more or less regarded as naïve and even infantile since values were inherently conflictual and beyond scientific jurisdiction. Both, however, engaged anew with the Kantian legacy of moral structure and freedom. Weber concluded that a recognition of the complexity and irreducibility of the conflict of values was essential to sociology. Durkheim, with his study of suicide rates (1897), and Weber with a study of the importance of Protestantism for the development of capitalism (1904) produced classic studies. These studies have proved to be lasting foundational analyses for modern sociology, not the works of Comte or Spencer. Yet both studies were still embedded in evolutionary frameworks, and were in different ways indebted to the earlier writers.

Durkheim worked with an evolutionary six-stage model: the elementary horde, simple clan-based tribe, tribal confederation, ancient city-state, mediaeval society and modern industrial nation.[18] This linear chain is underpinned by a simple theory of two fundamental forms of social solidarity: mechanical and organic. Societies that are 'mechanical' add together elements (kinship groups) as 'compound' or 'doubly compound' compositions in Spencer's terms; this form of solidarity was based on bonds of similitude. Societies that are organised on the basis of an 'organic' division of labour and interdependent specialisation of function (including mediaeval society and the modern nation) have a form of social solidarity that is more and more complex and based on contract. Here Durkheim added an essential idea: there are decisive non-contractual elements in contract stemming from the moral structures in which it is embedded – conceived as a negative externality, it is a fundamental condition of the validity of contract and legitimates its binding nature.

Weber also worked with an evolutionary framework that was never formalised as such. It suggests a first primitive civilisation, then archaic and historic civilisations and finally modern civilisation; these are cross-cut by three modes of domination: traditional, charismatic and modern (legal-rational). A major methodological turn was realised by a theorising of these three modes as three ideal types – conceived explicitly as fictionalised utopias rationally constructed as one-sided exaggerations of elements abstracted from real complex wholes. Ideal types could then be used for comparative analysis of historical formations. In fact his ideal type of bureaucracy instituted a minor revolution in the way sociologists understood administrative structures: they were far more efficient than any other type of administration.[19] The concept of discipline became central to the study not only of religion and industry but also that of war and the military machine. Weber's basic question was how to explain that modern capitalism emerged only in Western Europe in the Protestant period and nowhere else. To that end he wrote extensive studies of the major world religions that have been taken to complement those of the Durkheim school's extensive programme of research into the 'elementary forms' of religion (totemism, ritual, gift exchange, sacrifice, magic, prayer, kinship, classification) all first published around 1900.

Durkheim developed his sociological theories as his research grew more extensive. He began by suggesting that the earlier the society, the more likely it was to have physically repressive sanctions. He later revised this view completely. In his early lectures on moral education, for example, he argued that there was a plague of violent punishment in the schools of the Middle Ages, and the lash remained in constant use in schools up until the eighteenth century. He faced up to the issue of punishment as a practical issue for teachers in his pedagogy classes. Between the offence and the punishment he observed there is a hidden continuity. It is because this link is not understood that erroneous theories of punishment arise. One such theory sees punishment as expiation or atonement, another sees punishment primarily as a way of intimidating or inhibiting further offences. From a pedagogical point of view, he argued, the problem concerns the capacity to neutralise the demoralising effects of an infringement of group norms. The effectiveness of punishment should be judged by how far it contributes to the solidarity of a group as a whole; misapplied punishment can contribute to the creation of further immoral acts. Once applied, punishment seems to lose something of its power. A reign of terror is, in the end, a very weak system of sanctions. It is often driven to extremes by its own increasing ineffectiveness. Corporal punishment also involves a serious contradiction, since it is an attack on the dignity of the individual, a dignity valued and fostered in modern societies. After researching his lectures on educational thought in France, he revised the thesis of the violent mediaeval colleges; it was, he concluded, simply 'a legend' as he could not find empirical evidence to support it. He discovered that these educational communities remained essentially democratic and suggested that such forms never have very harsh disciplinary regimes. The new analysis suggests that the turn towards a more oppressive disciplinary regime began at the end of the sixteenth century just at the moment when the schools and colleges in France became detached from the community, a finding that directly refuted Spencer's analysis.

Durkheim's theoretical sociology then did not shy away from the issues of the nature of the modern state and political power. Durkheim's argument suggests social theory is often mistaken in thinking the state is either a purely repressive machine, or that the purely political division of powers can deliver political and social liberty in the fullest sense.[20] Durkheim's analysis of the family reveals how the modern family is born out of a struggle against wider kin dominance. This historic struggle, central to Durkheim's 'grand narrative' of the movement from societies based on mechanical to those based on organic solidarity, is also the narrative of the way the modern state played a key role in the construction of the moral and social system of contract and individual liberty.

The central theoretical issue here was addressed in an article of 1900 called 'Two Laws of Penal Evolution'.[21] Durkheim criticised Spencer for thinking that the degree of absoluteness of governmental power is related to the number of functions it undertakes and the more or less absolute character of central power is independent of the degree of social complexity. Durkheim presents an account of French society that is diametrically opposed to that, say, of Marx but consistent with that of Comte: seventeenth-century France and nineteenth-century France belonged to the same social type. To think there has been a change of type is to mistake a conjunctural event in the society (revolution) with its fundamental structure, since absolutism arises, not from the constituent features of a social form, but from contingent conditions in social evolution. In principle, the form of state (absolutist or democratic) is never a fundamental constituting feature of any society. It seems clear, however, that Durkheim was reworking the Spencerian thesis of the military versus industrial alternation that could cross-cut evolutionary classification of stages of development.

Durkheim investigated this basic idea in a different way in his study of suicide rates where such intensities are realised in actions of self-destruction. With earlier writers analysis stopped with the demonstration of regularity between two variables. Durkheim's own strategy was to examine the parallelism of rankings between the substantive series he analysed and called 'concomitant variation'.[22] Durkheim does not work with conflicts that arise from the constitution of the individual (conflict of drives, instincts in a Freudian manner), but in relation to the social forces theorised as currents, flows of energy, conceived as social causes. His 'morphological' classification of suicides suggests the fundamental forms are always associated with certain highly specific emotional states: egoistic suicide is performed with apathetic emotional detachment, altruistic suicide performed with calm resolve and anomic with agitated irritation and disgust. More complex forms are discussed subsequently as combinations of these fundamental ones. Analytically then there is the major division between morphology and aetiology, between the actual forms of the act itself and the social causes of suicide. The important discovery of the absence of a causal link between the morphology (the way the act was committed) and the suicide rate itself led to a re-thinking of suicide as an act subject to multiple causation.

Durkheim's attempt to put together a scientific ethics derived from sociology was cut short by his death in 1917, and only indicative sketches of his position remain. In effect his sociological legacy was not to be a completed moral science, but rather a model of sociology as leading to a social therapeutics in which the idea of social pathology was given a scientific foundation. This project, however, was largely abandoned in the twentieth century, as sociology became more profoundly influenced by the alternative – Weberian – formulation of what constitutes a social science. Comte, Spencer and Durkheim all embraced the radical Enlightenment view that the development of knowledge through a set of specialised scientific disciplines would produce conclusive knowledge that any rational mind would have to accept as the basis for ethical life. Weber, following a different tradition, did not accept this view: no science could resolve the problem of conflicting value systems.

Weber's work was also cut short by an early death in 1920, but his last writings present a very clear analysis of the complexity of the inherent oppositions of values in social life and, as this indeed becomes clearly recognised in modern culture sociology, itself becomes part of the reflexive equipment that enables us to escape naivety. Instead of leading to a therapeutics, Weber insisted on the irreducible nature of ethical choice and responsibility, and that sociology belongs to a kind of knowledge that provides at best a critical clarification of the structures and forces at work in modern civilisation: it does not itself, and cannot, produce values, ultimate, intermediate or provisional. Weber seems to work at one level with a Comtean idea that scientific progression is part of a wide process of rationalisation of cultures that produces out of traditional religion new forms of secular metaphysics. And with Spencer, the idea that far from eliminating metaphysical speculation science widens the spheres for such reflection. In addition to this it is his engagement with Marx and the analysis of the emergence of capitalism that marks his distinctive difference with Durkheim.

Weber found, on the one hand, Marx's analysis and 'historical materialism' generally reductive and, on the other, that the tradition of Comte, Spencer and Durkheim, which focused on industrialism alone (rather than capitalism and industrialism), missed an essential level of analysis. His sociology identified spheres of analysis, and included for the first time the 'erotic sphere'. His studies of the rise of capitalism outline the decisive role of religion in opening the economic to modern rational capitalism, and to do that Weber worked towards a conception of types of capitalism that has become, in addition to the analysis of the division of labour, essential to modern sociology. The term is to be differentiated from simple exchange, money, banking, trading and 'booty' or even finance capital, which are widespread in many different cultures. What interests him is the continuous activity of production in the form of the employment of wage labour and that products are marketable in a way that is calculable as a commercial exchange. This conception is very close to that developed by Marx of course, but what is new is the emphasis on rationality, calculation in relation to markets, including labour markets, and competition, as well as rational administration and law. Above all it only came into existence within one unique cultural configuration – not in Asia, nor in European antiquity, but only with the emergence of the Protestant-dominated cultures of northern Europe.[23]

But what was Weber's objective and why did he need a sociology? Certainly Weber clearly comes from a tradition that regards science as having nothing to offer an ethics as such. What Weber wanted was clarification of the specifically German set of problems leading up to 1914: the spectre of communism, authoritarian state formation, militarism, nationalism, imperialism and the question of the place of parliamentary democracy and administrative bureaucracy. Bismarck's legacy, the unification of modern Germany, included a strong central authority and bureaucracy but a weak parliament. Politicians were unprepared for independent political leadership. When Wilhelm II took power in 1890, Bismarck retired from the scene, paving the way to absolute monarchy. Weber's sociological analyses of political and legal systems, economy, law and religion, made it possible for him to diagnose the particularity of the tragedy of 1914, in a completely different way from either Durkheim or Veblen who both saw Germany's Prussian militarism and increasing absolutism as the key problem. Weber saw not only a failure of the German political system (absolutism, weak parliament and strong bureaucracy) but also the failure of the system of the European Great Power politics. Weber's vast and great studies of world religions and his system of sociology (as voluminous as any) were only fully published in 1916–20; and they belong to a different century inaugurated, as was the nineteenth, in war. Veblen advised the American government to press for punishing reparations against Germany. Weber was a member of the German delegation at Versailles in 1919 and warned of the danger of a treaty that made such a war beneficial to the victor.

Conclusions

In the interpretation developed here it is evident that the mature writings of Veblen, Durkheim and Weber, though arising from a tradition established in the nineteenth, belong essentially to the twentieth century, in the same way that the war of 1914–18 was on a different scale from any war before. The writings of Comte and Spencer, as well as those of Marx, nevertheless continued and continue to have effects throughout the world today as neo-liberalism and its discontents have revitalised the debates of the mid-nineteenth century. In fact the writings of that heroic age have been utilised to overturn some of the social democratic conclusions of Durkheim and Weber. But the heroic age theorists diverged dramatically in their diagnosis of the future, elaborating quite contradictory utopian visions. In the world today it would not be completely absurd to argue that what is at work is still a struggle between status and contract, hierarchy and equality, honour and right, regulation and freedom. If the struggle to roll back, or to preserve and reform the state seems perennial, so too will be a return to the debates of mid-nineteenth-century sociologists who tried to set the terms of the debate in the clearest possible way, even though, as Mill pointed out, their arguments often appear absurd and ridiculous because they took the risk to force the logic of their premises to ultimate conclusions. The sociology that eventually emerged from the controversies of the nineteenth century, developed principally in France, Britain and Germany, was concerned with certain dualities (egoism and altruism, anomie and fatalism, dependence and independence, sacred and profane) in the context of highly complex sets of power struggles. But the question of whether sociology should dispense with the category of social pathology or evil was never entirely resolved.

Sociology was not born in the generation of Durkheim and Weber. Sociology had its huge first success in the mid-nineteenth century with the voluminous writings of Comte and Spencer and their disciples. The word itself coined in 1839 was immediately popularised by the positivists and by liberals such as J. S. Mill. The Marxists did not identify with it and critiqued it as they did political economy. Marxist sociology was a much later concession. But the very separate and distinct notions of the 'social' and 'society' became a topic of scientific investigation in the mid-nineteenth century out of liberal and socialist debates, though it had been known from previous centuries that there were regular and stubborn characteristics of the social (its birth and death rates). In its first era sociology pronounced itself queen of the sciences, unifying methodologies in an overarching philosophy of evolution and progress. The failure of this project was clear by 1920, as sociology became a university discipline in its own right. The sciences remained divided and went their own ways within a loose ensemble: the natural sciences on one side and the arts on the other, with what are now called the human sciences in between. But the conception of society itself had been revolutionised irreversibly: it was now conceived as both highly structured but with inner tensions, inner currents and emotions and with an uncertain future.

NOTES

1 These are collected in *Comte: Early Political Writings*, ed. H. S. Jones (Cambridge: Cambridge University Press, 1998). Also available as an appendix in *System of Positive Polity*, 4 vols. (Bristol: Thoemmes Press, 2001).

2 For Comte's intellectual life covered in extensive detail, see M. Pickering, *Auguste Comte: An Intellectual Biography*, 3 vols. (Cambridge: Cambridge University Press, 1993–2009).

3 *The Positive Philosophy*, trans. and ed. H. Martineau (Chicago: Belford, Clarke & Co., 1880), the initial chapters 1–2, pp. 25–50. Martineau's reduction of the French six volumes brought Comte's work to an Anglophone audience. Her version of Comte is explored in 'The Elusive Disciple: Harriet Martineau', in Pickering, *Auguste Comte*, vol. 3, pp. 132–58.

4 Principally the studies by M. Francis, *Herbert Spencer and the Invention of Modern Life* (Stocksfield: Acumen, 2007), and J. Offer, *Herbert Spencer and Social Theory* (Basingstoke: Palgrave, 2010).

5 M. Hawkins, *Social Darwinism in European and American Thought 1860–1945* (Cambridge: Cambridge University Press, 1997).

6 H. Spencer, *Facts and Comments* (London: Williams & Norgate, 1902), pp. 162–3.

7 H. Spencer, *The Man versus the State* (London: Williams & Norgate, 1884), p. 143.

8 The materials he worked for *Principles* were also published separately with subeditors and compilers, in the eight volumes of *Descriptive Sociology*. After 1910 this series continued with more volumes.

9 Spencer began 'Religion: a Retrospect and Prospect', pp. 17–35. Harrison replied with 'The Ghost of Religion', pp. 37–58. Spencer counter-attacked 'Retrogressive Religion', pp. 59–99. Harrison responded with 'Agnostic Metaphysics', pp. 101–47. Spencer again: 'Last Words About Agnosticism and the Religion of Humanity', pp. 149–72. And Harrison concluded with 'Mr Herbert Spencer and Agnosticism', pp. 172–82. In E. Youmans, ed., *The Nature and Reality of Religion. A Controversy* (New York: Appleton, 1885).

10 'Re-Barbarisation', in *Facts and Comments*, pp. 172–88.

11 'Professional Institutions', in *Principles of Sociology*, vol. 3, pp. 177–324.

12 Cited in Offer, *Herbert Spencer and Social Theory*, pp. 44–5.

13 H. Spencer, *The Principles of Sociology* (London: Williams & Norgate, 1896), vol. 3, pp. 322–4.

14 H. Spencer, *Education* (London: Williams & Norgate, 1861).

15 H. Spencer, *The Principles of Ethics* (London: Appleton, 1910).

16 H. Spencer, *Autobiography* (London: Williams & Norgate, 1904), vol. 1, p. 578.

17 George Fitzhugh, *A Sociology for the South; or, The Failure of a Free Society* (Richmond: A. Morris, 1854).

18 Clarified in E. Wallwork, 'Religion and Social Structure in The Division of Labor', *American Anthropologist* 86 (1984), 43–64.

19 'Bureaucracy', in Weber, *Economy and Society* (Berkeley: University of California Press, 1922), vol I, pp. 956–1005.

20 For Durkheim the Spencerian thesis that freedom is freedom from the state ignores the fact that it is the state 'that has rescued the child from family tyranny [and] the citizen from feudal groups and later from communal groups'. Indeed the state must not limit itself to the administration of 'prohibitive justice … [it] must deploy energies equal to those for which it has to provide a counterbalance'. Against the political illusion of power Durkheim in effect tried to show that liberty is based on a particular form of the total social division of power: the state 'must even permeate all those secondary groups of family, trade and professional association, Church, regional areas, and so on'. *Professional Ethics and Civic Morals* (London: Routledge, 1992), p. 64.

21 'Two laws of Penal Evolution', in *The Radical Sociology of Durkheim and Mauss*, ed. M. Gane (London: Routledge, 1992), pp. 21–9.

22 Stephen Turner has noted that 'the novel feature of Durkheim's treatment of suicide is neither the thesis of social determination, which was conventional, [and] not the actual explanation … but the specific statistical reasoning he uses and the way he interprets his results … to produce a genuinely novel result' since 'relations between rates in which perfectly equivalent rank-orderings at some level of aggregation can be discovered … [indeed] he uses the term "law" to describe these relationships, and these relationships alone'. S. Turner, *The Search for Methodology of Social Science* (Dordrecht: D. Reidel, 1986), p. 367.

23 He insisted that 'we are dealing with the connection of the spirit of modern economic life with the rational ethics of ascetic Protestantism. Thus we treat here only one side of the causal chain'. His other studies, he says, 'follow out both causal relationships, so far as it is necessary in order to find points of comparison with the Occidental development. For only in this way is it possible to attempt a causal evaluation of those elements of the economic ethics of the Western religions which differentiate them from others, with a hope of attaining a tolerable degree of approximation'. M. Weber, *The Protestant Ethic and the Spirit of Capitalism* (London: Unwin, 1930), p. 27.

6

ADAM BUDD

Historical Methods in Europe and America

In the West, the bloody and costly Napoleonic Wars (1803–15) were followed by economic depression, political reform, famine in Ireland, civil war and imperial assertion. But the immediate global political consequence was the creation of the 'nation state' at the Congress of Vienna (1815–16), where Europe was carved up into countries that mirrored the languages, religions and traditions of the people who would rule them. The newly created governments were eager to justify their legitimacy as nations by employing historians to celebrate their 'imagined community'. Russians were the first to see the publication of a crown-supported national history, not long after Napoleon's retreat from Moscow in 1812. Alexander I's court historian, Nikolai Karamzin, published his evocative *History of the Russian State* in 1818. Even at twelve volumes, it sold out within weeks, and its heroic story of the royal family defined the historical consciousness of generations. In 1826, the newly anointed King William I of the Netherlands held a competition for the best plan for a general history of his newly united country: the winner would take the title of *Geschiedschrijver des Rijks* ('state history writer') a position that still exists. The challenge was to submit a plan rather than a history because William's kingdom was barely eleven years old.

This rush to glorify the nation by supporting historical scholarship was clearest in France, where the regime of Louis-Philippe (1830–48) empowered a respected historian, François Guizot, to endow new departments dedicated to celebrating the royal French state. This national effort to collect and publish its archival holdings featured a three-year training course in its associated École des Chartes. Upon graduation, jobs awaited the newly minted *archiviste-paléographistes* in newly built libraries. Guizot's method was more structured and enduring than Napoleon's suggestion to l'abbé Halma, back in 1808. When Halma had asked the Emperor to support his plan for a new history of France, Napoleon replied by telling him that unless readers breathed a visible sigh of relief upon reading of the rise of his Empire, the book and its author would be suppressed by force.

It was obvious, even at the time, that history writing was an exercise in self-fashioning, driven by economic forces that included state patronage and the open market. Entrepreneurs in Scotland rode this lucrative wave of patriotic historical feeling. Between 1842 and 1846, the Allen brothers published treatises that cited works of art, archaeology, literature and oral traditions, to argue that a particular type of Highland dress was 'the fossil relic of the universal dress of the Middle Ages ... [when] Celtic Scotland had been a flourishing part of cosmopolitan Catholic Europe: a rich, polished society'.[1] These claims were pure invention, but they were welcomed, and faith in them endures through the belief that the one-piece kilt is a traditional Scottish design.

Soon after, invention of the action photograph (1847) and undersea telegraph cable (1850) brought the perception of immediacy to news reports from distant battlefields. The Crimean War (1853–6) was the first modern battle for its adoption of an embedded photojournalist, and for the unprecedented editorial shaping of the public's perceptions of national sacrifice. Two generations later an American, Van Wyck Brooks, coined the term 'a usable past' to describe the selection of facts that historians employ to create a favourable historical record. This might seem surprising, because national origins were not a pressing issue among Americans before the Civil War (1861–5), which helps explain why their federal government could refuse public access to its Library of Congress and National Archives until the end of the century (1897 and 1934). In the United States, the opening of libraries was left to individual states and philanthropists. Shaping the nation through government-sponsored history was largely a European and not an American endeavour during the nineteenth century.

This chapter will reflect on those historical celebrations of the nation that were produced not merely by market forces and political expediency. Intellectual developments, which arose in the wake of the Revolution in France (1789–93), ensured the importance of narrating a progressive development of the nation state and documenting it through archival work. Tracing the ideas that inform historical methods – the choice of histories we read, write and study – are fundamentally important, because they reveal how the past was understood by those who lived in it. This chapter opens with Napoleon's invasion of Prussia, and will address developments in England, the German lands and America, before concluding in Paris on the eve of the Great War.

Foundations

The academic training of teachers and scholars of modern history emerged first in what is now Germany. This place also was the source of this century's most powerful historical concept. With the sound of Napoleon's gunfire heralding the defeat of Prussia, seen then as 'the most startling and unforeseen occurrence that had been witnessed in modern Europe', the philosopher G. W. F. Hegel completed his prophetic theory of history.[2] At Jena in 1806, Hegel wrote that the rise of the nation state is a natural manifestation of God's will to extend the virtues of law, reason and freedom on earth: 'The state consists in the march of God in the world', he wrote, even as he mourned his country's defeat.[3] Hegel's position grew from an idea that the philosopher Immanuel Kant had expressed twenty years earlier, on the eve of the French Revolution: 'The history of mankind can be seen, in the large, as the realization of Nature's secret plan to bring forth a perfectly constituted state as the only condition in which the capacities of mankind can be fully developed.'[4] It is easy to see this idea's appeal during a demoralising military invasion, particularly its promise that political conflict is, ultimately, constructive: 'the process of development ... is not the harmless and peaceful progress that is in the realm of organic life. Rather, it is a severe and unwilling working against itself', Hegel wrote, defining a basic concept in Romantic thought.[5] A short time later, Hegel's colleague in Berlin, the great historian Leopold Ranke, revealed his own Romantic idealism by observing that war is a clash of spiritual forces whose outcome expresses God's historical plan: 'you will be able to name few significant wars for which it could not be proved that genuine moral energy achieved the final victory'.[6] It is easy to see why Ranke retained little authority among military historians of later generations, particularly after the moral horror of the Great War and the Second World War.

Since God inspires military struggle, war is a natural and rational source of historical and moral progress. Hegel argued that this is embodied in the very origins of the nation state. It is not possible to overstate the influence of this idea during the nineteenth century. Hegel's concept urged historians either to take up the task of documenting and narrating national progress through its political developments, or to argue against doing so. His emphasis on moral progress encouraged the French philosopher Auguste Comte to construct a 'positive philosophy' that taught universal laws of historical progress, free of any contingencies. With its rules based on apparently empirical data, positivism brought the conceptual prestige of the natural sciences to the study of history, and inspired the *esprit de système* of Émile Durkheim's sociology, the psychoanalytic models of Sigmund Freud, the evolutionary psychology of Herbert Spencer and the cultural anthropology of Edward Tylor. Using a term coined in 1829, 'social scientists' and their disciples professed lawful models of historical development passing through progressive stages – from primitive to modern society; from infantile sexual instinct to creative sublimation and so on, using the language of the natural sciences.

Europe's leading university-based historians, in Prussia and in England, disliked philosophical commentary on historical processes, which the poet Samuel Taylor Coleridge also dismissed as 'the hollowness of abstractions … and its unenlivened geneneralising'.[7] But Hegel's prophetic philosophy was flexible: it led even the atheist Karl Marx to write a theory of 'retrogressive development' whose focus on 'real men' promised to ignore 'German philosophy' entirely.[8] Most historians in England sought a 'splendid isolation' from Continental upheavals in ideas as well as politics, but they too created a variation of Hegel's model. Indeed, Hegel's prophetic writings influenced Europe's leading establishment historians, such as Ranke at Berlin and William Stubbs at Oxford. Neither mentioned Hegel, but both believed that 'God dwells, lives and is recognizable in all history' – and that this justified the 'impartial' narration of European political progress to which they dedicated their careers.[9] As we shall see in the next section, Stubbs drew on the theological model of his predecessor at Oxford, Thomas Arnold, to establish an enduring undergraduate curriculum that taught a national 'consensus' on England's past, based on values held in the present, nicely consistent with Hegel's 'progressive' theory.

Leopold Ranke, whose teaching and research methods defined the professionalisation of history across Europe and America, reacted against the methods and claims of philosophy. For Ranke, 'Philosophy always reminds us of the claim of [a] supreme idea. History, on the other hand, reminds us of the conditions of existence.'[10] Like biologists, chemists and physicists, philosophers considered 'every particular only as part of the whole'. Ranke argued that historians should not work in this way. Historians understand the meaning of a historical event only after they have interpreted circumstances whose ultimate significance never can be settled. Unlike philosophers and scientists, historians do not seek conclusions that they confirm by testing. Rather, historians will disagree over a shared set of research findings, and argue over their merits to reach the best interpretation. This is why Ranke's *Historismus* ('historicism'), his concept that guides historical research and teaching, entailed the critical examination of primary sources, interpreted through discussion among students and their professor in a 'seminar' (from *Seminarium*: a place where seeds grow). Training in historicism was politically useful because it entailed a basic element of *Bildung* ('self-formation'), the cultivation of critical and imaginative sensibility, which was a domestic priority in Prussia during its occupation by France. When historians reach conclusions, which takes place only after they reach agreement on the meaning of facts, they cultivate their own minds as well as their narratives of the past. And unlike philosophers and scientists, according to Ranke, historians do not close the door to further discussion.

A recent commentator has described *Historismus* and *Bildung* as a joint project within Romantic thought: 'it is a fierce, sustained protest against living just only one life' – or against understanding historical truth according to a single authority, or seeing history as a process that had been fixed by an ideology.[11] Some of Ranke's students adopted *Historismus* as a religious doctrine, declaring their devotion to historicism and to *Bildung* as a 'life calling'. In contrast to Ranke, Stubbs' theological approach to history used a lecture- and textbook-based teaching method. British liberals like Stubbs stopped short of requiring a critical interpretation of a primary source once they had established its historical place in a theologically sanctioned, forward-moving plot. In other words, Ranke's theory and methods could cast Stubbs as a 'philosophical' rather than an 'empirical' historian, despite their shared concern for clarifying the past in national terms. It is ironic that Ranke has been understood as the father of history as a science. For only once 'science' is understood in appropriately historical terms can one see that by *Geschichtwissenschaft* ('historical science'), Ranke tried to distinguish the infinite search for historical *knowledge* from the definite arrival at *certainty* characteristic of investigation in philosophy, theology and the natural sciences.

The State of History in England

Isaiah Berlin, whose Oxford diction never masked his Latvian accent, observed that 'ideas do not breed ideas; some social and economic factors are surely responsible for great upheavals in human consciousness'.[12] Europeans and Americans endured the violence of revolution, reform and civil war during the nineteenth century. But in England, economic power and global influence only increased during the century, and its governments suppressed every outbreak of domestic unrest. Despite famine in Ireland, clearances in Scotland and rioting in English towns, no social, political or economic upheaval shook the British establishment's view of itself and of its past. There was no English equivalent to Prussia's subjection under Napoleon. British historiography shifted, from celebrating the triumph of England's unique constitution to examining the historical significance of social and economic problems, comparatively late in the century. This shift was made through the efforts of historians who understood the national importance of training 'working men' and university students in the analytical skills needed to address real-world challenges. This group included Arnold Toynbee, T. E. Cliffe Leslie and Henry Sumner Maine: they considered themselves readers and teachers of 'political economy', 'law' or 'moral philosophy' rather than modern history. We could describe them using the term 'economic historians'. Not only did these men focus on the more recent past, but they were concerned also with explaining the relationship between social values and government policies. These concerns held urgent meaning, in part because they observed the rough social experiences of industrialisation. Their influence on historical reading, teaching and writing were enormous, even though much of their scholarship was ignored by the establishment historians of their time.

So it was paradoxical that, at the height of its imperial reach and economic power, England in the nineteenth century was an intellectually vulnerable place. Childhood education had been compulsory from 1880 but it was not funded across England until 1899. The Education Act of 1902 had committed the government to instilling in its children 'a shared sense of national identity, national loyalty, and national pride ... knowledge of national history was deemed of the first importance'.[13] However, at the same time, an Assistant Master at Eton College worried in print about 'the lack of trained teachers' of English history.[14] Throughout the century, the country's fee-paying schools had been attacked for failing to teach history and science. Nevertheless, parents from the landed classes, whose sons were unlikely to require paid work, largely did not care. Elsewhere on the class spectrum, working-class readers participated in an 'autodidact culture [that] flourished up to the First World War'; Samuel Smiles' treatise *Self-Help* (1859) was consumed across class lines. But Jonathan Rose has shown that it was through reading *fiction* that working-class readers in Britain and in France learned their history.[15] Charles Dickens had borrowed insights from the social reformer Henry Mayhew, but for the most part neither author held aspirations for historical accuracy, nor depicted the past earlier than the present century. This reflected widespread uncertainty over the roles historians should play in the country's institutions of learning, at all levels.

Upon its founding in 1823, University College London could not find a candidate to appoint as Professor of Modern History. The eventual appointee remarked in 1833 that the study of modern history was unpopular because it was unnecessary: 'History is one of those departments of study in which most persons conclude that they are quite competent to become their own teachers.'[16] In 1866, a leading newspaper voiced surprise when the medievalist William Stubbs was appointed Regius Professor of Modern History at Oxford, since the Regius Professor at Cambridge was Charles Kingsley, a novelist.[17] The situation in Scotland was less confused, but only by default: John Stuart, Professor of Classics at Edinburgh, said in 1888 that 'the historical department of our Scottish universities is either blank or a farce', a view shared by a visiting Belgian diplomat in 1884.[18] Neither Edinburgh nor Glasgow had a professorial chair in modern history until 1894. Government neglected the state of education in other ways: England was the last country in Europe to develop a public library system. In 1849, libraries in England held less than half the number of books per capita than in France.

Still, Britain boasted a population of discerning readers of history. Readers demanded new editions of Edward Gibbon's massive *History of the Decline and Fall of the Roman Empire* (1776–87) throughout the nineteenth century. In 1823 a bookseller in Edinburgh commissioned an English translation of the editorial footnotes to a German edition of *Decline and Fall*, with the view that money could be made from providing elaborate references to the classical sources. The resulting volume was priced cheaply and marketed to general readers. In 1853, rival London publishers competed for readers by publicly attacking each other over matters like misplaced consonants, a geographical ambiguity in a footnote and a misspelled name in Greek.[19] This shows that even low-cost publishers were sensitive to the needs of critically minded readers of middling social ranks. Wealthy readers and colonial masters also sought the prestige of classical knowledge through Gibbon. Cecil Rhodes was unlikely to have been the only powerful reader of the time to memorise passages from *Decline and Fall*, with references to its footnotes, so that he could display in company the classical education he wished he had. This historical education had material benefits: knowledge of the classical world improved one's chances of landing a position in the Indian Civil Service. Aspiring families were eager to provide their sons with the classical knowledge taught at expensive fee-paying schools, for throughout the century the state did not provide a classical education.

Men could take a degree in modern history at Oxford from 1872 and at Cambridge from 1873, but training in 'the practical business of historical investigation', and not merely to pass the exam, was formally offered at Oxford only from 1895 and at Cambridge from 1907. Despite this, in 1898 an exasperated lecturer at Oxford told a room of colleagues that the Modern History School 'turns [students] out unable to read historical documents'.[20] During the full length of the century, when it was women who were expected to instruct children in most subjects at primary and secondary levels, they were unable to take a university qualification in the very subject that the government had paid them to teach. History tutors at Oxford were not required to allow women to attend lectures until well into the twentieth century, further sabotaging efforts to raise historical standards among teachers: the first woman to receive a graduate degree in history at Oxford was Eleanor Lodge, in 1928. Cambridge allowed women to take degree examinations in 1880, but would not allow them to graduate until 1948. Remarking on this state of affairs in 1906, the Manchester historian (and Oxford alumnus) Thomas Tout referred his colleagues to 'our national sin of self-complacency'.[21] The Royal Historical Society, founded in 1868, was a club run by 'noblemen and gentlemen of eminence', and its first President was assured that he was 'held fully exempted from duties of every kind'. This was a place for society rather than scholarship, for no particular historical expertise was required of its members.[22]

So how should students make sense of the founding of those other great Victorian historical institutions that include the Historical Manuscripts Commission (1869); the comprehensive *Dictionary of National Biography* (1885–1900); the prestigious *English Historical Review* (1886); the National Trust for Places of Historic Interest or Natural Beauty (1895); and the Royal Commission on Historical Monuments (1908)? For David Cannadine, these institutions fostered merely the appearance of Victorian 'historical-mindedness'. He observes that 'their memberships were limited, their finances were precarious, and they wielded little influence in Westminster or Whitehall'.[23] The historical curriculum at Oxford and Cambridge shaped the ideological tenor of the country's ruling class, not by training its sons in historical skills but by teaching them 'a national consensus about moral progress and social order'.[24] With graduates in modern history taking up administrative offices across Britain's global empire, this consensus mattered.

British intellectual life flourished through the work of independent scholars working in the new archival libraries, such as Samuel Rawson Gardiner and Agnes Strickland, but none of them made any impact on university teaching. Stubbs did not leave any comments on their contributions to scholarship, but his Cambridge colleague Frederic Maitland remarked: 'We had our swallows, and beautiful birds they were; but there was spring in Germany.'[25] Stubbs' successor, E. A. Freeman, was not troubled by his view that 'the ablest works in philosophy and history proceed from university men, indeed, but not, as a rule, from those who were resident' at a university.[26] By 1904, the incoming Regius Professor of Modern History at Oxford claimed that 'nearly all of us who [are] teaching history in Oxford have no training ... we are self-taught'.[27] This combination of the Oxford consensus on social values, uneven provision of historical teaching at all levels and the peculiar fact that the best scholarship was conducted by self-funded amateurs, led to an intellectually fragile state of national historical understanding among British readers. This partly explains why the publication in 1918 of an intellectually superficial venture between history and literary criticism was so clever and so devastating. Paul Johnson overstated the case when he said that Lytton Strachey's irreverent biographies of recent worthies, *Eminent Victorians*, 'destroyed the values of patriotism and [left] behind a national emptiness', but it is easy to see his point.[28] Shifts in the concerns of historical scholars contributed to the impression that 'eminent Victorians' represented authority that could be trusted no longer – indeed that it ought to be mocked.

The History of Consensus

Appointed Regius Professor of Modern History at Oxford in 1841, Thomas Arnold's vision of English history saw the nation emerging through a continuous process that moved inexorably forward through time, clarifying itself through the gradual improvement and perfection of the state's political institutions: Parliament, Church and judiciary.[29] His successor taught that the origins of this progression lay in the ethnic makeup of 'the English race', which, he wrote, emerged in early-medieval Germany. The white racial basis of this theory was essential to its core argument: the historical study of England will determine its students' understanding in a specific way, given their genetic roots in an ongoing family drama. In his inaugural lecture, Arnold declared that

> Britons and Romans had lived in our country, but they are not our fathers ... the history of Caesar's invasion has not more to do with us, than the natural history of the animals which then inhabited our forests ... So far can we trace our blood, our language, the name and actual divisions of our country, the beginnings of our institutions. So far [therefore] our national identity extends; so far history is modern, for it treats of a life which was then, and is not yet extinguished.[30]

William Stubbs retained Arnold's emphasis on race by asserting that those political institutions that comprise the students' objects of study are the living embodiment of a past 'we' share with other Englishmen. Since the nation is a moral entity whose goodness is self-evident to white and wealthy English students, their recognising its documentary record simply was an exercise in reverent patriotism. This led to historical studies on the presumption of an ideological consensus that was constructed, rather than substantiated, by historical scholarship. The cultivation of *Bildung* through critical scholarship was not required, for according to this consensus, England's forward-moving history had been ordained in the divine nature of things.

Thomas Arnold's devout Anglicanism, and his historical vision of English history, reads like a theological mission. Stubbs too was an ordained minister when he was appointed at Oxford, and he retired in 1884 upon his consecration as Bishop of Chester. Stubbs declared upon his inauguration that the study of English political development shows that 'we are growing into a perception of the Almighty Ruler of the world; that we are growing able to justify the Eternal Wisdom; and that by that justification to approve ourselves His children'.[31] He combined liberal Anglican doctrine with Arnold's racial theory of national origins – it is Hegel's plot without the internal Romantic conflict. For Stubbs, the English people are 'a people of German descent in the main constituents of blood, character, and language, but most especially ... in the possession of the elements of primitive German civilization and the common germs of German institutions'. These people had sown their genetic, psychological and intellectual seeds through political means and without resistance: 'the body of kindred freemen, scattered over a considerable area ... used a domestic constitution based entirely primarily [*sic*] on the community of land tenure and cultivation'.[32] The success of their unique political constitution enabled its adherents to migrate further, spreading their roots geographically, taking footholds in new territory before assuming their natural – and therefore rightful – dominance. This theory provided an immediate and prestigious justification of British imperial success, from Ireland to Canada and from India to Australia, as well as American westward expansion. J. R. Green provided a bright picturesque vision of this racial seed spreading from northern Germany to East Anglia in his immensely popular *Short History of the English People* (1874). In *The Descent of Man* (1879), Charles Darwin adopted the theory to explain the superior number of 'intellectual, energetic, brave patriotic, and benevolent men' in the United States.[33] J. A. Froude's *Oceana, or England and Her Colonies* (1887) broadened the geographical scope to show that 'wherever they went ... [the English] would carry with them the genius of English freedom'.[34] The American writer Frederick Jackson Turner disagreed with the theory, but it provided the basic paradigm of the most influential essay in American historical studies, 'The Frontier in American History' (1893).

Thomas Arnold's anticipation of a particular kind of student, who could realise the high promise of English origins in the present moment, should bring some colour to his reputation as Britain's first student of *Historismus*. Arnold had taught himself German so he could study Barthold Niebuhr's *Roman History* (1811–12) before it was available in translation (1827). This meant that Arnold reenacted for himself an essential step in Niebuhr's own scholarly process that mirrored elements of *Bildung*: following the Enlightenment philosopher Giambattista Vico, Niebuhr had approached Roman history by studying the languages its people spoke, the stories they told and poetry they knew, along with the agrarian traditions that marked key stages in the Romans' growing awareness of their world. Vico had taught, and Niebuhr had shown, that it is only through the recovery and critical study of primary evidence of past experience, understood through its own means of expression, that one could truly understand the past. Both Arnold's own critical edition of *Thucydides* (1830–5), and his own *History of Rome* (1838–42), reflected Niebuhr's historicism: both books were unique for their richness and range of linguistic and geographical details, which enabled readers to envision the conceptual world of the Roman past, free from the omniscient narration of a latter-day historian. This scholarship would cultivate *Bildung* by training readers to decipher a historical world of past languages, ideas and customs. Reading Niebuhr, and following Arnold's *Thucydides*, requires critical and imaginative exercise.

This historicism distinguished Arnold's scholarship from Gibbon's *Decline and Fall of the Roman Empire*. Gibbon's historical narrative had elaborated a moral argument that addressed original sources, but it did so entirely through paraphrase. Even Gibbon's footnotes referred to the sources only in translation. It is clear that Arnold found Niebuhr's focus on the linguistic and imaginative elements of Roman life more intellectually robust than Gibbon's description of the decadence and corruption that ruined the Roman Empire. As headmaster of the elite Rugby School, Arnold introduced the study of modern history there, the first school in Britain to do so. But Arnold's social commitment to locating England's past through a celebration of the present, limited the appeal of *Bildung* for his purposes.

Niebuhr knew the great Prussian explorers and scientists of this period, and like them, he taught that primary research must comprise the basis for meaningful study. Only these experiences can lead to a broader understanding of the world beyond the local. This is knowledge beyond oneself. Niebuhr expressed this in poetic terms that revealed his affinity with German Romanticism: 'He who calls what has vanished back into being, enjoys a bliss like that of creating.'[35] Niebuhr's theory of knowledge valued study for its widening of imaginative and intellectual understanding and not for validating an ideology or realising any religious mission. In this way, it expressed the national goal of *Bildung* that came to define the study of history at Berlin at the turn of the nineteenth century. Ranke was eager to point out that 'other sciences are satisfied simply with recording what has been found; history requires the ability to *recreate*'.[36] History enabled a primary understanding of the past that, for Niebuhr and for Ranke, set history apart from other academic disciplines. Also influenced by Vico, Ranke agreed that since it was people who lived in the past, people in the present are capable of understanding past achievements.

Niebuhr had collaborated with those poets and philosophers in Berlin who were associated with the cultural elements of German Romanticism, represented by the poet Friedrich Schiller and the philosopher Herder. But Niebuhr's emphasis on the unique character that defined each nation was an expression of an optimistic universalism and not the narrow nationalism for which Herder was famous. Niebuhr was anticipating the happy prospect of making new scholarly discoveries relating to nations other than his own. When his friend, the Prussian Minister of Education Wilhelm von Humboldt, described the kind of historical thinking that should inform the creation of modern history as a new discipline, he said that historicism was not compatible with national or theological determinism: 'Teleological history can ... never properly locate the ultimate goal of events in living things but has to seek it, as it were, in *dead* institutions.'[37] All historians held national improvement as their ultimate goal, but in Germany this entailed an understanding of nature as an unpredictable and dynamic force: 'the improvement of the human race', Humboldt wrote, 'is not a step-like education, [but] rather it is nature and always surprises through its novelty'.[38] This means that historians must study the past free of ideological influence and ready to accept its surprises. If history referred to the present, critical investigation of it would not be possible; national allegiances would ruin its scientific focus and challenge its cosmopolitan objectives.

Throughout Arnold's inaugural lecture, he defined the English nation as a material thing, as 'blood and institutions'. Arnold then distinguished modern history through its continuing development in his English students' own lives. It is here that Arnold parted company with Niebuhr and Humboldt, and this is why Arnold carried only superficial debts to the German historicism that would reach its greatest institutional statement in Ranke's seminar training. By envisioning the past as a thing that exists in the present, and that has exclusive meaning to particular students, for Arnold the past ceases to comprise an object of critical analysis or of meaningful investigation. Stubbs only rephrased Arnold's words when he said directly to his students: 'in modern history you are dealing with the living subject: your field of examination is the living, working, thinking, growing world of today' – that is, in institutions that are not dead.[39] Its sources always would comprise medieval documents in constitutional history, taught in the context of an abiding historical consensus, narrated by a national authority, within an institutional structure that did not elicit discussion, debate or training. As intellectual historians have shown, Victorian liberalism comprised a number of domestic goals and international priorities, but they all required the protective or enabling role of government institutions. This presumed a steady focus on the history of England's unique constitutional structures, married to a racial theory of its people.

William Stubbs' curricular and intellectual leadership in Oxford (1867–84) combined Arnold's quasi-theological mission with the national triumphalism of Macaulay's *History of England* (1848), probably the most popular work of English history ever published. Macaulay intended his book as a toast to national unity and its moral purpose: 'to excite thankfulness in all religious minds and hope in the breasts of all patriots'.[40] Combined with Arnold's race theory, Stubbs' optimism steered students away from the incisive 'political philosophy' of J. S. Mill and others among the emerging fields of social science, who recognised the establishment's emphasis on 'inherent natural differences' as a 'vulgar mode of escaping from the consideration of social and moral influences on the human mind'.[41]

Despite various curricular reforms, research skills were not taught at Oxford during the nineteenth century. Moreover, Stubbs' historical theory depended on arriving at a particular vision of the national past, which justified limiting the scope for further research. Since the teaching curriculum at Oxford was based on scholarship produced by its founder, who wrote with the needs of Oxford's own students in mind, students had structural and intellectual reasons not to extend, or to engage critically, with the history they were learning. W. J. Ashley recollected that 'when the new Honour School called for a new body of tutors, these tutors were then emerging from pupilage; and [Stubbs' theories] became in an amazingly brief period of time the accepted tutorial doctrine'.[42] After obtaining a first-class degree in modern history at Balliol in 1886, Andrew Little complained that he could learn 'the principles and practices of the critical examination of original historical documents' only by visiting the University of Göttingen.[43] Historical methods in Germany remained a source of fascination for British students but were ignored by their professors: Little said he had longed to join a research seminar for years. Oxford did not introduce a research degree in modern history until 1895, more than a decade after Stubbs had retired. In 1921, the Regius Professor of Modern History at Cambridge retained the convention that professors would not be compelled to undertake any teaching.[44]

When politicians approved an annual grant to support *The Rolls Series* of historical documents in 1857, it soon became the greatest publicly funded scholarly endeavour of the century. The labour on its 255 volumes was undertaken by 'private individuals, usually clergymen, often recruited by word of mouth, working alone and in their spare time, having very little contact with one another and none with the universities'.[45] Students did not take degrees in modern history to become historians, and the tutors who interacted with them did not provide such training. One Oxford tutor who taught during Stubbs' tenure recalled that 'only exceptionally untrammelled spirits regard independent reading as more important than the ministrations of their tutor'; for the tutor's role was to provide 'that combination of authority and comradeship, of dignity and *bonhomie*'.⁴⁶ As far as the students were concerned, studies at Oxford and Cambridge were 'but the continuation of the sixth form of Eton, Harrow, or Rugby'.⁴⁷ This was a curriculum designed to turn boys into gentlemen, and not to create the *Bildung* of cultured individuals within a cosmopolitan community of nations. When Lord Acton was appointed Regius Professor of Modern History at Cambridge in 1895, he retained Stubbs' presentism: modern history, he said, 'is a narrative told of ourselves, the record of a life which is our own, of efforts not yet abandoned to repose, or problems that still entangle the feet and vex the heart of men'.⁴⁸ This presumed inclusiveness, with its firm assumption that English history will be written by and for English men, illustrates the enduring centrality of Arnold's ethno-theological vision, across the full length of the nineteenth century.

Historicism and the Task of Historical Training

England's two ancient universities enjoyed independent wealth and patronage from the Church of England, whose documentary history comprised a central pillar of the modern history curriculum, defined by a royal appointee (hence the title of Regius Professor). Continental universities were forced to reform in ways that reflected creative responses to serious political threats, without the support of a national church or reigning monarch. The nationalisation and then abolition of every university in French territory under Napoleon's First Republic of 1793 held financial and ideological appeal to revolutionaries across Europe until the restorations of 1815. In the German-speaking lands the calls for abolition were sufficient to shut down its most prestigious and storied centres of learning: Halle and Wittenberg. As *Bildungsdiktator* in the Prussian government of Baron vom Stein, Wilhelm von Humboldt drew on Romantic principles to invent the research-based university, providing historical studies with an obvious duty to the state. The historical training curriculum at Berlin set the standard for historical education at all levels, in Germany, France and in the United States, in part because it created professional standards that justified a civic role for historians in post-Revolutionary nation states.

This meant that, in continental Europe, historical study entailed the cultivation of critical skills through scholarly training: historical studies comprised a professional and cultural apprenticeship in the name of civic duty. Preparing students to contribute to a growing field of editorial and narrative publications served the extended educational programmes of state governments. Similarly, when administrators in America founded its first graduate programme in modern history (at Johns Hopkins in 1876), they did so on civic grounds, to prepare young men to find well-paid work. Unlike the sons of the aristocracy or commercial elite who attended tutorials at Oxford and Cambridge, most students who studied history in Germany attended publicly funded secondary schools, and sought paid employment. Even at the University of Göttingen, which had been founded by a British king and held a reputation for erudition, the undergraduate curriculum was designed to train men for the professions.

Humboldt's recommendations to King Frederick Wilhelm in 1809 made a case for state support that would enrich the nation by fostering the cultural and intellectual sensibility of its students. Not unlike the Scottish universities of the previous century, whose innovative teaching and research enriched the country in specifically practical ways (by training physicians in community health and churchmen who could minister abroad, for example), this new university would advance a tangible and professional ideal: it would foster Humboldt's theory of *Bildung*. Its teaching would celebrate equality among peers and support a shared commitment to strengthening the morality and culture of the state. Humboldt began by clarifying the university's social responsibility: 'It is the calling of these intellectual institutions to devote themselves to the elaboration of the uncontrived substance of intellectual and moral culture, growing from an uncontrived inner necessity.' The debt to Hegel's vision of the state as a realisation of the nation's inherent goodness is evident here; the association to teaching as an expression of free inquiry refers directly to Kant and to Schelling, a young philosopher who theorised the Romantic writings of his friend, the great poet Goethe. With a critique of current methods elsewhere in the educational system, Humboldt proposed formalising Romantic concepts of freedom, collaboration, and open-ended learning that had never been considered by a state administration before:

> One unique feature of higher intellectual institutions is that they conceive of science [i.e., knowledge] and scholarship as dealing with ultimately inexhaustible tasks: this means that they are engaged in an unceasing process of inquiry... The relation between teacher and pupil at the higher level is a different one from what it was at the lower levels. At the higher level, the teacher does not exist for the sake of the student; both teacher and student have their justification in the common pursuit of knowledge.

This argument for collaborative learning yielded practical means of training the mind while exercising the creativity and imagination of each individual. Humboldt's reference to doing so in the context of a broader group adopted the imperative language of republicanism: 'the state must understand that intellectual work will go on infinitely better if it does not intrude'.[49] King Frederick William agreed: 'the state must replace through intellectual power what it has lost in material power'.[50] Humboldt's petition led to the founding of Humboldt University in Berlin, whose faculty included Hegel as Professor of Philosophy and, from 1825, Ranke as Professor of Modern History.

It is difficult to imagine a more striking contrast between the dynamic intellectual atmosphere that Stein and Humboldt organised in Berlin, a 'centre of *Bildung*', with 'the amateur zeal and scholarly isolation' that characterised the social context of historical research in England.[51] By the time Ranke arrived in Berlin, more than ten years had passed since Stein had commissioned the *Monumenta Germaniae Historica*. This massive documentary research project reveals the degree to which erudite scholarship on the principles of *Bildung* predated Ranke's seminar training. Since the documentary record of the German people could not be located in one place, preparation involved scholars collecting documents from towns and cities across Europe. They were organised by G. H. Pertz, who had graduated in History from Göttingen, and J. F. Böhmer, a gifted archivist, but one who was not sympathetic to the simmering Prussian nationalism held by several of his contributors. This pairing of Pertz with Böhmer ensured that the *Monumenta* would sustain the broadly cosmopolitan ideals of German Romanticism, without resorting to triumphant narration or ideological abridgements. When Humboldt had visited Paris in 1796–7, he had disapproved of French scholars 'keeping other nations in servility' through the superior resources that the *ancien régime* had committed to textual scholarship in its own archives; Humboldt had resolved to enable, through his education ministry, 'that a new historical thinking [would] be the German nation's mission to the world'.[52] Under Stein, Prussia would lead a truly cosmopolitan project, which explained in part why Ranke prided himself on the broadly European scope of his own research: 'nothing but universal history can be written', he taught.[53] Ranke's research took on an international scope that no academic historian elsewhere attempted. J. R. Seeley, Regius Professor of Modern History at Cambridge (1870–95), wrote a three-volume *Life of Stein* (1878) but this was 'a historical moralization of a national idea', and Seeley was disappointed that neither British readers nor government ministers were inspired by its practical hints.[54] Seeley's prescriptive book mistook Stein's own goals for the philosophical complexity of civic duty and state support within *Bildung*.

Arnold, Stubbs and other liberals understood British political institutions as the legacy of national progress, which they narrated through a progressive history of their constitution. Humboldt's programme for *Bildung*, on the other hand, accepted the state as 'a transitional arrangement' within the process of humanity's emergence from 'mechanical forms of social cohesion' towards a truly universal brotherhood, free from political institutions and state interference.[55] In his treatise *The Limits of State Action* (1791–2), Humboldt had argued that the only positive role for the state is to guarantee that individual citizens could cultivate their natural talents as they progress towards freedom from all necessities, material and intellectual: 'the state only occupies the place of a spectator', he wrote: it should assure citizens of their safety to develop and nothing more.[56] This meant that historical training should carry out a civic duty by enriching the state's moral aims through *Bildung*, but doing so would mark just a stage in human development. All progress towards and through the nation state, Hegel told his students, was animated by a universal spiritual push for freedom from material and structural constraints.[57] For this same reason, Ranke believed that historians could 'relive' past experiences by appreciating past values, but only when this 'empathy' with the past sustained a persistent championing of human individuality and the uniqueness of their historical circumstances. His student Jacob Burckhardt drew on this in a lecture he gave on the eve of the Franco-Prussian War. Reflecting on the likelihood of war between powerful states, he declared that 'studying history is not only a right and a duty, but it is also a supreme need. *It is our freedom* in the very awareness of universal bondage and the stream of necessities.'[58]

Ranke taught at Berlin from 1825 to 1871, and throughout this long tenure, students from across the globe treated his seminars as 'pilgrimage sites'. Although many likened the seminar to a fraternity of candid critics, working together to ensure the highest standards of historical analysis on shared principles, one American student reported that the seminar was 'a workshop in which the experienced master teaches his young apprentices the deft use of the tools of the trade'.[59] This pedagogical method set professional standards across Europe and America, with a fundamental emphasis on 'the understanding of the uniqueness of historical characters and situations'. This entailed 'a reconstruction of the past "*wie es eigentlich gewesen*" (to show what, essentially, happened), which begins with a strict dedication to the relevant facts; therefore the insistence on strict critical method'.[60] This meant identifying original evidence in a comparative context, clarifying what it says through reference to other documents, and by analysing how and why it says this. Such examination may require skills in philology (classical sources and antiquities), linguistics, law, politics and philosophy, so this method would entail working collaboratively with a broad research team. Only once one had generated these insights could one begin to narrate the history implied by these facts. Historical understanding was therefore inductive: it could be reached only *after* students unravel the meaning of facts through critical practice. These are the methods and sequence that define nineteenth-century historicism under Ranke. Unlike self-evident truths that can be uncovered through mathematics or the natural sciences, truth in history requires critical analysis, argument, revision. One of Stubbs' contemporaries focused on the contrast between Ranke and his English colleagues by pointing out that, for Ranke, 'there is no finality in scientific progress' – hence the union of research with teaching.[61] Like any scientific endeavour, the authority of historical method rests on its ability to enable and assimilate new discoveries. Burckhardt's wry observation was sharper: 'for a time, "the present" was literally synonymous with progress, and the result was the most ridiculous vanity, as if the work were marking towards a perfection of mind or even morality'.[62]

Ranke's conceptual emphasis on the uniqueness of each historical circumstance logically ensured that one could not impose any moral, ideological or determinist framework on the past. It also carried an important point for the professionalisation that was taking place through the specific methods, writing styles, publication venues and credentials that Ranke's students were acquiring. For by adhering to the preservation of historical uniqueness, historians could circulate their work among their peers, confident of their general agreement that their professional work comprised an 'exact, impartial, critical investigation of events'.[63] By the end of the century, German universities could encourage their faculty members to specialise, for this suited their comparative wealth of powerful teaching resources: by 1850 Germany had twenty-seven professorial chairs in history, forty-five in 1875 and more than sixty in 1900.[64] This speedy process of professionalisation drew on a division of labour fostered by the prevalence of conservative social values, for German universities excluded women until 1908, insisting on traditional definitions of *Bestimmung* ('women's place').[65]

From Social Science to Historical Synthesis

The previous sections have explained why historical thought, in British and German universities, largely took parallel paths. This concluding section will complicate that picture by pointing to a rift that took place among German historians at the end of the century. This *Methodenstreit* ('conflict over methods') exposed the assumption of national authority that seven decades of *Bildung* had brought to the academic bearers of Ranke's legacy. The responses to the *Methodenstreit* in France and America are informative, because they reveal shifts in the historical concepts that had emerged in Germany but adapted according to these different social contexts. There was no explicit reaction among historians in Cambridge and Oxford to the controversy that engulfed the historian Karl Lamprecht at the University of Leipzig, but it is interesting to consider that British readers followed it in newspapers and magazines.

In March 1896, while readers consumed volumes of his *German History* (1893–1905), Lamprecht declared that 'psychology must be the basis of the study of history'. This claim infuriated the dozens of Ranke's disciples who held posts at universities across Germany. Lamprecht gestured to his scientific colleague Wilhelm Wundt, one of Europe's leading experimental scientists and the first to call himself a 'psychologist', when he explained that 'collective feeling' is a cause and not merely a condition or outcome of historical events. Aiming to provoke a reaction, Lamprecht suggested a debt to Ranke by citing the master's own student, the art historian Burckhardt: 'The most attractive task of historical research consists in establishing the character of the psychic view which issues [from] a given combination of natural, economic, political, and social forces.'[66] With the great Hegel in his sights, Lamprecht proposed that there was nothing inevitable about the emergence of nation states. The nation state was just one expression of human agency, which will create different institutions at different times. For Lamprecht, historians should consider those structural forces that shape human expression before they interpret the past through the emergence of this particular institution. This was a clear challenge to *Historismus*. Not only did Lamprecht's emphasis on social and mental structures question whether every historical circumstance was unique (for structures will unify and distinguish things), but he also suggested that new scientific theories can organise and clarify what the past should mean. The associated research could draw upon economic, political and social evidence, leaving aside Ranke's elementary focus on archival documents and on critical method.

After nearly a century of emulating *Bildung* as a national policy and fundamental principle for research, German historians had come to themselves as teachers of the national past through their commitment to *Historismus*. This meant that Lamprecht's turn to the social sciences, and its deductive rather than inductive methods, threatened their authority and their state-sponsored jobs. Even Lamprecht's narrative style suggested a populist threat to their professorial status, for his thirteen-volume monograph cited no authorities, in a style that sought and won general readers, far more than any work by Ranke or his disciples. One historian suggested a further threat within Lamprecht's methodology: his writing sought a return to 'our early bondage to theology, philosophy, and law'.[67] By turning to the social sciences such as psychology and sociology, historians could lose the institutional independence and intellectual freedom that modern history had won, under Humboldt, so many years earlier. Ranke's disciples wrote letters to deny Lamprecht promotion, describing this historian as a dangerous subversive.

This conflict was followed closely in America and France, whose own research centres had been founded by Ranke's pupils and that had modelled themselves on German examples, particularly after France's defeat in 1871. Upon its founding in 1884, Ranke had been elected the first honorary member of the American Historical Association. More than twenty years later, the AHA president called Ranke 'our first leader'.[68] But the 'progressive' social policies touted by Theodore Roosevelt and Woodrow Wilson, along with the academic leadership of historians including Charles Beard, James Harvey Robinson and Frederick Jackson Turner, sought to reorient American historical studies to address social problems. The 'New Historians' of the early twentieth century were attracted to the quantitative methods and objective data characteristic of social science, and they taught that 'subjective framing' was an essential element of historical scholarship. Explicitly admiring Lamprecht, Beard challenged those historical principles that had defined the German-trained professoriate in America. His *Economic Interpretation of the Constitution* (1913) even questioned the conventional belief that the republic's basic principles emerged from 'the whole people'. Beard pointed to numerical evidence that illustrated the Founding Fathers' economic stakes in the legislation that they drafted, and observed that: 'Law is not an abstract thing. Separated from the social and economic fabric by which it is, in part, conditioned and which in turn, it helps to condition, it has no reality.'[69] This material observation shocked historians who had been bred on Hegel's spiritual vision of national emergence as it was taught by Ranke. For Stubbs, whose textbook on the British constitution understood law as a sacred genetic inheritance, this view was heresy. Beard's colleagues had invited Lamprecht to deliver a series of five lectures on the 'inner national development of psychic values' at Columbia University in 1904.[70] Robinson, Beard and their colleague Carl Becker joined the sympathetic audience. Then they awarded Lamprecht an honorary doctorate before he returned to Leipzig, signalling that America's second-oldest Department of History supported the challenge Lamprecht had brought to historians well beyond the Rhine.

German historians had reason to fear a merger of historical research with the social sciences. These historians at Columbia were advocates of progressive policies that fostered the institutional rise of the social sciences at the expense of historical studies. Upon Robinson's return to America after he was awarded a PhD from Freiburg (1890), he joined a government committee to revise national educational policy. In 1911, he recommended that schools drop ancient and medieval history and focus instead on recent American history, so that historical education could enable citizens to address domestic social problems. The committee's report quoted extensively from Robinson's collection of essays, *The New History* (1912), formally aligning itself with a growing movement within Columbia. By 1919, Beard and Robinson would resign from Columbia to establish the New School for Social Research, which did not have a history faculty. The committee's final report (1916) called for a synthesis, bringing history into the social sciences: '[History] must confess that it is based on sister sciences, that it can only progress with them, must lean largely on them for support, and in return should repay its debts by the contributions which it makes to our general understanding of our species.'[71] When the government's committee specified the methods that historical studies in schools should adopt, it specified that these should be 'rich in their economic, sociological, and political connotations'.[72] Ironically, this committee called for synthesis on the strength of support from America's German-trained historical scholars, who now sought to provide historical training by founding new departments using new methods.

In France, a similar call for synthesis helped facilitate an interdisciplinary merger of modern history with sociology. With the founding of Henri Berr's journal, *Revue de Synthèse Historique* in 1900, France provided an unlikely platform for intellectual diplomacy that was truly international in scope. Its goal of historical synthesis reflected the scholarly gains that professional ruptures, brought on by the *Methodenstreit*, had created. When the Third Republic reformed state education after France's defeat in 1871, its government invested heavily in the text-based philological training of historians, led by specialists who had studied in Germany. The state retained its concentration on the modern history of France in secondary schools, but its policy was guided by a curriculum that was 'obsessed by national borders, xenophobia, and anachronistic national enemies'.[73] Much like Humboldt had noted nearly a century earlier, the nationalism of French scholars prevented them from promoting the cosmopolitanism of *Bildung*. One might expect that French historians were moving towards a *Methodenstreit* of their own, given the differences between the philologists who published solely on academic matters and did not seek historical readers beyond the academic institutes, and the public whose children were taught an explicitly populist history that focused on the dangers of current political tensions.[74] Instead, state investment in specialists who worked in the universities and in teachers who worked in the schools led to intellectual malaise. This meant that France lacked a shared professional terrain on which a methodological conflict could be fought.

This was the context into which, from 1886, the sociologist Émile Durkheim launched his campaign to wrest 'academic hegemony' away from historical studies towards the social sciences. In dozens of articles and lectures, Durkheim drew on French nationalism to claim that modern history had tainted French education with German ideology, arguing that 'the homeland of Descartes and Comte was better equipped than the land of Ranke and Waitz to develop a truly scientific approach to social reality'. Like Lamprecht, Durkheim knew how to provoke his colleagues, depicting historians as mere 'laboratory technicians' who have no scientific wisdom. Durkheim referred to their seminar training as a means to develop interpretations and not conclusions. By addressing present concerns to readers at all levels, including ministers in government, Durkheim's arguments for teaching and research on 'social reality' over the historical past found a responsive audience. At the height of the *Methodenstreit* in Leipzig, Durkheim asserted that 'academic sociology is uniquely capable of developing those *idées directrices* to orient the historical researcher in his specialized investigations'.[75] For Durkheim, ideas led to the social formation of institutions: they fulfil a human need to create and sustain systems of belief.[76] Both Durkheim and Lamprecht were influenced by Wundt, and indeed Lamprecht would make a similar claim that 'history is nothing but applied psychology' when he defended his *German History* in 1904, before Durkheim was appointed to a professorial chair at the Sorbonne.[77] Durkheim seemed to have chimed in with Lamprecht by declaring that 'history cannot be a science without rising above the individual', and that when it did so, 'it ceases to be itself and becomes sociology'.[78] If historical scholarship was to retain Ranke's defining insistence on the contingencies of unique circumstances in our understanding of the past, the field faced a genuine crisis of legitimacy on both sides of the Rhine and of the Atlantic.

Finally, on the eve of the Great War, Henri Berr called for 'a historical and scientific synthesis' to breathe new life into historical studies and to direct sociological research. Berr used new professional tools – the research article, periodical publication and the referencing of scholarly resources – to foster dialogue across those disciplines that had been created through conflict. In the first issue of his *Revue de Synthèse Historique*, Berr wrote that the journal would seek 'common ground between the different disciplines of historical study, to neutralise the unfortunate effects of excessive specialisation … and support all that is truly scientific in the researches of sociology … it will also provide a meeting ground for the different fields of history, and for philosophy as well'.[79] By assuming a mutually comprehensible value of knowledge across different methods and fields of research, Berr's definition of the 'truly scientific' evoked the historicism of *Geschichtwissenschaft* from earlier in the century. Although Berr himself believed that history and not sociology was 'the organic master science', his unique capacity for accommodating debate on such matters led the *Revue* to become the leading intellectual journal in France between 1900 and 1914. Interestingly, its popularity beyond academia helped both to legitimate social science by reaching more readers and to familiarise specialists with the concerns of the general public whose 'social reality' they sought to understand – the *Revue* published a large number of letters to its editor. This was the only journal in Europe to carry articles by historians, economists and sociologists. These included both Durkheim and Lamprecht. Soon the *Année Sociologique* featured summaries of articles that appeared in the *Revue*. By 1905, the *Revue de Synthèse Historique* had taken on such prestige that Berr was able to persuade the Académie Française, which recommended academic appointments across the country's research institutes, to endow 'a chair for the study of the problems of historical writing'. It agreed, and the new chair was created at the Collège de France in 1905.[80]

Berr's ability to accommodate those methodological debates that had ruined careers in Germany and created an institutional crisis in America reflected itself in the positivist elements of his own historical thinking. Like Durkheim, Berr accepted that historical progress should be understood through a series of distinct stages based on the universality of human nature. In his monograph *Synthesis in History* (1911), Berr identified 'two degrees of synthesis'. The first was the 'erudite synthesis' that comprises the analytic decisions that justify the limit that researchers place on the number of facts they will consider. Since erudition, like the process of *Historismus*, could proceed indefinitely, an analytic position must justify its limit. The second degree, 'scientific synthesis', is the result of our synthesising instances of erudite analysis. Historians reach a synthetic understanding through our awareness of a relationship between investigation and analysis, a relation-ship that we have generated as individuals and as adherents to a given discipline. Berr associated historical studies with erudition and sociology with science, but his original contribution lay in his belief that historians need a combination of these two degrees of synthesis, for both are 'inherent in our human nature. Analysis and synthesis are logically inseparable'.[81] It is this logical and natural necessity for a balance between the accumulation of detail and with the formulation of cognitive synthesis that enabled Berr to identify 'a community of all the sciences over and above the distinctive-ness of the historical'.[82] Berr's position provided an intellectual liberation for historians and social sciences across Europe at the turn of the century, one that justified scholarly specialisation with a diplomatic curiosity about developments in other disciplines.[83]

In terms of his own writing, Berr made only theoretical contributions to historical synthesis. But in his role as an editor, Berr facilitated and moderated exchanges between scholars that, cumulatively, allowed the task of synthesis to take place in their readers' own minds. No one scholar such as Stubbs, Ranke or Robinson would provide a synthesis of erudition with analysis; unlike Durkheim, synthesis required more than intellectual leadership. It also required critical thinking by individual readers, thinking that could account for the contingencies and necessities that only a broad understanding of the human sciences may provide. In this sense, Berr's *Revue de Synthèse Historique* facilitated a cosmopolitan exercise in *Bildung* that brought together an eclectic range of sources and perspectives predating the divisive emergence of modern history as a professional discipline. After the Great War, the two historians Marc Bloch and Lucien Febvre, who would found the journal *Annales d'Histoire Économique et Sociale*, cited Henri Berr as the intellectual parent of their commitment to interdisciplinarity in historical studies. This journal, and the collegial school it fostered, has been described as 'the most influential single orientation in historical research and writing in the twentieth century'.[84] Looking back a further century later, few readers or writers of history consider themselves scientists. Those who defend the humanities and the broad vision that historical inquiry can provide, may seem to invoke vom Steim and Humboldt, by arguing for the special quality of understanding that emerges from critical debate over the changing meanings of primary sources.[85] English-speaking historians seldom use the associated German vocabulary, though we remain in its debt. Its guiding concepts persist.

NOTES

1 H. Trevor-Roper, 'The Highland Tradition of Scotland', in *The Invention of Tradition*, eds. E. Hobsbawm and T. Ranger (Cambridge: Cambridge University Press, 1983), p. 63.

2 J. Seeley, *Life of Stein* (Cambridge: Cambridge University Press, 1878), vol. 1, p. 167.

3 G. Hegel, *Elements of the Philosophy of Right*, ed. A. Wood, trans. H. Nisbet (Cambridge: Cambridge University Press, 1991), pp. 373–4.

4 I. Kant, 'Idea for a Universal History from a Cosmopolitan Point of View' [1784], in *On History*, ed. L. W. Beck (New York: Macmillan, 1963), p. 21.

5 G. Hegel, *Introduction to the Philosophy of History*, trans. Leo Rauch (Indianapolis, IN: Hackett, 1988), p. 59.

6 L. Ranke, 'A Dialogue on Politics' [1836], in *On the Theory and Practice of History*, ed. G. Iggers (London: Routledge, 2011), p. 66.

7 S. T. Coleridge, *The Statesman's Manual* (London: Gale & Fenner, 1816), p. 34.

8   K. Marx, *The German Ideology*, 1845, trans. S. Ryananskaya (New York: Prometheus, 1998), p. 41.

9   See G. Iggers, 'Introduction', in *On the Theory and Practice of History*, p. xvi.

10 L. Ranke, 'On the Character of Historical Science', in *On the Theory and Practice of History*, pp. 10–11.

11 J. W. Burrow, 'Introduction', in *The Limits of State Action*, by W. von Humboldt (Cambridge: Cambridge University Press, 1969), p. xxxiv.

12 I. Berlin, *The Roots of Romanticism*, ed. Henry Hardy (London: Pimlico, 2000), p. 7.

13 See D. Cannadine, J. Keating and N. Sheldon, 'History Goes to School, 1900–18', *The Right Kind of History* (London: Palgrave, 2011), p. 19.

14 C. H. K. Marten, 'The History of Teaching History in Schools', ed. W. Archbold, *Essays on the Teaching of History* (Cambridge: Cambridge University Press, 1901), p. 80.

15 J. Rose, *The Intellectual Life of the British Working Classes* (New Haven, CT: Yale University Press, 2001), pp. 189, 68–70.

16 N. B. Harte, *One Hundred Years of History Teaching at University College London* (London: UCL Press, 1982), pp. 5–6.

17 See 'Professor Stubbs's Inaugural Lecture', *Saturday Review* (2 March 1866), 279.

18 See P. Fredericq, *Science* (9 December 1887), 283.

19 See *A Survey of the Roman, or Civil Law*, trans. Rev. W. Gardiner (Edinburgh: W. Aitchison, 1823). The volume appeared in duodecimo, the cheapest format possible.

20 C. Firth, *A Plea for the Historical Teaching of History* (Oxford: Oxford University Press, 1904), p. 17.

21 See 'Schools of History', *Collected Papers of Thomas Frederick Tout*, vol. 11, p. 96.

22 R. Humphreys, *The Royal Historical Society, 1868–1968* (London: RHS, 1969), p. 3.

23 See Cannadine et al., 'History Goes to School', p. 1.

24 R. Soffer, 'Nation, Duty, Character, and Confidence: History at Oxford, 1850–1914', *Historical Journal* 30 (1987), 77.

25 See J. Kenyon, *The History Men* (London: Weidenfeld & Nicolson, 1983), p. 150.

26 Quoted in A. J. Ashley, *Essays in Economic Method*, ed. R. L. Smyth (London: Duckworth, 1962), p. 454.

27 Firth, *A Plea for the Historical Teaching of History*, p. 1.

28 See M. Holyrod, 'On the Borderline Between the New and the Old: Bloomsbury, Biography, and Gerald Brenan', *Biographical Passages*, eds. J. Law and K. Hughes (London: University of Missouri Press, 2000), p. 42.

29 In one of Arnold's few surviving poems, he describes this process as a river through time. See T. Arnold, 'The River of Life or Time', in M. Arnold, *The Poems of Matthew Arnold*, ed. K. Allott (New York: Longman, 1965), pp. 610–11.

30 T. Arnold, *An Inaugural Lecture on the Study of Modern History* (Oxford: John Henry Parker, 1841), p. 32.

31 W. Stubbs, *Seventeen Lectures on the Study of Medieval and Modern History* (Oxford: Clarendon Press, 1887), p. 23.

32 W. Stubbs, *The Constitutional History of England* (Oxford: Clarendon Press, 1874), vol. 1, pp. 2, 35.

33 C. Darwin, *The Descent of Man*, eds. J. Moore and A. Desmond (Harmondsworth: Penguin, 2004), p. 168.

34 J. Froude, *Oceana, or England and Her Colonies* (London: Longmans, Green & Co., 1887), p. 2.

35 See S. J. Gould, *Time's Arrow, Time's Cycle* (Harmondsworth: Penguin, 1988), p. 155.

36 L. Ranke, 'On the Character of Historical Science', in *The Theory and Practice of History*, ed. G. Iggers (London: Routledge, 2010), p. 8.

37 W. Humboldt, 'On the Historian's Task', *History and Theory* 6 (1967), 64. My emphasis.

38 Quoted in P. Hans Reill, 'Science and the Construction of the Cultural Sciences in Late Enlightenment Germany', *History and Theory* 33 (1994), 358.

39 Stubbs, *Seventeen Lectures*, p. 14.

40 Lord Macaulay, *History of England*, ed. Hugh Trevor-Roper (Harmondsworth: Penguin, 1968), p. 52.

41 See I. Hesketh, 'Diagnosing Froude's Disease: Boundary Work and the Discipline of History in Late-Victorian Britain', *History and Theory* 47 (2008), 373–95.

42 A. Ashley, 'The History of English Serfdom', *Surveys Historic and Economic* (London: Longmans, Green & Co., 1900), p. 40.

43 See F. M. Powicke, 'Little, Andrew George (1863–1945)', rev. Mark Pottle, *Oxford Dictionary of National Biography* (Oxford: Oxford University Press, 2004).

44 J. B. Bury's elusiveness was legendary. See 'Sir Steven Runciman', *Daily Telegraph* (2 Nov. 2000).

45 See Kenyon, *The History Men*, pp. 150–1.

46 Ashley, 'The University Ideal', in *Surveys Historic and Economic*, pp. 452–3.

47 This was Matthew Arnold's view in 1864. See *The Complete Prose Works of Matthew Arnold*, ed. R. H. Super (Ann Arbor: University of Michigan Press, 1977), vol. 4, p. 331.

48 Lord Acton, 'Inaugural Lecture', *Lectures on Modern History* (London: Macmillan, 1906), p. 32.

49 W. Humboldt, 'On the Spirit and Organizational Framework of Intellectual Institutions in Berlin', trans. E. Shils, *Minerva* 8 (1970), 243, 244.

50 F. William, *Bredow-Venturinischen Chronik* (Berlin: Raurer, 1808), p. 5.

51 R. Chickering, *Karl Lamprecht: A German Academic Life* (Atlantic Highlands, NJ: Humanities Press, 1993), p. 35; Kenyon, *History Men*, p. 151.

52 See U. Muhlack, 'Universal History and National History', in *British and German Historiography, 1750–1950*, eds. B. Stuchtey and P. Wende (Cambridge: Cambridge University Press, 2000), pp. 29–30.

53 Quoted in Bert James Loewenberg, *American History in American Thought* (New York: Simon & Schuster, 1972), p. 385.

54 R. T. Shannon, 'John Robert Seeley and the Idea of a National Church', in *Ideas and Institutions of Victorian Britain*, ed. R. Robson (London: Bell, 1967), p. 255. My vote for the most cosmopolitan British historian of the period goes

to S. R. Gardiner (who turned down the chair of modern history at Oxford in 1894).

55 P. Vermeulen and O. de Graef, '*Bildung* and the State in the Long Nineteenth Century', *Partial Answers* 10 (June 2012), 244.

56 W. Humboldt, *The Limits of State Action*, trans. and ed. J. W. Burrow (Cambridge: Cambridge University Press, 1969), p. 145.

57 See Hegel, *Introduction to the Philosophy of History*, p. 20.

58 J. Burckhardt, *Reflections on History*, trans. M. D. Hottinger (London: Allen & Unwin, 1944), p. 20. My emphasis.

59 See B. G. Smith, 'Gender and the Practices of Scientific History: The Seminar and Archival Research in the Nineteenth Century', *American Historical Review* 100 (Oct. 1995), 1153, 1156, 1157.

60 G. Iggers, 'Introduction', in *The Theory and Practice of History* by Leopold von Ranke (London: Routledge, 2010), p. xxvii.

61 See S. Gardiner, *The Academy* 734 (29 May 1886), 382.

62 Burckhardt, *Reflections on History*, p. 208.

63 Humboldt, 'On the Historian's Task', p. 59. For a history of historical journals, see Margaret F. Steig, *The Origin and Development of Scholarly Historical Periodicals* (New York: University of Alabama Press, 1986).

64 See G. Lingelbach, 'The Institutionalization and Professionalization of History in Europe and the United States', in *Oxford History of Historical Writing, Vol 4: 1800–1945*, eds. S. Macintyre et al. (Oxford: Oxford University Press, 2001), p. 81. For a comparative visual illustration, see I. Porcianai and L. Raphael, *Atlas of European Historiography* (London: Palgrave, 2010).

65 J. Albisetti, *Schooling German Girls and Women: Secondary and Higher Education in the Nineteenth Century* (Princeton, NJ: Princeton University Press, 1988).

66 Quoted in Chickering, *Karl Lamprecht: A German Academic Life*, p. 53.

67 Ibid., p. 215.

68 See G. Burton Adams, 'History and the Philosophy of History', *American Historical Review* 14 (1909), 236.

69 C. A. Beard, *An Economic Interpretation of the Constitution* (New York: Macmillan, 1913), pp. 10, 12.

70 These lectures were published simultaneously in America, Britain and Germany. See K. Lamprecht, *What Is History? Five Lectures on the Modern Science of History*, trans. E. A. Andrews (New York: Macmillan, 1905) p. 190.

71 J. H. Robinson, *The New History: Essays Illustrating the Modern Historical Outlook* (New York: Macmillan, 1913), p. 74.

72 The Committee on Social Studies of the Commission on the Reorganization of Secondary Education, *The Social Studies in Secondary Education* (Washington, DC: Government Printing Office, 1916), pp. 53–4.

73 P. den Boer, 'Historical Writing in France, 1800–1914', in S. Mcintyre, ed. *The Oxford History of Historical Writing* (Oxford: Oxford University Press, 2011), vol. 4, p. 197.

74 William Keylor and Isabel DiVanna have noted how few historical monographs were purchased by non-specialists during this period. See I. DiVanna, *Writing History in the Third Republic* (Newcastle: Cambridge Scholars, 2010), p. 226.

75 W. Keylor, *Academy and Community: The Foundation of the French Historical Profession* (Cambridge, MA: Harvard University Press, 1975), p. 113.

76 É. Durkheim, *The Rules of Sociological Method*. Preface to the 2nd edn, trans. W. D. Halls (New York: Free Press, 1982), p. 45.

77 Lamprecht, *What Is History?* p. 29; Durkheim was appointed Professor of Education at the Sorbonne in 1906.

78 É. Durkheim, *Contributions to L'Année Sociologique*, ed. Y. Nandan (New York: Free Press, 1980), p. 71.

79 H. Berr, 'Sur Notre Programme', *Revue de Synthèse Historique* 1 (1900), 9.

80 M. Siegel, 'Henri Berr's *Revue de Synthèse Historique*', *History and Theory* 9 (1970), 328, 333.

81 H. Berr, *La Synthèse en Histoire: Essai Critique et Historique* (Paris: Alcan, 1911), p. 19.

82 See L. Krieger, *Time's Reasons: Philosophies of History Old and New* (Chicago: University of Chicago Press, 1989), p. 148.

83 See R. Fritz, *The Decline of the German Mandarins: The German Academic Community, 1890–1933* (London: Harvard University Press, 1969), pp. 334–73.

84 A. Megill, 'Coherence and Incoherence in Historical Studies: From the *Annales* School to the New Cultural History', *New Literary History* 35 (2004), 209.

85 See J. Guildi and D. Armitage, *The History Manifesto* (Cambridge: Cambridge University Press, 2014).

7

KEITH TRIBE

Capitalism and Its Critics

It could be said that, during the nineteenth century, capitalism took over the world. Developments in trade, finance, manufacturing, farming, energy sources and population growth in Western Europe converged to create a new kind of economy whose rhythms were no longer primarily dictated by pestilence, the seasons, climatic cycles or wars of religion and of succession.[1] Warfare in particular became a contest between nation states, and periodic revolutionary upheavals came to focus upon the institutions of the modern state: a key text of the Russian Revolution was Lenin's *State and Revolution* (1917). Competition between European states for resources and markets extended capitalism across the globe, creating a new imperial order. As working populations grew, and communications extended, towns and cities mushroomed in Western Europe and North America, attracting a new urban working class whose productive powers were exploited by the owners of capital: financiers and industrialists driven by the urge to accumulate on an ever-increasing scale. The prophet of this new system is usually thought to be Karl Marx, who in 1867 published the first volume of a treatise intended to reveal the source of these rhythms pulsing through the world economy, the 'laws of motion' of the capitalist mode of production. He wrote in the preface to this first volume of *Das Kapital* that his analysis was based upon England, where the 'capitalist mode of production' had developed in its classic form. As a system, however, this was destined to engulf the world: 'The country that is more industrially developed shows to the less industrially developed only the image of its own future!'[2]

This is the way that nineteenth-century economic development is often thought about today; but it does not entirely correspond to the way in which those who lived through the nineteenth century thought about their own world. To begin with, 'capitalism' as a generic term for a specific social, political and cultural system is an invention of the twentieth, not the nineteenth, century. The theoretical object of Marx's analysis in *Kapital* is not 'capitalism', but the 'capitalist mode of production', conceived primarily there as a system of production organised around large factories. When in 1894 J. A. Hobson published The *Evolution of Modern Capitalism*, the subtitle 'A Study of Machine Production' also made clear that 'modern capitalism' was a form of industrial organisation, not a socio-political system – this perspective marked even the final chapter of the book, on 'Civilisation and Industrial Development'. This conception of capitalism as chiefly an industrial system was widely shared; when in 1899 Lenin published *The Development of Capitalism in Russia*, this was a mainly empirical investigation of rural production, forms of labour, industrial production and market organisation in contemporary Russia. The idea that 'capitalism' is rather more than one form of economic organisation, but a form of economic organisation whose rationality eventually invades all areas of public and private life, was first elaborated not by Karl Marx, or indeed any nineteenth-century Marxist; instead this idea comes from Max Weber, articulated in his two essays on 'The Protestant Ethic and the "Spirit" of Capitalism', published in 1904 and 1905. And the idea of endless consumption, of capitalism as a self-sustaining race of emulation and acquisition, originates in Thorstein Veblen's *Theory of the Leisure Class* (1899), in which he developed a conception of social emulation as 'conspicuous consumption'.[3]

While we might today think of nineteenth-century Western Europe and North America as the cradle of a modern capitalism that is as much cultural as economic, what is presumed to be intrinsic to this understanding of 'capitalism' – an economic system that has come to suffuse the entire social world – is a comparatively recent invention. Many who lived through the nineteenth century did indeed conceive their world as one undergoing a fundamental transformation; but this transformation had many aspects, and 'capitalism' did not serve as a widely accepted term representing the totality of these aspects. If we are to properly understand the way in which contemporaries thought about what *we* think of as 'nineteenth-century capitalism', we need to start from recognition of this disjunction.[4] Otherwise we risk succumbing to a solipsistic and counterfeit 'history', presuming ourselves to be standing at the 'end of history' – as did the 'modern men' who Max Weber excoriated in the closing passages of the 'Protestant Ethic'.

Instead, we can approach the question of 'capitalism in the nineteenth century' along two linked paths: first of all, examining the actual emergence of the term 'capitalism' and its various cognates, asking just when and where this terminology was used, and what was meant by the usage. The term is a relatively recent invention; it can be said straight away that there is little evidence for widespread usage during the nineteenth century, and none at all for its usage in anything like the modern sense alluded to above. Second, we can reverse this philological approach, and consider instead how those phenomena that we today talk of in terms of 'capitalism' were examined and argued over by their contemporaries.

There were 'capitalists' before 'capitalism', and 'capital' before either. The last, deriving from the Anglo-Norman *capitall, capitale*, Middle French *capital*, first gained its specifically financial sense in the later sixteenth and early seventeenth centuries, contrasting a sum of capital to the interest payable upon it.[5] However, it was not until the mid- to later eighteenth century that this term was attached to persons – in French, Dutch and English, 'capitalists' were those who possessed capital and who used it for the purpose of investment. This remained, however, a relatively esoteric usage, certainly not commonly encountered. In chapter 4 of David Ricardo's *Principles of Political Economy and Taxation* (1817) it is the activity of the capitalist that reconciles the market and natural prices of a commodity:

> It is then the desire, which every capitalist has, of diverting his funds from a less to a more profitable employment, that prevents the market price of commodities from continuing for any length of time either much above, or much below their natural price. It is this competition which so adjusts the exchangeable value of commodities, that after paying the wages for the labour necessary to their production, and all other expenses required to put the capital employed in its original state of efficiency, the remaining value or overplus will in each trade be in proportion to the value of the capital employed.[6]

And when in the third edition of 1821 Ricardo added chapter 31 'On Machinery', the capitalist becomes a central character, conducting the 'joint business of a farmer, and a manufacturer of necessaries'.[7] Plainly, the 'capitalist' is here the agent representing and employing (fixed and circulating) capital, in the same way that the labourer is the agent directed by the capitalist and receiving wages in return: Ricardo's analysis is built around the factors of land, labour and capital, and the associated income streams of rent, wages and profit, represented in turn by the landlord, the labourer and the farmer/manufacturer who, for the sake of symmetry, is called the capitalist. The landlord owns land; the labourer owns his own physical capacities; the capitalist owns capital. As the coordinator of production, the 'capitalist' here is a close equivalent of Jean-Baptiste Say's 'entrepreneur', the agent initiating and organising production.

Ricardo used the term 'capitalist' quite unselfconsciously, simply describing one of the parties to a process of production and distribution. During the 1820s in England radicals adopted the terminology of political economy to argue that the labourer, as the owner of his own labour, thereby had a right to its entire product. This line of argument was later characterised as 'Ricardian Socialism',[8] although British writers such as

Robert Owen and William Thompson looked back rather to Adam Smith's *Wealth of Nations*, a work that opened with the statement that: 'The annual labour of every nation is the fund which originally supplies it with all the necessaries and conveniences of life which it annually consumes, and which consist always, either in the immediate produce of that labour, or in what is purchased with that produce from other nations.'[9] In the hands of Robert Owen, Smith's *Wealth of Nations* was a treatise concerning employment, machinery and social progress, social wealth hinging upon the expenditure of social labour. Insofar as the political economy of Robert Malthus, James Mill and David Ricardo had anything to do with arguments developed among English radicals of the 1820s, it was their emphasis upon distribution – between wages, profit and rent – that was of importance. William Thompson, for example, added to this a concern with the 'right distribution' of wealth that drew directly upon Jeremy Bentham's utilitarian calculus: 'The distribution to be here inquired into, is that which will promote the *greatest possible quantity* of human happiness, or the *greatest happiness of the greatest number*.'[10] This was also linked to a nascent conception of marginal utility: that the forced alienation of the products of labour will lower average happiness, since it brings about a greater loss of happiness to the loser, than an increase to the gainer.[11]

The basic principles of political economy were, however, open to more than one kind of transformation through critique. Thomas Hodgskin moved in the same radical circles – Jeremy Bentham, James Mill, Francis Place – as William Thompson, but instead of Thompson's co-operative socialism, Hodgskin's more libertarian inclinations stemmed from the influence of Godwin. The labourer, argued Hodgskin, was the 'real maker of the commodity':

> The only advantage of circulating capital is that by it the LABOURER is enabled, *he* being assured of his present subsistence, to direct *his* power to the greatest advantage. HE has time to learn an art, and *his* labour is rendered more productive when directed by skill. Being ASSURED of immediate subsistence, he can ascertain which, with his peculiar knowledge and acquirements, and with reference to the wants of society, is the best method of labouring, and he can labour in this manner.[12]

Hodgskin also argued that what was 'stored up or previously prepared' was the skill of the labourer; and that it was the 'command the capitalist possesses over the labour of some men, not by his possessing a stock of commodities, that HE is enabled to *support* and consequently employ other labourers' – that this was the substance of circulating capital.[13] Fixed capital on the other hand is of advantage to the capitalist not because it represented stored-up labour, 'but because it is a means of obtaining a command over labour'.[14] Capital and labour, 'the shovel and the digger' as John Bray later put it,[15] were antagonistic when linked to particular classes, 'for the gain of the capitalist is always the loss of the working man, and the poverty and toil of the last is a necessary consequence of the wealth and idleness of the first'.[16]

While the capitalist is present in the writings of these radicals as a figure with interests inimical to those of the working man, this trope does not form an axis around which a critique of an industrial system as such is organised. 'Capitalism', or 'capitalist society', is notable by its absence here. The traditional idea that an Industrial Revolution beginning in the early nineteenth century created an English working class that quickly developed a critique of capitalism is anachronistic and misconceived in all three elements, but well expressed by Max Beer's classical formulation:

> The communist and socialists, or anti-capitalist writers, based themselves, in addition to these self-evident truths [that land was originally held in common, and that originally members of society were free and equal], on Locke's theory that labour was the real title to property, or, as Adam Smith puts it, 'the produce of labour constitutes the natural recompense or wages of labour'. The industrial revolution had shown, however, that the produce of labour belonged, not to the labourer, but to the capitalist. This experience, joined to Adam Smith's emphasis on labour being the source of wealth and the standard of value, and Ricardo's apparently irrefragable logic of the theory of labour value and the inverse ratio of wages and profit, gave to Locke's argument on labour and property a social-revolutionary turn, and turned it into a weapon against the social system which was emerging from the economic revolution.[17]

This idea that Owenite and other radical arguments of the 1820s and 1830s seized on contemporary political economy and inverted it into autocritique is something in fact effected much later, by Friedrich Engels' *Condition of the Working Class in England in 1844*, which borrowed freely from both Owenite thinking and French criticism of the emergent 'English model', converting it into a critique of 'industrialism', not of 'capitalism'.[18] Since Engels' writing was subsequently linked to Marx, and given the supposition that the latter's writings turned on a critique of 'capitalism', it is easy to see how two ideas became telescoped into a third, that English radicals before 1848 identified a nascent capitalist system as the source of the evils that they denounced. This was always a historical fiction.

'Capital' was not in any case a central organising idea of early nineteenth-century political economy; it turned instead upon 'value', economic activity being condensed into the idea that 'labour' endowed goods with their (exchange) value. All the same, the political economists did assume that in return for this a fixed portion of the product of labour flowed back to workers as wages; but it was this idea that led them to oppose the amelioration of poverty and pauperism by raising wages. Further, Ricardian political economy set forth an economic model in which production was generated by factors of production (land, labour and capital), which in turn received revenues (rent, wages and profit). In this world there were abstract landowners, labourers and 'capitalists', but the system within which these operated was conceived in concrete terms, of industrialism and commerce, not of 'capitalism'. While the Ricardian model set forth a social mechanism, this mechanism was not thought of as 'capitalism'.

English conditions and English critiques of these conditions did play a role in the development of the idea that there was a new mechanism at work in society, but this idea came not from Owen, Thompson or Bray, nor initially from Engels or Marx, but from French writers in the 1840s considering the path upon which England was developing, and arguing against its emulation in France. Of central significance here was Louis Blanc's critique of the 'English model' in a series of articles that were first published in 1839, then as a separate pamphlet in 1841 under the title *Organisation du travail*. This then went through many editions during the 1840s, Blanc adding extensively to it; but the striking feature of the first version was its clear division of society into the rich and the poor, shackled together by a merciless process of competition that resulted in the impoverishment of all. 'Systematic reduction in wages, bordering on the suppression of a certain number of workers, this is the inevitable effect of unlimited competition. It is therefore only an industrial process by means of which the proletarians (*les prolétaires*) are forced to exterminate each other.'[19] This also fostered exploitation by '*capitalistes*'[20] who furthered the process of economic concentration and monopolisation. Blanc argued that the most advanced development of this system was to be found in England, and that Ricardo was its most heartless prophet.[21] England presented to the world both extreme poverty and extreme opulence, and France was on the same path: 'In 1789 France adopted all the traditions of English political economy; it became an industrial people like the English people ... France and ... England, ruled by the same economic laws, and as a consequence animated by the same spirit.'[22] The dating of this to 1789 carries an echo of Adolphe Blanqui's contention in 1837 that England had undergone an 'Industrial Revolution' comparable in scope to the political revolution that had convulsed France.[23] This usage of 'Industrial Revolution' caught on, together with its characterisation in terms of new types of machinery displacing craft labour and natural sources of energy.[24] As already noted, Engels adopted this schema in his *Condition of the Working Class in*

England in 1844, creating a channel through which the entire idea would eventually become attributed to Marx.

Blanc elaborated his own ideas through the 1840s, adding to and revising *Organisation du travail*, in the process transforming his 'capitalist' into the epitome of an entire economic system: 'One can see quite what the sophism that serves as the foundation of all M. Bastiat's arguments consists of. The sophism involves a constant confusion of the use of *capital* with that which I will call capitalism, that is to say, the appropriation of capital by one group, excluding all others.'[25] Nonetheless, he does not elaborate this neologism, and continues to talk of 'capital' and 'capitalists'; although it should also be noted that in so doing he retained a strongly financial sense to these terms, a sense that would eventually be lost when they became identified with a conception of 'capitalism' organised around a confrontation of capital and labour in a process of (factory) production.

That 'industrialism' was the term of choice in mid-century, linked to many of the ideas that would later become part of this conception of 'capitalism', is demonstrated by the explanation of what this term meant in one of the many German lexica of the nineteenth century. 'Industrialism' was defined as

> materialism ... transferred to the commercial domain, the pathological eco-
> nomic and social condition in which big industry predominates over all other
> kinds of sustenance and vocation. Its objective is the greatest possible fabrica-
> tion of products on the basis of unlimited division of labour and completely
> free competition. It is only concerned with what is produced, and how much;
> not with how this is produced, it is more concerned with the commodity than
> with men, and makes these into a commodity, as an auxiliary machine. It
> heaps big capital in the arms of the few and thereby causes mass impoverish-
> ment ... The bond which especially unites the workers generally in society is
> supposed to be active love; but in industrialism it is instead selfishness; and
> here those who rule do not have the position of a moral order governing men,
> but of a chained watchdog guarding a sack of money.[26]

Combined with the writing of Blanc, this supports the idea that a critique of the economic system in terms of competition, commodification and pau-perism was, if not routine, at least unsurprising in mid-century. But the term of choice on all sides was 'industrialism', not 'capitalism'.

This is rather lent emphasis by the publication in 1870 of Schäffle's *Kapitalismus und Socialismus*, a bulky work of 732 pages that is aimed, so the title page states, at reconciling the contradictions of capital and labour.[27] Based on public lectures at the Austrian Museum of Industry, the text is extremely discursive and does not get around to defining what is meant by capitalism until the fifth lecture (of fifteen), maintaining that 'capitalism is the articulation of millions of units of labour and property into one unique national and international organism of production *supervised by "entre-preneurial", capitalists competing for the highest possible entrepreneurial profit* ... Socialists are right when they say that the contemporary economy is characterised by the "capitalist mode of production", by the hegemony of "capitalism".'[28] What does this 'hegemony of capitalism' involve? It turns out on the following page that what Schäffle has in mind is rather similar to what we have already seen in Ricardo: that the capitalist is an entrepreneur combining factors of production and deriving a profit as a reward for so doing. It is simply a way of describing the functioning of an economy continuous with that outlined in early nineteenth-century political economy, and without the inherent critique that we have seen in the Wagener entry on 'Industrialism'. This, at least, demonstrates plainly that to talk of 'capitalism' in no way automatically implies a critique of the prevailing economic order and that, in the German context, such a critique could be effected through use of the term 'industrialism', as with Wagener's *Lexicon*.

So if 'industrialism' was in mid-century doing the work that is now customarily attributed to 'capitalism', where does this term come from? As with 'capital' and 'capitalist', the economic conception of 'industry' preceded 'industrialism', and 'industry' came in the early nineteenth century to mean something rather different to what it did in the eighteenth. In *Wealth of Nations* Smith used the term 'industry' synonymously with 'economic activity' – arguing, for example, that the 'industry of the town' was everywhere in Europe superior to 'that which is carried on in the country'.[29] The superiority of the former is owed to its focus upon trade and manufactures, whereas the 'industry of the country' is devoted to 'the raising of rude produce by the improvement and cultivation of land'.[30] Note that while 'trade and manufactures' are superior, they do not exhaust the activities associated with 'industry'.

The transformation of this particular usage can be attributed to Saint-Simon, who in November 1819 opened his new publication, *L'Organisateur*, by supposing that France suddenly lost fifty of its leading physicians, chemists, physiologists, mathematicians, painters; its fifty leading mechanics, civil and military engineers, artillerymen, architects; bankers, traders, agriculturalists, blacksmiths, gunsmiths, tanners; masons, carpenters and so on. These were, he said, the flower of French society, the most useful to the country; France would become lifeless without them.[31] By contrast, the entire aristocracy and all their hangers-on could vanish without having the least negative impact upon anyone but themselves. French prosperity depended on the progress of its arts and sciences, to which those in the first list all contributed, while the aristocracy and their flunkies made no such contribution.[32] Saint-Simon then proceeded to consider political systems, in particular, the model of the English constitution, before returning to this issue in the eighth letter.[33] He comes back to his starting point, and states: 'Industrial capacity, or that of *arts et métiers*, is what must be substituted for feudal and military power.'[34] Feudal society is associated with military power; modern society with industrial power, this last understood as power based upon all kinds of productive activity. And modern society would be guided by the leading 'industrialists', instead of being commanded by military rulers: 'Let us observe that the progress of industry, of the sciences and arts, by multiplying the means of subsistence, by reducing the number of those without work, by enlightening minds and improving *mœurs*, tends to the gradual disappearance of the three great causes of disorder: poverty, idleness and ignorance.'[35] This conception of 'industriousness' was given further point in late 1823 when a *Catéchisme des industriels* began to appear, opening with the question: 'Qu'est-ce que un industriel?': 'An industrial is a man who works to produce, or contribute for the support of different members of society, one or more material means for satisfying their needs or their physical tastes ... they form three great classes, which are called cultivators, manufacturers and merchants.'[36] This industrial class, he went on, should occupy the first rank of society, being the most important of all; but in present society it was the most lowly, since the social order lent greater consideration and power to secondary works. The purpose of the catechism was to show how this condition could be overcome without the need for violent upheaval. And in a second appendix, Saint-Simon argued that while those concerned for the public good were known as liberals, they should be invited to inscribe on their banner 'industrialism' instead of 'liberalism'.[37]

It is this conception of industrial society, a society based upon productive activity, which enabled the broad reception of Saint-Simonian ideas, on the one hand among radical artisans, on the other among engineers and bankers. Industrialism was here a positive idea, an idea that in its transmutation from a kind of human activity to a particular sector of the economy became contaminated by an existing critique of manufacturing and exploitation. As we can see with Wagener, by the 1860s this transformation was more or less complete; but it is already prefigured in the writings of Lorenz von Stein in the later 1840s.

Stein contrasted an era in which work was primarily done by hand to that in which the machine held sway. The master in the workshop was replaced by the owner of capital who commands by virtue of owning machinery; the work done becomes increasingly simple and repetitive, the worker tied to the machine by the need for work and wage. No longer can the worker advance in time to become a master; the worker is a simple wage labourer, a factory worker, defined by the nature of his work and with no way of acquiring the capital needed to become his own master:

> Labour itself becomes therefore a pure commodity. And the price of this commodity is determined by the same principles determining that of all other commodities, by the volume of supply and demand ... Capital, and through it the capitalists, determine the wages of labour, holding in their hands the entire life of this factory worker. And in this way the emergence of machine labour fosters a distinction between capital and labour.[38]

This contrast between capital and labour is what Stein considers to be characteristic of modern society, open to resolution only through the principles of equality and liberty, through a redistribution of property, however difficult this might be.

This resolution of the 'social danger',[39] as Stein called it, was not the one that Marx had in mind; nonetheless, Marx would take these and other ideas and lend them a new synthesis, arguing that the revolutionary potential of the capitalist mode of production lay in the manner that it created the basis for its own supersession, in the radicalisation of factory workers who, oppressed by the yoke of capital, ever more proletarianised, would eventually rise up and throw it off. This line of argument, exposed in the later chapters of *Capital* vol. 1, was continuous with the arguments of those, like Proudhon and Stein, who identified machine production as the agent that had transformed the nature of work and life. The identification of industrialism with factory production turned attention to the new working class and its organisations; although Marx considered the trade unions that he encountered in the 'workshop of the world' too respectable for their own good, and in his later years reserved his political endorsement for the Communards of 1871, and the prospects offered by the Russian peasant *mir*. In any case, the vision of the future as a proletarian factory existence was itself out of time: it was eventually realised in Fritz Lang's *Metropolis* and Charlie Chaplin's *Modern Times*, but not in any nineteenth-century European city, where factory workers were always a minority of the urban working population, which itself was everywhere, apart from in Britain, a minority of the working population as a whole.

If we return our focus to the use of the term 'capitalism', it can be said that in the later nineteenth century it was, when employed, strongly associated with conceptions of 'industrialism' and 'industrial society', adding to these little more than a slight critical force. If 'capitalism' was by the early 1900s already becoming a way of referring to modern society, however broadly, this was still firmly linked to the kind of critique of industrialism that had first developed in the mid-nineteenth century. When Weber proposed in 1904 that there was a 'spirit' of capitalism that could be related to what he called the 'Protestant ethic', and that was distinct from the simple domination of production by capitalists, the idea itself owed nothing directly to Marx: for as a theorist of capitalism Weber treated Marx as a particular kind of economist. The long genesis of this new conception of 'capitalism' is traced in Peter Ghosh's definitive intellectual biography of Max Weber, both in regard to his understanding of Christian religion, and to the conception of capitalist development embedded in his agrarian writings of the 1890s.[40] However, the idea of a specific 'spirit' of capitalism was mooted first not by Weber, but by Werner Sombart, who had introduced the idea in his *Modern Capitalism* of 1902. In this work Sombart divided human history since antiquity into three major epochs: the peasant–feudal organisation of economic life; the dissolution of agrarian bonds and the creation of property-less urban-based industrial labour; and the current epoch, characterised by the dominance of mercantile life, of calculative-speculative organised activity, in which the object of economic life was the acquisition of money. This drive had, he argued, created the form of organisation best described as *capitalistic*.[41] He later defines *capitalism* as follows:

> We call capitalism a kind of economy in which the specific economic form is the capitalist enterprise ... I call a capitalist enterprise that economic form whose purpose is the valorisation of assets by means of a collection of contracts regarding monetised reciprocal services, that is, reproducing the owner of these assets inclusive of gain (profit). An asset used in this way is called capital.[42]

For Sombart, accordingly, 'capitalism' is an economy typified by an enterprise form that he defines in such a way that it had existed since the early modern period of European history. The reciprocal relationship established between contracting parties gives rise to rational calculation, and the development of this rational relationship is embedded in the development of the enterprise form. Having elaborated the historical evolution of the enterprise, Sombart then turns to what he calls the 'Genesis of the Capitalist Spirit', the title of section 3 of the first volume. Here he first of all considers the 'awakening of the capitalist acquisitive drive',[43] which he primarily associates with the existence of money. However, it is also clear that this acquisitive drive is unique to European peoples, resulting from culture, climate, race and the conditions of natural and popular development: the 'willingness to work, the lively temperament, the down-to-earth world view' of Europeans.[44] This is not, however, sufficient to explain the development of capitalism in Europe; nor, Sombart thinks, is it adequate to attribute the development of capitalism to particular religious communities, for the idea that 'Protestantism, whether in its Calvinist or Quaker variations, has essentially furthered capitalism is too familiar for it to require further argument'.[45] Moreover, he goes on to suggest that the Protestant religious system is more effect than cause of the 'modern-capitalist spirit'. Elaborating his argument regarding the role of rationality in promoting capitalist development, he ends up identifying the development of double-entry book-keeping as the turning point, stating that if pushed he would not hesitate to identify the year 1202 as marking the birth of modern capitalism.[46]

The absence from this first edition of *Der moderne Kapitalismus* of any systematic treatment of banking, trade and mass production is one of its most striking features. While this was in part related to the contemporary demarcation of 'economic history' as, broadly, a discipline devoted to the study of the period up to 1800, it could be said with some justice that the problem with Sombart's account of 'modern capitalism' in 1902 is that it was not very modern. By making 1202 the year in which 'modern capitalism' originated, Sombart hindered any linking of the emergent nineteenth-century critique of 'industrialism' to his own account of 'capitalism'.

It would have been clear to Weber's contemporaries that the title of the 1904/1905 essays, 'The Protestant Ethic and the "Spirit" of Capitalism', was a direct reference to Sombart. While this allusion to Sombart recurs both in the subsequent criticism of the 'Protestant Ethic' and in Weber's defence of it,[47] the association of Protestantism with capitalism that Sombart casually noted as being 'too familiar' transmuted in time to the 'Weber thesis',[48] that Protestantism in some way 'caused' capitalism. Noting Sombart's remark is important here since it establishes that the 'Weber thesis' pre-existed *The Protestant Ethic*, that Weber would have been aware of this, and that as a consequence this cannot reflect what Weber was seeking to argue in 1904/1905. Nevertheless, the common presumption that Weber in some way argued that Protestantism 'caused' capitalism has long become embedded in the commentary. Weber himself put it like this:

> *Today's* capitalist economic order is a monstrous cosmos, into which the individual is born and which in practice is for him, at least as an individual, simply a given, an immutable shell, in which he is obliged to live. It forces on the individual, to the extent that he is caught up in the relationships of the 'market', the norms of its economic activity. The manufacturer who consistently defies these norms will just as surely be forced out of business as the worker who cannot or will not conform will be thrown out of work.[49]

While individuals were 'trained', what needed to be explained was 'The origin of this attitude';[50] and here Weber goes on to state clearly that what he intends to develop is distinct from the 'view of naïve historical materialism, according to which such "ideas" come about as a "reflection" or "superstructure" of the economic base'.[51] This 'spirit' is, in the pursuit of a calling, that which 'strives systematically for profit for its own sake'.[52] And:

> The question of the motive forces behind the development of capitalism is not primarily a question of the *money* reserves to be used, but a question of the development of the capitalist spirit. Wherever it emerges and is able to make its influence felt, it creates the money as the means of achieving its effects, although the reverse is not true.[53]

Hence 'capitalism' for Weber was not so much a particular form of industrial organisation, but a particular rationality that both shaped individuals and was created by the way in which they led their lives. It is this conception that his two essays of 1904 and 1905 introduced, a conception more recognisably continuous with present-day usage than Marx's own focus upon the world of factory labour and the appropriation of surplus value.

While 'capitalism' is thus a twentieth-century concept, it is also important to recognise that it is routinely used to imply criticism of the conditions to which it refers. However, since it is largely empty of specific content, as such it is also a term that defies very clear definition. What loss would there then be, besides some rhetorical force, if it were simply replaced by the term 'industrialism'? The insistence in the foregoing of adhering to the language used by those contemporary with the nineteenth century is intended in part to make an answer to this question possible.

Marx's place in all of this is especially complicated; while he never relied analytically on the term 'capitalism' in his published writings, it is often assumed that he did: after all, he wrote a book called *Capital*. However, the writings left unpublished at his death in 1883 did contain a rather more substantial conception of 'capitalism' as an economic system than the one exposed in the first volume of *Capital*. The drafts that Engels assembled and published as the second and third volumes presented some building blocks – in the circuits of capital, discussions of money and the relationship of value and price – permitting the elaboration of capitalism as a process in which the production of commodities was primarily a means for the accumulation of capital, and only secondarily a means for the satisfaction of human wants and needs. The difficulty with Marx's actual writings is that, too often, this very sound idea was elaborated in obscure and repetitive philosophical language and never given the kind of analytical form to which Marx elsewhere aspired. Rudolf Hilferding's *Finanzkapital* (1910) went some way to rectify this, removing the analysis of capitalism from the conflict of capital and labour to focus upon the creation of credit, the circulation of capital, the role of limited liability and the relationship of the stock and commodity exchanges in creating and destroying value in periodic crises.[54]

However, effective analytical development of this idea by Marx himself would have required him to begin with an entirely different conception of the 'English model' that he made the locus of his work for the first volume of *Capital* – abandoning the history of labour and of the organisation of work, and opting instead for an institutional history of finance, money and banking. In this way it would have been possible to demonstrate quite how the production of commodities used by people simply became an instrument for, subordinate to, the never-ending extension of finance capital. What became lost in arguments during the later twentieth century about the relationship between a 'young' and a 'mature' Marx, the Hegelian philosopher and the political economist, was that *Capital* seeks to realise a philosophical idea in terms of a political economy. The critique of religion with which Marx began – that man created spiritual beliefs that in turn came to dominate him – was transformed into a mechanism in which a worker created a world of commodities that then weighed on him as a crushing force. The worker, the creator of goods, became the creature of capital, of a system in which goods used him. This is the theme of the later sections of *Capital* vol. 1, which trace the development of the capitalist labour process as large-scale factory production.

In this way Marx eventually became the pre-eminent theorist of 'capitalism', but his own view remained one trapped in the 1840s – of French critiques of industrialism and of English political economy. Charles Kindleberger's classic account of economic crises[55] identifies the 1857 crisis, spreading from the United States to England to continental Europe, as the first world financial crisis. This was what prompted Marx to begin drafting the manuscripts now known as the *Grundrisse*, frantically writing until he made himself ill, so that he might complete his work before crisis turned into revolution. The next major financial crisis, marked by the collapse of Overend & Gurney in May 1866, went more or less unremarked by Marx; the crisis developed while he was working on the final draft of *Capital* vol. 1, and in taking note of the crisis he confined himself to some brief remarks made in the later pages of the work. It was only in September 1868, a year after the publication of *Capital* vol. 1, that he began making detailed notes on the course of the 1866 financial crisis. In correspondence with Engels he reiterated his view that its ultimate cause could be located in the early 1860s, with the accumulation of substantial stocks in the cotton industry, and the avoidance of an overproduction crisis only because of the shortages of raw material related to the American Civil War. He had in mind using this notebook material in a section of *Capital* vol. III on credit; but when Engels assembled that text from Marx's manuscripts, he found nothing that he could build on.[56] And so Marx treated what is today understood to be a major financial crisis as at root an industrial crisis. For him, the recent creation of limited liability, the financial overtrading this made possible, and the role of the Bank of England in policing banks that had every incentive to issue large amounts of short-term debt against assets that had a tendency to evaporate in a crisis – all of these features were treated as so many 'phenomenal forms' of a real underlying industrial crisis.

Marx lived exactly through the era during which, in Britain, the transition from agricultural to industrial to financial crises occurred – in Britain the last phase was marked by the rise of railway finance, and the succession of financial crises that it brought in its wake. Looking back on the nineteenth century from the early twenty-first, this transition in mid-century seems to mark a clear shift in the rise of capital: as a disorderly force that has worked its way forwards through successions of boom and bust, as an all-consuming 'modern capitalism'. But while Marx lived through this transition, he did not grasp its significance; for him, 'capitalism' was an industrial system in which capital exploited workers. To make the necessary leap to an understanding of capitalism as the domination of money, banking and finance over the world economy would have meant more than the work of critique and synthesis that he achieved; he would have had to begin again in the 1850s on very different foundations from the ones that he had constructed in the years preceding the 1848 Revolutions out of English political economy and French socialist thought.

NOTES

1 The best brief account of this transformation can be found in E. A. Wrigley, *Continuity, Chance and Change* (Cambridge: Cambridge University Press, 1988), esp. pp. 98–102.

2 Karl Marx, 'Vorwort', *Das Kapital*, Bd. I (Hamburg: Otto Meissner, 1867), p. ix.

3 The title of ch. 4 – Thorstein Veblen, *The Theory of the Leisure Class* (London: Penguin Books, 1994). Veblen does not employ the term 'capitalism' here at all, but refers for example to 'the modern industrial system' (p. 86); his analysis was only later assimilated to critiques of capitalism. It could also be pointed out that Veblen in many respects here resumed an already-existing eighteenth-century critique of luxury in commercial societies.

4 A stance that runs counter to the *Cambridge History of Capitalism*, 2 vols., eds. Larry Neil and Jeffrey Williamson (Cambridge: Cambridge University Press, 2014), which presumes that 'capitalism' is a universal idea around which one can write a universal history.

5 The OED dates the first instance to Peele, *Pathe Way to Perfectnes* (1569), with Vaughan, *Golden groue* (1600) ii. xxi. sig. P3 having: 'He that receiueth any thing ouer and aboue the capitall summe that was lent, is an vsurer.'

6 David Ricardo, *Principles of Political Economy and Taxation, The Works and Correspondence of David Ricardo*, eds. P. Sraffa with M. H. Dobb (Cambridge: Cambridge University Press, 1951), vol. I, p. 91.

7 Ibid., p. 389. Hence as used by Ricardo, the term is close to Jean-Baptiste Say's conception of the *entrepreneur*.

8 Anton Menger's *The Right to the Whole Produce of Labour* (London: Macmillan, 1899; first German edn 1886) is the classic study of the development of this idea in France, Germany and Britain during the nineteenth century. H. S. Foxwell's lengthy 'Introduction' (pp. v–cx) to the English translation focused exclusively on British writers, and linked them clearly to Ricardo (pp. lxxii–lxxiii); this in turn led to their subsequent identification as 'Ricardian socialists', Foxwell himself referring to 'Ricardian socialism' (p. lxxxi).

9 Adam Smith, *An Inquiry into the Nature and Causes of the Wealth of Nations* (Oxford: Oxford University Press, 1976), vol. 1, p. 10.

10 William Thompson, *An Inquiry into the Principles of the Distribution of Wealth most Conducive to Human Happiness* (London: Longman, Hurst, Rees, Orme, Brown & Green, 1824), pp. ix, 1. See also here Gregory Claeys, *Machinery, Money and the Millennium: From Moral Economy to Socialism, 1815–1860* (Princeton, NJ: Princeton University Press, 1987), p. 92. It should also be said that Thompson's use of Jeremy Bentham's formulation regarding the greatest happiness of the greatest number was untypical of contemporary mainstream English political economy.

11 Thompson, *Inquiry*, pp. 68ff.

12 Thomas Hodgskin, *Labour Defended Against the Claims of Capital* [1825] (London: The Labour Publishing Co., 1922), pp. 38, 36–7, emphasis in original.

13 Ibid., pp. 46, 52.

14 Ibid., p. 55.

15 John Bray, *Labour's Wrongs and Labour's Remedy* (Leeds: David Green, 1839), p. 60.

16 Ibid., p. 61.

17 Max Beer, *A History of British Socialism* (London: G. Bell & Sons, 1929), vol. 1, p. 102.

18 Claeys, *Machinery, Money and the Millennium*, ch. 7.

19 Louis Blanc, *Organisation du travail* (Paris: Administration de librairie, 1841), p. 13.

20 Ibid., p. 45.

21 Ibid., p. 153.

22 Ibid., pp. 56, 62–3.

23 Adolphe Blanqui, *Histoire de l'économie politique en Europe depuis les anciens jusqu'à nos jours* (Paris: Guillamin, 1837), vol. 2, pp. 166ff.

24 'The condition of labour underwent the most profound alteration since the origin of societies. Two machines, henceforth immortal, the steam-engine and the spinning machine, overthrew the old commercial system and gave birth almost at the same moment to material goods and social questions unknown to our fathers.' Blanqui, *Histoire de l'économie politique*, vol. 2, pp. 207–8.

25 Louis Blanc, *Organisation du travail*, 9th edn (Paris: Au Bureau du *Nouveau Monde*, 1850), p. 161.

26 Hermann Wagener, 'Industrialismus', *Neues Conversations-Lexicon: Staats- und Gesellschafts-Lexicon* Bd. 10 (Berlin: F. Heinicke, 1862), pp. 61–2. Lucian Hölscher notes that this is the first such entry in a German reference

work – 'Industrie, Gewerbe', in *Geschichtliche Grundbegriffe* Bd. 3, eds. O. Brunner, Werner Conze and R. Koselleck (Stuttgart: Klett Cotta, 1982), p. 291. There is no entry for 'Capitalismus' in Wagener; that for 'Capital und Capitalgewinn' deals with capital purely as an economic category discussed in the literature of political economy – Bd. 5 (Berlin, 1861), pp. 54–73.

27 A. E. F. Schäffle, *Kapitalismus und Socialismus mit besonderer Rücksicht auf Geschäfts- und Vermögensformen* (Tübingen: Verlag der H. Laupp'schen Buchhandlung, 1870).

28 Ibid., p. 116, emphasis in original.

29 Smith, *Wealth of Nations*, vol. 1, x.c.21.

30 Ibid.

31 Henri Saint-Simon, 'Premier extrait de *l'Organisateur*', in *Œuvres complètes*, eds. Juliette Grange, Pierre Musso, Philippe Régnier and Franck Yonnet (Paris: Presses Universitaires de France, 2012), vol. 3, pp. 2119–20.

32 Ibid., p. 2122.

33 Which can be attributed to Auguste Comte – see Saint-Simon, 'Premier extrait de *l'Organisateur*', pp. 2119–20.

34 Saint-Simon, ''L'Organisateur. Huitième lettre', *Œuvres complètes* vol. 3, p. 2152.

35 Saint-Simon, 'L'Organisateur. Neuvième lettre', *Œuvres complètes* vol. 3, p. 2188.

36 Saint-Simon, *Catéchisme des industriels*, in *Œuvres complètes* vol. 4, p. 2876.

37 Ibid., pp. 2962–3.

38 Lorenz von Stein, 'Die socialen Bewegungen der Gegenwart' [1848], in *Schriften zum Sozialismus. 1848, 1852, 1854* (Darmstadt: Wissenschaftliche Buchgesellschaft, 1974), p. 8.

39 Ibid., pp. 10–11.

40 Peter Ghosh, *Max Weber and The Protestant Ethic: Twin Histories* (Oxford: Oxford University Press, 2014), Part 1.

41 Werner Sombart, *Der moderne Kapitalismus* (Leipzig: Duncker und Humblot, 1902), Bd. 1 pp. xxxi–xxxii.

42 Ibid., Bd. 1, p. 195.

43 Ibid., Bd. 1 Abt. 111 K. 14.

44 Ibid., Bd. 1 p. 302.

45 Ibid., pp. 380–1.

46 Ibid., p. 392. 1202 is the date of Leonardo Pisano's *Liber Abaci*, which for the first time combined commercial arithmetic, the rules of algebra, and Arabic numerical notation.

47 Max Weber, *The Protestant Ethic and the 'Spirit' of Capitalism and Other Writings*, eds. Peter Baehr and Gordon C. Wells (Harmondsworth: Penguin Books, 2002), pp. 223, 236, 247, 287.

48 Wilhelm Hennis, *Max Weber's Central Question* (Newbury: Threshold Press, 2000), p. 14.

49 Weber, *The Protestant Ethic*, p. 13.

50 Ibid.

51 Ibid., pp. 13–14.

52 Ibid., p. 19.

53 Ibid., p. 22.

54 Rudolf Hilferding, *Das Finanzkapital. Eine Studie über die jüngste Entwicklung des Kapitalismus* [1910] (Frankfurt am Main: Europäische Verlagsanstalt, 1968).

55 Charles P. Kindleberger (with Robert Aliber), *Manias, Panics, and Crashes: A History of Financial Crises*, 5th edn (New York: John Wiley and Sons, 2005), p. 298.

56 João Antonio de Paula et al., 'Notes on a Crisis: The *Exzerpthefte* and Marx's Method of Research and Composition', *Review of Radical Political Economics* 45 (2013), 162–82 esp. 175–7.

8

ROGER SMITH

Individuality, the Self and Concepts of Mind

Friedrich Nietzsche, writing in the 1880s, foretold a time when 'psychology shall be recognized again as the queen of the sciences, for whose service and preparation the other sciences exist'.[1] As always with this 'dancing' philosopher, the statement invites different interpretations. It seems to say that psychology is the end point of knowledge, yet it gives no hint as to what this psychology is. It appears a prophecy about individuality and ethics, both a belief and a demand that disciplined truth, that is, science, should and will lead a few elect people out of the Christian and bourgeois moral framework of the age to build life on what actually is the being of a person. Nietzsche expected psychology to reveal the true feelings and motives underlying what people do, in contrast to the polite tales normally told. He initiated what was later known as the hermeneutics of suspicion, and this suspicion was directed against many ideals and sentiments common in the nineteenth century. Certainly elevating psychology as a science, Nietzsche did not have in mind the laboratory experimentation, the physiological psychology or the statistical studies of individual difference then developing and that were to support claims about psychology's scientific status over the next century. Nor did he foretell the huge number of practices in therapy, childcare, education, management and lifestyle that were to give shape to psychological society, society organised and administered around the psychological activity of individuals. Rather, Nietzsche proposed a dangerous experiment: he offered the future to an individual who could with honesty and dignity look himself in the face (for Nietzsche it was a he), not a self-indulging individual but a self-questioning, self-'overcoming' individual. The future, he proposed, lay not, as Christian, Jew and Muslim hold, in the hands of the one God, nor in reason as a historically transcendent reality, nor in the material world transformed by science and technology, nor in collective aspirations to nation, community or humanity. Rather, a future that would really be able to claim knowledge of truth belonged to 'the will to power' that lies at the root of the individual psyche.

This was, and is, radical. Nietzsche took the theme of psyche as his own, and he developed it far beyond what most of his contemporaries imagined or allowed. In so doing, he drew on, if often enough to mock and throw overboard, a century and more of changing ideas about being human. I characterise the subject as being human, not the self or mind, seeking a term under the cover of which to describe the historical, contingent ways apparently basic notions as self, mind and individual acquired the prominence they did in the nineteenth century, with a palpable legacy in the present. There was no natural reality of self or mind or individual discovered in the nineteenth (or in any other) century. Nor is the theme simply the history of psychology. The creation of a discipline and profession of psychology, in all its variety, is itself part of the story.

Moreover, there is no thought isolated from practice: just as practice is the mother of thought, so thought about what is human recreates the thinking human. An ideal history would therefore take account of how people lived, and how that changed. All I shall do, though, is emphasise a central feature of nineteenth-century intellectual culture, the ardent belief that thinking and knowledge make a difference, that they shape individual agency and, in so doing, achieve value.

For exposition, I organise this historical sketch under three headings: idealism, naturalism and practices of the self. I use these headings to suggest ways in which the elaboration of discourse about psychological life contributed to recognisably modern, twentieth- and twenty-first-century presumptions about individuality, self and mind.

The nineteenth century stands out for the range and quantity of its publications and readers. This was the case for books and also for journals, and 'the thick journals' (to use a Russian expression for widely published and read fortnightly, monthly or quarterly 'high-brow' periodicals) carried a high-level of detail and debate to communities only slowly accepting a division between specialist and non-specialist, amateur and professional. Throughout the century, and at all levels of society, with the partial exception of the very lowest, and sometimes in the very highest, there was a formidable commitment to education. Reading and education were themselves practices creating individuality, for women and children as well as men, even if opportunity varied enormously. With the spread of literacy, these activities became the means for each person to advance capacities of self and achieve some level of agency. Changes in the technology of printing and distribution put the written word, often illustrated, into the hands of everyone able to read or to listen to someone who could read, and people borrowed from lending libraries when they could not afford to purchase.

Institutions for formal education greatly expanded in many countries, especially when national interests encouraged the setting up of compulsory schooling. There were new institutions for training people for work and specialist knowledge, and many of these became the universities of the industrial centres. (In England, compulsory schooling dates from the Elementary Education Act of 1880, though extensive provisions for schooling preceded this, as in other countries.) Beginning in the opening years of the century, the universities expanded and transformed (the University of Berlin opened in 1809–10, University College, London, in the 1820s), establishing institutions for learning at the highest level. These universities were committed to a combination of teaching and research as a cultural value in its own right, a system that lasted in substantial respects until the 1980s. This created university teaching as a profession – an expert service from trained scholars offered for the public good in exchange for social status and independence to pursue the truth.

One consequence, in practice, was discipline formation, the structuring of knowledge into specialised departments. This brought with it challenges, often and disturbingly said to be unaddressed, to demonstrate the relations between different areas of knowledge and the relations between expert scholarship, the newly constituted second-class 'amateur' interest in learning and the public interest. There were initially hopes that philosophy would be the unifying, rational force; but as the specialist sciences, the natural sciences and the human sciences and humanities alike (or, roughly, in German, *Naturwissenschaften* and *Geisteswissenschaften*, and in French, *sciences physiques* and *sciences morales* or *sciences humaines*), appeared to make rapid progress and have social impact, in ways philosophy did not, many scholars preferred to invest in the empirical sciences. These institutional and disciplinary developments changed the social framework of both informal and systematic thought about the mind and the self.

Idealism

The Abrahamic religions, passed down as living cultures from earlier centuries, posited the soul, created by God and answerable to God and to the laws of his divinely instituted communities, as the individual human essence. Under the influence of ancient philosophy, thought about the soul was not narrow and dogmatic but at the centre of debate about the nature of life, of immortality and of intellect and reason as the capacities that marked humankind's special place between the material world below and the spiritual world above. The language of the soul persisted in religious communities, and it also flourished in sensitive everyday human relations, where it voiced the preciousness of the subjective world of passionate and aesthetic feelings, and also of devotion to poetry, music, art and novels as the shared and refined expression of feeling.

A wide range of nineteenth-century thinkers, however, took reason to be the core of what creates a person as a self. Philosophical discussion of reason was transformed and given its canonical modern statement by Immanuel Kant, and he separated analysis of reason from both theological and psychological discussion of the soul. The philosophers known as the German idealists, notably J. G. Fichte, F. W. J. Schelling and G. W. F. Hegel, took this further, advancing, in their terms, the logical-rational, as opposed to faith-bound or psychological, analysis of the human essence. Fichte undertook the most extreme attempt to derive all science from the prior reality of the 'I', claiming in logic that the 'I', understood as the active and striving being, had to be the starting point of knowledge. For knowledge, he instructed, 'attend to yourself: turn your attention away from everything that surrounds you and towards your inner life; this is the first demand that philosophy makes of its discipline'.[2]

This was language that easily became, and was often understood to be, psychological – language recommending the empirical study of the psyche. Indeed, throughout the century, most authors did not sharply differentiate philosophical and psychological, rational and empirical, treatments of the self. Only late in the century, in the work of Gottlob Frege and others, was there the clearly articulated declaration (going back to arguments in Kant), opposing 'psychologism', that logical and empirical statements are categorically distinct.

Idealist approaches to the self underwrote two significant aspects of higher education in the German-language world, followed elsewhere, if with local adaptations. The first was philosophical anthropology, a name for the science of reasoning about humankind concerned with the human spirit (*Geist, esprit*), the spirit of creative activity in individual persons and in cultural life collectively. Artistic genius stood as a popular model for the activity of spirit, while individual peoples, increasingly imagined as nations, were thought to possess a 'national spirit'. It was presupposed that spirit had rational content and unfolded over the centuries in the achievement of language, political civilisation, the arts and the sciences. Such thought gave an identity and a place to individuals and peoples as participants in progress.

The second idealist dimension was commitment to *Bildung* (roughly, 'formation'), a value and goal of integrated thought and action, the harmony of the individual and the harmony of the historical community of which the individual was intrinsically part. Thus, if the writings of the idealists at times had a dauntingly opaque philosophical character, they nevertheless added authority to a very widely distributed faith in the essential capacity of 'the human spirit' to make progress. Very significantly, this way of thought gave identity and meaning to both individuals and communities. It markedly contributed to binding the individual to national aspirations by envisaging the nation as the bearer of the spirit of a people with shared historical roots. Idealists found in language and in the arts of language, especially poetry, the native voice of the true identity of a person as part of a particular community. Hence, for example, the enormous importance of Aleksandr Pushkin, writing in the language of the people, not in French, in the 1820s and 1830s, for the sense of Russian identity and Russian character.

Philosophical anthropology maintained strong connections with religious faith, though in dialogue with it rather than through a stable relationship. Many discussions of identity and progress began to refer to the human spirit without implying any particular theological commitment. In social worlds emphatically divided by status, race, class, gender, political agency and education, discussion enforced division as much as it encouraged a feeling of common humanity. It depended on local context. For many conservatives, the ideal of the human was something achieved, at best, by special individuals and elite groups of people, and they demanded that the masses defer to this reality. Liberal reformers, by contrast, looked to national independence, economic exchange, legislation and education to make access to the ideal open to all. At its most radical, the philosophical anthropology of the young Karl Marx underpinned a revolutionary programme that had as its ideal the achievement of true humanity, though the political movement that followed was at times notorious for sacrificing individuals to the march of collective history. Looking forward to 'the practical overthrow of the actual social relations which give rise to this idealistic humbug', Marx turned to the argument that human identity comes from the ways people 'produce their means of subsistence': 'What they are … coincides with their production, both with what they produce and with how they produce.'[3] Nevertheless, he retained the ideal of a cultured, fulfilled person, a person free to choose rather than bound in exploited labour.

Idealism frequently had romantic expression, romantic in the sense of referring to individual lives shaped around intimate personal feelings, and romantic in the sense of supporting an aesthetic and moral culture ('Romanticism') that valued personal sensibility and creativity. Such expression profoundly informed the modern conception of the individual self. In rich imagery, romantic writing envisaged each self a 'lamp', shining with its own source of light, rather than a 'mirror', merely reflecting the passing impact of experiences. To be sure, almost no earlier writer on soul and mind had treated the person as completely passive; John Locke, to take the key instance, had attributed to the mind the active capacity of reflection along with the capacity to receive sensations. Idealist and romantic writers, however, took over descriptive analysis of mind in terms of active faculties (earlier understood as faculties of the soul), broadly divided into cognitive, affective and conational (or volitional), and stressed the desiring, active modalities.

Writing and teaching with increased frequency under the heading of psychology, authors markedly enriched attention to the affective and volitional side of the life of mind. The English poet, Samuel Taylor Coleridge, influenced by Schelling's philosophy and in dialogue with the poetic sensibility he developed with William Wordsworth, most clearly carried this into the British setting. For Coleridge, the free self was the ground of knowledge: 'If then I know myself through myself, it is contradictory to require any other predicate of self but that of self-consciousness ... The self-conscious spirit therefore is a will; and freedom must be assumed as a *ground* of philosophy, and can never be deduced from it.'[4] In France, Maine de Biran, building on the work of a group of intellectuals, the *idéologues*, who had sought a comprehensive theory of human nature with which to order post-revolutionary society, turned introspectively to 'inner experience'. In experience, he determined on the sense of volition as the irreducible ground of being human. Revealing much about this way of conceiving individual identity, he wrote down intimate reflections in a diary, a diary that aimed, as one of its objectives, to lay out a psychology. 'Psychology is thus a science of interior facts', the science of the 'I' ('*le moi*').[5] The diary, in this like the novels of his contemporary, Stendhal (Marie-Henri Beyle), stressed the riches, and rich confusions, of the inner life that created, while it expressed, identity.

Romantic idealism gave particular prominence to 'genius', the special ability of the spirit of a remarkable individual to create, or indeed to love or to wage war; yet it also set out ideals that every person could feel and imitate, fostering her or his own individuality, or *personnalité*, a word in use in French. The characters of novels, such as Pechorin in Mikhail Lermontov's *A Hero of Our Time* (1840) or Charles Dickens' Mr Pickwick (first serialised, then published in book form in 1836), became models of individuality, individuality that nevertheless exemplified local or national characteristics with which readers could identify or on which they could pass judgement.

An idealist sensibility to nature also profoundly influenced the social process of shaping character. As industrial production and a massive shift to urban living took hold, first in Britain and then elsewhere, Nature (with a capital 'N') became in imagination the repository of ideals of purity, naturalness and truth. In Wordsworth's poetry, or in the writings of John Ruskin or Ralph Waldo Emerson, sensibility to nature, formalised in an aesthetics of the natural world, became the touchstone of the moral life. Belief that one might find who one truly is, and thereby set a course for one's true humanity, in the presence of nature, took firm hold. Thus, beginning in the 1840s, generations of young people, a number of extremely tough and determined women included, employed local guides and opened up the Alps, and then other ranges, to mountaineering. Leslie Stephen, who enjoyed scrambling alone, described the mountains as 'felt rather than perceived ... like the tapestry of some gorgeous chamber which one watches with half-closed eyes'; and, more sternly, he recognised the power of nature to form character – 'the mountains represent the indomitable force of nature to which we are forced to adapt ourselves'.[6]

As Stephen's feelings when he climbed high above the snowline exemplify, belief in the innate capacity of the spirit in each person had strong moralistic content. This, indeed, gives the notion of being 'Victorian' one of its central components. It was far from a uniquely British phenomenon. Belief in the obligation to do one's duty in God's world gave rise to and merged with belief in the innate capacity of spirit to direct individuals according to their duty and responsibility within the social order. This had long been enacted in legal systems and in the enforcement of political power. In the nineteenth century, the language of responsibility and policing more clearly and more often took psychological form. In bourgeois society, especially in the respectable middle class and among those aspiring to belong to it, people learned to be self-conscious of themselves as willing and hence responsible selves. They also learned, dealing with people in whom will and responsibility appeared minimal or absent, people like children, the mentally ill, the uneducated working classes, colonial subjects and, in certain respects, women, to develop practices of management in schools, asylums, administration and the family. Management ensured that a competent individual took control. As the century passed, the claim became more and more common that this control over individuals required expertise, the kind of medical, educational, criminological and psychological expertise needed to identify, to know and thus to regulate different human types.

The leadership of both the Orthodox and Catholic branches of Christianity set itself against new ways of thought about mind and spirit for much of the century. Nevertheless, in the 1880s, a new pope directed Catholic intellectuals to shape an academic response to modernity, and this (especially at the University of Louvain, or Leuven, in Belgium under F.-F.-J. Mercier) recreated the medieval synthesis, built on knowledge of the soul as the principle of reason, of Thomas Aquinas. In Orthodox Russia, in the last decades of the century, there was a strong move, led by Vladimir Solov'ev, to bring philosophical idealism into harmony with the mystical traditions of the church.

Long before, at the beginning of the century, Friedrich Schleiermacher, in Protestant Berlin, had inspired a reinterpretation of the essence of religion as primarily an affective or emotional reality. This subsequently opened up a conception of Jesus as the ideal human personality, the model for ordinary people of how to live well and to develop individual character and the capacity for love. Strikingly, when 'the new psychology', forms of psychology claiming scientific status, became established in the decades before 1900, not a few priests turned to embrace it in the hope that it would address the emotional and existential concerns of their congregations, and they did not turn away as from a threat to Christian faith. This influenced the way a field of psychology of religion developed, from the 1890s to the 1920s, with William James' *The Varieties of Religious Experience* (1902) as its masterpiece.

Naturalism

No one should underestimate the persistence, into the twentieth century and beyond, in everyday discourse and personal relations and in the social institution of law, of historical presuppositions originating with notions of soul, spirit and will. Yet, also, no one should doubt the impact of science in the nineteenth century, science that would seem to have no place for such notions. If it is a commonplace to refer to the nineteenth century as an age of scientific progress, it is a commonplace that smoothes over deep tensions and ambiguities about both science and progress. These tensions and ambiguities were extensively and passionately debated.

In modern English, 'science' is more or less equivalent to 'natural science' (and claims to knowledge or expertise based or modelled on it). By contrast, in the nineteenth century, as still in continental European usage, 'science' denoted systematic and disciplined knowledge with a claim to truth, and science thus included subjects in the humanities like history and philology as much as the emerging specialities of physics, geology, physiology and such like.

The whole range of the sciences had consequences for thought about human nature. Thus, a very important instance of the impact of science – on some estimates more important than the impact of Darwin – was the impact of 'the higher criticism', systematic historical study, based on analysis of the content and provenance of the available primary sources, of the life of

Jesus. The reconfiguration of Jesus as a historical, as opposed to divine, personage had consequences for all aspects of personal lives ordered on scriptural authority. In addition to this, though, there was indeed an articulate, intense awareness of the manner in which the natural sciences were making huge strides, advancing knowledge of the history of the earth and of animals and plants, unifying the forces of nature in the science of energy, revealing the chemical structure of life and propounding the germ theory of disease. For Christian observers, the question was whether all this new knowledge constituted real progress, that is, moral and spiritual progress. The English geologist Adam Sedgwick was extreme, but not alone, in reacting to early evolutionary theory as having 'annulled all distinction between physical and moral': it left, he felt, the personal moral life and Christian society without meaning.[7] Work in natural science indeed transformed what was thought about human nature in ways that made reference to psyche, soul and the human spirit problematic.

By 'naturalism', I denote belief that 'the nature' of being a person is the source of values to live by, it being understood that this nature originates in the world as natural scientists portray it. It is the theory that values are immanent in nature. (The contrast is with beliefs that locate the source of values in a transcendent god or spirit, or in the nature of humanity as understood in a different way, for example, in Aristotelian thought, or as created by history of civilisation.) This position in the nineteenth century had roots especially in English-speaking intellectual culture, going back to Hobbes and Locke, amplified in the Scottish and French Enlightenments and further elaborated in the political economy and utilitarian ethical, legal and social programmes promoted by Jeremy Bentham, James Mill, John Stuart Mill and their successors.

Idealists and writers influenced by Locke alike (I generalise) thought within the frame of what one may call the Cartesian ego: the knowing self is a principle that must be supposed to be prior to knowledge, and acquiring knowledge therefore involves shaping or looking on an 'outer' world from 'within' a knowing self, a 'subject' in cognitive relation with 'objects'. Within this frame, the idealists gave logical priority to the reasoning self, while English-language writers mostly argued from the base of the experiential self. Those who I call naturalists described the self as the sum of conscious experience, experience that leads to action, they maintained, as a consequence of the feelings of pleasure and pain that are intrinsic to it. For the naturalist, human nature consisted of the capacities to have and to respond to experience. Following from this, the utilitarians deduced that what is good is what increases pleasure, or happiness, and decreases pain; and it was then a small step to conclude that the greatest good, and the goal of social arrangements, should be the greatest happiness of the greatest number of people. The outcome was a way of thought providing a rational calculus for the formulation and assessment of individual ethical action and social policy. The natural self, with its affective responses to the world it finds itself in, provides what it is necessary to know in order to make both material and moral progress. The task, which many nineteenth-century writers took up, was therefore to understand human nature more fully, beginning, as Alexander Bain, the Scottish exponent of the psychological basis of this way of thought explained, with 'a systematic and precise account of the states of human consciousness, – a Natural History of the Feelings'.[8] The argument was enormously influential in gathering authority for the psycho-logical and social sciences, not least economics, from the late nineteenth cen-tury to the present. It powerfully voiced and reinforced individualism: the means and purpose of social policy is the pleasures and pains of individuals. It provided the template for Darwin's own thought about human nature and the mechanism of evolution. Yet, then and now, critics held that it was an impoverished view of human desire and aspiration, the ideology of a capit-alist view of the self rather than the means to realise human ends.

Naturalistic argument to bring knowledge of the self, in moral as well as in factual respects, into line with knowledge of nature was at the heart of the debate over evolutionary theory. Evolutionary science, in the most literal way, located the origin of what it was to be human in nature. If there are large complexities to the historical story and to philosophical examination of what evolutionary knowledge implies, in the public domain, horror and humour that 'man is a monkey' had a field day. Charles Darwin, as by far the most authoritative and empirically grounded writer on evolution, then became, as he has continued to be, the figurehead for a naturalistic concep-tion of human identity.

Evolutionary naturalists pushed towards understanding mind as the col-lective term for a range of adaptive processes, shared with the animals, rather than for a number of faculties giving humans unique human capacity for reason and morality. They argued that the examination of self should concern not the subjective sensibility of spirit or abstract reason, but activity of mind in making a difference to life. This promoted a shift in psychology from the study of mental content to the study of mental function. In philo-sophical reflection, it directed questions, including questions about the self, away from judging truth in connection with an ideal and towards judging truth in terms of what knowledge makes possible. It pointed towards the appreciation of moral codes as means of adaptation rather than absolute standards. The attempt to be systematic about these ways of thinking then created the philosophy called American pragmatism. James gave this its most accessible form, relating it to personal concerns in 'The Will to Believe', a lecture (1896) that related the idea of the self to a choice about what to believe. This was a long way from the positing of rational spirit with which the century had opened.

Many people, who held implicitly if not explicitly to some species of idealism, tarred scientists with the brush of 'materialism'. They feared that scientists treated the self as if it were nothing but the product of the chance relations of material stuff giving rise to one experience rather than another. In fact, few scientists accepted being labelled in this way. They took cover in philosophical theories of matter that denied it was the crude stuff their critics supposed it was, while in day-to-day life they acted, at least as much as anyone else, as if there were a human spirit. 'Materialism' was first and foremost a social label, used to brand an intellectual position with, at best, the odour of philistine working-class or bourgeois culture, and at worst, the stench of radical and revolutionary politics. Given Victorian sensibility about the romantic, ideal and volitional self, 'materialist' was a self-description only for those who put themselves firmly into opposition to the established order.

All the same, there was endless debate about how mind or soul could be said to have relations with matter or brain. In English, from the late seventeenth century, 'mind' rather than 'soul' was increasingly the word of choice in disciplined empirical and philosophical discussion of the content of reason, passion and will. Such discussion took place in the nineteenth century under the title of mental philosophy or mental science; only from the mid-century was it, to any significant extent, called psychology in the English-speaking world. Reference to 'mind' marks the spread of naturalism in English-language thought. Taking the argument further is difficult, however, because of the absence of exact cognates in other languages: French continued with *âme* (soul) and *esprit* (spirit), German, *Geist* (spirit) and *Gemüt* (mind), Russian, *um* or *razum* (intellect), and so on. There was no common language or body of knowledge with the self as its subject. Rather, discussions that in modern eyes have psychological content were part of a process shaping bodies of knowledge. I now picture this shaping, which significantly expanded naturalistic views of mind and self while proposing new methods for their study, under four headings: evolutionary theory, physiological psychology, experimental psychology and the study of individual differences.

Darwin's argument on human evolution, in *The Descent of Man* (1871), turned on showing empirically that there were no differences in kind, though there were obvious differences in degree, between the mental (or psychological) life of animals and humans. If there were no difference in kind,

Darwin argued, there was no impediment to accepting that humans have evolved from animals. Animals possess memory, he thought it clear, show affection, reason, exhibit curiosity and so on. Language, consciousness, conceptual thought and moral action gave him pause, though he discerned their roots in animals too. Some readers thought the argument demeaned being human; others found in it a grand vision of humanity as the highest stage of cosmic progress. Evolutionary belief implied that the self derives a significant portion of its character from the animal past, character that cannot be shed even if it can be regulated or inhibited. Writers pointed to what they maintained was the natural instinct of aggression, or to sexual differences, for instance. This enriched and underwrote with science prevalent imagery of the tenuous control of the mind over the body, the willing self over the instincts, civilisation over barbarism, reason over madness, male logic over female emotion and so on. These polarities were deeply embedded in the rhetoric that went with hierarchical social order. Yet writers of a radical political persuasion also pointed to the natural characteristics of individuals. Petr Kropotkin, the anarchist Russian prince in exile in London, focused on an innate capacity for sympathy, the basis, he believed, for social co-operation – if only the distortions imposed by governments could be eliminated. This was an influential statement of anarchism.

The emphasis in evolutionary thought on inheritance strengthened belief that individual selves and social order related through parentage, race and biological factors generally. Male physicians, for example, on the basis of their claim to knowledge about the different natural bodily economies of the two sexes, quite commonly opposed women's call for education and emancipation. Belief about the inherited character of individual selves reached something of a high point as the twentieth century opened, just as it was to do again a century later. In addition, acceptance that inheritance of acquired characteristics was a mechanism causing the evolution of species, the view put forward by J.-B. Lamarck at the beginning of the century, accepted to a fair extent by Darwin and given pride of place in Herbert Spencer's evolutionary vision, had a place for mental activity in bringing about long-term change, and this enhanced its appeal. If there were such inheritance, it was thought, individual effort (but also individual failure, for example, alcoholism) would have consequences for subsequent generations. By contrast Darwin's (and A. R. Wallace's) mechanism of natural selection appeared to leave the direction of evolution to chance, as people said, that is, to the working of natural laws blind to human interests.

The comparative psychology of animals and humans ambivalently elevated the animals and mocked the human spirit. Before attributing this to evolutionary theory, it is worth remembering just how familiar the evidence was to ordinary people, who lived in close proximity to working animals, kept pets or used commonplace language to describe people, for example, as 'wild beasts' or 'as gentle as a dove'. The evolutionary framework, however, systematically shifted descriptive language for the mind away from capacities like reason and will towards mental functions – perception, cognition, attention, etc. – understood as processes with consequences for behaviour, processes that could be observed in animals. For the evolutionist, it was behaviour that appeared to matter, and the turn to study behaviour firmly united terms for the analysis of the individual person with the animal world. This gave shape to much of twentieth-century psychology.

A second area of scientific work in the nineteenth century, physiological psychology, contributed to later psychology. From ancient times, medicine had taken for granted the intimate relation, if not in some way identity, of soul, or mind, and body. The physician P.-J.-G. Cabanis, in his *Rapports du physique et du moral de l'homme* (presented to his colleagues in Paris between 1796 and 1802), gave a classic reformulation, which drew special attention to the internal bodily feelings and their importance for the well-being of the self. Then, from about the 1830s, physicians trained with some knowledge of the emerging discipline of physiology turned to the study of the brain and nervous system as the empirical, factual rather than speculative, preparation for the study of mind and self. They sought knowledge in the light of reflex action and localisation of function models of the nervous basis of mind. Bain in Britain and Hermann Lotze in Germany are examples of transitional figures, writers on mind rather than medicine (though Lotze had a medical degree), who promoted descriptive psychology tied to knowledge of nervous activity. Many writers were especially interested in abnormal minds, and because so little was in fact known about brain and nerves, in spite of large claims about progress, the clinical case, the living experiment provided by abnormal function, played a large part in imagination about mind. If a considerable number of claims turned out to be speculation, physiological psychologists nevertheless shifted the attention of those interested in character and identity on to the body.

It is tempting to think that much of what can be said about physiology and naturalistic views of the self in the nineteenth century can also be said about the neurosciences in recent decades. The difference surely lies in the modern capacity to re-engineer the brain prosthetically and chemically, and equip it with information technology, re-configuring the self as a construction, indeed, as a commercial product. The similarity lies with the debates: what is the relation of mind to brain, are humans automatons or moral agents, what is inherited and what is acquired in individual development, is there no essential self? In the nineteenth century, such questions provoked limitless disagreement. Debate, not agreed answers, gave people the vocabulary, the phrasing, with which to frame discussion of the self. They often enough wrote and talked with a startling degree of self-righteousness, intolerance and ill-founded confidence; but they also created an open and optimistic culture with faith that it was indeed possible to debate in public and to arrive at answers.

Two examples. In 1863, Ivan Mikhailovich Sechenov published 'Reflexes of the Brain' in a Russian medical journal, the first version of a subsequently expanded essay on representing all mental activity in terms of the reflex model, in which a stimulus automatically leads to action. (Sechenov was important in Russia for his contribution to making physiology part of scientific medicine.) His critics, liberal as well as conservative, said that the reflex model rendered the human person a machine, which performs from necessity, and that this threatened belief in the individual responsibility required for social order. Sechenov denied this threat and, in effect, argued that human progress, moral as well as material, would be better served by advancing knowledge of the natural workings of the self.

A decade later, Thomas Henry Huxley read an address to the British Association for the Advancement of Science on 'The Hypothesis that Animals Are Automata and Its History'. He clearly extended what he said about animal automata to humans and ended up with the notorious comparison of conscious awareness to the sound when a bell of a clock is struck, which pictured the conscious life of mind as a decorative feature without causal consequences. By contrast, in his energetic life, Huxley (like Sechenov) fiercely and consistently exercised the volition of a rational self. It will hardly do to dismiss this as inconsistency: this was the general form of the culture of individualism – a necessitarian view of causal relations alongside a personal culture of dynamic agency. The debates make clear, in retrospect, that statements about the self with a claim to factual status were also endorsements of social values. For many of the spokesmen for natural science, like Sechenov and Huxley, those values were naturalistic ones.

Physiological psychology, along with evolutionary theory, promoted views of the self grounded in embodied experience. This was, of course, far from new. Nevertheless, the empirical arguments were advanced and received as having powerful new authority. In dispute was how far, and in what ways, the embodied self was intrinsically a social self. There was a conception of the self as literally bounded by its individual body, a picture of the self looking out through the windows of the senses on to the world and becoming a social self only by interaction with other such selves. This was a profoundly individualist view, perhaps the kind of view appropriate to self-made entrepreneurs. Opposed to this, though existing side by side with it, was the view of the self as by nature being of a particular social type, a type set by the group (race, nation, gender, class and so forth) in which the mind was embodied. The latter position reached its extreme at the end of the century in the writings of numerous theorists of race, and also in the work of the Italian scientist and reformer, Cesare Lombroso, who classified criminality, prostitution, genius and social phenomena generally in terms of biological types.

A third contribution to naturalistic views of the self came from experimental psychology, a collective activity from the 1860s or so but acquiring large-scale institutional presence only in the twentieth century. In the nineteenth century, in Europe, but less in North America, this science continued to be intellectually and institutionally connected to philosophy. It was initially primarily a German science; by the 1890s, though, much the largest expansion was taking place in the United States. If in the short run the impact on publicly articulated notions of the self was small, in the long run it provided the means to treat the self as analysable into parts, or functions, each of which was subjected to quantitative investigation. It dissolved any empirical conception of self as unitary reason. At the end of the nineteenth century, 'the new psychology' was extremely diverse and generated a multiplicity of cross-cutting descriptions of the contents and functions of mind. It was common to comment that psychology was a science in its earliest stages.

German experimental psychologists pursued a general science of mind, that is, knowledge of a sort of idealised mind. Alongside this, however, throughout the century, there was a large interest in individual differences, in the individual character of actual selves and in the distinctive characteristics of groups such as national peoples (*les peuples* or *das Volk*). This made a very large contribution to naturalistic ways of thought about mind and self. The systematic, quantified study of individual differences began in the nineteenth century, with the work in the 1830s of the Belgian astronomer and social scientist, Adolphe Quetelet, followed by that of Francis Galton and later by the much more refined mathematical techniques of Karl Pearson and others. A precise language was created, statistics, for describing individual selves in relation to the characteristics of populations. Measuring individual differences, and then mapping the distribution of differences in a population, investigators showed that each self, however individual, could be assigned a place in relation to a norm, or median point, in the distribution. Techniques, which began as the description of differences in character like the height of conscripted soldiers, demonstrated regularity in the distribution of such apparently individual events as murders. The character and conduct of individuals in social groups conformed to law-like patterns that could be measured and pictured (as in the bell-shaped curve of normal distribution). Modern statistics developed and began to play a large part in rendering selves subject to precise study and precise administrative policies.

Nineteenth-century observers were enormously impressed by the way individual events or characteristics, which to everyday perception looked to be subject to chance, emerged as part of an ordered pattern. If individuals exercised will, as people commonly believed they did, and thus acted as moral selves, en masse they nevertheless conformed to a predictable order. The study of the self, it appeared, would have to be a social science. In the 1890s, Émile Durkheim, opposing Spencer's individualistic approach to social and ethical evolution, systematically laid out the conceptual and methodological arguments for this social science, arguments that made the very notion of the individual self a social phenomenon.

The statistical definition of normality powerfully reinforced belief that it was possible objectively to identify abnormality. The abnormal self was certainly a nineteenth-century preoccupation. Enhanced methods of clinical observation in medicine, associated with the Paris medical school in the opening years of the century, together with the growth of institutions like state schools, asylums and prisons, which grouped individuals where they could be systematically observed, brought abnormality into empirical focus. The study of the abnormal became the royal road to a general science of the normal self. This was exemplified in the study of neuroses, study that led to a range of so-called depth psychologies in the early years of the twentieth century. Sigmund Freud then achieved a reputation for a way of thinking about mind, psychoanalysis, which, in attributing so much to the unconscious, questioned the unity of the self and pictured the self divided against itself. But this emphasis had a long history before Freud. So much is this so, and so important were techniques and beliefs connected to the individual character of selves, that I discuss the issues in a separate section. If both idealist and naturalist reasoning upheld belief in the norms of a unified self, many people were also well aware just how malleable and fragile that unity was.

Practices of the Self

There was recognition of the value of the individuality of each person, but it was very far from universal. In Russia, for example, the decree ending serfdom dates from 1861, while in the United States legal slavery ended with the conclusion of the Civil War in 1865. Throughout the century, authoritarian governments, rising nationalist sentiment, racism and colonial occupations fostered collectivist rather than individualist ideals. Yet observers a century later were to think of the century as bequeathing a culture of individualism, exemplified, to take British examples, in the entrepreneurial confidence of the engineer Isambard Brunel or in the brilliance and eccentricity of Sherlock Holmes. The individualist and authoritarian stances were not at all incompatible. Thus, the British liked to glorify their individuality in order to demonstrate their collective superiority, and many fierce individuals (such as David Livingstone and Cecil Rhodes) were firm proponents of the imposition of the collective institutions of Christianity and Empire. I argue for the contribution to nineteenth-century thought of psychological techniques available to the individual, techniques taken up by a large public and not only by specialists. This connects to what was noted earlier about the development of psychological society.

The social movement known as phrenology was exemplary. Flourishing especially in Britain and the United States between the 1810s and 1840s, phrenology was a theory of individual differences holding that the strength of different mental capacities, for philanthropy or for memory, for example, reflected the size of the different parts of the brain in which each capacity is supposedly localised. It was further believed that the relative sizes of the parts of the brain were reflected in the conformation of the skull, and it was thus thought possible to read off a person's capacities and incapacities, a man or woman's character, by feeling, or even measuring, the bumps on the head. Phrenologists recreated the ancient art of physiognomy, reading character from appearance. They also consolidated public belief that there is no mind without brain – and no study of the self without study of its foundations in this organ of the body. It was a popular movement because it addressed the topic of individual character, of interest to everyone, a topic on which there was a huge reservoir of everyday ('folk') knowledge. Phrenology was a technique to acquire knowledge of character, on the basis of which to take eminently practical decisions about upbringing, schooling, career choice, illness, predilection for criminality and so on; the technique was relevant to both individuals and groups (studied by physical anthropologists who compared brain size and skulls from women and men and from different classes and ethnic groups in the second half of the century); and it undertook all this in terms accessible to ordinary people. Though critics indicted phrenologists for a deterministic way of thought that denigrated the unity and freedom of the soul, advocates emphasised that it put power, agency, into the hands of people. This double-face was to remain characteristic of the social life of modern theories of the self.

Phrenology was a kind of model of the practices the sociologist Nikolas Rose called 'governing the soul'. These practices did not develop in expert scientific communities, then to be imposed on the public as social control; rather, they developed within non-expert communities as accessible ways to manage individuals in their social relations or for individuals to manage themselves. The practices greatly contributed to an individualist way of thinking about the self, as they worked (insofar as one may think of them 'working') through the internalisation of patterns of understanding and control within individual selves. There was a publication industry on self-help, which merged with the literature of advice, the work of priests, physicians, moralists, pedagogues and writers of children's books, all of which aimed to equip the self with the tools and the energy to shape itself in line with social values and norms. Focused on the individual, the practices appeared non-political; in fact, though, they came to be most characteristic of liberal democracies that placed value on the individual as the locus of agency.

The writing of the nineteenth century overflowed with stories about the achievement of people, most definitely women as well as men, pulling themselves up socially and morally by their own bootstraps, by individual application of intelligence, discipline, will and spirit. Thomas Carlyle, the editor of Cromwell's letters and speeches, uniting idealism and exhortation, influenced a whole generation of English-language readers in the mid-century with a language of the self-determining hero. It perhaps hardly needs to be said, but, in spite of all this, local and national circumstances hugely influenced the degree to which individual effort had results. Desolation and hope destroyed abounded, as we know, for instance, from Anton Chekhov.

In what were still different German states in the first half of the century, and in France after the restoration of the monarchy in 1815, there was an extensive literature on psychology as the science of knowledge of the subjective self. This was a science of the feelings of individual selves known through reflection and introspection, building on knowledge represented in the arts of fiction, theatre and of illustration as much as on fact. The proponents of this science intended to provide a more empirical, and hence, they believed, constructive approach to philosophical questions, and to contribute the knowledge necessary for the way of life proper to a human being. In a discussion that later historians of philosophy were to identify as the basis of existentialism, Søren Kierkegaard, in *The Concept of Anxiety* (1844), subtitled 'a simple psychologically oriented deliberation', defined anxiety 'as freedom's self-disclosure of itself in possibility'.[9] Separating his study of 'subjective spirit' from theology (concerned with the dogmatics of the soul), Kierkegaard in effect translated the Christian concern with sin into discourse about subjective states of the individual self. In France in the same years, led by Victor Cousin, an eclectic, moralistic psychology based on the introspective analysis of the self was taught to teachers and promoted as preparation for sound philosophy. In Scotland and in the colleges of the eastern United States, mental science, with its descriptive analysis of mind, was a compulsory part of a young gentleman's education, designed to foster Christian character, social responsibility and the qualities necessary for leadership.

Yet another significant dimension of public debate about the self concerned numerous phenomena of altered states of consciousness (e.g. somnambulism), hypnotism, spiritualism and psychical (or, in later language, paranormal) experiences. Interest in mesmerism dated from the 1770s, and it acquired new life as the psychological phenomenon of hypnotism in the 1850s. Modern spiritualism dated from 1847. Dream analysis and mystic experiences were, of course, ancient, but writers from the late eighteenth century onwards once again found them an endless source of fascination The bizarre and the exceptional (like genius, like moral madness – as when a young mother kills her child), and exceptional states of consciousness (as in visions or the display of multiple personalities), all demanded to be accommodated by the notion of the self. At their extreme, such phenomena seemed to call the very notion into question, as Robert Louis Stevenson well understood in Dr Jekyll and Mr Hyde (1886).

Belief that there were hidden, unconscious aspects to mental life and to the self was widespread, in addition to the fact that there was ubiquitous adjectival reference to 'unconscious' nervous processes not accompanied by conscious awareness. Nevertheless, there continued to be religious and philosophical circles where such talk was thought, at best, questionable, a threat to rational moral discourse. Arthur Schopenhauer made this threat explicit in terms of philosophical argument itself. His metaphysical account of the self as the contingent expression of blind will, without individuality, published in The World as Will and Representation in 1818, had considerable influence half a century later. It conveyed a pessimistic vision of the human condition, in marked conflict with the hopes invested in reason and in self-help.

Pessimistic writers also stood out against the longings placed, across the social classes, in an unseen spirit world. Engaged in séances or activities like table-turning, groups of people and individual mediums claimed to extend the boundaries of the self and find wisdom and support in forces, also understood as selves, lying beyond the limits of the ordinary material world. Spiritualism was a technology of empowerment, especially but by no means only for women, of the affective self. It was akin to practices of religious conversion, or of hypnotic suggestion, that gave people a feeling of agency by breaking boundaries conventionally thought to delimit the self. These practices also prompted a large debunking literature from medical, scientific and psychological experts, a literature that put forward alternative stories about the self as vulnerable to deception and disorder and hence in need of a wise, expert guiding hand.

In these and other ways, people expressed who they were, and made choices about who they were to be, in practices of the self, practices increasingly couched in explicitly psychological language. If the practices were not always new, they had new forms and were more extensively spread in the nineteenth century. They fed into and reinforced an intense preoccupation at virtually all levels of society in 'character', a term with both individuals and groups as its referent. (The term 'personality' did not, at least in English, compete with it until the twentieth century.) Fictional writing, the diary and the letter were means for reflection on and debate about the character of selves; and so were the writings of physicians, educators and moralists, who never tired of putting pen to paper.

By beginning with a sketch of idealism, I stressed the continuity of much nineteenth-century discussion of the self with the monotheistic beliefs and philosophical thought of earlier centuries. Both naturalistic argument and disciplinary practices of the self cut into this. The result was unsettlement, destabilisation, open equally to optimistic and to pessimistic readings.

The optimism contributed to what was later to be called the Enlightenment project, the development of techniques of knowing, and their distribution through education, in order to shape the future, both political and intimate, of human relations. Educated people drew on the way of thought that had proved so successful in advancing the natural sciences in order to intervene in human life. In the nineteenth century, the project embraced the language of the human spirit: proponents did not doubt that this was the way forward for humanity in general and the moral individual in particular. In one of the syntheses of knowledge as knowledge of progress, for which the century is known, Auguste Comte thus combined a historical theory of the successive stages through which each of the sciences passes, before achieving positive knowledge, with a 'Religion of Humanity' founded on what he took to be universally shared sentiment or feeling.

For each expression of optimism, however, it is possible to find a matching statement of pessimism. The perpetuation or, as some observers argued, the expansion of gross poverty (leading to mass emigration from Europe), appalling housing conditions in many rapidly growing cities, the relentless growth in the numbers of the insane held in asylums, alcoholism, purported evidence for degeneration and even the ennui, restlessness and neurosis so often felt and portrayed in modern life, suggested limits to hopes for the self. In certain famous instances, this fostered critique of the belief that the human spirit, reason, knowledge of human nature or new technologies of the self were enough to ensure progress.

Fyodor Dostoevsky, now among the most widely read of these critics beyond the authors of the Bible and the Qur'an, began to be known in translation at the end of the century. Readers found in his fiction a view of the self that at one and the same time profoundly excited, because it discarded bourgeois niceties to portray the wild and variegated irrationality of the inner self, and shocked, because it implied that only a return to spiritual values could save humankind from disaster. Nietzsche's writing – to return to where this sketch began – started to be known at more or less the same time. There readers found both a call to life, portrayed in metaphors of dance, and the most searing critique of the Christian morality that had underpinned both idealist and naturalist approaches to the moral self throughout the century. Both Dostoevsky and Nietzsche adopted the individual as the subject of value, the category in terms of which to say what had to be said about being in the world, but, in revolt against the superficial notions of the self with which they felt surrounded, they pointed in radically divergent directions. Dostoevsky, providing unequalled portraits of the disorder and sheer contradictions of the forces at play in the self, turned towards an ideal of the unified Christian soul. Nietzsche, though reasoning on behalf of truth with a rigour that led him to question claims to truth as then understood, and particularly to question belief that introspection had a superior claim as a way to arrive at it, provided terms in which to recognise the dissolution of the self, its contingent status and its construction in the service of drives and passions. For Nietzsche, as Gilles Deleuze observed, 'power is not what the will wants, but on the contrary, the one that wants in the will'.[10] Both Dostoevsky and Nietzsche exposed incoherence in the aspiration to make philosophical anthropology a coherent and systematic view of the self as the concrete, individualised instance of humanity. Yet, by the time they had readers at the end of the nineteenth century, belief that human self-knowledge lay with psychology, a science of mind, had become far too well embedded to be shifted by what they had to say. To the contrary, commentary represented them as if they themselves were psychologists.

NOTES

1 F. Nietzsche, *Beyond Good and Evil: Prelude to a Philosophy of the Future* [1886], trans. W. Kaufmann (New York: Vintage Books, 1966), sect. 23.

2 J. G. Fichte, *Science of Knowledge with the First and Second Introductions*, trans. P. Heath and J. Lachs (based on 3rd edn, 1802) (Cambridge: Cambridge University Press, 1982), p. 6.

3 K. Marx and F. Engels, *The German Ideology Parts I & III* [1845–6], ed. R. Pascal (New York: International Publishers, 1947), pp. 28–9, 7.

4 S. T. Coleridge, *Biographia Literaria or Biographical Sketches of My Literary Life and Opinions* [1817], ed. G. Watson (London: Dent, 1956), p. 153.

5 P. Maine de Biran, *Journal*, ed. Henri Gouhier, 3 vols. (Neuchâtel: Editions de la Baconnière, 1954–7), vol. 1, p. 148.

6 L. Stephen, *The Playground of Europe* [1871] (Oxford: Basil Blackwell, 1936), pp. 109, 181.

7 Quoted from Sedgwick's review, 'Natural History of Creation' [1845], in *Victorian Sensation: The Extraordinary Publication, Reception, and Secret Authorship of Vestiges of the Natural History of Creation* by J. A. Secord (Chicago: University of Chicago Press, 2000), p. 245; original italicised.

8 A. Bain, *The Senses and the Intellect* [1855], 2nd edn (London: Longman & Co., 1864), p. 88.

9 S. Kierkegaard, *The Concept of Anxiety: A Simple Psychologically Oriented Deliberation in View of the Dogmatic Problem of Hereditary Sin* [1844], trans. A. Hannay (New York: Liveright, 2014), p. 134.

10 G. Deleuze, *Nietzsche and Philosophy* [1963], trans. H. Tomlinson (London: Athlone Press, 1993), p. xi.

9

GREGORY CLAEYS

Social Darwinism

Introduction

Viewed retrospectively, the most influential thinkers of the nineteenth century were Karl Marx (1818–83) and Charles Darwin (1809–82). Two of
their central concepts, class struggle and evolution, both focused on the
idea of 'struggle', and clearly had some common origin, as Marx at least
recognised. Together they provided a definitive leitmotif for *fin de siècle*
Europe and America, whose inheritance was bequeathed to the twentieth
century, at least to 1945 (for Social Darwinism), and to 1991 (for Marxism).
These legacies are now mostly exhausted, however. Marx's relevance today
is limited.[1] Social Darwinism, tainted by its identification with eugenics
and the Holocaust, is even less popular. Both isms, in their worst and most
brutal incarnations, now appear harsh and punitive, sharing a common
condemnation of 'non-productive' groups (the idle poor, and some races;
and the idle rich, respectively) who became increasingly viewed as doomed
to extinction.

This chapter examines the origins and development of the language of
the 'survival of the fittest', and the concepts of scarcity, competition and
productivity from which it stems. Commencing with Malthus, it focuses
on Darwin and some of his followers and contemporaries. The quite varied
cluster of ideas we refer to as 'Social Darwinism' is often assumed to have
been deduced from Darwin's *On the Origin of Species* (1859) and even
more his *The Descent of Man* (1871). More loosely, they are also, however, metaphors describing an age of overcrowded urban masses, and the
search, especially in Germany, for *Lebensraum*, or space to expand; as well
as of the democracy of the crowd, and the constant disorder that technological modernity threatened throughout the period. United with ideas of
racial and class struggle these concepts fuelled a 'Machiavellian' morality of
expediency, where 'the end justifies the means', which would come to dominate the two most destructive ideologies of the twentieth century, Nazism

163

and Stalinism. To understand how this emerged we need some sense of how groups were designated as 'inferior' or 'unfit', and thus how political economy and racial ideology became interwoven. We will see that much of the ethos we associate with Social Darwinism was initially popularised by T. R. Malthus' *Essay on Population* (1798). Incorporated into the new science of political economy, whose authority gradually displaced that of theology across the century, this provided a social model based upon market competition that was easily assimilated into a quasi-scientific language of racial and international struggle during the later nineteenth century. By the *fin de siècle* period such ideas had come to serve as a primary defence for economic and cultural elites as well as an aristocratic radicalism stressing the need for 'higher types', which became associated with Friedrich Nietzsche in particular. They also became a principal justification for the most genocidal imperial occupations of the period, notably in Africa, as well as for warfare in Europe. By his death in 1882, Darwin himself came to accept some of the more negative implications of the 'survival of the fittest' concept. Others, however, turned the concept towards the deduction that humanity required a more co-operative ethos in order to evolve successfully.

The Origins: Competition and Political Economy

As defined by Mike Hawkins, the Social Darwinist world view consists in four key assumptions: (1) biological laws govern all organic nature, including humans; (2) the pressure of population growth on resources generates a struggle for existence among organisms; (3) physical and mental traits confer an advantage on their possessors in this struggle, or in sexual competition, which advantages can, through inheritance, spread through the population; (4) the cumulative effects of selection and inheritance over time account for the emergence of new species and the elimination of others.[2]

This standpoint needs to be augmented by considering how the language of race came to be coupled with assumptions about humanity's evolution as a species. The idea of 'favourable variants' or 'best types' within the species had no necessary bearing on race as such. But by the 1870s a civilisational narrative, in which so-called advanced, mostly European nations distinguished themselves from 'savage' or 'barbarian' peoples, merged into Social Darwinism to promote both a hardened form of racist discourse and an apology for genocide. This narrative initially began to gel in Robert Knox's *The Races of Men* (1850) and Joseph Gobineau's *Essay on the Inequality of the Human Races* (1853), both of which suggested more rigid, ontological racial categories and the natural predominance of Europeans over the rest of the world. In the United States, racialist ideas of

'Manifest Destiny' came to play a major role in the expansion westwards of settlers and conquerors. Such developments, however, merely extended profound racial prejudices already evident by the 1830s (and much earlier) in North America, Australia and North Africa. From this perspective much of the racial discourse identified with Darwinism was a post facto justification of conquests already well under way by 1859, and indeed since the conquest of the 'new world' began in the late fifteenth century.

Any account of Social Darwinism must commence with the Reverend Thomas Robert Malthus' *Essay on Population*, a key source independently for both of the co-discoverers of natural selection, Charles Darwin and Alfred Russel Wallace. Malthus adapted the phrase, the 'struggle for existence', in the first edition of the book, published in 1798, in the context of scarcity of resources. In the second edition of the *Essay* (1803) he used the pretext to close the doors to newcomers to 'nature's mighty feast'.[3] Darwin recalled that in reading Malthus in 1838, 'being well prepared to appreciate the struggle for existence which everywhere goes on from long-continued observation of the habits of animals and plants, it at once struck me that under these circumstances favourable variations would tend to be preserved, and unfavourable ones to be destroyed. The result of this would be the formation of new species.'[4] In 1859 he thus described his own view as 'the doctrine of Malthus applied with manifold force to the whole animal and vegetable kingdoms'.[5] Wallace wrote that on recollecting in 1858 a passage from Malthus he had read some twelve years earlier 'it suddenly flashed upon me that this self-acting process would necessarily *improve the race*, because in every generation the inferior would inevitably be killed off and the superior would remain – that is, *the fittest would survive*'.[6]

'Fitness' eventually became the central concept in the new world view. Although it has earlier antecedents, the background to this idea, which is intertwined with conceptions of a work ethic and of the duty to labour, can be explored by introducing Adam Smith's extraordinarily influential discussion of productive and unproductive labour in the *Wealth of Nations* (1776). Here the process of capital accumulation and by extension social progress more generally were made contingent on maximising productive labour and minimising the unproductive labour of servants and others who made no physical object that could be exchanged in the market.[7] Malthus regarded it as 'natural and just' that those who possessed a surplus should normally only assist others in need who could themselves help create a surplus.[8] Here individuals were thus valued primarily in terms of their labour capacity and ability to increase social wealth. Idleness and parasitism on the part of the poor thence would be increasingly condemned by the well-to-do.

'Efficiency' would later come to define the 'fitness' of this group most exactly. 'Productivism' describes the overall set of ideas.[9]

Surprisingly, perhaps, radical and socialist critics of these assumptions rarely disagreed with this overall assessment of human worth. Most presumed that labour ought indeed to define the value of people's contribution to society. But in their view this also implied the eradication of the idle rich through universal mandatory labour. The parasitism of the idle aristocracy and of assorted opera-dancers and purveyors of pleasure had already been hinted at by Smith. (But whatever their other sins, Marx never accused the bourgeoisie of inactivity.) Moreover, besides classes, other groups, like more sedentary races, could be viewed as obstacles to the progress of the species or parasitic on production. Those reclining in the shade in the hotter climes were natural targets for such assumptions. Anti-Semitism, too, was often cast in these terms. The stage was set for the bloodbaths of race and class that would besmirch much of the subsequent century.

Malthus did not of course hint at improvements in physical type in the human species as a result of a struggle for resources. His categories are moral rather than ontological. The language of 'fitness', as suggesting the need to assist only those most likely to assist society's well-being, was however certainly present in the distinction between the 'deserving' and 'undeserving' poor that became central to the Poor Law Amendment Act (1834), in which Malthus' influence is clearly evident, and which demanded harsher treatment of the poor. With David Ricardo's *Principles of Political Economy and Taxation* (1817) Malthusian precepts were integrated into mainstream political economy. Now the idea of an inevitable struggle between landlords, capitalists and labourers for a larger share of the social product became central to the logic of social development. This became a key source for Marx's idea of class struggle. Even John Stuart Mill would regard a 'systematic antagonism' as 'the only condition under which stability and progressiveness can be permanently reconciled to one another', instancing François Guizot's account of the promotion of the 'spirit of liberty' 'by the struggles of the middle class'.[10] The general theme came increasingly to coincide with the spirit of the age. Commentators conceded by mid-century that: 'The struggle for existence of the lower and middle classes, at home, annually becomes more difficult as population increases and wealth consolidates in the hands of those already rich.'[11] The Russian radical Alexander Herzen went so far as to describe the system of aristocratic landholding as 'a more or less civilized form of cannibalism: a savage who eats his prisoner' being no different from landowners who drew enormous rents from their estates or manufacturers who grew rich at the expense of their workmen.[12]

What was true for classes domestically was equally so for nations at large. The idea that countries in the international arena were subject to laws of intense competition and thus the requirements of increasing efficiency was a commonplace in political economy by 1800.[13] Such competition was increasingly portrayed as a law of nature rather than the result of custom and convention. Here the natural sciences also furnished an idea of contest. Darwin noted that Charles Lyell's *Principles of Geology* (1833) already contained the idea of a 'universal struggle for existence'. The *Origin* and even more *The Descent of Man* (1871) then promoted the idea of a universal system of competing organisms in which strife, triumph and failure were constant.

It was not Darwin, however, but the social theorist Herbert Spencer who coined the term 'survival of the fittest', as an alternative to Darwin's 'struggle for existence'. As early as 1851, Spencer later recalled, he had reflected 'on the benefits resulting from survival of the fittest among mankind', adding that 'the survival of the fittest, as I construe it in its social applications, is the survival of the industrially superior and those who are fittest for the requirements of social life'.[14] His *Social Statics* (1851) described evolution as 'pitiless in the working out of good: a felicity-pursuing law which never swerves for the avoidance of partial and temporary suffering'. Here the need to conform to this 'law' is associated with a minimal government, laissez-faire political economy and hostility to poor relief and collectivism.[15] In 1852, writing on population, Spencer expressed the view that 'those left behind to continue the race are those in whom the power of self-preservation is the greatest – are the select of their generation'.[16] This brought him 'within measurable distance of Darwin's great contribution to biology'.[17] Reading Darwin then revealed the full consequences of the hypothesis. But Darwin's 'natural selection', thought Spencer, carried 'a decidedly teleological suggestion' not warranted by the theory itself, which his own phrase aimed to avoid.[18] Spencer is accordingly often not described as an advocate of 'Social Darwinism'. His *The Principles of Biology* (1864) described 'the preservation of favoured races in the struggle for life'. He later recapitulated that his general principle meant that: 'If left to operate in all its sternness, the principle of the survival of the fittest, which, ethically considered, we have seen to imply that each individual shall be left to experience the effects of his own nature and consequent conduct, would quickly clear away the degraded.'[19]

These themes were prominently defended in Spencer's *The Man versus the State* (1884), where maximum liberty and individualism and minimal state interference are deduced from the need to allow the principle to operate unimpeded. In the United States such ideas were also prominently associated with William Graham Sumner, and would later resurface in some forms of neo-liberalism. Yet late in life, in 1893, Spencer began to doubt his earlier conclusions, maintaining with T. H. Huxley that the 'process of evolution must reach a limit, after which a reverse change must begin', and that 'the survival of the fittest is often not survival of the best'. In 'denouncing the brutal form of the struggle for existence' and contending 'that the ethical process is a part of the process of evolution', he thought that 'the struggle for life needs to be qualified when the gregarious state is entered, and that among gregarious creatures lower than man a rudiment of the ethical check is visible'.[20]

Darwin and Wallace recognised the superior utility of Spencer's phrase, the 'survival of the fittest' as early as 1866. Wallace thought it preferable to 'natural selection', and inserted it into *The Varieties of Animals and Plants Under Domestication* (1868). Darwin added 'survival of the fittest' to the fifth edition of the *Origin of Species* (1869), remarking that 'I have called this principle ... by the term Natural Selection, in order to mark its relation to man's power of selection. But the expression often used by Mr. Herbert Spencer of the Survival of the Fittest is more accurate, and is sometimes equally convenient.'[21] Here he meant by 'fitness' the fact that an organism was 'better adapted for [its] immediate, local environment'.

From Darwin to Social Darwinism

Much of the early controversy over *Origin of Species*, and even more *The Descent of Man*, emanated from the threat to Christian orthodoxy that evolution posed. Many thought that Darwin implied that mankind had not been created in God's image, like the angels, but had evolved from the apes, and perhaps no great distance either. Agnosticism might be one reasoned conclusion from these premises. Another might be that war and unrelenting aggression were natural human behaviour. Another was that the more highly evolved might naturally rule over and even exterminate the more primitive in the name of efficiency and industrial progress.

This assumption was not particularly novel. Justifications for imperial occupation based upon inefficient use of and/or non-ownership of land by hunter-gatherers occur even in Thomas More's *Utopia* (1516), and appear as late as John Hobson's notionally anti-imperialist tract, *Imperialism* (1902).[22] To most Europeans the dominant historical narrative in 1800 as well as 1900 involved a conflict between the progressive triumph of civilisation over barbarism, with occasional setbacks. Gibbon's readers knew that the social and national weakness induced by debilitating luxury in particular threatened conquest from without by barbaric peoples. In such struggles success was counted by strength, especially military might. In the later eighteenth century the salutary effects of war had been promoted by writers like Adam Ferguson and G. W. F. Hegel. To many, Napoleon evidenced the civilisational, even radical and democratising possibilities of conquest. In *On War* (1832) Clausewitz urged the maxim that war was the continuation of politics by other means. Violence could be understood as legitimating national, racial and species goals. It was common in domestic life, against wives, children and servants. It was normal, even essential, in the ever-expanding empires. As early as 1830 it was reported in the Australian colonies that the native inhabitants were 'treated, in distant parts of the colony, as if they had been dogs, and shot by convict-servants, at a distance from society, for the most trifling causes'.[23] Violence also governed class relations within the supposedly civilised nations. Brutality in the factory and workhouse was common. Strikes and demonstrations were routinely suppressed by force. Retaliation by the working classes was also widely justified after the French Revolution of 1789, notably by Auguste Blanqui in France. The government's suppression of the Paris Commune involved a stupendous bloodbath. Anarchist and 'terrorist' violence killed many heads of state and lesser officials in the decades up to 1914. The French social theorist Georges Sorel would dramatise the positive virtues of armed resistance in his *Reflections on Violence* (1908), as would the anarchist Michael Bakunin, famous for asserting that destruction was a creative process too. What, after all, was revolution, but force? What was the state, but legitimised force? What was history but the record of force imposed and resisted? Darwin's reception needs to be read as reinforcing rather than fundamentally altering these assumptions. But with Darwin a civilisational imperative was transformed into a biological one.

Marxism came to share many of these assumptions with Social Darwinism. It was Engels rather than Marx who most prominently identified the theory of class struggle with Darwin's writings. Marx did not, as he was once supposed to have done, seek to dedicate *Capital* to Darwin. Nonetheless in 1860 he wrote Engels that *Origin* 'provides the basis for our views'.[24] In 1861 he reiterated that 'Darwin's writing is very important and suits me as the basis in natural history for the historical class struggle'. But a year later he added more sceptically that 'Darwin rediscovers, among the beasts and plants, the society of England with its division of labour, competition, opening up of new markets, "inventions" and Malthusian "struggle for existence"'. He thus did not simply assume a parallel between his historical theory and Darwin's account of nature, much less Malthus, whose 'utter baseness of mind … a baseness which can only be indulged in by a parson' he deplored.[25] But at Marx's graveside Engels insisted that: 'As Darwin discovered the law of the development of organic nature, so Marx discovered the law of development of human history.'[26] The association remained a popular one on the left. Though almost all were anti-Malthusians, many of Marx's followers became Darwinians, with Enrico Ferri and Karl Kautsky, among others, indicating the parallels between the two great scientific world views. 'It is because I am an evolutionist that I am a Socialist', enthused Annie Besant.[27] Marx's son-in-law, Edward Aveling, was anxious to cement the association.[28] The most important 'revisionist' Marxist, Eduard Bernstein, adapted a theory of evolution to argue against the 'catastrophist' account of capitalism and for a gradual, democratic replacement of capitalism.[29] On Lenin's Kremlin desk was a statue of a monkey holding a skull, sitting on a volume of Darwin. Marxism, indeed, came to portray itself as essentially heralding a higher evolutionary stage of human morality in its vision of communist society. It came to see its own 'scientific socialism' as the social equivalent of Darwinism; thus shortly after the Chinese Revolution of 1949 two new courses were introduced into Shanghai's educational system, Darwin's theory of evolution and the Marxist theory of social development.[30] Social Darwinism was thus clearly as amenable to collectivist as to individualist interpretations.[31]

The cases of Spencer and Marx alike indicate that Social Darwinism cannot be conceived as a series of deductions from the *Origin of Species* and/or *The Descent of Man*. Darwin himself, curiously enough, can be best described as converting to rather than originating Social Darwinism. Between 1859–71 his ideas shifted from defining fecundity as the factor that helped explain the predominance of particular species, to the normative claim vis-à-vis humanity that intelligence was the quality that best promoted a desirable evolutionary outcome. In Darwin's original account the 'fittest' did not survive, in the later meaning of the term: 'success in leaving progeny', or those able to breed the most, did.[32] In animals this might imply that the strongest produced the most offspring. In humans, however, since the poor had much larger families, evolution from their stock, rather than the 'best' or most able, seemed most likely. France, it was claimed, for instance, was

> practising Darwinism the wrong way about. She is relying, for the recruiting of her population, on the selection of inferior types. The more wealthy classes, who by means of work and intelligence have arrived at a certain degree of ease, and by this very fact exhibit a certain intellectual superiority, are precisely those who are eliminating themselves by a voluntary sterility. On the other hand, imprudence, unintelligence, idleness, insanity, and misery intellectual and material, are prolific, and are responsible for a great proportion of the national population.[33]

The message was clear: the weak bred irresponsibly while the most intelligent had fewer progeny and thus faced extinction. The same logic might apply in the world to different races. Between 1865 and 1871 Darwin came round to the view that 'fitness' involved the triumph of 'the intellectual and moral' races over the 'lower and more degraded ones'. In *Origin* Darwin had used 'race' in a loose manner to describe species in general. By *The Descent of Man* (1871) he warned that 'civilised races' 'encroach on and replace' the savage, with the 'lower races' being displaced through the accumulation of capital and growth of the arts. He now warned too of the 'degeneration of a domestic race' because humanity allowed its worst members to breed so wantonly and injuriously. Darwin even wrote in 1881 that: 'The more civilized so-called Caucasian races have beaten the Turkish hollow in the struggle for existence. Looking to the world at no very distant date, what an endless number of the lower races will have been eliminated by the higher civilised races of the world.'[34] Beyond this, an obsession with degeneration through the inheritance of negative traits now haunted an entire epoch like the ghostly spectre of a monstrous past. Here Bénédict Morel (*Treatise on Degeneration*, 1857), Cesare Lombroso (*Criminal Man*, 1896) and Max Nordau (*Degeneration*, 1898) were key figures, while in Britain Edwin Ray Lankester's *Degeneration: A Chapter in Darwinism* (1880) led the way.

Accordingly genius mounted a counteroffensive against degeneration. In Britain this strategy originated with Darwin's cousin, Francis Galton (1822–1911), who in 1883 defined the term eugenics to mean 'the science which deals with all influences that improve the inborn qualities of a race; also with those that develop them to the utmost advantage'.[35] This clearly implied strengthening the social regulation of marriage, a proposal that gained strength in the second half of the century. In a brief utopia, 'Kantsaywhere', Galton described a system of marriage certificates, with the morally and physically 'unfit' excluded from bearing children and treated with 'sharp severity' if they failed to abide by the rules.[36] Such extreme ideas were, however, not so distant from Malthusian proposals to restrict the right of marriage to those able to support a family, which even liberals like John Stuart Mill promoted.[37] What eugenics added was the need to either promote specific attributes in the population regarded as germane to progress, especially 'genius', Galton's own preoccupation,[38] or to limit the breeding of defective or delinquent individuals, including criminals, alcoholics, the insane and drug addicts. The former of these schemes became known as 'positive' eugenics, and the latter, 'negative' eugenics.

Besides its application to domestic populations, the language of Social Darwinism had particular relevance to debates over imperial expansion. Here its widespread casual justification for not only the conquest but also the extermination of subject populations is noteworthy. Writing in 1909, the German-born British homeopath J. Ellis Barker insisted that if 'might is right in international politics', then 'the law of the survival of the fittest and strongest, which rules the whole animal and vegetable creation, applies with equal force to man and to his political associations'. 'This world', he added, was

> not a world of ease and peace, but a world of strife and war. Nature is ruled by the law of the struggle for existence and of the survival of the fittest and the strongest. States, like trees and animals, are engaged in a never-ending struggle for room, food, light, and air, and that struggle is a blessing in disguise, for it is the cause of all progress. Had it not been for that struggle, the world would still be a wilderness inhabited by its aboriginal savages.

Thus, thought Barker, 'The abolition of war would be a misfortune to mankind. It would lead not to the survival of the fittest and strongest, but to the survival of the sluggard and the unfit, and therefore to the degeneration of the human race.'[39]

It was already a truism by 1880, then, to suggest, as Lord Derby did, that: 'The struggle for existence between races, as between individuals, is incessant. The strongest must win in the end; and the very first condition of a strong race is that it shall be physically healthy.'[40] Such observations were particularly widespread in relation to the conquest of Africa. Here a key convert to the idea that the struggle for existence was a direct instrument of divine rule was the business magnate Cecil Rhodes, who played a prominent role in conquering southern Africa.[41] Explorers noted of apparently defeated groups (here the Mashona in their struggles with the Zulu) that: 'Respecting these people, the impression left upon my mind is that they are a declining race, exemplifying strongly the Darwinian doctrine of the survival of the fittest.'[42] This lent an air of inevitability to such proceedings. Nature willed such destruction. So Rhodes' ambitions were explained in terms of the fact that 'the African natives, as weaker races manifestly unfit to govern the land they hold, must sooner or later give way before the irresistible advance of the stronger white people. It is the old doctrine of the survival of the fittest – a brutal theory, no doubt, but one impossible to alter or amend.'[43]

Cruel, merciless, but necessary, even inevitable and Providential: such was the general consensus. The same was said in the American West, where one witness to the disappearing Winnebago tribe noted that 'the doctrine of the "survival of the fittest" must be carried out, I suppose, and the Red Indian does not seem to be fit for much in the Great West'.[44] (Indigenous settlement had lasted some 15,000 years at this point.) An early governor of California, too, insisted that 'a war of extermination will continue to be waged between the two races until the Indian race becomes extinct'.[45] 'Scientific investigation', it was suggested in 1902, had dispelled the idea that the 'lower races' could be quickly raised to a higher level of civilisation.[46] Yet others, assessing the same peoples under the impact of white penetration, protested that: 'Along with drink come debasing and demoralising influences which sooner or later end in the utter annihilation of the race. Can this be the survival of the fittest? Surely no. It is the strong and intelligent killing the weak and ignorant.'[47]

Still others noted that the spirit of jingoism, that curious reaction against peaceful and industrial civilisation, as well as against international morality may perhaps be said to have partly had its source in a philosophy of materialism; Darwin's doctrine of the survival of the fittest being misconstrued, as if the strongest were the fittest, which, though true in the case of brutes, is untrue in the case of the moral and intellectual being, Man.[48]

Among the most devastating applications of these assumptions came with Belgium's occupation of the Congo and Germany's conquest of the Herero and Nama peoples in south-west Africa. In the Congo some 10 million may have died under King Leopold's savage regime, in which entire villages were enslaved for rubber production. Under the Germans the Hereros and Nama were massacred mercilessly, denounced as a race unfit to survive, even as *Unmenschen*, or subhuman, and herded into concentration camps, where they were killed through forced labour, in tragic anticipation of the treatment of the disabled, Jews and others some forty years later. Here the justification was that peoples who created nothing had no reason to survive; the overlap between biological racism and productivist logic is complete. Through writers like Ernst Haeckel and Friedrich Ratzel, Social Darwinism attained an ascendancy in Germany unmatched elsewhere in Europe. The explanation for this lies at least partly in the immense population boom in late nineteenth-century Germany, which led to the idea of a *Volk ohne Raum* (people without space), and thence to the adaptation of ideas of struggle for existence to a demand for *Lebensraum*.[49]

Yet many did not accept these supposed deductions from Darwinian premises. Those who refused to embrace the harshest implications did so from various political perspectives. Some liberals contended that whatever value a crude struggle for existence had in the earliest stages of society had now been superseded. 'The "survival of the fittest" is a cruel theory now', argued one, instancing the occupation of Egypt: 'Have we lived in vain? Are the old beliefs and ideas at their worst to linger yet?' 'With a barbarous people in ancient days', wrote another, 'this may have been held to be a natural law, but under enlightened and civilized conditions it should be reduced to a minimum'.[50] Referring to New Zealand it was asserted that:

Darwin's new gospel of 'the survival of the fittest' may satisfy the conscience of the Philistine and the Pharisee in their struggles to be rich; but though, for a time, it may continue to be the fashionable philosophy of the day – inasmuch as it justifies tyranny and wrong on the condition that they survive and succeed – it is nothing less than a crime against humanity.[51]

The British journalist and social philosopher Walter Bagehot's *Physics and Politics* (1872) contended that liberal democracy guaranteed evolutionary progress and suited higher forms of social growth. Many liberals assumed that hereditary aristocracy was incompatible with natural selection, and urged a meritocratic application of Darwin's principle. In the 1880s New Liberals like David Ritchie argued that the state could act as a benevolent institution fostering cultural evolution by freeing individuals from a 'perpetual struggle for the mere conditions of life'. In *Evolution and Ethics* (1893), T. H. Huxley, too, asserted that a crude struggle for existence characterised only the early stages of human existence, while the later were influenced by moral factors, which necessitated, among other things, educating the poor. The sociologist Benjamin Kidd's *Social Evolution* (1894) took the view that social improvement increased in the degree to which present society subordinated its interests to future members. Here, too, religion might play an important role by promoting solidarity, efficiency and a sense of sacrifice to the community. If nothing else, this proved that Darwinism and Christianity were not completely incompatible. But Kidd added that 'the weaker peoples disappear before the stronger, and the subordination and exclusion of the least efficient is still the prevailing feature of advancing humanity'.[52]

On the left, like some liberals, many later Socialist writers, such as Enrico Ferri, saw inherited wealth and prestige as a barrier to promoting 'fitness'.[53] Alfred Russel Wallace took evolutionary principles to imply a socialist outlook early on, and became a prominent advocate for land nationalisation.[54] Anarchists like the Russian prince, Peter Kropotkin, stressed that the growth of social solidarity and the interdependence of everyone's happiness on others indicated an evolutionary trend towards mutual aid.[55] Another Russian, the revolutionary anarchist Michael Bakunin, wrote that 'there is very little true morality within this world with the exception of a small number of strong and highly moral characters which have emerged, by Darwinian selection, from sordid oppression and inexpressible poverty. They are virtuous, i.e. they love the people and stand for justice against any injustice, for all oppressed against all oppressors'.[56]

One of the most severe critics of crude Social Darwinism was the New Liberal political economist John Hobson, who rejected, as Michael Freeden puts it, 'the attempt to endow the struggle for survival with positive ethical content'.[57] Instead, ethical imperatives had to be factored into the evolutionary process. Like Saint-Simon and Comte, Hobson believed that social evolution required that 'on the one hand, militarism is displaced by industrialism, and, on the other hand, political limits of nationalism yield place to an effective internationalism based upon identity of commercial interests'.[58] Reviewing Kidd's *Social Evolution* in 1895, Hobson summarised Kidd's position as being that while 'modern physiological science establishes as the first condition of all progress the maintenance of that struggle among the individuals of a race which continually eliminates the less efficient and enables the more efficient to survive and multiply', it was not true that any 'successful attempt to suspend the struggle and to secure the survival of the unfit members will not merely check further progress but will inevitably cause a deterioration of the race'. Reason could intervene to mitigate the attendant pain and misery of such a process. Equality of opportunity and democratisation might increase the pace of struggle. Kidd thought socialism would inhibit this by equalising outcomes and suppressing competition. Religion might nonetheless alleviate the effects of unbridled competition. Hobson, however, thought 'Mr. Kidd shows no grasp of the evolutionary character of socialism'. Socialism in fact aimed at an 'equalization of opportunity by putting down some lower form of struggle, in order that the struggle may take a higher and intenser form. When all mankind was placed upon absolutely equal terms of competition in the rivalry of life, the ideal of socialism would be attained.' Rebutting Herbert Spencer's dismissal of poor laws and sanitary legislation because they would 'keep alive those "unfit" persons whose sacrifice was demanded in the interest of society', Hobson contended that

> No socialist community could fail to recognize that marriage and production of children were the most important social acts; that society had a clear right to determine what sort of children should be born, seeing that society had both to support them and to depend upon them for support ... Every intelligent society, socialist or other, would consider it as a first duty to prohibit unsocial unions, would prevent the propagation of physical, mental and moral disease.[59]

No discussion of the philosophical adaptation of Social Darwinism would be complete without mentioning Friedrich Nietzsche (1844–1900), the writer most famously associated with the proclamation that 'God is dead' and the deduction that moral 'nihilism' results. Nietzsche's defence of intellectual elitism had of course many precedents. This theme was indeed a constant refrain in response to the democratisation of European culture, Samuel

Taylor Coleridge's 'clerisy', John Stuart Mill's 'individuality' and Matthew Arnold's 'culture' all responding in Britain to the same problem, the potential threat to 'high' culture of the increasingly enfranchised but scarcely literate masses. After Darwin, W. H. Mallock in *Aristocracy and Evolution* (1898) avowed similar arguments. Nietzsche's far greater influence lay in part in the overlapping of his language with the central assumptions of Social Darwinism, including its most racialist applications. Invocations of the 'superb blond beast wandering in search of prey and carnage' suggest such comparisons.[60] This, again, seems to be an invitation by Nature to cruelty and conquest in the name of creating a 'higher' civilisation, an exercise in which pity and compassion play no role, and are indeed held in contempt.

This is even more the case with Nietzsche's supposed master-principle, the 'will to power', which implied that all human beings were engaged in a constant struggle with one another. In what sounds like a distant echo of the German individualist anarchist Max Stirner's doctrine of egoism, all striving for distinction was 'the striving after ascendancy over one's neighbour, be it only a very indirect one, or one only felt or dreamt of'.[61] Amidst the clamour for egalitarianism of modern feminism, trades unionism and socialism, all of which he contemptuously dismissed, Nietzsche's response was that the fate of mankind 'depends on the success of its highest types', and that the 'goal of humanity' lay in 'its highest specimens'. This implied an aristocracy of artists and philosophers willing to break free from the mores of the epoch. In one of the most extreme formulations of this idea, Nietzsche insisted that: 'The aim should be to prepare a transvaluation of values for a particularly strong kind of man, most highly gifted in intellect and will, and, to this end, slowly and cautiously to liberate in him a whole host of slandered instincts, hitherto held in check: whoever meditates on this problem belongs to us, the free spirits.' Thus 'the democratization of Europe will tend to the production of a type prepared for slavery in the most subtle sense of the term, the strong man will necessarily, in individual and exceptional cases become stronger and richer than he has perhaps ever before'.[62]

While Darwin's direct influence seems unlikely, the vagueness of some of Nietzsche's formulations invariably invited comparisons with Social Darwinism.[63] The 'free spirits' turned out, not surprisingly, to have little concern for the freedom of the majority, and much disdain for human life as such.[64] Nietzsche's role in transmitting a particularly vicious form of Social Darwinism to Nazism is undoubted. A book appeared in 1935 by one Dmitry Gavronsky entitled *Friedrich Nietzsche und das Dritte Reich*. 'All Nazis rightly stress their descent from Nietzsche', it was claimed shortly after.[65] This does not make Nietzsche a Social Darwinist, much less an anti-Semite or proto-Nazi. It does suggest that a Social Darwinist reading of his ideas in this period would have appeared perfectly acceptable. His much-vaunted appeal to a new Superman to lead modern Europe out of the intellectual anarchy that reducing all morals to the will to power had created proved immensely influential. Nietzsche's *Übermensch* idea represented another affectation of living in a state of grace 'beyond good and evil', where the 'transvaluation of all values' permitted 'free spirits' to define as 'good' only 'all that enhances the feeling of power'.[66] This hinted at an affinity with the antinomianism of some sixteenth-century Anabaptists, and others for whom the state of grace permitted any act, as well as Stirner's individualist anarchism. But Nietzsche's was not a confused and childish 'Aryan' biological conception of racial superiority many Nazis probably associated with him. To Nietzsche, the Superman ideal represented self-mastery as much as the dominance of any superior group over the rest.

Conclusion

The excluded 'others' in Social Darwinist discourse were those whose technologies were too primitive to resist the champions of progress, expansion and civilisation, and the supposed imperatives of 'efficient' industrialisation. Most were non-whites. In colony after colony the natives were dismissed as unproductive, worthless members of lower races doomed to extermination because they fell behind in the race to modernity. Imperial policies of exploitation made this a self-fulfilling prophecy. The first to be almost completely exterminated were the Palawa, or Indigenous Tasmanians. Some 80 to 90 per cent of Indigenous American peoples died. In India as many as 10 million died in the 1876–8 famine alone, many of whom might have been saved, since record exports of wheat from India to Britain occurred at the same time. Here and elsewhere in the imperial heartlands a few among the conquering races resisted such exploitation and oppression. Most did not.

During the *fin de siècle* period growing international commercial and military competition fused with an obsession with evolution and the possibility of species degeneration. Social Darwinism came to permeate almost every strand of social and political thought as ideas of fitness, efficiency and military preparedness were widely discussed. During the Boer War it became evident that Britain's cannon and Maxim fodder, drawn from the factory districts, were physically unfit for the task. A movement for 'national efficiency' was a partial result. The First World War strongly reinforced ideas of national and international struggle.

Perceptions of diminishing territory also doubtless fuelled anxieties about overpopulation and the need to expand elsewhere. Such propensities equally promoted despotic longings; as Elias Canetti writes, there is not the 'slightest doubt that a ruler's desire to own a whole people like slaves or animals grows stronger as their numbers increase'.[67] Malthus' prophecy thus came to define the entirety of the later modern epoch as the 'survival of the fittest' became the dominant metaphor of the age. The idea of competition at the centre of Social Darwinism thus originates in a shrinking planet and the growing claustrophobia and quest for *Lebensraum* that accompany population growth. Its source, initially, is Malthus rather than Darwin. It indicates the collapse of societies based upon privilege and the emergence of a generalised ethos of competition rooted in supposed merit, at best, but mere strength at worst.

Only later in the twentieth century did the idea of the 'survival of the fittest' come fully into its own. Today the verdict on Social Darwinism is usually defined by the Holocaust and the eugenics initiatives that preceded it, especially Hitler's infamous T4 programme, in which some 70,000 disabled and feeble persons were killed, and the key criterion was 'not medical but economic: was the patient capable of productive work or not?'[68] Hitler's crude variation on Social Darwinism resulted from the message of the trenches 'that life is a cruel struggle, and has no other object but the preservation of the species'.[69] To the Nazis, 'right is what serves us, what serves the German people. Injustice is what does not serve the German people.' And to Mussolini 'Fascism … conceives of life as a struggle' in which 'a people, historically perpetuating itself' became 'a multitude unified by an idea and imbued with the will to live, the will to power, self-consciousness, personality'.[70] The Bolshevik equivalent was (in Lenin's words) the view that: 'Morality is that which serves to destroy the old exploiting society.'[71] Pity was not among the Nazi, fascist or Bolshevik catalogue of virtues, and we rarely encounter it among their actions.

Indisputably this perspective stems from several sources besides Social Darwinism. From an ethical viewpoint some thought that removing God from the human moral equation simply resulted in achievement being defined solely by success, and success by power over others. By the 1880s and 1890s power worship became a dominant variant of the struggle for existence. This was in fact only a variant in turn on the 'might makes right' principle. In *The Science of Power* (1918) Benjamin Kidd explained that a new pagan ethic based on collective emotion represented the 'supreme principle of efficiency' in the modern world. The history of the West had been defined by 'the fittest', who, having survived 'successive layers of conquest', had proven 'the fittest in virtue of the right of force, and in virtue of a process of military selection probably the longest, the sternest, the most culminating which the race has ever undergone'. Only the barrier of a religion that was 'the utter negation of force' prevented this from being realised.[72]

We cannot here consider in detail how the worship of success in national and individual types viewed from a Social Darwinist perspective fed into and was derived from the worship of technology and machinery more generally, from whence most of the stress on 'efficiency' derived. The introduction of Henry Ford's assembly line for producing Model T automobiles in 1913 clearly did much to cement the fusion of mechanisation with industrial labour and maximum efficiency. The revolution in efficiency associated with Frederick Winslow Taylor's 'scientific management', dating from 1911, which focused on rationalising and speeding up production, aided this process. All the great discoveries of the latter decades of the nineteenth century, including radiation, electricity, photography, the telegraph, the internal combustion engine and the aeroplane, fuelled a militant enthusiasm for the construction of scientifically based social utopias. Sadly not only did human behaviour not improve apace, but most of the new inventions turned out to have destructive applications as well. Machine and power worship, which helped produce the cult of 'efficiency', came to imply a disdain for human life, and the human costs of attaining the mechanical utopia.

The great problem of twentieth-century totalitarianism has sometimes been accounted for by reference to nineteenth-century Social Darwinism as the source of an anti-religious dehumanisation. But reducing human beings entirely to economic units, as in Auschwitz, to be exploited unto and even after death, is a function more directly of an economic world view, which defines productiveness as the sole criterion of human worth. Valuing human beings primarily if not exclusively according to their productivity and a constantly increased striving for efficiency and intensified 'struggle' defines both the capitalist and Marxist variants of later modernity. (There are many extreme instances of this: under the Khmer Rouge communist regime in Cambodia in the late 1970s women's attractiveness was deliberately concealed because, as a regime slogan put it, 'physical beauty hinders the will to struggle'.)[73] Here, it is not implausible to argue, Marx substituted the myth of the chosen class – the proletariat – for an original myth of the chosen people, harnessing this in turn to a theory of historical evolution or 'myth of the species'.[74] The class struggle, however, would turn out to be little more helpful to humanity's progress than many applications of the theory of organic evolution. As much blood, indeed, was spilt ensuring purity of class as purity of race, to the ultimate benefit of neither. Discourses on national, racial and class struggle nonetheless persist in many forms today, and with overpopulation and scarcity of resources are likely to rise to prominence again.

NOTES

1 See Gregory Claeys, *Marx and Marxism* (Harmondsworth: Penguin Books, 2018).

2 Mike Hawkins, *Social Darwinism and European and American Thought 1860–1945* (Cambridge: Cambridge University Press, 1997), p. 31.

3 T. R. Malthus, *An Essay on the Principle of Population* (London: J. Johnson, 1798), p. 48; 1803 edn, 2 vols. (Cambridge: Cambridge University Press, 1989), vol. 2, pp. 127–8. For context see Gregory Claeys, 'Malthus and Godwin: Rights, Utility and Productivity', in Robert Mayhew, ed., *New Perspectives on Malthus* (Cambridge: Cambridge University Press, 2016), pp. 52–73.

4 Charles Darwin, *Autobiography* (London: Watts & Co., 1929), p. 57.

5 Charles Darwin, *On the Origin of Species*, 2nd edn (London: John Murray, 1860), pp. 5, 63.

6 Alfred Russel Wallace, *My Life*, 2 vols. (London: Chapman & Hall, 1905), vol. 1, pp. 361–2.

7 See Gregory Claeys, 'The Reaction to Political Radicalism and the Popularization of Political Economy in Early 19th Century Britain: The Case of "Productive and Unproductive Labour"', in *Expository Science: Forms and Functions of Popularization*, eds. Terry Shinn and Richard Whitley (Dordrecht: D. Reidel; Sociology of Science Yearbook, vol. 9, 1985), pp. 119–36.

8 Malthus, *An Essay on the Principle of Population*, p. 205.

9 For details see Gregory Claeys, *Machinery, Money and the Millennium: From Moral Economy to Socialism, 1815–60* (Princeton, NJ: Princeton University Press, 1987).

10 John Stuart Mill, *Collected Works*, 33 vols. (London: Routledge & Kegan Paul, 1985), vol. 20, p. 269.

11 J. C. Byrne, *Twelve Years Wandering in the British Colonies. From 1835 to 1847*, 2 vols. (London: Richard Bentley, 1848), vol. 1, p. 7.

12 Alexander Herzen, *From the Other Shore* (London: Weidenfeld & Nicolson, 1956), p. 64.

13 See Istvan Hont, *Jealousy of Trade. International Competition and the Nation-State in Historical Perspective* (Cambridge, MA: Harvard University Press, 2005).

14 Herbert Spencer, *Various Fragments* (London: Williams & Norgate, 1897), pp. 106–7.

15 Herbert Spencer, *Social Statics* (London: John Chapman, 1851), pp. 322–3.

16 Herbert Spencer, 'A Theory of Population, Deduced from the General Law of Animal Fertility', *Westminster Review*, ns 1 (1852), 500, 469, 501. The message of this piece he later described as being that 'fertility is inversely proportionate to the size and heterogeneity of the species and the activity and complexity of its life'. Herbert Spencer, *Autobiography*, 2 vols. (London: Williams & Norgate, 1904), vol. 2, p. 131.

17 William Henry Hudson, *Herbert Spencer* (London: Archibald Constable & Co., 1908), p. 36. Rogers describes 1852 as the moment when the 'struggle for existence' was conceived by Spencer: 'Darwinism and Social Darwinism', *Journal of the History of Ideas* 33 (1972), 277.

18 *Nature* (1 Feb. 1872), 263.

19 Herbert Spencer, *The Principles of Ethics*, 2 vols. (London: Williams & Norgate, 1893), vol. 2, p. 393.

20 Spencer, *Various Fragments*, p. 117.

21 Charles Darwin, *On the Origin of Species* (London: John Murray, 1902), pp. 76–7.

22 See Gregory Claeys, *Imperial Sceptics: British Critics of Empire, 1850–1920* (Cambridge: Cambridge University Press, 2010), pp. 235–81.

23 Robert Dawson, *The Present State of Australia* (London: Smith, Elder & Co., 1831), p. 58.

24 Karl Marx and Frederick Engels, *Collected Works*, 50 vols. (London: Lawrence & Wishart, 1975–2005), vol. 41, p. 232.

25 Marx and Engels, *Collected Works*, vol. 31 p. 347; vol. 41, p. 381.

26 Quoted in Jonathan Sperber, *Karl Marx: A Nineteenth-Century Life* (New York: W. W. Norton, 2013), pp. 394, 547.

27 Annie Besant, *Is Socialism Sound?* (London: Freethought, 1887), p. 147.

28 Edward Aveling, *Charles Darwin and Karl Marx: A Comparison* (London: Twentieth Century Press, 1893). Aveling's other works included *The Student's Darwin*, *Darwinism and Small Families*, *Darwin Made Easy* and *The Gospel of Evolution*.

29 Eduard Bernstein, *Evolutionary Socialism* (London: Independent Labour Party, 1909). It was not, however, based on Darwinism.

30 Harry Wu and Carolyn Wakeman, *Bitter Winds: A Memoir of My Life in China's Gulags* (New York: John Wiley & Sons, 1994), p. 8.

31 On the range of interpretations see David Stack, *The First Darwinian Left. Socialism and Darwinism 1859–1914* (Cheltenham: New Clarion Press, 2003).

32 Darwin, *On the Origin* (2nd edn, 1860), p. 62.

33 Quoted in Gustave Le Bon, *The Psychology of Socialism* (London: T. Fisher Unwin, 1899), pp. 134–5.

34 *The Life and Letters of Charles Darwin*, ed. Francis Darwin, 3 vols. (London: John Murray, 1887), vol. 1, p. 316.

35 Francis Galton. *Essays in Eugenics* (London: Eugenics Education Society, 1909), p. 35.

36 Reprinted in Claeys and Lyman Tower Sargent, eds., Francis Galton, '"Kantsaywhere" and "The Donoghues of Dunno Weir"', *Utopian Studies* 12 (2001), 188–233. On eugenics and literature, see Gregory Claeys, *Dystopia: A Natural History* (Oxford: Oxford University Press, 2016), pp. 294–315.

37 See Gregory Claeys, *Mill and Paternalism* (Cambridge: Cambridge University Press, 2013), pp. 43–6.

38 Francis Galton, *Hereditary Genius: An Inquiry into Its Laws and Consequences* (London: Macmillan & Co., 1869).

39 J. Ellis Barker, *Great and Greater Britain* (London: Smith, Elder & Co., 1909), pp. 23, 25. In this period Barker warned constantly of the danger of war between Britain and Germany.

40 *Speeches and Addresses of Edward Henry XVth Earl of Derby*, 2 vols. (London: Longman, Green & Co., 1894), vol. 2, p. 91.

41 *The Last Will and Testament of Cecil John Rhodes* (London: Review of Reviews, 1902), p. 95.

42 Walter Montagu Kerr, *The Far Interior: A Narrative of Travel and Adventure from the Cape of Good Hope across the Zambesi*, 2 vols. (London: Samson Low, Marston, Searle & Rivington, 1886), vol. 1, p. 119.

43 Howard Hensman, *Cecil Rhodes. A Study of a Career* (London: William Blackwood & Sons, 1901), p. 110.

44 George Augustus Sala, *America Revisited*, 2 vols. (London: Vizetelly & Co., 1882), vol. 2, p. 164.

45 Peter Burnett's inaugural address, 20 December 1849.

46 Ramsden Balmforth, 'Darwinism and Empire', *Westminster Review* 158 (July, 1902), 6.

47 John Buchanan, *The Shirè Highlands (East Central Africa) as Colony and Mission* (London: William Blackwood & Sons, 1885), p. 79.

48 Goldwin Smith, *Commonwealth or Empire: A Bystander's View of the Question* (London: Macmillan & Co., 1902), p. 37.

49 David Olusoga and Casper W. Ericsen, *The Kaiser's Holocaust. Germany's Forgotten Genocide* (London: Faber & Faber, 2010), pp. 75, 86, 109, 203, 220.

50 *Letters from an Egyptian to an English Politician Upon the Affairs of Egypt* (London: George Routledge & Sons, 1908), p. 88.

51 J. C. Firth, *Nation-Making: A Story of New Zealand. Savagism v. Civilisation* (London: Longmans, Green & Co., 1890), p. 286.

52 Benjamin Kidd, *Social Evolution* (London: Macmillan and Co., 1894), p. 65.

53 Enrico Ferri, *Socialism and Positive Science (Darwin-Spencer-Marx)* (London: Independent Labour Party, 1905), p. 21.

54 See Gregory Claeys, 'Wallace and Owenism', in *Natural Selection and Beyond: The Intellectual Legacy of Alfred Russel Wallace*, eds. Charles Smith and George Beccaloni (Oxford: Oxford University Press, 2008), pp. 235–62.

55 See, most recently, Ruth Kinna. *Kropotkin: Reviewing the Classical Anarchist Tradition* (Edinburgh: Edinburgh University Press, 2016).

56 Quoted in *Bakunin on Violence: Letter to S. Nechayev* (New York: Anarchist Switchboard, n.d.), p. 27 (2 June 1870).

57 Michael Freeden, 'John Hobson as a New Liberal Theorist', *Journal of the History of Ideas* 34 (1973), 428.

58 J. A. Hobson, 'Free Trade and Foreign Policy', *Contemporary Review* 74 (1898), 168.

59 J. A. Hobson, 'Mr. Kidd's "Social Evolution"', *American Journal of Sociology* 1 (1895), 299–312.

60 Friedrich Nietzsche, *The Twilight of the Idols* (London: T. N. Foulis, 1911), p. 45.

61 Friedrich Nietzsche, *The Dawn of Day* (London: T. Fisher Unwin, 1903), p. 105. See Stirner, *The Ego and His Own* (London: A. C. Fifield, 1912).

62 Friedrich Nietzsche, *The Will to Power*, aphorisms 955–7 (London: T. N. Foulis, 1910, pp. 361–3).

63 Nietzsche himself claimed that only 'learned cattle' had understood his Superman concept in terms of Carlyle's hero-worship and Social Darwinism: *Ecce Homo* (London: T. N. Fouis, 1911), p. 58.

64 The satire on Nietzsche in Alfred Hitchcock's film, *Rope* (1948) captures this brilliantly.

65 Aurel Kolnai, *The War Against the West* (London: Victor Gollancz, 1938), p. 14. See also M.-P. Nicolas. *From Nietzsche Down to Hitler* (London: William

Hodge & Co., 1938), and generally Jacob Golomb and Robert S. Wistrich, eds., *Nietzsche, Godfather of Fascism?* (Princeton, NJ: Princeton University Press, 2002).

66 Friedrich Nietzsche, *The Twilight of the Idols … The Antichrist* (London: T. N. Fouis, 1911), pp. 128, 139.

67 Elias Canetti, *Crowds and Power* (Harmondsworth: Penguin Books, 1992), p. 445.

68 Richard J. Evans. *The Third Reich At War* (Harmondsworth: Penguin Books, 2009), p. 85.

69 *Hitler's Table-Talk 1941–1944* (London: Weidenfeld & Nicholson, 1953), p. 44.

70 Benito Mussolini, *The Doctrine of Fascism* (Florence: Vellecchi Editore, 1936), p. 15.

71 Quoted in Robert Conquest, *Lenin: A Biography* (London: Macmillan, 2000), p. 41.

72 Benjamin Kidd, *The Science of Power* (London: Methuen & Co., 1919), p. 5.

73 Loung Ung, *First They Killed My Father* (London: Harper Perennial, 2006), p. 158; Moeung Sonn with Henri Locard, *Prisoner of the Khmer Rouge* (Phnom Penh: Editions Funan, 2007), p. 149.

74 This is suggested by Jules Monnerot, *Sociology of Communism* (London: George Allen & Unwin, 1953), pp. 41, 280–1.

10

WENDY HAYDEN

Feminist Thought

In 1888, women representing nine different countries convened in Washington, DC, for the first International Council of Women. Comparing the early women's rights efforts at the Seneca Falls conference of 1848 to this International Council of Women, speaker Frederick Douglass remarked: 'Then its friends were few – now its friends are many. Then it was wrapped in obscurity – now it is lifted in sight of the whole civilized world, and people of all lands and languages give it their hearty support. Truly the change is vast and wonderful.'¹ Douglass' observations illustrated how the event was a culmination of the efforts of nineteenth-century women's rights activists and signalled the progress they had made in forty years. The product of international correspondence and connections among women activists, the conference demonstrated the wide-ranging scope and interests of nineteenth-century women's rights advocacy, which would soon be called feminism. Suffrage would not be granted in many countries until the twentieth century, but feminist thought encompassed more than suffrage; nineteenth-century feminist thought was characterised by activism and by its commitment to analysing the role of gender in order to achieve equality for women.

The efforts of nineteenth-century activists produced significant advances for women across the United States and Europe. Women entered the workforce as teachers, factory workers, nurses and doctors, among other professions. They gained access to higher education, from female seminaries teaching religious values to single-sex and co-educational colleges and universities emphasising the humanities, social sciences and sciences. The groundwork for twentieth-century reforms such as suffrage came from the nineteenth-century women who found their voices and detailed their feminist thought, philosophies and arguments through making speeches and writing fiction, pamphlets and articles in periodicals. Among the topics they discussed were suffrage, property rights, education, abolition of slavery, racial injustice, temperance, birth control, dress reform, marriage reform and labour reform.

Although the feminist thought espoused by nineteenth-century thinkers existed prior to the turn of the century, it was in the nineteenth century that it became widespread. The emergence of feminist thought as a more cohesive philosophy is often attributed to several factors: the Industrial Revolution that transformed the workforce, taking it out of the home; the Enlightenment focus on individual sovereignty; the legacy of the French Revolution; the activism for the abolition of slavery; and the religious revivals of the early nineteenth century that encouraged women's participation. All of these factors influenced the thinkers who embraced feminist sensibilities, but it is the growth of literacy, and the number of men and women who gained access to literacy, which led to more women developing, articulating and distributing feminist philosophies.

Contemporary readers may question the characterisation of nineteenth-century women's rights advocacy as feminist because the use of the term 'feminism' was not widespread until the twentieth century and because of the concern of applying modern definitions to past practices. The term 'feminism' did not emerge until the late nineteenth century, when it was often employed in a pejorative sense, a charge against women who did not fit certain ideals of womanliness. The term gained prominence in the 1880s and 1890s, first in France, then throughout Europe, before moving across the Atlantic to the United States. It became more commonly applied – sometimes losing its derogatory connotations – in the early twentieth century.[2] Speakers and writers integral to the development of feminist thought often used terms such as 'woman's rights', 'woman's emancipation' or 'woman's equality' to discuss their views. Though 'suffragist' is a term used to name the activists of this first wave of feminism, it does not encompass the breadth of concerns of nineteenth-century feminist thinkers, limiting them only to calls for the vote for women. Some historians prefer to discuss 'feminisms' rather than 'feminism' to show that feminist thought in the nineteenth century – as in other periods and in contemporary contexts – was not monolithic. Furthermore, feminist thought was not and is not exclusive to women. John Stuart Mill, Frederick Douglass and other men advocated for women's rights and helped to shape what would become a feminist philosophy. 'The woman question', as it was called in the nineteenth century, became the focus of debates among women and men, men and men, women and women, those we would call feminists and those we would call anti-feminist.

Feminist thought arose both in response to and within restrictive ideologies and institutions. Though many ideologies and institutions seemed to oppress women, nineteenth-century women also adopted some of these ideologies and entered these institutions, transforming them into feminist principles and feminist spaces in the process. Thus, the feminism of many nineteenth-century women does not always resemble the feminism of twenty-first-century women. Nineteenth-century women adopted ideologies about gender roles that contemporary feminists might define as anti-feminist. And there was much anti-feminist ideology embedded in institutional structures, such as the church. Nineteenth-century feminists, however, often adopted these ideologies and adapted these spaces to their own ends. Whether they did so strategically or because they agreed with ideologies based in gender differences varies. The rise of feminist thought, then, should not be seen as a heroic narrative or as a story of particular remarkable women. Rather, telling the story of the rise of feminist thought in the nineteenth century should forefront the development of the use of gender as a category of analysis. The growth and variations of feminist thought within nineteenth-century ideologies propelled the sometimes conflicting identities within feminism and women's rights advocacy and the widening scope of issues perceived as women's issues. These conflicts did not hinder but enabled feminist thought to develop, often in unexpected places.

Separate Spheres and Nineteenth-Century Women

Studies of nineteenth-century feminist thought have concentrated on several metaphors to both explain the restrictions placed on women and the arguments used to combat those restrictions. However, even though these metaphors proliferate in discussions of the status of nineteenth-century women, they are not without conflict about their use. The metaphors of 'separate spheres', 'the cult of true womanhood' and 'passionlessness' have dominated scholarly discussions of nineteenth-century thought and are often perceived as literal interpretations of nineteenth-century women's experiences.

'Separate spheres', a term first used by Alexis de Tocqueville to describe the gender demarcation he observed on a visit to the United States in 1835, became frequently used among both nineteenth-century thinkers and the historians who study them.[3] It was both a descriptor and an argument. Woman's sphere was the domestic; she was the 'angel of the home' while men's sphere was the public. Strict gender roles differentiating masculine from feminine qualities and concerns characterised the division of these spheres. Thus, 'separate spheres' serves as a metaphor to discuss women's subjugation to the home.

Many historians studying gender and feminist thought in the nineteenth century use the concept of separate spheres as a framework for analysis. Some of their narratives describe feminist action in the Victorian period as women finding ways to break out of their confining sphere to assert full rights to citizenship. Such a characterisation is problematic, as is a strict reliance on a separate spheres framework of analysis to describe gender roles in the nineteenth century. Many feminist scholars of the twentieth and twenty-first centuries have employed the framework, but they have also analysed and acknowledged the limitations of that framework.

For example, separate spheres seems a helpful category of analysis when we look at the role of women in the economy, in religion and in national identities. The Industrial Revolution transformed the workforce and economy in the United States and Europe. The result of its transformation on women in industrialised countries was the idea that work was done outside of the home; 'women's work', which often took place inside the home, was thus no longer categorised as work. However, women also benefited from industrialisation by going outside the home to work, especially in factories. The growth of what we now call a middle class affected these roles. Women workers outside the home then became a threat to a male-dominated workforce; therefore, a separate spheres ideology emerged to valorise women's work within the home. Religion also affected the development of an ideology of separate, gendered spheres, such as when religious leaders emphasised the woman's role in keeping the home a place of purity and piety, a sanctuary from compromised morals outside the home. Finally, separate spheres ideology benefited nationhood. Women's sphere was tied to the need to reproduce sons who would be good citizens of the nation. The result of many factors, the domesticity of women was celebrated and prescribed through separate spheres ideology.

Historian Barbara Welter described the prescriptive qualities placed upon nineteenth-century women as 'the cult of domesticity' or 'the cult of true womanhood':

> The attributes of True Womanhood, by which a woman judged herself and was judged by her husband, her neighbors and society could be divided into four cardinal virtues – piety, purity, submissiveness and domesticity. Put them all together and they spelled mother, daughter, sister, wife-woman. Without them, no matter whether there was fame, achievement or wealth, all was ashes. With them she was promised happiness and power.[4]

The cult of true womanhood explained the ideologies behind women's sphere. When women gained rights that took them out of that sphere, such as the right to be educated, they were often still relegated to a more feminine approach to that right. For example, higher education for women started in seminaries, where the feminine virtues of piety and purity were at the forefront of the curriculum. Such ideologies provided a justification for separate spheres to delineate the masculine from the feminine and were even written into law, such as marriage and divorce laws that assumed women's sexual purity.

Historian Nancy Cott has traced the origins and uses of the idea of 'passionlessness', a metaphor perpetuating the erasure of women's sexual feelings and the perception of women as pious, pure and morally superior to men. The evangelical religions of the late 1700s and early 1800s arose to counter what many considered the lack of mores brought about by the French Revolution; as a result of their efforts, the idea of passionlessness equated 'Christian values' to 'women's virtues'.[5] This ideology reversed previous assumptions of women as more sexual, and thus more dangerous, than men. Instead, women were presumed to lack sexual appetites. The new ideas were codified in religious institutions, medical literature and didactic fiction. Viewing women as passionless and thus more virtuous than men had both advantages and disadvantages for women. On the one hand, their perceived lack of sexual feeling kept them from gaining knowledge about the body and its pleasures; women contesting the characterisation of women as lacking sexual feeling pointed to the harms that could come from lack of knowledge and lack of ownership of their bodies within sexual relations – both outside and inside marriage. On the other hand, their perceived moral superiority to men became the foundation for many women's rights.

The framework provided by the metaphors of separate spheres, the cult of true womanhood and passionlessness becomes more complicated under further examination and reveals itself as location – and class – specific. Cott and Welter focused their research on early nineteenth-century white women living in New England in the United States, deriving their material from their careful study of letters, didactic manuals, fiction, magazines and other primary sources. Those with access to these tools of literacy would be more likely to leave records behind, so these terms do not represent all women's experiences, which are not monolithic, even within a given region or social standing. Once class and race come into the discussion, these metaphors as descriptions of the status of nineteenth-century women – and as the restrictions they fought against – become even more problematic so some scholars have questioned or avoided these terms.

These frameworks, however, facilitate analysis of power relations since they help to show who benefited from these ideologies. For example, the idea of true womanhood emerged as industrialisation arose, inferring a stake in keeping women's place in the home. Ideas of separate spheres, and the stakes in them, are also not specific to the northern United States, the context of Cott's and Welter's conclusions, but occurred in other countries as well. Whether a society embraced the gendered division of spheres depended upon factors like industrialisation, economy and literacy. For example, the ideals of true womanhood did not become a part of Latin America's national identities and ideologies until the twentieth century, owing to the lower rates of literacy and an economy that required both men and women to work outside the home. Once Latin American countries shifted to a more industrial economy in the early twentieth century, women's domesticity was celebrated in order to foster the formation of a middle class.[6] Social and economic class contributed to the rise of true womanhood as an ideal in Britain as well, where a stigma towards the working class led many to identify with the ideals of true womanhood as a marker of their higher-class status.[7] In the United States, womanhood was not only classed but raced. Harriet Jacobs' (1813–97) slave narrative, *Incidents in the Life of a Slave Girl* (1861), detailed the sexual degradations women slaves were subjected to because they were not seen as 'true women' lacking passion and promoting piety.[8]

It would be too simple to explain the status of nineteenth-century women using these ideals and ignoring the other, larger cultural factors at work. But it would also be too simple to ignore these terms in analysing the status of nineteenth-century women. Furthermore, the ideologies represented in these terms were not always restrictive; some nineteenth-century women found the basis of liberation rather than oppression within these ideas of the cult of true womanhood or domestic ideals, for example, making them defining features of nineteenth-century feminist thought. Therefore, instead of these metaphors supporting a view of feminist history of the nineteenth century as a heroic narrative featuring strong women who found ways to break out of the sphere that marginalised them, using these metaphors to understand feminist history helps to forefront the role of gender.

Historians have identified two lines of argument that indicate two types of feminist thought, one based on natural rights or justice and the other based on the perceived gender differences and higher morality of women. Historians have different names for these, such as those who categorise the two as 'natural rights feminism' versus 'domestic feminism'. Natural rights feminism had its basis in the Enlightenment focus on individual sovereignty. Domestic feminism had its basis in gender differences. Hence, these two types of feminism are also called 'equality feminism' versus 'difference feminism', based on beliefs about gender roles: equality feminists believed in the sameness of men and women and argued that women should be granted the natural rights given to men; difference feminists believed in gender differences and argued that women should be given rights because those feminine qualities provided a balance to men and benefited the public sphere. In some cases, these two types of feminism can be distinguished by whether their adherents believed gender differences were biological or social in nature. The difference feminists often saw gender differences as innate and biological while equality feminists would characterise them as the result of socialisation. Also called 'rational feminism' versus 'ethical feminism', ethical feminism emphasised femininity and feminine values.[9] These adherents of a 'relational feminism' believed in the uniqueness of women and their feminine values while 'individualist feminism' emphasised the rights of the individual.

Gender differences were not always the distinguishing characteristics between types of feminism, however. Historians studying feminism in a European context also distinguished between what they called 'bourgeois feminism' and 'socialist feminism', with the first putting women's rights at the forefront of their agenda and the second putting them as part of a larger socialist agenda.[10] In a US context, these types of feminist thought have been identified as the 'argument from justice' and 'the argument from expediency',[11] the latter so-named because emphasising women's beneficial attributes proved to be an expedient – and effective – argument for reform.

Feminist Foundations: True Women and Their Rights

A feminism based on gender differences that emphasised feminine values was more common across both the United States and Europe. Though the ideology of gender differences can seem confining in contemporary contexts, nineteenth-century women found arguments for rights within these apparent restrictions. For example, the perception of women as more moral than men provided the means to argue for their participation in public forums. Not surprisingly then, religious institutions and the movement for the abolition of slavery were the first areas where women asserted their rights in the public sphere.

For example, the Grimké sisters, Sarah Grimké (1792–1873) and Angelina Grimké Weld (1805–79), both devout Quakers involved in the church, participated in the movement for the abolition of slavery by making speeches throughout the United States during the 1830s. Grimké Weld delivered her *Speech at Pennsylvania Hall* on 17 May 1838, which argued for women's difference having a positive effect on the public sphere. She emphasised feminine values as the most effective approach in changing the hearts and minds of men and women on the subject of slavery: 'The great men of this country will not do this work; the church will never do it. A desire to please the world, to keep the favor of all parties and of all conditions, makes them dumb on this and every other unpopular subject.' Grimké Weld suggested that their lack of rights was a strength for women advocating for abolition; because women were not in a position of power, they were in a better position to make unpopular arguments. She also urged women to utilise the form of the petition as an alternative to the ballot box.[12] The Grimké sisters, two of the earliest women to spread a feminist consciousness, faced much resistance, not only for the abolitionist ideas they advocated but also for their daring act to proclaim this advocacy through public speeches. The speech at Pennsylvania Hall was protested by those who believed women should not speak in public, especially in front of a mixed audience of both men and women – what was called a 'promiscuous audience'. Because the act of speaking to a promiscuous audience countered the definition of a true woman, women activists needed to assert their true womanhood and position their advocacy as a feminine value in line with the actions of a true woman.[13]

The Quaker church supported the Grimké sisters' initial efforts for abolition as moral reform and defended their public speaking as the Quakers were one of the few religious sects allowing women to speak in religious meetings and to become ordained. When the Grimké sisters became more explicit about women's rights, important male figures in the Quaker church who had supported their abolitionist goals, including Theodore Weld, the husband of Angelina Grimké Weld, condemned their efforts, causing Sarah Grimké to publish *Letters on the Equality of the Sexes* in 1838.[14] The sisters demonstrate how many women came to a feminist consciousness through their involvement in religious movements and those movements' moral reform goals. They thus framed these efforts as their duty as women, using an argument from expediency that positioned feminine values – and the true women that held them – as morally superior.

In an address given in 1832, African American activist Maria Stewart (1803–79), adopted the sermonic style of a pastor to frame her speech for abolition and to justify her speaking as a Christian duty 'to promote the cause of Christ'. She emphasised the role of women as pious moral guardians and implored them to exert their influence:

> O woman, woman! Upon you I call; for upon your exertions almost entirely depends whether the rising generation shall be any thing more than we have been or not. O woman, woman! Your example is powerful, your influence is great; it extends over your husbands and children, and throughout the circle of your acquaintance. Then let me exhort you to cultivate among yourselves a spirit of Christian love and unity, having charity one for another … And, O, my God, I beseech thee to grant that the nations of the earth may hiss at us no longer![15]

Grounding feminist claims in religion allowed the difference feminists to assert the power to educate on moral issues. In order to educate men and help them be more moral and pious, they needed to have rights. Both Stewart and the Grimké sisters relied on ideologies of gender differences and religious values not to restrict women but to show the importance of women's voices in these debates.

Religious values brought many women to a feminist consciousness, whether it was by encouraging their participation in the church and in moral reform advocacy or by providing a space in which it was possible for equality to exist. For example, Russian feminist Marie Zebrikoff (1835–?) noted how the radical Christian societies in Russia modelled after similar organisations in the United States helped to bring Russian women to a feminist consciousness. She said that '[the Christian woman] feels raised to a condition of equality and independence by her faith in a religious doctrine' that places men and women on equal moral footing. Thus, these women found a basis for why they did not deserve to be oppressed both within the home and by the state.[16]

Greater access to education for women came from these arguments from expediency and from the value of Republican motherhood to national and racial identities. Republican motherhood, an idea whose origins can be traced to the Enlightenment (and even further back to ancient Greece), made women the chief producers and reproducers of the values of a nation's new male citizens. Republican motherhood connected to the idea that women were morally superior; they became the 'custodian[s] of civic morality'.[17] Towards the late nineteenth century, a Darwinian discourse emerged that also placed responsibility on women for producing the 'fittest' citizens, whether 'fit' was described as pertaining to health or to intelligence. What has been called Republican motherhood and Darwinian motherhood[18] actually enabled women to argue for specific rights in order to improve themselves and thus their sons – the future citizens of a country. Frances Ellen Watkins Harper (1825–1911) urged 'Enlightened Motherhood' to uplift African Americans after the abolition of slavery:

> No race can afford to neglect the enlightenment of its mothers. If you would have a clergy without virtue or morality, a manhood without honor, and a womanhood frivolous, mocking, and ignorant, neglect the education of your daughters. But if, on the other hand, you would have strong men, virtuous women, and good homes, then enlighten your women, so that they may be able to bless their homes by the purity of their lives, the tenderness of their hearts, and the strength of their intellects.[19]

To achieve this enlightenment, women needed to have rights and access to opportunities. Harper's argument also illustrated another popular tenet of nineteenth-century women's rights advocacy: the idea that nations could not become strong if they restricted the women responsible for nurturing an engaged and knowledgeable future male citizenry.

Emphasising feminine attributes and true womanhood was essential to gaining adherents to feminist principles. Anti-feminists and anti-suffragists of the nineteenth century based their arguments on fear that giving women rights would take them out of their natural place and would make them more masculine than feminine, and more male than female. Some feminist thinkers dealt with these objections by agreeing that women's place was not in public and redefining the public spaces they entered as an extension of the home, which emphasised their roles as moral guardians of the home. They could argue for rights based not on their status as humans or citizens, as natural rights feminists would, but on their status as women and all the gendered attributes that came with it. Theodore Stanton (1851–1925), discussing French debates on the woman question, answered the argument that granting women rights would destroy their womanhood by emphasising a belief in 'equality in difference' ('*l'égalité dans la difference*'): 'The question is not to make woman a man, but to complete man by woman.'[20]

Thus, much feminist thought in the nineteenth century combatted restrictive ideologies of gender by accommodating and adopting them. The adoption of an ideology of gender differences, whether strategic on the part of feminists or in collusion with it, created a conflict: women accepted gendered ideologies, maintaining the status quo, while also challenging it by asserting rights for women. Women claiming motherhood as a reason for giving them rights did nothing to change gendered thinking. As a result, gendered appeals for women's rights may seem negative, even when they led to positive reforms. To nineteenth-century feminists, though, gendered segregation of spheres – physical spaces, intellectual concerns, and personal attributes – created positive spaces for women to connect with each other.

Historian Caroll Smith-Rosenberg identified a 'female world of love and ritual', a female culture based in homosocial networks. Segregation by gender into separate spheres, Smith-Rosenberg argued, led to the emotional segregation of men and women, and, consequently, to intense emotional relationships between women.[21] These intense relationships are documented by the letters they sent each other, which often resemble the types of letter lovers might exchange, but, as Smith-Rosenberg explained, were not always an indication of a lesbian identity despite their seemingly sensual content. Their intense friendships and attachment to each other often began in childhood and extended well into their marriages with men. Even letters between sisters have elements that may remind modern readers of a sensual relationship. These women depended on each other emotionally. In a gender-segregated culture, women were left to develop strong attachments to each other and to feel isolated without those attachments. Through relationships with their mothers, sisters and cherished women friends, nineteenth-century women in the United States and Britain gained a support system unparalleled in other eras.

A women's culture also emerged during the French Revolution, leading to the first time women formally organised into political societies and women's clubs aimed at political representation, such as the Society for the Amelioration of the Condition of Women and the Woman's Rights Society.[22] Historian Estelle Freedman has identified 'separatism as strategy' in the creation of a separate public female sphere, exemplified in the late nineteenth century by the growth of women's political organisations, women's clubs and the settlement house movement.[23] Thus, these relationships among women in both their private communications and their contributions to literature and magazines created an alternative public female sphere and separate 'women's culture', which served as important prerequisites to the rise of a feminist consciousness and more formal feminist organising.

Justice, Equality and the 'New Woman'

Though a majority of feminists in the nineteenth century endorsed beliefs in gender roles, others responded to these restrictive ideas with natural rights arguments: that women should receive rights not based on what they would do with those rights but based on the values of individual sovereignty and democratic citizenship. These equality feminists challenged prevailing gender ideologies rather than adopting them. Mary Wollstonecraft (1759–97) pioneered this argument in her *Vindication of the Rights of Woman* published in 1792. This document pointed to gendered differences as a result of socialisation rather than inherent qualities in men and women. To Wollstonecraft, women were not inherently inferior to men; rather they were not given the same opportunities as men. She turned, then, to the role of education, believing, 'the neglected education of my fellow creatures is the grand source of the misery I deplore'. She attributed the idea of women as fragile and inferior in body and mind to 'a false system of education' maintained by men.[24] Wollstonecraft crafted the argument that would be taken up by many nineteenth-century feminists: women deserved every right given to men and the opportunity to reach equality with men. These women, by the end of the century, were called 'new women', a term that arose in 1894 to show the progress and new identities feminism enabled.

Many equality feminists resented the privileges males received as citizens, especially when those men did not possess the attributes, such as literacy, needed to be fully engaged citizens. John Stuart Mill (1806–73) in *The Subjection of Women* (1869) explained this disparity and pondered how men learned to subjugate women:

> Think what it is to a boy, to grow up to manhood in the belief that without any merit or any exertion of his own, though he may be the most frivolous and empty or the most ignorant and stolid of mankind, by the mere fact of being born a male he is by right the superior of all every one of an entire half of the human race.

In characterising this inequality as an 'evil' done to half the human race, Mill invoked the values of democracy, moral reform and religion.[25]

Equality feminists often challenged restrictive ideologies and traditional roles for women in institutionalised religion by leaving religious sects that subjugated women for sects that allowed women to become ordained. They also confronted gender disparities in religion through writing their own religious texts that refuted the inferiority of women. American feminist Elizabeth Cady Stanton (1815–1902) spearheaded the writing of *The Woman's Bible* in 1895 as a reaction to new editions of the Bible from the Church of England. Cady Stanton characterised the Bible as the source and 'the fountain of all tyranny'.[26] Indeed, religion had often been used as a justification for women's subordinate status. Cady Stanton and others argued that

> it is evident that our demands for equal recognition should now be made of the Church for the same rights we have asked of the State for the last fifty years, for the same rights, privileges and immunities that men enjoy. We must demand that the canon law, the Mosaic code, the Scriptures, prayer books and liturgies be purged of all invidious distinctions of sex, of all false teaching.[27]

Lucretia Mott (1793–1880), ordained as a Quaker minister, charged, 'It is not Christianity, but priestcraft that has subjected woman as we find her.'[28] These women challenged male dominance in the church by responding to what they deemed the 'false teachings' that kept women in an inferior status. Rejecting these teachings brought many women to a feminist consciousness.

This feminist consciousness most often took the form of arguments for suffrage to promote equal rights for women. Emphasising how it would heal the wrongs inflicted on women and enable them to assert full rights to equality, some feminists made suffrage the focus of their platform, often at the expense of other reforms. For example, British feminist Frances Power

Cobbe (1822–1904) praised the developments that had resulted in women accessing education, working outside the home and receiving property rights, but added, 'But the crown and completion of the program must be the attainment of the Political Franchise in every country wherein representative government prevails.' Cobbe also addressed how women lacked the ability to employ the methods available to men to combat oppression: through battles, revolutions and violent protests. They could only appeal to men as 'daughters to fathers; of sisters to brothers; of wives to husbands; of the women, who make the charm of society, to the men who call them friends'.[29] Cobbe recognised the conflict though: using these appeals and their influence – the influence celebrated by those arguing for rights based on women's feminine virtues – could not work if women had no power or influence to begin with. She explained, '[Women] have not the minutest political influence at their disposal wherewith to coerce their opponents. Never was there a case of such pure and simple Moral Pressure – of an appeal to justice, to reason, to men's sense of what is due, and right, and expedient for all.' To Cobbe, '"Suffrage is the key of woman's position." Obtaining it, every privilege she can reasonably desire must follow. Failing to obtain it, nothing – not even such instalments of her rights as she has hitherto enjoyed – is secure.'[30]

Other feminists, however, saw the vote as futile if women could not achieve full equality within the home. Tennessee Claflin (1844–1923), for example, urged a broader platform of reform that started with the rights women lost within marriage:

> If the enfranchised woman should still be compelled to remain the servile, docile, meekly-acquiescent, self-immolated and self-abnegative wife, there would be no difficulty about the voting. At the ballot-box is not where the shoe pinches, nor where the corn stings. It is at home where the husband, as in pre-historic times of anarchy, is the supreme ruler, that the little difficulty arises; he will not surrender this absolute power unless he is compelled.[31]

For some, property rights would address the inequities of women inside the home. Laws of coverture prevented women from having a legal identity once married. By the end of the century, many of these laws would be eradicated in the United States and Europe, though some tenets of them remained until well into the twentieth century.

Equality feminists often urged universal methods in challenging restrictions on women, even when these methods did not apply in all cases. Russian feminist Marie Zebrikoff spoke to the conflicts Cobbe addressed: that women could not fight inequality through government when they did not have a voice in the government. She noted that women in Russia could not employ the same means as American women because not even men in Russia had the rights they sought. But she also noted how movements for men to achieve these rights instigated the calls for women's enfranchisement as well: 'The spirit of liberty and equality is like rising water: it cannot mount in one portion of society without reaching the same level in every part. In England, to take another example, the women's movement sprang into life when the emancipation of the workman became a burning theme in the press, in public meetings and in parliament.'[32] Zebrikoff presented several examples that illustrated how feminist thought based on the principles of equality and individual sovereignty emerged from other movements addressing inequities, whether they urged the abolition of slavery or equality for workers. Once people began to believe in equal rights for certain populations, women could bring their calls for women's equality into those platforms.

Biological Determinism: Medical Science and the Female Body

Both difference and equality feminists needed to attend to the role of a belief in biological determinism in excluding women from the rights and privileges men enjoyed. Many debates and discussions of the woman question focused on how the attainment of these rights and privileges might affect women's bodies. Supporters and opponents of women's rights turned to medical science in considering a strict separation of spheres. Medical discourse shaped and was shaped by positions on women's social roles. Some literature from the scientific and medical communities resulted in defining women as 'diseased', 'hysteric' and controlled by their reproductive physiology. Thus, it would seem that science and medicine were unlikely spaces for developing feminist ideas. On the contrary, while there were those who used science and medicine to maintain restrictions, there were also those who found liberation for women within science and medicine, even while agreeing with gendered ideas of the body and women's social roles. The ideas of medical science could be turned to feminist and anti-feminist ends.

The idea that women's bodies made them inferior persisted throughout the nineteenth century, often despite scientific and medical advances. The most prominent argument for women's bodies restricting them from entering male-dominated spheres came from American physician Edward Clarke's bestselling and often republished volume *Sex in Education: A Fair Chance for Girls*, first published in 1873. Clarke (1820–77) argued that educating women in the same manner as men would damage women's bodies. He attributed women's illnesses to the energy women must expend in higher education taking energy away from the reproductive organs. However, he did not argue against all forms of education for women, but specifically attacked educational systems that pursued the 'identical' education of men and women. Clarke instead advocated 'appropriate' education for women that would not harm their reproductive health. Interestingly, Clarke made an argument similar to equality feminists in defining women's bodies as naturally healthy. He countered other physicians who viewed women's bodies as naturally weak and debilitating; instead he pointed to lifestyle choices and environment – in particular the education of women that was identical to the education men received – as the cause of a greater number of ill women in the United States.[33] In his ideal system of education, women would be given education 'appropriate' for their sex, one that does not unduly tax the mind and one that allows for rest during their 'periodical function'. He also responded to the naysayers who pointed to institutions of co-education that graduated healthy women; Clarke insisted that the long-term physiological effects could not yet be known and that these women would most likely end up with the same ailments as found in his sample of patients.

Clarke's ideas provoked response from female physicians such as British physician Elizabeth Garrett Anderson (1836–1917), who in 1874 attacked Clarke's logic in *The Fortnightly Review*'s ongoing discussion of his work. Anderson offered alternative causes in her repudiation of Clarke:

> The cases that Dr. Clarke brings forward in support of his opinion against continuous mental work during the period of development could be outnumbered many times over even in our own limited experience, by those in which the breakdown of nervous and physical health seems at any rate to be distinctly traceable to want of adequate mental interest and occupation in the years immediately succeeding school life.

She pointed out that these illnesses were more prevalent in 'fashionable and idle American women – those guiltless of ever having passed an examination – than they are among those who have gone through the course of study complained of'.[34] Anderson's argument also critiqued the limited number of women in Clarke's study. Indeed, Clarke's sample size was extremely small and drawn from the same higher education institution – Vassar College.

Feminist thought did not arise only in response to arguments like Clarke's that relied on biological determinism; there were those who used the differences in women's bodies not for restrictions but for rights. For example, some women used the same line of argument – that women's bodies were not naturally weak and that the higher number of illnesses could be attributed to lifestyle and environment – to make an argument for giving women rights, such as not restricting them to the home or curtailing their physical exercise. They also embraced arguments that highlighted anatomical differences to show how women's bodies made them the vessels for a new generation; in order to nurture this new generation within their bodies, they needed rights.

In fact, women were able to professionalise as physicians by conceding to gender roles: they endorsed a belief in biology determining a woman's nature by arguing that women would be better physicians than men because of their femininity. British physician Elizabeth Blackwell (1821–1910) addressed the London School of Medicine for Women in 1889 to argue for women's special influence on medicine because they are 'nobler creatures' who can provide 'moral guidance'.[35] They thus needed a scientific education to fulfil their roles in combining 'sympathy and science – the hard and soft sides of medical practice'.[36]

Those who embraced the work of Charles Darwin and applied it to social roles, such as sociologist Herbert Spencer (1820–1903), discussed the woman question as central to evolution. Though many employed this thinking to support the biological inferiority of women, there were also those who made a case for women's rights as central to progress. The role of motherhood, then, turned into a central feature in debates on the woman question. While many difference feminists argued for rights based on their roles as mothers who could influence the next generation, more radical feminists instead argued for the reclassification and professional-isation of motherhood – making it into a tool for Social Darwinism and a public good. Charlotte Perkins Gilman (1860–1935) made this argument in the influential *Women and Economics* (1898), which was translated into seven languages. Gilman used Darwinian arguments to show that women's economic reliance on men was not natural but a result of social factors and that keeping women subordinate to men impeded progress. For Gilman, women's rights were not necessarily a matter of natural rights or justice but a matter of social evolution. She framed women's inequality in economic terms: though women do not produce wealth, their labour in the household has economic value, which is not compensated. She defined motherhood as 'an exchangeable commodity given by women in payment for clothes and food': 'He is the market, the demand. She is the supply.'[37] Thus, she argued, motherhood should be a more professional activity: it should be taught as a science – including instruction in nutrition and physiology, which can be classified as 'preventative medicine' – and recognised as a professional skill in line with other compensated and trained professions.[38]

Throughout the nineteenth century, many thinkers debated whether women's bodies should limit them from certain occupations and pursuits. Though their dispositions were often cited as a reason to prevent women from achieving certain rights, as more women gained these rights, the reasons for restricting them disappeared. Anna Julia Cooper (1858–1964) on 'The Higher Education of Women' (1892) pointed out that the education of women had not led to 'upheaval' and 'collapse'. Cooper also praised the 'special influence of women' in the fields of 'religion, science, art, economics, [which] have all needed the feminine flavor'.[39] Equality and difference feminists often responded to biological determinism by accepting it. In the twentieth century, though, true women arguments fell out of favour with new women. The more successful suffragists of the twentieth century relied on philosophies of justice and individual sovereignty.

Conclusion

The exclusion of women from the 1840 World Slavery convention in London resulted in the first women's rights convention in Seneca Falls, New York, in 1848. In her opening remarks to the convention, Cady Stanton insisted that the time had come for women's rights and that 'woman herself must do this work; for woman alone can understand the height, the depth, the length, and the breadth of her own degradation. Man cannot speak for her, because he has been educated to believe that she differs from him so materially, that he cannot judge of her thoughts, feelings, and opinions by his own.' Women did this work through the nineteenth century as they debated the woman question and developed the philosophies that would become feminist thought. Cady Stanton's speech enumerated the principles that made their way into women's 'declaration of independence' from men, the *Declaration of Sentiments* of 1848:

> We are assembled to protest against a form of government, existing without the consent of the governed – to declare our right to be free as man is free, to be represented in the government which we are taxed to support, to have such disgraceful laws as give man the power to chastise and imprison his wife, to take the wages which she earns, the property which she inherits, and, in case of separation, the children of her love; laws which make her the mere dependent on his bounty. It is to protest against such unjust laws as these that we are assembled to-day, and to have them, if possible, forever erased from our statute-books, deeming them a shame and a disgrace to a Christian republic in the nineteenth century.[40]

Cady Stanton's remarks illustrated the multiple fronts of the battle women needed to wage, from ideas of women's mental and physical inferiority to their disenfranchisement in law and religion.

Instead of segregating the women's rights advocates who argued for more conservative causes, the International Council of Women in 1888 welcomed all women's groups working to improve women's conditions, going beyond suffrage goals and including women in temperance and Christian societies, labour reform and moral reform movements. They made no distinctions based on a belief in gender differences. The line between equality feminism and difference feminism was not always clear because some women made arguments that contained both an argument from justice and an argument from expediency. Wollstonecraft and Cady Stanton, for example, could not afford to ignore the power of arguments for rights based in motherhood. In some cases, women may have adopted the argument from expediency and agreed with ideologies of gender differences strategically, but there were also women who subscribed to and celebrated women's difference. These difference feminist arguments should not be seen as lesser arguments than the true feminist arguments of the equality feminists, however. One did not lead to the other; rather, both co-existed-and both were feminist.

NOTES

1 Frederick Douglass, 'Frederick Douglass on Woman Suffrage', *Woman's Journal* (14 April 1888), Blackpast.org, www.blackpast.org/1888-frederick-douglass-woman-suffrage#sthash.093GvNII.dpuf.

2 Karen Offen, 'Defining Feminism: A Comparative Historical Approach', *Signs* 14 (1988), 126–8.

3 Linda K. Kerber, 'Separate Spheres, Female Worlds, Woman's Place: The Rhetoric of Women's History', *Journal of American History* 75 (1988), 9–10.

4 Barbara Welter, 'The Cult of True Womanhood: 1820–1860', *American Quarterly* 18 (1966), 152.

5 Nancy Cott, 'Passionlessness: An Interpretation of Victorian Sexual Ideology, 1790–1850', *Signs* 4 (1978), 221.

6 Donna J. Guy, 'True Womanhood in Latin America', *Journal of Women's History* 14 (2002), 170–1.

7 Philippa Levine, *Victorian Feminism 1850–1900* (Gainesville: University Press of Florida, 1994), p. 15.

8 Harriet A. Jacobs, *Incidents in the Life of a Slave Girl*, ed. Lydia Marie Frances Child (Boston: Ticknor & Fields, 1861), Documenting the American South, http://docsouth.unc.edu/fpn/jacobs/jacobs.html.

9 Minike Bosch, 'History and Historiography of First-Wave Feminism in the Netherlands, 1860–1922', in *Women's Emancipation Movements in the Nineteenth Century: A European Perspective*, eds. Sylvia Paletschek and Bianka Pietrow-Ennker (Stanford, CA: Stanford University Press, 2004), p. 54.

10 Levine, *Victorian Feminism*, p. 16.

11 Aileen S. Kraditor, *The Ideas of the Woman Suffrage Movement 1890–1920* (New York: Columbia University Press, 1981).

12 Angelina Grimké Weld, *Speech in Pennsylvania Hall* (17 May 1838), Women's Speech Archive, www.womenspeecharchive.org/women/profile/speech/index.cfm?ProfileID=102&SpeechID=457.

13 Susan Zaeske, 'The Promiscuous Audience Controversy and the Emergence of the Early Women's Rights Movement', *Quarterly Journal of Speech* 81 (1995), 191–2.

14 Sarah Grimké, *Letters on the Equality of the Sexes, and the Condition of Woman: Addressed to Mary S. Parker, President of the Boston Female Anti-Slavery League* (Boston: Isaac Knapp, 1838), Archive.org, https://archive.org/stream/lettersonequalitoogrimrich/lettersonequalitoogrimrich_djvu.txt.

15 Maria Stewart, 'An Address Delivered Before the Afric-American Female Intelligence Society of Boston', in *With Pen and Voice: A Critical Anthology of Nineteenth-Century African-American Women*, ed. Shirley Wilson Logan (Carbondale: Southern Illinois University Press, 1995), pp. 11, 16.

16 Marie Zebrikoff, 'Russia', in *Selections from The Woman Question in Europe*, ed. Theodore Stanton, compiled by D. G. Rohr (New York: MSS Information Corporation, 1974), p. 149.

17 Linda K. Kerber, *Women of the Republic: Intellect and Ideology in Revolutionary America* (Chapel Hill: University of North Carolina Press, 1980), p. 11.

18 Amanda Frisken, *Victoria Woodhull's Sexual Revolution: Political Theater and the Popular Press in Nineteenth-Century America* (Philadelphia: University of Pennsylvania Press, 2004), p. 136; Wendy Hayden, *Evolutionary Rhetoric: Sex, Science, and Free Love in Nineteenth-Century Feminism* (Carbondale: Southern Illinois University Press, 2013).

19 Frances Ellen Watkins Harper, 'Enlightened Motherhood: An Address Before the Brooklyn Literary Society' (15 November 1892), Gifts of Speech: Women's Speeches from Around the World, http://gos.sbc.edu/h/harperf.html.

20 Theodore Stanton, 'France', in *Selections from The Woman Question in Europe*, p. 21.

21 Carroll Smith-Rosenberg, 'The Female World of Love and Ritual: Relations between Women in Nineteenth-Century America', *Signs* 1 (1975), 9.

22 T. Stanton, 'France', 27.

23 Estelle Freedman, 'Separatism as Strategy: Female Institution Building and American Feminism, 1870–1930', *Feminist Studies* 5 (1979), 512–29.

24 Mary Wollstonecraft, *Vindication of the Rights of Woman*, 1792, Project Gutenberg, www.gutenberg.org/ebooks/3420.

25 John Stuart Mill, 'The Subjection of Women', in *Feminism: The Essential Historical Writings*, ed. Miriam Schneir (New York: Vintage, 1992), pp. 176, 178.

26 Elizabeth Cady Stanton, 'The Degraded Status of Women in the Bible', in *Bible and Church Degrade Women* (Chicago: H. L. Green, 1896), p. 8.

27 Elizabeth Cady Stanton, 'Speech at Metropolitan Opera House in New York City on November 12, 1895', in *Women Without Superstition 'No Gods-No Masters': The Collected Writings of Women Freethinkers of the Nineteenth and Twentieth Centuries*, by Annie Laurie Gaylor (Madison, WI: The Freedom from Religion Foundation, 1997), p. 107.

28 Lucretia Mott, 'Not Christianity, but Priestcraft', in *Feminism: The Essential Historical Writings*, ed. Miriam Schneir (New York: Vintage, 1992), p. 100.

29 Frances Power Cobbe, 'Introduction', in *Selections from The Woman Question in Europe*, p. 11.

30 Cobbe, 'Introduction', p. 8.

31 Tennie C. Claflin, *Constitutional Equality, a Right of Woman* (New York: Woodhull, Claflin, & Co., 1871), p. 114.

32 Zebrikoff, 'Russia', p. 138.

33 Edward Clarke, *Sex in Education: A Fair Chance for Girls* (Boston: James R. Osgood & Company, 1874), p. 167.

34 Elizabeth Garrett Anderson, 'Sex in Mind and Education: A Reply', *Fortnightly Review* 15 (1874), in *Gender & Science: Late Nineteenth-Century Debates on the Female Mind and Body*, ed. Katharina Rowold (Bristol: Thoemmes Press, 1996), pp. 64–6.

35 Elizabeth Blackwell, *Essays in Medical Sociology* [1902] (New York: Arno Press, 1972), pp. 8, 10.

36 Regina Markell Morantz-Sanchez, *Sympathy and Science: Women Physicians in American Medicine* (New York: Oxford University Press, 1985), p. 5.

37 Charlotte Perkins Gilman, *Women and Economics: The Economic Factor between Men and Women as a Factor in Social Evolution* (New York: Harper & Row, 1966), pp. 13–15, 86.

38 Gilman, *Women and Economics*, pp. 230–1.

39 Anna Julia Cooper, 'The Higher Education of Women', in *Available Means: An Anthology of Women's Rhetoric(s)*, eds. Joy Ritchie and Kate Ronald (Pittsburgh, PA: University of Pittsburgh Press, 2001), pp. 165, 168.

40 Elizabeth Cady Stanton, 'Opening Address at Seneca Falls Convention', and 'Declaration of Sentiments', Gifts of Speech: Women's Speeches from Around the World, http://gos.sbc.edu/byyears/1800s.html#1848.

II

SAREE MAKDISI

Race and Empire in the Nineteenth Century

'Of the thousand millions of human beings that are said to constitute the population of the entire globe, there are – socially, morally and perhaps even physically considered – but two distinct and broadly marked races, viz., the wanderers and the civilized tribes', announces Henry Mayhew (1812–87) at the very beginning of his widely influential *London Labour and the London Poor*. Moreover, Mayhew adds, not only are all humans divisible into either the wandering or civilised races, but each civilised population has attached to it a wandering horde that preys on it – and this, he argues, goes for England as much as anywhere else. 'It is curious that no one has as yet applied the above facts to the explanation of certain anomalies in the present state of society among ourselves', he goes on.

> That we, like the Kafirs, Fellahs, and Finns, are surrounded by wandering hordes – the 'Sonquas' and the 'Fingoes' of this country – paupers, beggars, and outcasts, possessing nothing but what they acquire by depradation from the industrious, provident and civilized portion of the community; that the heads of these nomads are remarkable for the greater development of the jaws and cheekbones rather than those of the head; and that they have a secret language of their own – an English 'cuze-cat' or 'slang' as it is called – for the concealment of their designs: these are points of coincidence so striking that, when placed before the mind, make us marvel that the analogy should have remained thus long unnoticed.[1]

At a single stroke, Mayhew's mid-century assessment of race in imperial Britain renders any hard and fast distinction between inside and outside – England and the colonies, metropolis and colonial peripheries – unstable. This must be the point of departure for any consideration of the relationship between race and empire in the nineteenth century. Seen from Mayhew's vantage point (and he is an exemplary figure, representative of a dominant way of viewing the world at the time), there were whole populations within England – people who would today be considered white and English – who were seen as racially different from the settled and 'civilised' portion of the population for whom Mayhew was writing. 'We' are indeed superior to other races, Mayhew suggests; but those other races aren't just out there in the imperial contact zone, but right here among 'us' – not merely in the form of immigrants from Africa, Asia, Ireland or elsewhere (who were also present in England of course), but in the form of native-born Englishmen. Indeed, Mayhew adds, we can study 'the moral characteristics of the nomad races of other countries, as a means of comprehending the more readily those of the vagabonds and outcasts of our own'.[2] That is, we can use our knowledge of other places and societies, including in the empire, to better understand England itself.

Thus Europe did not have to look beyond its shores to find its Other; the Other, it turns out, was already in Europe, and was European. This of course throws open the whole question of what it means to be European in the first place. If Europeans would eventually think of themselves not simply as more advanced than other peoples but really further ahead in the stream of developmental time, Europe itself might be thought to inhabit several different and contradictory stages of development, different moments in time, as it were.[3] For, as complicated as it might have been, precisely the same colonial claims and logics of historical time were used to understand certain territories and populations within Europe itself, who were understood to be misaligned with the temporal pressures of modernisation, and hence holdovers of some kind from a premodern era, closer to the savage and the primitive than to their more urbane and sophisticated compatriots (hence their formidable jaws and cheekbones).[4] Indeed, while European imperialists imagined themselves to be engaged in a civilising mission overseas, they also came to think of the need for a civilising mission within Europe: processes of either elimination or assimilation of these internal racial Others that would ultimately enable a clearer and cleaner geographical differentiation between civilisation and its others on a global scale by the end of the nineteenth century.

As a result, England (let alone Britain's Celtic periphery[5]) at the turn of the nineteenth century could hardly be considered unambiguously a 'civilised', modern nation. Long before Mayhew himself, when sophisticated or educated middle-class English writers looked at the lower orders of their own country, 'savagery' was what they saw – and in exactly the same terms that they saw it in Africa or Asia or the Pacific. Native-born Englishmen (again, let alone the Irish, the Welsh or Scottish Highlanders, all of whom were subjected to formal processes of colonial intervention) were thought of in precisely the same terms that defined their encounters with 'primitive' people in the colonial realm.[6] England itself was thought of as largely a country awaiting civilisation and even a kind of domestic imperialism. 'I recollect the awkward gaze wherewith the people looked upon me, and the painful feelings of my heart when I retired to a little hovel from among them', the Reverend George Greatbatch recalled after arriving in the village in Lancashire ('probably one of the most unenlightened and uncivilized parts of the kingdom') to which he was sent as a missionary in 1801. 'I had little thought there was a station for me at home which so much resembled the ideas I had formed of an uncivilized heathen land.'[7] Greatbatch was by no means unique; other missionaries found in England a 'heathenism as dense as any in Polynesia or Central Africa', and the population of England's rural towns and villages 'as heathen and barbarian as the natives of darkest Africa'.[8] Greatbatch was only one of many clergymen dispatched by missionary societies either to what they regarded as the heathen districts of London or of the English countryside or to faraway locations throughout the empire; in any case, from their point of view, there wasn't much difference among these geographically dispersed places and populations. In his classic work on the working people of England, Friedrich Engels quotes a clergyman who notes that people in the fashionable West End of London knew as little of the inhabitants of the impoverished eastern districts of the metropolis 'as of the savages of Australia or the South Sea Isles'.[9]

These dynamics were hardly restricted to England but were a generalised European phenomenon. Throughout Europe, the view of the civilising mission that emerged alongside modern colonialism was never restricted solely to overseas subjects; other 'savage' populations at home were also seen to be in need of civilisation and development – these erstwhile Europeans were viewed in the same racial terms as Africans and Arabs and other 'primitive' or 'inferior' people in the overseas colonial realm.[10] In Britain, France, Russia and Italy, this set of attitudes developed alongside and in inextricable relationship to exterior processes of colonisation.[11] Thus, racial discourses tying the national interior to the colonial exterior were inseparable from the emergence of identifiably modern forms of class identity through the nineteenth century. 'While social historians generally have assumed that racial logics drew on the ready-made cultural disparagements honed to distinguish between middle-class virtues and the immorality of the poor, as well as between the "undeserving" and the "respectable" poor among themselves, it may well be that such social etymologies make just as much sense reversed', Ann Stoler argues. 'The racial lexicon of empire and the sexualized images of it, in some cases, may have provided for a European language of class as often as the other way around.'[12] In other words, the language of race gave a way for European writers to think through and describe their attitudes towards and relations to their social inferiors at home.

As we have seen, church missionaries were active participants in this process, but they were by no means unique. The language of race was consistently deployed by radical thinkers and writers from the late eighteenth century through much of the nineteenth. Consider the description of Grimes, a 'common labouring man' in William Godwin's 1794 novel *Caleb Williams*. 'He was not precisely a lad of vicious propensities, but in an inconceivable degree boorish and uncouth', the narrator says.

> His complexion was scarcely human; his features were coarse, and strangely discordant and disjointed from each other. His lips were thick, and the tone of his voice broad and unmodulated. His legs were of equal size from one end to the other, and his feet misshapen and clumsy. He had nothing spiteful or malicious in his disposition, but he was a total stranger to tenderness; he could not feel for those refinements in others, of which he had no experience in himself.

He was, in short, an 'uncouth and half-civilized animal'.[13] Nor is Grimes the only character described in such racial and indeed animalised terms in the novel. Caleb at one point encounters a terrifying woman who he describes in something more than merely loathsome terms:

> Her eyes were red and blood-shot; her hair was pendent in matted and shaggy tresses about her shoulders; her complexion swarthy, and of the consistency of parchment; her form spare, and her whole body, her arms in particular, uncommonly vigorous and muscular. Not the milk of human kindness, but the feverous blood of savage ferocity, seemed to flow from her heart; and her whole figure suggested an idea of unmitigable energy, and an appetite gorged in malevolence.[14]

Like Grimes, this woman is native-born and English; but, far from serving as the basis for a neat contrast with colonial savagery, characters like this serve to confirm the sense that the domestic and the foreign savage are one and the same, equally in need of the ministration of civilisation.

Nowhere are these kinds of racial characterisations of the lower orders more starkly depicted through the nineteenth century than in London, the very heart of the empire. Entire districts of the metropolis were seen from a 'respectable' point of view (like Godwin's or Mayhew's) to be inhabited by wandering hordes. In these areas, in fact, the language of race and a more stripped-down discourse of animalisation were collapsed into one another. By the second third of the nineteenth century, the term 'rookery' came into wide use as a way to describe the darkest and densest slums of London. A rookery – still used today to refer to a place of dense animal habitation – is a place where people take on a degraded existence so shorn of individuality that they become seen as animals living densely packed together (imagine the beach of a seal or walrus rookery and you get the point) as dictated by what one observer called their 'common wants and a common nature'.[15] This sense of commonness precludes the kind of individualisation that came to be seen as foundational for the development of individual subjectivity in the modern liberal sense, and of its social and architectural corollary, privacy.[16] Indeed, 'There is no privacy here for any of the over-crowded population; every apartment in the place is accessible from every other by a dozen different approaches.'[17] That is to say, just as the people themselves have a kind of common existence (i.e. both shared but also mean, low), the spaces they inhabit are common in the most degraded sense of the term. To the outside viewer, as Dickens writes in one of the pieces in *Sketches by Boz*, this is shocking and alienating: 'He traverses streets of dirty, straggling houses, with now and then an unexpected court composed of buildings as ill-proportioned and deformed as the half-naked children that wallow in the kennels.'[18] Notice how the animalisation of the spaces directly leads to the animalisation of the people 'wallowing' in their 'kennels'.

In these kinds of slums, the worst of the worst end up merging together. There, as one mid-century writer puts it, 'everything that is squalid, hideous, debauched and immoral, makes its dwelling; – there woman is as far removed from the angel as Satan is from the Godhead, and man is as closely allied to the brute as the idiot is to the baboon'.[19] It becomes impossible to imagine species – let alone racial – allegiance with the kinds of degraded creature who inhabit such spaces. Even the narrator of Mary Wollstonecraft's politically radical 1798 novella *Maria* admits, 'in viewing the squalid inhabitants of some of the lanes and back streets of the metropolis', feeling 'mortified at being compelled to consider them as my fellow-creatures, as if an ape had claimed kindred with me'.[20] Baboons and apes, then, are what one comes across in these parts of the imperial capital; or Africans or Arabs, who were in any case not much higher on the biological scale that started to emerge at around this time (indeed it is worth noting that these kinds of attitude, anticipating modern racism, were still only in formation in the nineteenth century, not yet hardened into the attitudes that would reach full development only in the twentieth century).

Recalling Mayhew's global differentiation of two races becomes essential here, pitting 'us', the civilised, settled, respectable and industrious inhabitants of the city against 'them', the degraded and animalised wandering Others among us, with their small heads and large cheekbones, their disregard for private property, female chastity and (shudder) hard work. Thus, even as an imagined community of national belonging was developing in the nineteenth century, emerging right alongside it was a biological and racial logic and lines of separation that cut right through the nation, rather than separating the national space neatly from the outside. In other words, being one of 'us' was not simply a matter of national identity, but rather a question of racial belonging that did not clearly align with the national space.

'A few years ago', George Godwin wrote in the mid-1850s, 'it was a fashion to visit the "Rookery'" of St. Giles', and wonder at the peculiarities of that strange land'. He notes that even if there have been various improvements, these are still dangerous spaces hostile to outside intruders: 'To investigate the condition of the houses of the very poor in this great metropolis is a task of no small danger and difficulty: it is necessary to brave the risks of fever and other injuries to health, and the contact of men and women often as lawless as the Arab or the Kaffir.' He continues by noting that, 'there is amongst the very poor a strong feeling against intrusion few persons venture into these haunts besides the regular inhabitants, the London missionaries, the parish surgeon, and the police, and thus the extent of this great evil is imperfectly understood'.[21] Such gestures had to a certain extent been made before. Henry Fielding, for example, had famously written of London that 'the whole appears as a vast wood or forest, in which a thief may harbour with as great security as wild beasts do in the deserts of Africa or Arabia'.[22] But both in Fielding and in Godwin what is being proposed is a comparison: London and its more problematic residents are *compared* to Africa or Arabia and their inhabitants; they are not collapsed into them. Quite consistently from the second third of the nineteenth century on, however, the comparison – as *comparison* – would be dropped and certain segments of the English lower orders would be transformed into outright 'Arabs' themselves.

'Of all the dark and dismal thoroughfares in the parish of St. Giles, or, indeed, in the great wilderness of London, few, we think, will compare with that known as Church Lane, which runs between High Street and New Oxford Street', Walter Thornbury writes in the 1870s.

> During the last half century, while the metropolis has been undergoing the pressure of progress consequent upon the quick march of civilisation, what remains of the Church Lane of our early days has been left with its little colony of Arabs as completely sequestered from London society as if it was part of *Arabia Petræa*. Few pass through Church Lane who are not members of its own select society ... none else have any business there; and if they had, they would find it to their interest to get out of it as soon as possible. Its condition is a disgrace to the great city, and to the parish to which it belongs.[23]

The 'Arabs' being referred to here are not from – and indeed have nothing to do with – the region to the south and east of the Mediterranean. Rather, they are the racial embodiments of the wandering population that Mayhew had warned of two decades previously. If Arabs wander, the reasoning went (with reference to Bedouin rather than the inhabitants of the great Arab cities of Cairo, Baghdad, Damascus or Jerusalem – for they, in Mayhew's schema, were actually more like sophisticated Englishmen than the human refuse of St Giles), then wanderers must be, if not literally Arabs, then virtual Arabs of some kind; that is, restless, untrustworthy, violent and ill-disposed to any person of property and reputation.

There was an explosion of this kind of language through the nineteenth century, beginning in the 1830s. In his well-documented campaign to develop Ragged Schools for urban youth, Thomas Guthrie argued that London's slum children needed attention because 'these Arabs of the city are as wild as those of the desert'.[24] Lord Shaftesbury, after whom the great avenue that smashed through densely packed rookeries from Piccadilly Circus to Holborn is named, complained that these 'city Arabs ... are like tribes of lawless freebooters, bound by no obligations, and utterly ignorant or utterly regardless of social duties'.[25] Others could not disagree. 'Observe the vast number of the "city Arabs", to be encountered in a walk from Cheapside to the Angel at Islington', writes James Greenwood in the 1860s; Dickens, in the same decade, points out the 'wild tribes of London or City Arabs' and the 'London Hassaracs or Abdallahs, in laced boots and velveteen jackets' who seem to defy all known norms of conduct.[26] By the late nineteenth century, the 'street Arab' had become a popular subject for photographs and drawings and also a well-known literary type, and there was a proliferation of fiction and theatrical productions featuring London's street Arabs.

Thus, even as the British empire was mapping out and bringing under control territories and populations on the other side of the globe, there was a concurrent discovery at home of all kinds of interior spaces and populations that subverted and made impossible any clean demarcation of the difference between a settled and civilised metropolis and a wild and unruly colonial sphere. The main question was what could be done about these racial Others within the national space: could they be assimilated in some way, or would they need to be eliminated, purged from the nation? The territories and spaces these people inhabited also needed redemption, but this at least seemed a more straightforward proposition: if the places where London's wandering Arabs were densely packed and cut off from the wider forms of circulation tying the metropolis together, the obvious solution was to break open these pockets of dissolute backwardness and to integrate them with the rest of the city. Thus, narrow streets and courts were obliterated and replaced with wider boulevards and packed tenements were pulled down and replaced with more modern structures that would allow just those forms of privacy and individuated development that the rookeries had seemed to preclude.

Throughout the worst parts of the west-central side of the metropolis, then, new streets were developed and ploughed through the older urban fabric. In addition to Shaftesbury Avenue (already mentioned), New Oxford Street was pushed through the rookery nestled between the eastern end of Oxford Street and the western terminus of Holborn. In 1887, Charing Cross Road was opened, cutting through the slum districts between Trafalgar Square and Tottenham Court Road. Similarly, Farringdon was broadened and Clerkenwell Road laid out to demolish the slums around the eastern end of Holborn leading towards Clerkenwell. And so on through the entire city. Each of these developments displaced thousands of people at a time, so that as one area was being torn down and developed other areas became even worse as people displaced sought new shelter.[27] Towards the end of the nineteenth century, even as the western side of London was being more or less brought under control, the East End seemed to get worse and worse. Here too it was impossible to distinguish the language of race and empire as applied outside Britain from that applied domestically as well. The Ripper murders in Whitechapel in the 1880s – involving grisly disembowelments of prostitutes by an unknown assailant – brought together a number of explicitly racial and colonial forms of discourse to imagine (more often than not in grotesquely exaggerated ways) the fears of settled and respectable Londoners and to set them ever further apart from the restless wandering population – including the streetwalkers preyed upon by Jack the Ripper – to the East.

Such districts were seen to be in need of eradication, but they were also seen explicitly in connection with overseas colonial situations. More than one mid-century observer suggested that London's slums were the nurseries of convicts whose inevitable (and appropriate) fate was the colonial penal settlement.[28] And, more to the point, the project to settle and civilise London and indeed the rest of England (plus the more technically colonial Celtic parts of Britain) was seen as a kind of parallel project to the settlement and civilisation of the outside colonial world at large. From the point of view of colonial officials such as John Stuart Mill or Thomas Macaulay, just as India had stopped developing at some point in the distant past and hence needed assistance on its 'progress towards the high attainments of a civilised life',[29] so too did whole parts of London and England more generally, which were seen to lie outside of time and history and locked in moribund antiquity. Officially speaking, indeed, discourses of power and surveillance were freely transposed back and forth between England and the explicitly colonial overseas empire, particularly India.[30] And at the same time, policies developed for the one could be shifted to the other, given that they were seen to be more or less the same in any case: policies of policing and incarceration, to be sure, but also policies of development, education and improvement in general.

Great improvements were made through the nineteenth century in infrastructure, transportation, education and public health across Britain, and especially in London, which eventually made British cities cleaner and healthier places to live at the end of the century than they had been at the beginning.[31] But, for all the innovations and the material improvements inspired by investigators like John Snow or reformers like Chadwick, there was always also a price to be paid, principally by those 'human beings who live amidst – and are swept aside with – the old rubbish'.[32] What had to be eliminated from the national space, however, was 'the offensive mass', the Arabised horde of wanderers; that de-individualised, animalised form of being seen as both spatially and temporally out of sync with modernity. What could be allowed back in, or generated from out of all the flux and commotion, were redeemed individuals more appropriate to a white and fully occidental stage of development.

Race and empire can be seen as the discursive and material engines that brought about these transformations. And what emerges in depictions of the national interior as these practices developed through the century is an unstable mixture of racial types, corresponding to different degrees of access to civilisation and Westernisation. Sometimes social inferiors were depicted as decent, clean, aspiring and appealing. If in certain characters we can recognise the lineaments of savagery, in other words, we can see in others the traces of civilisation and improvement. What this suggests is not so much the extent to which attitudes were shifting in this period, but rather the extent to which these objects of surveillance were themselves shifting and developing. Some of them were showing the emergent capacity for inclusion in the still very emergent categories of whiteness and Englishness, while others proved themselves to be still feckless savages deserving of the axe or the gallows.

What distinguishes the putative metropolitan centre from the outer reaches of the empire at this stage is that, whereas the development and deployment of a racial language to depict overseas Others is, and would remain until the twentieth century, more or less comprehensive and all-encompassing,[33] the deployment of the same language in the domestic interior of England through the nineteenth century is uneven, and actually being dismantled as 'civilisation' and occidentalism are spread: 'they' out there in India or Africa or Arabia may be all the same, but 'we' are still only gradually coming together as a collective with even a claim of cultural and social unity and connectedness. What distinguishes imperial from domestic space, in other words, is a matter of degree: 'they' are completely uncivilised; 'we' are at least partly civilised – and we are working on civilising the rest of 'our' countrymen.

How, then, was this civilising process brought about? It is no coincidence that what has been identified as the great transformation of modern Britain – the process of making it a genuinely modern nation – took place at exactly the same time as Britain's overseas imperial policy was undergoing a massive shift in gears, as the guiding concept of the empire went from an exchange of difference to its transformation and improvement.[34] Race would prove to be essential to both projects at once – and in relation to one another. The process of civilising labouring people – turning them into moral, formally equal self-regulating individuals – was one of the defining features of state formation through the nineteenth century; indeed, the process of state formation and cultural regulation involved the subjugation of the working class, capturing it to the demands of the new social system.[35] Karl Polanyi famously describes this process in explicitly colonial and racial terms, noting: 'What the white man may still occasionally practice in remote regions, namely, the smashing up of social structures in order to extract the element of labor from them, was done in the eighteenth century to white populations by white men for similar purposes.'[36]

The civilising process was not merely a phenomenon exported by Europeans along racial lines overseas, in other words, but also a process that unfolded at home. The moral revolution this process involved transformed not only individuals, but the entire society. People had to be taught – by whatever means necessary – the importance of all those things that Mayhew found missing or underdeveloped in the wandering hordes of London: the value of sobriety, chastity and industry, the importance of morality, the sacred status of private property and, above all, the need to work hard. The value of self-control, self-regulation, self-discipline, the management of appetite and desire, were all pivotal to the radical thought that emerged in the late eighteenth century and would be institutionalised in the decades after the Great Reform Act of 1832.

Thus a racial and at times an explicitly colonial set of discourses was developed to think through relations within England and Britain more generally who were subject to the authority of other social groups. We can think of this as a kind of class racism, but the tensions between categories of race and of class are more profound then even this formulation allows.[37] The concept of racial difference was so fluid that the very same population or part of a population could be variously identified as either racially similar or racially different depending on shifting circumstances and contingencies. The project of a domestic civilising mission in parallel to a foreign one involved ultimately the gradual smoothing out of these contradictions so that all these forms of racial difference within the national space could be reduced to the point where 'we' can have a sense of collective national or racial identity (these two categories obviously never did align very smoothly – but that is more a story of the twentieth century and later than of the nineteenth[38]).

Thus the often fraught encounters between different social groups within England, which we might be tempted to think of in terms of class, are actually more productively thought through in terms of race. Indeed, it is essential here not to confuse questions of race with those of class, or to collapse the one category into the other. Bernard Porter, for instance, quite rightly argues that 'there were millions of women and men [in Britain] who were as subjected and exploited by "imperialists" as anyone in the colonies'.[39] He adds that while ' "the British" are conventionally regarded as the imperialists and Australians, say – all of them – as colonial subjects, each of those populations in reality comprised mixes of both categories: the ruling classes in Britain lording it over their own lower classes in almost exactly the same way as they lorded over their colonial peoples'.[40] Thus he argues that 'broad-brushing all nineteenth- and early twentieth-century Britons as necessarily on the same side of the colonial master–subject divide is clearly misleading. Only the imperial ruling class can be unequivocally located there'.[41] Although Porter is raising a vitally important set of questions here, the problem is that he is thinking through these dynamics and tensions strictly in terms of class when – as we see in the case of Mayhew – the category of race is actually more significant. That is, the people Mayhew is considering do not form a class in any meaningful sense of that term: they neither constitute themselves as a class nor can they be located in terms of the class structures of industrial society. The tensions Porter is alluding to genuinely are racial tensions, in other words, not merely class tensions dressed up in the language of race.

Much more is at stake here than merely semantic quibbling. Thinking of class as the category that counts at home, and race as the category that matters more overseas in the imperial realm, reinforces the distinction between metropolis and periphery complicated or undermined altogether by Mayhew and countless others. It also elides the extent to which race and racism were built-in features of the modern state, inseparable from both its internal as well as its external operations.[42] As Paul Gilroy points out, 'seeing racism as something peripheral, marginal to the essential patterns of social and political life can, in its worst manifestations, simply endorse the view of blacks as an external problem, an alien presence visited on Britain from the outside'.[43] Thus, as we learn from Mayhew, racial fault lines can be traced within the space of the nation, not simply between the nation and external or imperial spaces, or between home-grown and immigrant communities.[44] Hence race and class have to be seen as articulated concepts, not so easily separable.[45]

Thus forms of alienation that might at other moments be expressed in class terms could in the nineteenth century be expressed in terms of race. In other words, structures of identity that it might be tempting to think through in terms of class also in this period have racial dynamics built right into them. The result, through the nineteenth century, is an amalgamation of often contradictory forms of identity, or a complex plurality of identities rather than a single one.[46] Consider, for example, the role that race and class play in Thomas Carlyle's mid-century *Discourse on the Nigger Question*. Seeking at times to differentiate, and at other times to collapse into one another, colonial black labour in the Caribbean and putatively white labour at home in England, Carlyle ends up mixing both sets of categories. 'Our own English labourers', he complains on the one hand, are paying high sugar duties and gradually starving through lack of work while 'beautiful Blacks sitting there up to the ears in pumpkins' are idly lazing without any inducement to labour. Here the noble and suffering English labourer – the freeborn Englishman – is contrasted with the ungrateful black colonial plantation worker. On the other hand, at other moments in the text Carlyle confounds the two, as when he complains that the putatively white working class in England are no better than the lazy blacks of the Caribbean, 'for they also have long sat Negro-like up to the ears in pumpkin, regardless of "work", and of a world going to waste for their idleness!'[47] How, in these circumstances, can one imagine a sharp differentiation of 'us' from 'them?' Sometimes 'our' people really do constitute an 'us', and at other times they are not 'us' at all, and on the contrary rather too much like the undesirable 'them' over there in the colonies.[48]

This reinforces the extent to which it is difficult or impossible to think of a single national or racial culture in the nineteenth century that was capable of neatly differentiating Britons from colonial peoples. Some parts, at some times, of the British population could be configured as a kind of racial or national or civilisational 'us', and at other times these same people were thought of as anything but 'us'. Some of 'us' could be marked for dispossession, alienation or expulsion, only to later be configured for various forms in inclusion or assimilation or reincorporation. And the instability of these forms of identity was tied into the instability, the inability to mark a clear line separating the metropolitan centre of empire from its distant peripheries.

And, as we have seen, both were subject to a colonial civilising process. Indeed, if we think of race as fundamental to the operations of imperialism, we have to reckon with the fact that not merely civilising but almost actually imperial processes were unfolding within England (and as I said Britain more generally) as much as they were in the overseas spaces over which Britain was extending its imperial reach. The encounters between higher and lower social orders in England hardly took place on an even terrain; one side wielded disproportionate – indeed, fatal – power over the other. Until the gradual development of a recognisably modern legal system later in the nineteenth century, social elites in England literally exercised the power of life and death over their social inferiors, and were able to prosecute them or grant them mercy in ways that would have been institutionally unthinkable the other way around.[49]

This literally sanguinary power is helpfully thought through with reference to Michel Foucault's observation that racism is most productively defined as a method of separating groups that share (however unevenly) a biopolitical continuum. 'When you have a normalizing society, you have a power which is, at least superficially, in the first instance, or in the first line a biopower, and racism is the indispensable precondition that allows someone to be killed, that allows others to be killed', he argues, with particular relevance here to the power of life and death that the English elites held over their plebeian counterparts. 'Once the State functions in the biopower mode, racism alone can justify the murderous function of the State', Foucault adds. 'If the power of normalization wished to exercise the old sovereign right to kill, it must become racist.'[50] According to Foucault, then, the logic of racism is inseparable from biopolitical logic of the state in the nineteenth century – it was deployed to negotiate relations with socially designated 'others' both within the borders of the state and in zones of formal colonial conquest and occupation.

As a result, representations of certain populations in both rural and urban England in the nineteenth century not only shared certain features in common with British representations of imperial India or Africa during the same period, they were often driven by the same imperial logics and mechanisms of surveillance. They were even structured by similar codes of counter-insurgency.[51] Especially when confronted with political restlessness or uprisings of various kinds (from the Luddite uprising to the ongoing struggle for democratic representation), those in power at home, as much as those in positions of authority in an overseas colonial setting, were interested in investigating the circumstances and attitudes of their social inferiors and racial others, amassing knowledge, tabulating figures, developing strategies of intelligence and containment.[52] And there were unmistakable parallels – in terms of personnel, intellectuals, theorists and institutions – between parallel projects to surveil and control subaltern groups at home and overseas.

Descriptions of criminality in India were easily adapted from those developed to reckon with domestic lawlessness in England, and vice versa, as domestic and colonial discourses of surveillance and power developed symbiotically, hinting at the interest that the colonial elite had in the policing of both territories. Specific policies and mechanisms developed for use in India could be imported wholesale to England, and the other way around, and the formation of a modern police system from the 1830s on had an impact on the British administration of India, where allegedly rampant criminality was also discovered, and was equally in need of reform.[53]

In both sites, more or less equally, the name of progress and reform was deployed to either civilise or eradicate the traces of racial difference. In both cases, the colonial and the domestic, there is a similar degree of alienation of the observed and represented from the elite observer; in both, similar questions about the Other are registered; and in both there are similar anxieties about the status and activity of these Others – whether they are working or resting, whether they are happy or suffering; whether they are docile or threatening. The sense of a potentially threatening population that needs to be surveyed, known, controlled, improved – in a word, civilised – turns out to be not substantially different when constructed in an English setting than it is in an Indian one.

Thus the project to transform the racial Other at home in a way that could be understood and framed in terms of racial commonality was a major component of the civilising mission from the late eighteenth century onwards. The most obvious work of the civilising mission consisted in the many projects to school, evangelise, convert, improve and instruct the common people of England, whether by evangelicals or radicals – hence the proliferation of, on the one hand, the Proclamation Society (founded 1787), Religious Tract Society (1799), Society for the Suppression of Vice (1801), British and Foreign Bible Society (1804) and, on the other hand, the Society for the Diffusion of Useful Knowledge, Mechanics' Institutes, Friendly Societies, Lancastrian day schools and so on.

But all this kind of work took time, and through much of the nineteenth century, even as the British empire was reaching its zenith overseas, Britain at home lacked a dominant and secure sense and space of racial and cultural identity. Instead, there was a struggle to try to secure the space in which such an identity could be constructed. When the British were viewing the unsettled colonial world in the nineteenth century, in other words, they were not doing so from a vantage point of their own racial or civilisational stability or sense of security, but rather with a sense of their own civilisational development still very much at stake. Or to put this differently: it is impossible to take for granted a white or English or Western sense of self in the nineteenth century that could clearly be thought of as calmly and indisputably in control of a territory from which it set out to conquer other races and nations. That sense of self was still very much in formation on both a national and a global scale, and it lacked a sense of its own territorial stability. It was only in the process of racially configuring the other – both at home and overseas – that the self could become racially defined in turn.[54] These processes took decades to unfold, however, and continually converged or overlapped with other categories of identity, including those of class and gender. In such a fluid field, where the domestic is not readily or cleanly separable from the foreign, and the stranger from one of 'us', it is difficult to seize stable points of reference and certain categories of identity that would eventually separate were often confounded together.

NOTES

1 Henry Mayhew, *London Labour and the London Poor* (London: Griffin, Bohn & Co., 1861), vol. 1, pp. 1–2. Much of the material I discuss in this chapter is also addressed in different parts of my book *Making England Western: Occidentalism, Race and Imperial Culture* (Chicago: University of Chicago Press, 2014).

2 Mayhew, *London Labour*, vol. 1, p. 5.

3 See Johannes Fabian, *Time and the Other* (New York: Columbia University Press, 1986).

4 Dipesh Chakrabarty, *Provincializing Europe: Postcolonial Thought and Historical Difference* (Princeton, NJ: Princeton University Press, 2000), p. 7.

5 See Michael Hechter, *Internal Colonialism: The Celtic Fringe in British National Development* (Berkeley: University of California Press, 1975).

6 See Susan Thorne, *Congregational Missions and the Making of an Imperial Culture in Nineteenth-Century England* (Berkeley: University of California Press, 1999); and '"The Conversion of Englishmen and the Conversion of the World Inseparable:" Missionary Imperialism and the Language of Class in Early Industrial Britain', in Frederick Cooper and Ann Laura Stoler, eds., *Tensions of Empire: Colonial Cultures in a Bourgeois World* (Berkeley: University of California Press, 1997), pp. 238–55.

7 Quoted in Thorne, 'Missionary Imperialism', p. 238.

8 Both quoted in Thorne, 'Missionary Imperialism', p. 247.

9 G. Alston, quoted in Friedrich Engels, *The Condition of the Working Class in England* (Harmondsworth: Penguin, 1987), p. 73.

10 See Robert Miles, *Racism After 'Race Relations'* (London: Routledge, 1993), pp. 88, 91.

11 See e.g., Eugen Weber, *Peasants into Frenchmen: The Modernization of Rural France, 1870–1914* (Palo Alto, CA: Stanford University Press, 1976).

12 Ann Laura Stoler, *Race and the Education of Desire* (Durham, NC: Duke University Press, 1995), p. 123.

13 William Godwin, *Caleb Williams* (Peterborough: Broadview, 2000), pp. 109–10.

14 Ibid., p. 305.

15 Thomas Beames, *Rookeries of London: Past, Present and Prospective* (London: Thomas Bosworth, 1851), p. 6.

16 I have discussed this issue at length both in *Making England Western* and in Saree Makdisi, *William Blake and the Impossible History of the 1790s* (Chicago: University of Chicago Press, 2003).

17 W. Weir, 'St. Giles's Past and Present', in Charles Knight, ed., *London*, vol. 2 (London, 1841), pp. 257–72.

18 Charles Dickens, *Sketches by Boz* (London: Penguin, 1996), p. 94.

19 George Reynolds, *Mysteries of London*, vol. 1 (London: John Dicks, 1845), pp. 406–7.

20 Mary Wollstonecraft, *Maria; Or, the Wrongs of Woman [1798]* (New York: Norton, 1998), p. 102.

21 George Godwin, *London Shadows: A Glance at the 'Homes' of the Thousands* (London: Routledge, 1854), pp. 1–2.

22 Henry Fielding, 'Enquiry into the Causes of the Late Increase of Robbers', in *The Complete Works of Henry Fielding: Legal Writings* (London: Heinemann, 1903), p. 83.

23 Walter Thornbury, *Old and New London* (London: Cassell, 1878), vol. 3, p. 202.

24 Thomas Guthrie, quoted in Lydia Murdoch, *Imagined Orphans: Poor Families, Child Welfare and Contested Citizenship in London* (New Brunswick, NJ: Rutgers University Press, 2006), p. 25.

25 Lord Shaftesbury, also quoted in Murdoch, *Imagined Orphans*, p. 25.

26 James Greenwood, *Seven Curses of London* (Boston: 1869), pp. 4–5; Dickens, 'Underground London', *All the Year Round* (30 July 1861), 390.

27 See Gareth Stedman Jones, *Outcast London: A Study in the Relationship Between Classes in Victorian Society* (New York: Pantheon, 1984), esp. pp. 159–214.

28 See, e.g., Beames, *Rookeries*, p. 214.

29 James Mill, *History of British India*, quoted in Saree Makdisi, *Romantic Imperialism* (Cambridge: Cambridge University Press, 1998), p. 114.

30 See Upamanyu Pablo Mukherjee, *Crime and Empire: The Colony in Nineteenth-Century Fictions of Crime* (Oxford: Oxford University Press, 2003).

31 See Michelle Allen, *Cleansing the City: Sanitary Geographies in Victorian London* (Athens: Ohio University Press, 2008), p. 2.

32 Ibid., p. 6.

33 See Edward Said, *Orientalism* (New York: Pantheon, 1978), pp. 32–3.

34 See Karl Polanyi, *The Great Transformation: The Political and Economic Origins of Our Time* (1944; reprint. Boston: Beacon Press, 2001), pp. 81–9; also see E. P. Thompson, *The Making of the English Working Class* (New York: Vintage, 1966), pp. 220–5; Eric Hobsbawm, *Industry and Empire* (New York: New Press, 1999), pp. 82–3.

35 Philip Corrigan and Derek Sayer, *The Great Arch: English State Formation as Cultural Revolution* (Oxford: Blackwell, 1985), pp. 114–15.

36 Polanyi, *The Great Transformation*, p. 173.

37 See Etienne Balibar and Immanuel Wallerstein, *Race, Nation, Class: Ambiguous Identities* (London: Verso, 1991), esp. pp. 204–15.

38 See Paul Gilroy, *There Ain't No Black in the Union Jack: The Cultural Politics of Race and Nation* (Chicago: University of Chicago Press, 1991).

39 Bernard Porter, *The Absent-Minded Imperialists: Empire, Society and Culture in Britain* (Oxford: Oxford University Press, 2006), p. xii.

40 Ibid., p. 308.

41 Ibid., p. 309.

42 See David Theo Goldberg, *The Racial State* (Oxford: Blackwell, 2002).

43 Gilroy, *There Ain't No Black in the Union Jack*, p. 11.

44 See Gilroy, *There Ain't No Black in the Union Jack*; also Ann Stoler, *Race and the Education of Desire* (Durham, NC: Duke University Press, 1995).

45 See Stuart Hall, 'Race, Articulation, and Societies Structured in Dominance', in *Sociological Theories: Race and Colonialism* (Paris: UNESCO, 1985), pp. 305–45.

46 See Stuart Hall, 'Gramsci's Relevance to the Analysis of Racism and Ethnicity', in *Proceedings of the International Seminar on Theoretical Issues of Race and Ethnicity*, Milan, Italy (Paris, France: UNESCO, 1985), p. 34.

47 Thomas Carlyle, 'Occasional Discourse on the Nigger Question', in *Collected Works of Thomas Carlyle* (London: Chapman & Hall, 1864), vol. XIII, pp. 1–28, esp. pp. 3, 4, 24.

48 See Carlyle, 'Occasional Discourse', p. 20.

49 See John Brewer and John Styles, 'Introduction', in *An Ungovernable People: The English and their Law in the Seventeenth and Eighteenth Centuries*, eds. John Brewer and John Styles (London: Hutchinson, 1980), pp. 11-20.

50 Michel Foucault, *Society Must be Defended: Lectures at the Collège de France, 1975–1976*, trans. David Macey (New York: Picador, 2003), p. 256.

51 See Ranajit Guha, 'The Prose of Counter-Insurgency', in *Selected Subaltern Studies*, eds. Ranajit Guha and Gayatri Spivak (Oxford: Oxford University Press, 1988), pp. 45–86.

52 See David Solkin, *Painting out of the Ordinary: Modernity and the Art of Everyday Life in Early Nineteenth-Century Britain* (New Haven, CT: Yale University Press, 2008) for a fascinating take on how this logic extended to visual culture.

53 Mukherjee, *Crime and Empire*, pp. 47–9, 123.

54 See Goldberg, *The Racial State*, p. 16.

12

NORMAN VANCE

Patterns of Literary Transformation

Between 1800 and 1900 the dominant literary mode of romanticism, with its various transformations, moved in the direction of modernism, accompanied and sometimes assailed along the way by different kinds of realism. More paradoxically, over the same period literature tended to become ever more international, indeed cosmopolitan, even as self-consciously national literatures developed and asserted themselves with growing confidence in Ireland and in the United States, in Russia and in Scandinavia. With better communications, cheaper machine-assisted book production and improved educational provision ensuring an expanding readership, books and ideas as well as people began to travel further and faster, in Britain and elsewhere. Eventually, by 1873, the age of steam made it possible for the French novelist Jules Verne to imagine and describe a more or less realistic journey around the world in eighty days.

Romanticisms

Romanticism was a broad, retrospectively applied literary and cultural category. Observing different timetables in different countries, it brought together themes and concerns first insistently voiced towards the end of the eighteenth century, particularly in Germany, Britain and France before and after the libertarian excitements of the French Revolution. It was international because of the international interests, reputations and influence of the leading writers who were eventually classified as Romantics: J. W. von Goethe and the Schlegel brothers (August Wilhelm and Friedrich), Sir Walter Scott and Lord Byron, Jean-Jacques Rousseau and François-René de Chateaubriand were avidly read at different times from Massachusetts to Moscow.

In eighteenth-century usage 'romantic' tended to mean outside everyday experience, fantastic or far-fetched, the stuff of improbable old romances. The label fitted nineteenth-century writers who imparted an emotional charge to the unfamiliar and the irregular, often appropriating for present purposes events and materials remote in time or place. Such writers often challenged time-honoured tyrannies, aesthetic as well as political, and called into question the cold, calm sense of order and proportion associated with the classicism of ancient Greece and Rome, particularly classical architecture. The term 'Gothic', describing a different architectural tradition, was often used in an extended sense to cover roughly the same rugged imaginative terrain as 'romantic'.

The romantic imagination might engage with the awesome grandeur and beauty of the natural world, particularly in little-visited locations, or with social and political visions of liberty and ideal possibility, or with turbulent personal feeling, perhaps touched with supernatural mystery. Hearts and minds could respond with enthusiasm to a new range of stimuli collectively representing a kind of antidote to the perceived dryness, even sterility, of Enlightenment rationalism and its approach to nature and society. Emotionally undernourished from his excessively rationalist upbringing by his father, the economist, philosopher and historian James Mill, John Stuart Mill describes in his *Autobiography* (1873) how he found healing and a richer and deeper humanity in the romantic poetry of William Wordsworth and the writings of Samuel Taylor Coleridge, not to mention Goethe and other German writers who Coleridge admired. In his romantic musings on God, man and nature in *Aids to Reflection* (1825) Coleridge repudiated the reductiveness and 'utter emptiness and unmeaningness' of what he called 'the vaunted Mechanico-corpuscular Philosophy', the atomistic, quasi-mathematical scientific outlook that he traced back to Descartes.[1] In poems such as 'The Song of Los' (1795) William Blake had been even more hostile to the rationalist tradition, which he particularly associated with Isaac Newton and John Locke almost a century earlier.

But romanticism had its own pre-history, drawing inspiration from Shakespeare, re-read as a romantic genius not just by the Schlegel brothers in Germany, but by Coleridge in England and Victor Hugo in France. Long before Shakespeare, disconcerting, awe-inspiring strangeness had been theorised in the ancient world by the Greek writer Longinus as the 'sublime'. European romantic theory was able to draw on revived interest in the sublime in eighteenth- and nineteenth-century France, England and Germany, inaugurated by Nicholas Boileau's French translation of Longinus (1674) and influentially revisited in the young Edmund Burke's *Philosophical Enquiry into the Origin of Our Ideas of the Sublime and the Beautiful* (1757) and in Immanuel Kant's *Critique of Judgement* (1790).

Romantic writers, exploring new territories of the mind, were travellers in imagination and sometimes also in reality. In *Lalla Rookh* (1817) Byron's friend and biographer, the Irish poet Thomas Moore, framed a series of oriental tales in verse with the (imagined) journey of the emperor's daughter from Delhi to Kashmir. Byron's increasingly conservative bête noir Robert Southey set his narrative poem *Madoc* (1805) in pre-colonial America, making his twelfth-century Welsh hero found a settlement and confront the Aztecs. Byron himself, more widely travelled than either of them, drew extensively on his own wanderings as far as Albania for his immensely popular *Childe Harold's Pilgrimage* (1812–18). He acquired an international reputation not just for his writing but for his sometimes scandalous personal life, redeemed by securing European fame as a Greek national hero from his association with the Greek struggle for independence from the Turks and his death at Missolonghi in 1824.

But more or less exotic locations and romantic episode and adventure, including what Wordsworth, thinking of the folk memory of the Scottish highlands, described as 'old unhappy far-off things/And battles long ago',[2] could be sampled more comfortably at home in the study, by dipping into old travel books and ballads, folk songs and folk tales. Antiquarians had begun to collect and publish some of this traditional material in the previous century, variously encouraged or irritated by James Macpherson's creative enhancements and distortions of ancient Scottish and Irish poems, published to European acclaim as the works of 'Ossian'. Thomas Percy's pioneering *Reliques of Ancient English Poetry* (1765) provided the model for subsequent collections such as Charlotte Brooke's *Reliques of Irish Poetry* (1789) in Ireland and J. G. Herder's *Volkslieder* (1778–9) in Germany. Among the most important subsequent collections were the German compilations of Jakob and Wilhelm Grimm, *Kinder- und Hausmärchen* (1812–14) (better known as *Grimms' Fairy Tales*) and *Deutsche Sagen* (1816–18). In Finland Elias Lönnrot collected ancient Finnish narrative poems preserved in oral tradition and synthesised them into a national epic, the *Kalevala*, published in its final form in 1849. This provided the American scholar-poet Henry Wadsworth Longfellow with a model and a metre for *The Song of Hiawatha* (1855), drawing on native American lore. The poem was a self-conscious contribution to the specifically American national literary tradition that was beginning to take shape. In Ireland the scholar-poet and translator Samuel Ferguson drew on the *Tain Bo Cuailgne* or 'Cattle-Raid of Cooley' and other ancient narratives preserved in manuscript for 'The Tain-Quest' and similar poems, collected as *Lays of the Western Gael* (1865). Using similar materials he went on to write *Congal: A Poem in Five Books* (1872), which was his own attempt at a national epic.

Ancient and medieval sources were constantly recalled in the nineteenth century in retold or invented stories and in poetic dreams and fantasies.

They were at the heart of the cult of 'romantic primitivism': simplified and idealised versions of primitive societies provided a means of critiquing contemporary society. They also supplied heroic role models to bolster national self-respect: Arminius (or Hermann) had resisted Roman advances in Germany, as had Vercingetorix in Gaul and Caractacus and Boadicea (or Boudicca) in ancient Britain. Increasingly nationalist Ireland's heroic warrior of choice was Cuchulain, invoked by poets such as William Butler Yeats. Legends about adventurous, often solitary, sea voyages in early Irish society had been formalised into the literary genre of the *immram* and some of the narratives were translated and published in P. W. Joyce's *Old Celtic Romances* (1879), Tennyson's source for his poem 'The Voyage of Maeldune' (1880). Matthew Arnold's poem 'St Brandan' (1860) was based on the Latin 'Navigatio Sancti Brendani', a Christianised *immram*. Icelandic saga, admired and translated by William Morris, provided the basis of his verse-epic *Sigurd the Volsung and the Fall of the Niblungs* (1876) and saga provided a model for novels of earlier and more violent times such as Charles Kingsley's *Hereward the Wake* (1866) and Rider Haggard's *Eric Brighteyes* (1891). The courtly fiction of forbidden love, *Aucassin and Nicolette*, a thirteenth-century legend of Provence, was adapted by late romantics such as Andrew Lang and Algernon Swinburne and attracted the interest of the Victorian critic Walter Pater.

The old stories stimulated new kinds of interest in Homer, Shakespeare, the Bible and classical mythology, all of which seemed to be close to nature and popular tradition. Friedrich Schiller's poem 'Die Götter Griechenlands' (1788), translated by the romantic novelist Edward Bulwer Lytton as 'The gods of Greece', was nostalgic for the days when nature was imagined as divine, before the old gods retreated to the world of the poetic imagination. In similar vein, in *The Marriage of Heaven and Hell* (1790), William Blake recalled a lost world when 'the ancient poets animated all sensible objects with gods or geniuses'. John Keats was fascinated by the worlds of Shakespeare and Homer and the classical past. His 'Ode to a Nightingale' (1820), ranging in imagination from classical mythology and the warm south of Provence to the Old Testament tale of Ruth, ends 'Was it a vision, or a waking dream?/ Fled is that music: – Do I wake or sleep?'

Sometimes the dreams and visions of romantic writers were troubling, even nightmarish. Exploration not just of the outer world but of the inner world of the imagination, of the experiencing self and of perhaps painful or extreme states of consciousness, became a characteristic romantic enterprise. Percy Bysshe Shelley's version of the sensitive romantic self, particularly in 'Mont Blanc' and his Odes, is both more ambitious and more questioning than most, and more disposed to fall upon the thorns of life, mingling doubt and a sense of personal pain with prophetic aspiration. The literary currency of suffering has precedents in tragic drama but it took on a new lease of life across Europe as 'Wertherism', a term taken from the extravagant sorrows of Goethe's hero in his sensationally successful and influential novel *Die Leiden des jungen Werthers* (1774). The calmer meditations and solitary ecstasies of Jean-Jacques Rousseau's *Rêveries du promeneur solitaire* (1782) darkened into the disturbed visions of Thomas de Quincey's *Confessions of an English Opium-Eater* (1822), translated by the French romantic Alfred de Musset in 1828. Long before Friedrich Nietzsche said it in *Die fröhliche Wissenschaft* ('The Gay Science') (1882), the 'Dream of the Dead Christ' incorporated in Jean Paul Richter's novel *Siebenkäs* (1796–7) floated the then deeply troubling imaginative possibility that 'God is dead', that we inhabit a godless universe. Coleridge explored moral guilt and outraged nature in the dream-like scenes of his 'Rime of the Ancient Mariner', written in ballad form and published in the landmark collection of *Lyrical Ballads* (1798) in which he collaborated with his friend Wordsworth.

Nature interacting with the romantic self is explored at length in Wordsworth's autobiographical *Prelude* (1850), his account of 'the growth of the poet's mind', and in the American poet Walt Whitman's all-encompassing, mystically pantheistic *Song of Myself* (1855), which had a considerable influence on the development of modernist writing in America and on the work of D. H. Lawrence in England. The English Romantics, particularly Wordsworth and Coleridge, contributed to the eclectic anti-rationalist humanism of New England 'Transcendentalism' as represented in the writings of Ralph Waldo Emerson and Henry David Thoreau. Thoreau, romantic individualist that he was, experimented with putting into practice romantic dreams of escape into a life in nature by living a self-sufficient existence in a cabin he built on the edge of Walden Pond near Concord, Massachusetts. *Walden, or Life in the Woods* (1854), his account of the experience, became a classic of the emerging national literature of the United States. It provided Yeats with theme and imagery for his poem of romantic escape 'The Lake Isle of Innisfree' (1890), written in London, which was soon added to the developing corpus of Irish national literature.

In Germany and elsewhere the *bildungsroman* or novel of personal development and self-realisation, particularly associated with Goethe's *Wilhelm Meister's Apprenticeship* (1795–6), an influential model, represented a prose version of the romantic concern with the growth of the individual. It also provided a way of integrating romantic and social concerns in novels such as Charles Dickens' *Great Expectations* (1861) where the protagonist's moral development is also a process of finding a better mode of functioning within his society.

Byronic romantic individualism, particularly as represented in Byron's satirical epic *Don Juan* (1819–24), characterises the hero of Aleksandr Pushkin's novel in verse *Eugene Onegin*, finally published in full in 1833, but other characters in the novel represent other romanticisms: Tatyana sees herself as the heroine of all the sentimental novels she has read in French, while Lensky, educated at Göttingen, is Pushkin's version of a German romantic.[3] Russian writers were becoming increasingly responsive to new writing in other European countries but constantly lamented that their own work was unknown outside Russia. International recognition of Russia's developing national literature came later, from the 1880s, with French and then English translations of Turgenev and Dostoevsky. Matthew Arnold read Tolstoy in French translation in 1887 and described him, after some criticisms, as both a great writer and a great soul.

Soul-baring and self-indulgent romantic individualism could be embarrassing and tedious in print. Shelley and Keats could usually get away with it, but few of their successors shared their genius. Some of the worst and most febrile excesses were mercilessly parodied in the critic William Edmonstoune Aytoun's *Firmilian, or The Student of Badajoz: A Spasmodic Tragedy* (1854) and Charles Kingsley held his 'spasmodic' poet-figure Elsley Vavasour up to ridicule in his novel *Two Years Ago* (1857). The young Robert Browning owed rather too much to Shelley and tried to be too like him as a poet: his *Pauline: A Fragment* (1833) was severely criticised for its intense and morbid self-consciousness. This seems to have spurred him to channel thought and feeling into 'dramatic monologues' spoken by a brilliant array of dramatised characters, sages and painters, madmen and murderers, for whose sometimes extreme attitudes and behaviour he could not be held responsible. Alfred Tennyson's strange self-consciously Shelleyan early poem 'Supposed Confessions of a Second-Rate Sensitive Mind Not in Unity with Itself' (1830) is to some extent redeemed by its preposterous self-mocking title and a degree of ironic impatience with its own rhetoric. Like Browning, Tennyson went on to establish ironic distance between his own identity and the feelings and situations he wished to explore by developing his own version of the dramatic monologue, even if one senses that his dramatic monologists in poems such as 'Ulysses', 'Locksley Hall' and 'Maud' are only partially disguised exaggerated versions of himself. The technique of dramatic monologue as distancing adaptation or transformation of romantic individualism and self-disclosure persisted into the twentieth century in the *Personae* of Ezra Pound and the 'masks' adopted by W. B. Yeats.

The inner life of the poet, personal growth, more or less painful consciousness, responsiveness to the natural world, what Wordsworth described as 'emotion recollected in tranquillity' and the nature and the power of the imagination all represent one strand of romanticism. There is another, more sociological strand, which engages with communities, shared dreams and passions and the often unsung moral dignity and resilience of ordinary people. Wordsworth's Lakeland shepherds and villagers, along with the world of the Ayrshire poet Robert Burns' *Poems, Chiefly in the Scottish Dialect* (1786), helped to establish a tradition of more or less democratic regionalism in verse and prose that carries on into the Yorkshire novels of the Brontë sisters and the 'Wessex' novels and poems of Thomas Hardy.

Regional consciousness, historical as well as geographical, was given European currency as a literary mode in the verse and fiction of Sir Walter Scott, particularly in his Scottish tales, and left its mark on the American tales of Washington Irving set in the Hudson valley such as 'Rip van Winkle' (1820) and 'The Legend of Sleepy Hollow' (1820). Historical fictions such as Fenimore Cooper's *The Last of the Mohicans* (1826) owed a lot to Scott's habit in *Waverley* (1814), *Old Mortality* (1816) and other novels exploring historical episodes off-centre, through the experience of apparently commonplace individuals caught up in them, rather than concentrating exclusively on the lives and deeds of the famous and historically celebrated. In France Honoré de Balzac's *Les Chouans* (1828), a tale of Royalist revolt in Brittany in 1800, was intended as the first instalment in a series of historical tales modelled on Scott's Waverley novels. Scott's influence also lay behind Alessandro Manzoni's pioneering Italian novel *I Promessi Sposi* or *The Betrothed* (1827), set in seventeenth-century Lombardy. In Russia, Pushkin's *The Captain's Daughter* (1836), set during the Pugachev rebellion of the 1770s, was partly modelled on Scott's novel of Jacobite rebellion *Rob Roy* (1817). Scott's humane and imaginative approach to history and his even-handed peacemaking sympathy with both victors and vanquished in historical conflicts also had a direct influence on historical writing such as the substantial narrative histories of the Norman Conquest written by Augustin Thierry in France (1825) and E. A. Freeman in England (1867–79) and on North American writing such as Francis Parkman's *History of the Conspiracy of Pontiac* (1851).

Romantic history and sanitised or mythologised historical memory, a collectivised version of the romantic emphasis on past emotion recollected in tranquillity, could provide a way of processing recent and painful historical experience and of salvaging damaged dreams of liberty. Some of the earlier poems in Thomas Moore's *Irish Melodies* (1808–34), such as 'The harp that once through Tara's halls', 'Let Erin remember the days of old' and 'Remember the glories of Brien the bold' responded to unsuccessful and brutally suppressed Irish rebellions in 1798 and 1803 by invoking earlier splendours and earlier champions, implying unspoken parallels and offering romantic dreams of recovery in a better future. This aspect of Moore provided a model for the writings of later cultural nationalists and patriots such as Thomas Davis and the 'Young Ireland' journalist, balladist and exiled rebel Thomas D'Arcy McGee. It contributed to the fusion of culture and nationalist politics in the Irish literary revival at the end of the nineteenth century.

But romantic ruralists and cultural nationalists always needed urban publishers and audiences. Rural remoteness from cultural and social centres such as St Petersburg or Paris or even provincial capitals such as Rouen had practical disadvantages and limited attractions for those with the leisure to reflect on such things, particularly for women, a theme in Anton Chekhov's plays. In Gustave Flaubert's *Madame Bovary* (1857) the discontented protagonist, bored with her commonplace husband and with country life, escapes into romantic dreams induced by memories of Alphonse de Lamartine's poetic reverie 'Le lac' (1820) and of Scott's *Bride of Lammermoor* (1818), encountered anew through the glamorising artifice of opera in Donizetti's *Lucia di Lammermoor* (1835). But the clash between romantic dream and unattractive reality ends badly, a recurring theme in realist fiction.

Realisms

Various motivations or compulsions to 'tell it like it is' gave rise to various forms of realism, sometimes as an aspect or development of romanticism and sometimes as a reaction against it. The long-established pastoral tradition, stemming ultimately from Theocritus and other classical poets, had used elegantly artificial, idealised country scenes to contrast with the life of the city or the court. In England this provoked harsher, less comfortable writing from rural poets such as the Suffolk parson George Crabbe, admired by Scott and Byron for his verse-tales. These included 'Peter Grimes' in *The Borough* (1810), a tale of savage brutality, guilt and remorse, which inspired Benjamin Britten's opera with the same title. Like Crabbe, the Northamptonshire farm labourer John Clare knew all about the realities and miseries of country life. He wrote about them in his poem *The Shepherd's Calendar* (1827), the title an ironic gesture towards Edmund Spenser's Theocritean *Shepheardes Calendar* (1579). Crabbe and Clare anticipate even if they do not directly influence the prose realism of later writing about country life such as Thomas Hardy's early *Far from the Madding Crowd* (1874). Hardy's central character in this novel is the shepherd Gabriel Oak and the story was originally published as a monthly magazine serial, with each episode carefully set in the month in which it was due to appear, so that it could be read as a more modern *Shepherd's Calendar*.

Other realisms were stirring in other parts of the world. As new territories were settled, and the American frontier moved further and further west, pioneer adventure and unfamiliar experience attracted myth-making romantic narratives, tall tales and 'local colour' stories. But something sterner and more serious was required by the influential literary journalist and novelist William Dean Howells, who had made his own contribution to American realism with novels such as *The Rise of Silas Lapham* (1885), the story of a *nouveau-riche* businessman in Boston. Hamlin Garland, who knew about the physical and economic hardships of farm life at first hand, came under Howells' influence and published several collections of scrupulously realistic stories about the poor and the weary in the rural Middle West, notably *Main Travelled Roads* (1891). He coined the term 'veritism' to describe his project of local-colour realism deployed for a democratic purpose.

In Italian fiction some realist writers followed the example of the romantic historical novelist Alessandro Manzoni, responding to his respect for democratic ideals and his strong sense of economic and social injustice, which he felt might be redressed by benign paternalism. But for others this was too close to bourgeois conservatism and they favoured an anti-bourgeois radical realism or *verismo*, drawing on French models. *Verismo* was particularly associated with the later work of Giovanni Verga, whose most important novel, *I Malavoglia* (1881), focuses on the economic decline and fall of a family in the Italian South. In nineteenth-century Spain *realismo* overlapped with *costumbrismo*, a special attentiveness to the manners and customs of specific regions, which was perhaps not very different in kind from the romantic regionalism of Wordsworth or Scott. *Realismo*, unlike other realisms, was quite respectful of moral, social and religious convention, but still attempted to draw attention to the more unvarnished aspects of contemporary life.

Public awareness of unglamorous realities became more widespread, in England at least, from the 1830s onwards. Meticulously detailed evidence of social conditions was collected by parliamentary commissions and published in voluminous 'blue books' (as they were called from their covers), which were mined by novelists as well as politicians engaged in debates about reform of everything from the Poor Law to factory conditions. The journalist Henry Mayhew's vivid pen-portraits of 'London Labour and the London Poor' in the columns of the *Morning Chronicle*, beginning in 1849, provided often disturbing raw material. Some of it was used by Charles Kingsley in *Alton Locke* (1851), his novel about the exploitation and appalling hardships of the London tailors. There were many subsequent social reports such as Andrew Mearns' *Bitter Cry of Outcast London* (1883),

George R. Sims' *How the Poor Live*, also published in 1883, and the Italian anarchist Paolo Valera's *Milano sconosciuta* ('Unknown Milan') (1879). In America the journalist Jacob Riis published *How the Other Half Lives* in 1890 and Jane Addams' *Twenty Years at Hull-House* vividly described the horrors facing immigrant settlers in the slum life in Chicago's West Side between 1889 and 1909. In 1906 Upton Sinclair's novel *The Jungle* presented an angry, moving, sometimes revolting account of the brutal conditions in the Chicago stockyards and the meat-packing industry.

Pioneer exploring under extreme conditions, particularly in tropical or equatorial regions, was, or could be, written up as a late nineteenth-century version of the romantic quest. Exploring and reporting on urban and indeed rural poverty closer to home at a time when explorers were finding out more about 'darkest Africa' suggested an ironic parallel to William Booth, founder of the Salvation Army, in *Darkest England and the Way Out* (1890). The parallel also underpins Joseph Conrad's *Heart of Darkness*, written in 1899 and published in 1902, a profoundly pessimistic modernist novella about the Belgian Congo and European civilisation in crisis.

A traditional responsibility of travel writers was to communicate what they had seen as vividly as possible. Pictures helped, and so did improved ways of reproducing them inexpensively. Mayhew's published travels among the London poor were accompanied by engraved illustrations. The versatile graphic artist Gustave Doré illustrated little-known aspects of the urban life encountered in Blanchard Jerrold's *London: A Pilgrimage* (1872). The *Illustrated London News*, founded in 1842, published meticulously detailed drawings of workhouse interiors and fish markets, scenes of famine and riot in India and elsewhere and action pictures from the defence of Paris and the bombardment of Sedan during the Franco-Prussian War of 1870–1.

But new technology was already starting to provide a more reliable and 'scientific' method of image capture. The Crimean War (1854–6) and the American Civil War (1861–5) were the first wars to be photographed. Photography, and the development of newspaper photo-journalism from the 1880s, made available graphic images not just of war but of country life and urban poverty, topics that it was no longer easy to glamorise or ignore.

It is tempting, if anachronistic, to link this later nineteenth-century development with the rise, at an earlier date, of painstaking literary realism. Yet writers too can be regarded as involved in a form of scientific image capture, an aspect of the new social science particularly associated with Herbert Spencer, author of *Social Statics* (1851) and *The Study of Sociology* (1873). Spencer's friend George Eliot used the language of science, of investigating 'the varying experiments of Time', in the Prelude to *Middlemarch* (1871–2), her novel of English provincial life, often identified as the classic realist text in English literature. Eliot shared with the art critic John Ruskin a sense of realism as a moral duty. She described it as 'the doctrine that all truth and beauty are to be attained by a humble and faithful study of nature, and not by substituting vague forms, bred by the imagination on the mists of feeling, in place of definite, substantial reality'.[4] Eliot's realist plots adjusted dreams and ambitions to the constraints of circumstance, but still allowed the individual some moral freedom and dignity, as did the American realism of William Dean Howells. The German romantic poet 'Novalis' (Friedrich von Hardenberg, 1772–1801) was invoked by Eliot and other novelists such as Thomas Hardy for the view that 'Character is Destiny'.

'Naturalism', an ostensibly scientific French variant of realism particularly associated with the fiction of Emile Zola, influential in America in the grim, often tragic novels of Frank Norris, Jack London, Theodore Dreiser and others, was much more determinist. The naturalists emphasised, and set out to demonstrate, what they saw as the overwhelming influence of heredity, blind instinct and environment on human behaviour. Their inspiration was the French historian Hippolyte Taine's sociological *Histoire de la littérature anglaise* (1864), which claimed in its introduction that moral as well as physical facts had identifiable scientific causes, that vice and virtue were products just as much as vitriol and sugar. In this scientific, documentary spirit Zola embarked on his Rougon-Macquart series of twenty novels (1871–93), subtitled 'The Natural and Social History of a Family Under the Second Empire'. Successive volumes ranging across several generations traced patterns of corruption and ambition, degradation and human misery, described in sometimes horrifying or disgusting detail. *L'Assommoir* (1877), about drunkenness and the misfortunes of a laundress, *La Terre* (1887), about the harshness and rapacity of peasant life on the land and *La Bête Humaine* (1890), featuring a homicidal maniac, murderous sexual desire and a runaway train, were regarded as particularly offensive. Zola's English publisher Henry Vizetelly was prosecuted and imprisoned for dealing in obscene publications.

'Zolaism' became a convenient if usually inaccurate and imprecise reviewers' shorthand for controversial social, sexual and economic realism in novels and plays, whether by the English novelist George Gissing or the Norwegian dramatist Henrik Ibsen, both of whom rejected and rather resented the label and the imputation. Ibsen growled that 'Zola descends into the sewer to bathe in it; I, to cleanse it.'[5] This was perhaps ungracious: Zola promoted the French production of Ibsen's play *Ghosts* in 1890, seeing in it his own sense of what naturalist drama could and should be doing. Thomas Hardy's *Jude the Obscure* (1895), reviewed by the London *World* under the title 'Hardy the Degenerate', brought allegations that Hardy had modelled himself on Zola, particularly the Zola of *La Terre*, and had developed a view of humanity as 'largely compounded of hoggishness and hysteria'. In fact his models for literary faithfulness lay closer to home, in Wordsworth and George Eliot, and Hardy had little appetite for quasi-documentary depiction or 'slice-of-life' realism, which he saw as an abandonment of creative responsibility.[6] An increasingly crusty Tennyson rhymed 'Zolaism' with 'abysm' in his old age.[7]

But literary realisms are older than Zola and older than the photographers. Crabbe and Clare have already been mentioned. The unreality of romantic glamour and excess, particularly as represented by Byron and some of the more lurid Gothic novelists, had sometimes been repudiated by the Romantics themselves, particularly by Wordsworth, an important influence on George Eliot's self-consciously realist fiction. The Italian poet Giuseppe Belli (1791–1863) wrote more than 2,000 sonnets in the Roman dialect, giving literary currency to plebeian speech and engaging realistically with power, sex, greed and hunger across a wide range of Roman life from Popes to prostitutes.

This encroached upon the domain of the novel, and indeed the Russian novelist Nikolai Gogol and the Irish novelist James Joyce both seem to have encountered and admired Belli's work. From its origins (or at least one set of origins) in eighteenth-century England the novel form aspired to realism, officially distinguished itself from 'romance' and took a stand against the distortions and improbabilities of eerie fantasy, the old tales of chivalry and lengthy pseudo-historical narratives of love and adventure such as Madeleine de Scudéry's *Artamène, ou le Grand Cyrus* (1649–53). But in practice elements of romance, including Gothic mystery, kept intruding themselves, particularly in the novels of the Brontë sisters. Even so, Jane Austen's *Northanger Abbey* (1818) is an entertaining warning against reading life as Gothic romance as her misguided heroine tries to do. Stendhal's unromantic and unheroic view of war in his novel *La Chartreuse de Parme* (1839) influenced Tolstoy's *Sebastopol Sketches* (1855–6) and *War and Peace* (1865–9), which challenged the view put forward by the romantic historian Thomas Carlyle and others that history was made by great men such as Napoleon, and indeed questioned whether it was significantly affected by any act of the individual will. Tolstoy in his turn contributed to Stephen Crane's anti-romantic novella of the American Civil War, *The Red Badge of Courage* (1895). Romantic illusion dissipated by objective realities might seem an inevitable development in an increasingly scientific age.

Romantic Survival and Resurgence

Yet romance refused to go away. Science and romance, or realism and romance, are not always at odds. As Mary Shelley's *Frankenstein, or the*

Modern Prometheus (1818) illustrates, visionary science and scientific ambition can be seen as versions of the romantic quest or the search for the unknown, even if the quest in *Frankenstein* is tainted with Gothic nightmare and Faustian lust for illicit power and knowledge. Romance and the realities accessible to scientific observation and verification can complement and support each other. One of the possibilities within the tradition of Gothic fiction, exploited in Ann Radcliffe's *The Mysteries of Udolpho* (1794) and in Charlotte Brontë's *Villette* (1853), is the unnerving, mysterious sequence of events that turn out to have a rational explanation, reassuringly returning to the less alarming realities of everyday life even while leaving the reader with an abiding sense of strangeness encountered.

This method of combining romantic and realist possibilities is important in the development of the detective story. The origin of the genre is usually traced to a handful of magazine stories from the 1840s by the American romantic fantasist Edgar Allan Poe. There is an element of romantic wish-fulfilment as well as ingenuity in the way in which Poe ensures his detective Auguste Dupin manages to solve at least some of life's apparently intractable mysteries by rigorously rational means. Half a century later, Dupin's most famous successor, Sherlock Holmes, invariably demonstrates that the most exotic and alarming mysteries can yield both exciting suspense and consolingly rational solutions.

Sherlock Holmes' creator, Sir Arthur Conan Doyle, had had a scientific training as a medical doctor. Holmes' brilliant deductions from minute observation can be seen as an extension or development of diagnosis from the systematic observation and identification of symptoms inculcated by medical training, but the development moves into the realm of fantasy. Despite the aura of scientific rationalism in the Holmes stories Doyle was less a realist than a romantic fantasist with a sense of adventure, author of historical romances such as *Micah Clarke* (1889), set in seventeenth-century England, and *The White Company* (1891), a medieval tale of chivalry, and of the Professor Challenger stories such as *The Lost World* (1912), which are science fiction romances renewing and transforming the romantic traveller's tale.

Science fiction had come into its own at the end of the nineteenth century in works such as H. G. Wells' Darwinian nightmare *The Island of Dr Moreau* (1896) and other unnerving fantasies such as *The Time Machine* (1895), alert not just to evolutionary theory but to the thermodynamic possibility of a cooling sun and a dying universe. A little earlier electricity, submarines and space travel had all been pressed into service in the science fiction romances of Jules Verne. Science fiction could lead on to the consideration of other kinds of future. Mary Shelley's *Frankenstein* incorporated a critique of society offered by the outcast and demonised man-made monster. Both Wells, sometime Fabian socialist and unsuccessful parliamentary candidate for the Labour Party in the 1920s, and Verne, who served as a radical mayor of Amiens, moved beyond science fiction to consider utopian and dystopian social and political themes, another aspect of their romantic heritage. The future visited in *The Time Machine* shows a leisure class that has evolved into the feebly elegant, incurious and ineffectual Eloi and a working class that has evolved into brutal, ape-like underground dwellers, the Morlocks.

Aestheticism and symbolism are further examples of romantic survival into and beyond the late nineteenth century. John Keats had yearned for a life of 'sensations rather than thoughts' in a letter to his friend Benjamin Bailey (22 November 1817). The yearning was echoed in the critic Walter Pater's elegantly polished, sometimes fantastic reflections on paintings and poets, republished in collections such as *Studies in the History of the Renaissance* (1873), which influentially privileged intense aesthetic experience as the supreme good. A more flamboyant, amoral and controversial version of Pater's aestheticism, usually identified as 'decadence', was developed in Oscar Wilde's *Picture of Dorian Gray* (1890), which alluded obliquely to J. K. Huysmans' novel *À Rebours* ('Against Nature') (1884) and its eccentric hero Des Esseintes who has tried to escape from the external world into a private world of colour and sound and extreme sensation. Pater's historical novel *Marius the Epicurean* (1885), set in second-century Rome, has little external action or even dialogue but stays with the developing consciousness and sensations of Marius as he experiences pagan religion, Epicureanism, Stoicism and early Christianity.

The nature and flux of individual awareness became ever more important to the novelist Henry James, notably in *What Maisie Knew* (1897), where an adult world of broken marriage, power games and emotional chaos is presented to the reader through the perceptions of a child. It was James' brother, the philosopher and psychologist William James, in his *Principles of Psychology* (1890), who first used the phrase 'stream of consciousness' to describe the succession of thoughts in the waking mind and the phrase was picked up to describe the experimental interior monologues developed early in the next century by modernist novelists such as Proust, Joyce and Virginia Woolf.

If realism and naturalism had presented themselves as reactions against romanticism, Symbolism as it developed in France could be seen as a reaction against realism and naturalism. It represented a kind of return to some of the themes and strategies of romanticism, concerned not with precise, mechanical representation but with connotation and evocation, seeking to convey mood and atmosphere through suggestion and unexpected association. Poets such as Paul Verlaine and Stéphane Mallarmé attempted to depict not so much things in themselves as the effect that they produced, which could almost stand as a description of the English romantic paintings of J. M. W. Turner, much admired in an earlier generation by John Ruskin. One of the most successful symbolist works was Mallarmé's *L'Après-midi d'un faune* (1876), well known through Claude Debussy's orchestral interpretation (1892–4). Arthur Symons helped to introduce symbolism to twentieth-century English readers and writers in his book *The Symbolist Movement in Literature* (1899).

Literary Themes: Social and Political Change, Religion, Science

Nineteenth-century writing is as bewilderingly varied in content as one might expect in a century that witnessed revolution, radical reform and knowledge explosion in many countries. 'Literature' was a much broader category in 1800 than it is now, often deemed to include historical and scientific writing and other forms of what we might now rather limply call 'non-fictional prose'. The intelligent nineteenth-century general readers implied and targeted in the great quarterly and monthly periodicals of the time were assumed to have broad literary and intellectual interests, and so were the essayists and reviewers who wrote for them. Even within a single text there could be multiple interacting themes, so single-theme readings of a novel by Dickens or Dostoevsky (much influenced by Dickens), focusing just on education or religion, could – and do – miss much of the point. In long poems such as *Milton* (1804–8) and *Jerusalem, the Emanation of the Giant Albion* (1804–20) the artist-poet William Blake responded imaginatively, and often disconcertingly, to the French and American revolutions, to social and political repression, religious orthodoxy, the scientific tradition of the eighteenth century and the literary modes and attitudes inherited from Greece and Rome.

But not all literary works ranged quite so widely. Revolutionary politics provided a specific focus and the French Revolution cast a long shadow. Even before it started, Rousseau's influential *Discourse on Inequality* (1755) and *Social Contract* (1762) had developed a radical – and romantic – theory of the social state, claiming that primitive man had lived free in a state of nature. The early stages of the French Revolution had excited short-lived romantic enthusiasm at the prospect of a new order: Wordsworth, conservative in later years, like Coleridge and Southey, claimed in retrospect that 'Bliss was it in that dawn to be alive/ But to be young was very heaven!'[8] Radical novels such as *Caleb Williams* (1794) by William Godwin, author of an *Enquiry Concerning Political Justice* (1793), revisited themes of injustice and misused despotic power. Blake and other radical figures had condemned the emperors and tyrants of classical times as fatal models for modern rulers, but Godwin admired the political virtue represented by the noble Greeks and Romans who had stood out against tyranny, many of them praised in Plutarch's enduringly popular *Lives*. The Brutus who assassinated Julius Caesar was particularly admired by radicals and revolutionaries and the execution of Louis XVI and Marie Antoinette in 1793 had prompted revivals of Voltaire's play *La Mort de César*.

Edmund Burke did his best to discourage revolutionary enthusiasm in England with his *Reflections on the Revolution in France* (1790). Even so, class antagonism persisted. Radical Shelley, who admired Godwin and married his daughter Mary, protested vigorously against heavy-handed counter-revolutionary government measures. His satirical 'Masque of Anarchy' (1819) angrily lampooned those he held responsible for the 'Peterloo' massacre outside Manchester when a popular protest meeting was suppressed by military force. In his lyrical drama *Prometheus Unbound* (1820) he revised the Greek myth of Prometheus the firebringer to pursue the revolutionary theme of the overthrow of Tyranny in the name of all mankind.

But Burke's prophetic warnings, and toxic memories of the guillotine and the reign of terror, helped to change the general mood from enthusiasm to apprehension. So did Thomas Carlyle's vividly impressionistic prose-epic *The History of the French Revolution* (1837), which inspired and fed into Charles Dickens' *Tale of Two Cities* (1859), set in Paris and London in the revolutionary era. Recurring fears of revolution in Britain, fed by unrest in continental Europe, rose to a climax with fears of physical force at the massive Chartist demonstration in London in 1848. This was, however, constrained by wet weather and passed off peacefully. Riots in Hyde Park, though a long way short of revolution, gave Matthew Arnold his opportunity to preach the potentially pacifying gospel of culture in *Culture and Anarchy* (1869). Trafalgar Square riots in 1886 provided a starting point for the revolution bringing in the post-industrial utopia of William Morris' fantasy *News from Nowhere* (1890).

Society itself, rather than revolution, became a dominant theme in nineteenth-century writing. Balzac responded in secular terms to Dante's all-encompassing *Divine Comedy* by presenting his wide-ranging collected fictions of contemporary social life as *La Comédie humaine*, published in sixteen volumes between 1842 and 1846. The long, densely populated novels of Dickens and Trollope present virtually complete societies. William Makepeace Thackeray's *Vanity Fair* (1847), taking its title from John

Bunyan's allegorical site of worldly folly and spiritual emptiness in *Pilgrim's Progress*, is set among the follies and vices of fashionable society some thirty years previously.

Britain, the first industrial nation, was the first to register the social shocks of rapid, unplanned urbanisation and an unstable industrial economy leading to periodic unemployment. The sometimes devastating human costs, particularly during the economic depression of the hungry forties, were registered in Carlyle's angry denunciations in *Past and Present* (1843) and reflected in poems such as Tennyson's *Maud* (1855) and in 'condition of England' novels. These include the politician Benjamin Disraeli's *Sybil, or the Two Nations* (1845), developing a vision of the country now disastrously split into two nations, the rich, politically self-interested and irresponsible, and the oppressed poor, and Elizabeth Gaskell's *Mary Barton* (1848), set in industrial Manchester where Friedrich Engels had already gathered graphic information for his *Condition of the Working Class in England*, published in German in 1845. A little later Charles Dickens' *Hard Times* (1854) caricatured industrial Preston as Coketown and attacked what he saw as the dehumanising consequences of utilitarian social and educational policy. Mechanised industry and the associated demand for ever more raw materials and mineral resources, including coal, soon spread to other countries. Zola's novel *Germinal* (1885) documented class conflict and the oppressed and brutalised life of a French mining community. In America Frank Norris' *The Octopus* (1901), which owed a lot to Zola, presented the pitiless and unscrupulous economic power of the railroad in a wheat-growing area as an irresistible inhuman force.

There were much older forms of oppression and of rebellion against it. Mary Wollstonecraft is usually credited with inaugurating feminist discourse in the revolutionary era with her *A Vindication of the Rights of Woman* (1792). The position of women is a common theme in Victorian novels such as Charlotte Brontë's *Jane Eyre* (1847) and George Eliot's *The Mill on the Floss* (1860) and the debate continues in John Stuart Mill's *The Subjection of Women* (1869). This work was immediately translated into Danish by George Brands and so became available to progressive northern thinkers such as the Norwegian dramatist Henrik Ibsen. Brands' admiration for Mill, and other contemporary European writers such as Hippolyte Taine and Ernest Renan, and his determination to make them better known in his own country, played a major role in the modernisation of Scandinavian literatures and the emergence of distinct national traditions.

The woman question emerged as a touchstone of modernity in the literatures of many countries from the 1870s onwards. In *A Doll's House* (1879) Ibsen's sense of social institutions standing in the way of freedom and truth focused specifically on marriage, the circumscribed position of his heroine Nora and the dawn of self-realisation. This helped to identify Ibsenism as a powerful reformist social force, espoused in Britain by George Bernard Shaw both in the theatre and in political debate. In Russia Tolstoy's tragic story of adulterous love, *Anna Karenina* (1875–6), narrated an unrealisable attempt to live by romance, but in the process created a defiant female heroine committed to fullness of life. Sarah Grand, six times mayor of Bath, usually credited with coining the phrase 'the new woman', attacked the sexual double standard in marriage in *The Heavenly Twins* (1893). In the same year George Gissing explored female friendship in his novel *The Odd Women* and the Australian-born George Egerton published her best collection of short stories, *Keynotes*. These identify moments of significant female and feminist consciousness, setting out fantasies of self-realisation and freedom for the 'new woman' within a realistic framework. Another, less sympathetic, version of the 'new woman' was offered in the Swedish dramatist August Strindberg's *Miss Julie* (1888): the enigmatic protagonist's quest for sexual fulfilment is caught up in a sexual politics complicated by class difference. The repressively and insensitively masculinist nature of the nineteenth-century medical profession is condemned in the American Charlotte Perkins Gilman's short story 'The Yellow Wallpaper' (1892).

Religion, along with children and cooking, had often been seen as women's business, an aspect of the severely limited sphere of activity to which they were notionally confined by patriarchal society. But religious writing provided at least some nineteenth-century women with a voice, an income and some professional standing. One of the most highly regarded was Christina Rossetti, whose extensive output, secular and sacred, included a devotional commentary on the Book of Revelation, *The Face of the Deep* (1892), as well as religious poems and hymns. Catherine Winkworth translated many of the finest German hymns, published in *Lyra Germanica* (1855–8) and other collections and often reprinted for congregational singing. The indefatigable Margaret Oliphant supported her family through writing more than 100 books, which included novels with religious themes such as *Salem Chapel* (1863) and her biography of the charismatic religious leader Edward Irving (1862). Susan Warner, author of the piously sentimental tale *The Wide, Wide World* (1850), and her sister Anna Bartlett Warner, both of Orange County, New York, were prolific and very successful novelists and hymn writers.

Religion and immediately post-religious concerns continued to provide not just the context but the form and substance of much of the writing of the period. Publishers issued a steady stream of religious periodicals, biblical commentary, theological reflection or polemic, tracts and missionary biographies. In Britain and America there was a market for religiously edifying novels, mainly intended as Sunday school prizes. While much of this material is of minimal literary or even historical interest, some of it is still read. John Henry Newman's poem *The Dream of Gerontius*, originally published in a Jesuit periodical in 1865, has acquired a kind of immortality in Edward Elgar's musical setting (1900). Poems by Newman, or Blake or Tennyson, as well as lyrics in John Keble's Wordsworthian *Christian Year* (1827), were sometimes detached from their original context and sung as hymns. Historical novels of early Christianity such as the American Lew Wallace's *Ben Hur* (1880) or the Polish Henryk Sienkiewicz's *Quo Vadis* (1896) became international bestsellers.

Tradition was an inescapable element of religious thought and practice, whether the models and examples came from antiquity or the Middle Ages or the protestant reformation or from some later period. Religious (and anti-religious) controversy sometimes focused on different interpretations of the early development of Christianity, rather sardonically reviewed in the sceptical Edward Gibbon's much-reprinted *Decline and Fall of the Roman Empire* (1776–88). There were responses not just in aggrieved pamphlets and dry and dusty nineteenth-century church histories but in polemical historical fictions such as Charles Kingsley's *Hypatia; or New Foes with an Old Face* (1853). This was based around a discreditable religious disturbance in fifth-century Alexandria described by Gibbon. The new foes of the title were those like Newman who looked to the church of the first five centuries as a model for contemporary Christianity. Newman himself published a religious historical novel, *Callista*, in 1855, a tale of Christian martyrdom set in North Africa in the third century.

Institutional Christianity of various kinds, and clergymen, good, bad and indifferent, were so much part of everyday life that secular novels accommodated them as a matter of course, not always in a complimentary fashion. The most satisfying example was probably Anthony Trollope's *Barchester Towers* (1857), dealing with various kinds of intrigue in a cathedral city loosely based on Winchester and Salisbury. Charlotte Mary Yonge, much influenced by John Keble, published a long series of novels and stories about families and village communities, often focused on the local church. *The Heir of Redclyffe* (1853) is perhaps the best known. The high seriousness of her output, widely admired, even by other writers, helped to vindicate the moral and religious dignity of the novel form, too often dismissed as a frivolous and worldly distraction in earlier generations by censorious clerics, puritanical parents and earnest librarians. By 1880 Dostoevsky's *The Brothers Karamazov* and some of his earlier novels were raising unnerving questions about God, man and society in a manner that prompted sustained theological commentary, including a book from an Archbishop of Canterbury in our own century.⁹ In 1888 Mrs Humphrey Ward's exploration of contentious religious issues in her best-selling novel *Robert Elsmere* prompted a long review from the former (and future) Prime Minister W. E. Gladstone.

Religious writing both emerged from and helped to shape the general course of literary history. Spiritual autobiography, in a long and varied tradition ranging from St Augustine's *Confessions* to John Bunyan's *Grace Abounding to the Chief of Sinners* (1666), provided a natural model for more secular autobiography and accounts of the inner life, particularly works such as Wordsworth's *Prelude* (1850), tracing the growth of the poet's mind and imagination. Rousseau's autobiographical and at times scandalous *Confessions*, posthumously published in 1781, gestured ironically at Augustine. James Hogg's *Confessions of a Justified Sinner* (1824) was a nightmare novel of Calvinistic religion gone badly wrong. John Henry Newman's account of his religious development, *Apologia pro Via Sua* (1864), took its title from Plato's narrative vindication of the life of Socrates, known as the *Apologia* or *Apology*: it embodied a defence of his own integrity and an account of the stages of his passage from Evangelical Anglicanism to his reception into the Roman Catholic Church. The title was mischievously adapted by the sceptical intellectual historian and biographer Leslie Stephen for his *Agnostic's Apology* (1900). Credit for coining the term 'agnostic' is usually given to the scientist T. H. Huxley, known as 'Darwin's bulldog' or aggressive populariser. Huxley took it from the New Testament reference to the altar to the unknown God (*agnosto theo* in the original Greek) that St Paul encountered in Athens (Acts 17:23).

There was a natural connection or overlap between romantic and religious discourses, both concerned with personal growth and with the inner life. In Germany F. D. E. Schleiermacher's *Reden über die Religion* (1794), translated as *On Religion: Speeches to Its Cultured Despisers*, emphasised emotional experience as the basis of religion, deeming creeds to be the expression rather than the foundation of religion. In France François-René Chateaubriand's influential *Le Génie du christianisme* (1802) incorporated a chapter concerned with a characteristic romantic hero, René, later published separately as a short novel. The parent work set out to demonstrate that (mainly Catholic) Christianity, intimately associated with beauty, the imagination and the emotions, was uniquely able to satisfy man's desire for the infinite.

In Britain Evangelical reactions against what was perceived to be the cold, dry, formal religious tradition of the eighteenth century, distrustful of 'enthusiasm' or religious frenzy, stimulated a more fervent 'religion of the heart' emphasising personal religious experience and 'conversion' to godly life. The poet William Cowper registered his own intense Evangelical spirituality in hymns of personal devotion such as 'O for a closer walk with God' or 'Sometimes a light surprises/The Christian while he sings' included in the *Olney Hymns* (1779) that he produced with his friend John Newton.

The novelist George Eliot, brought up in this tradition, parted company with it and early in her career undertook to translate the German texts of David Strauss' controversial *Life of Jesus* and Ludwig Feuerbach's *Essence of Christianity*, both of which called into question the literal truth of the gospel narrative. But Eliot's secular humanism did not take her far from the spirit of Christianity: from the outset of her career in fiction, in *Scenes from Clerical Life* (1858) and her first novel *Adam Bede* (1859), she did imaginative justice to the moral feeling, compassion and love deepened by suffering that were part of official church teaching but did not depend on it.

The experience of religious doubt, the felt absence rather than the felt presence of the divine, could attract the same kind of language as religious devotion and spiritual quest, the same archetypal imagery of light and darkness, birth and death, even if the meaning was not the same. There is a journey from darkness back to light in Tennyson's 'Diary of a Soul', *In Memoriam* (1850), his long poem about bereavement, loss of faith and direction and a rather precariously recovered sense of being able to trust in some larger hope. Newman's hymn 'Lead Kindly Light Amid the Encircling Gloom' or the Jesuit priest Gerard Manley Hopkins' bleak sonnet 'I Wake and Feel the Fell of Dark, Not Day' have their counterpart in James Thomson's poem of atheistic despair 'City of Dreadful Night' (1874). This draws selectively on Dante's *Divine Comedy* but turns away from the perpetual light of heaven to the darkness of Dante's hell, encouraged by the musings of the gloomy Italian romantic poet Giacomo Leopardi. Gérard De Nerval prefaced his poem 'Christ aux Oliviers' (1844) with an epigraph proclaiming 'Dieu est mort! Le ciel est vide' ('God is dead! Heaven is empty'). Matthew Arnold, sensitive to the French romantic tradition represented by Chateaubriand and Senancour, elegised dead or dying faith in poems such as 'Stanzas from the Grande Chartreuse' (1855) and 'Dover Beach' (1867).

There are more prosaic explorations of the loss of faith in the form of prose fictions such as Thomas Carlyle's eccentric *Sartor Resartus* (1836), J. A. Froude's *Nemesis of Faith* (1849) and Mary Ward's *Robert Elsmere* (1888). To some extent these follow the structure of the religious conversion-narrative, stemming ultimately from the New Testament account of the dramatic conversion of St Paul, but they trace turning away from rather than turning to religious certainties.

Old certainties were called in question by new knowledge, as often happens. The new technologies of the age of steam grew out of but also stimulated scientific discovery. The fossil record, which had been enhanced by fresh finds turned up by extensive and systematic quarrying and the massive excavations required to build the railway system, yielded disconcerting evidence of now-extinct species. Deeper and safer mines called for a better understanding of the structure and development of the earth's crust. The unimaginable abysses of geological time that were gradually revealed, stretching back millions of years before there was any trace of human or even animal life, served to make sensitive spirits feel less at home in the world and contributed significantly to the still pre-Darwinian moods of doubt and despair of Tennyson's *In Memoriam* (1850).

In the wake of Darwin's *Origin of Species* (1859) and the popularisation of Darwinian ideas, particularly by T. H. Huxley, science emerged as an ambiguous asset. The term 'evolution', modishly scientific and with associations of inexorable process, was recklessly and misleadingly applied to all kinds of development. To Huxley's horror, registered in his Romanes lecture on 'Evolution and Ethics' (1893), it was used to sanction ruthless and socially irresponsible economic self-interest and social processes that took no account of the damage caused to people's lives. On the other hand, the doctors, from whom the early science lecturers were often recruited, had led the way in establishing and demonstrating the social benefits of science. There were already significant improvements in medicine, retrospectively incorporated into George Eliot's *Middlemarch*, which is set in the 1830s, and there had been substantial advances in public health and the treatment of preventable disease. The scientific habit of mind, developing and testing principles on the basis of accumulated evidence rather than received wisdom, had triumphed on a heroic scale in Darwin's work and encouraged critical and sceptical enquiry in other areas, including historical scholarship. As Huxley kept pointing out, aspects of the Biblical narrative, particularly miracle stories, did not stand up particularly well to modern scientific scrutiny. Charles Kingsley, himself an enthusiastic amateur marine biologist, mocked the sceptical seriousness of the scientists in his children's novel *The Water Babies* (1863), a kind of religious allegory incorporating his own moralised version of evolutionary process.

More sceptical novelists, particularly Thomas Hardy, paid more attention to the challenge implicit in evolutionary theory to doctrines of Providence or divinely established order and development in nature. Hardy made narrative use of the sombre realisation that there was no merit about the biological survival of the fittest: it was a matter of physical suitability for a given environment and had nothing to do with moral or mental qualities or individual effort. Survival at the end of his bleakest novel, *Jude the Obscure* (1895), seems to be reserved for a couple of worthless opportunists while his painfully self-educated protagonist has perished, ill-adapted to the social and moral environment of his time, and his beloved Sue, a demoralised version of the new woman, is likely to follow him.

Romance, romantic love and conventional religious faith were all likely to have a difficult time under modern conditions understood in this way. But the tensions likely to be generated had enormous imaginative and emotional power. Darwin's Danish translator, Jens Peter Jacobsen, was both a romantic and a realist, a scientist who was also a poet and novelist. His novel *Niels Lyhne* (1880), the story of an aspiring poet, encompasses idealised love, lost faith and the melancholy disillusionment of vanished dreams. The novel was much admired by twentieth-century modernists such as the poet Rainer Maria Rilke, and it helped to shape Thomas Mann's early novel *Tonio Kröger* (1903). But Jacobsen did not live to hear their praise: he died of tuberculosis in 1885, before he was forty.

NOTES

1 Samuel Taylor Coleridge, *Aids to Reflection* [1825] (London: George Bell, 1884), p. 268.
2 William Wordsworth, 'The Solitary Reaper' (1807), ll.19–20.
3 T. J. Binyon, *Pushkin: A Biography* (London: HarperCollins, 2003), p. 407.
4 George Eliot, 'Contemporary Literature: Art and Belles Lettres', *Westminster Review* 65 (1856), 626.
5 Quoted by Michael Meyer, *Ibsen* (Harmondsworth: Penguin Books, 1974), p. 515.
6 Quoted by Michael Millgate, *Thomas Hardy: A Biography Revisited* (Oxford: Oxford University Press, 2004), pp. 341, 405.
7 Alfred Tennyson, 'Locksley Hall Sixty Years After' (1886), ll. 145–6.
8 William Wordsworth, *The Prelude* (1850), Book XI, ll. 108–9.
9 Rowan Williams, *Dostoevsky: Language, Faith and Fiction* (London: Continuum, 2008).

FURTHER READING

Chapter 2

Bourdeau, Michel, Mary Pickering and Warren Schmaus (eds.), *Love, Order, and Progress: The Science, Philosophy, and Politics of Auguste Comte* (Pittsburgh, PA: University of Pittsburgh Press, 2018).

Claeys, G., *Mill and Paternalism* (Cambridge: Cambridge University Press, 2013).

Comte, A., *Early Political Writings*, ed. and trans. H. S. Jones (Cambridge: Cambridge University Press, 1998).

A General View of Positivism, trans. J. H. Bridges (London: Trübner & Co., 1865).

System of Positive Policy: Or Treatise on Sociology, Instituting the Religion of Humanity, 4 vols. (London: Longmans, Green & Co., 1875–7).

Craiutu, A., *Liberalism Under Siege: The Political Thought of the French Doctrinaires* (Lanham, MD: Lexington Books, 2003).

Guizot, F., *The History of Civilization in Europe*, trans. W. Hazlitt, ed. L. Siedentop (London: Penguin, 1997).

The History of the Origins of Representative Government, ed. Aurelian Craiutu, trans. Andrew R. Scoble (Indianapolis, IN: Liberty Fund, 2001).

Hayward, J., *After the French Revolution: Six Critics of Democracy and Nationalism* (New York: Harvester Wheatsheaf, 1991).

Jaume, L., *L'individu effacé, ou le paradoxe du libéralisme français* (Paris: Fayard, 1997).

Jennings, J., *Revolution and the Republic: A History of Political Thought in France Since the Eighteenth Century* (Oxford: Oxford University Press, 2011).

Jones, H. S., *Victorian Political Thought* (Basingstoke: Palgrave Macmillan, 2000).

Manuel, Frank E., *The Prophets of Paris* (New York: Harper & Row, 1965).

Mill, John Stuart, *The Collected Works of John Stuart Mill*, eds. F. E. L. Priestley and John M. Robson, 33 vols. (Toronto, ON and London: University of Toronto Press, 1963–91).

Rosanvallon, Pierre, *Democracy Past and Future*, ed. Samuel Moyn (New York: Columbia University Press, 2006).

Le Moment Guizot (Paris: Gallimard, 1985).

Saunders, Robert, *Democracy and the Vote in British Politics, 1848–1867: The Making of the Second Reform Act* (Farnham: Ashgate, 2011).

Stedman Jones, Gareth, *Karl Marx: Greatness and Illusion* (London: Allen Lane, 2016).

Stedman Jones, Gareth and Gregory Claeys (eds.), *The Cambridge History of Nineteenth-Century Political Thought* (Cambridge: Cambridge University Press, 2011).
Tocqueville, Alexis de, *Democracy in America*. Historical-Critical Edition, Bilingual Edition, 4 vols., ed. Eduardo Nolla, trans. James T. Schleifer (Indianapolis, IN: Liberty Fund, 2010).
Urbinati, Nadia, *Mill on Democracy: From the Athenian Polis to Representative Government* (Chicago: University of Chicago Press, 2002).
Varouxakis, Georgios, 'Guizot's Historical Works and J. S. Mill's Reception of Tocqueville', *History of Political Thought* 20 (1999), 292–312.
Wright, T. R., *The Religion of Humanity: The Impact of Comtean Positivism on Victorian Britain* (Cambridge: Cambridge University Press, 1986).

Chapter 3

Bokenkotter, T., *A Concise History of the Catholic Church* (New York: Image Books, 1990).
Chadwick, O., *The Victorian Church*, 2 vols. (London: SCM Press, 1987).
Correll, M. R., *Shepherds of the Empire: Germany's Conservative Protestant Leadership, 1888–1919* (Minneapolis, MN: Fortress Press, 2014).
Dansette, A., *Religious History of Modern France* (Freiburg: Herder, 1961).
Dorrien, G., *The Making of American Liberal Theology*, vol. 1 (Louisville, KY: Westminster John Knox, 2006).
Edwards, D., *Christian England*, vol. 3 (Grand Rapids, MI: Wm. B. Eerdmans, 1984).
Elliott-Binns, L. E., *English Thought 1860–1900, The Theological Aspect* (London: Longmans, Green & Co., 1956).
Gjerde, J., *Catholicism and the Shaping of Nineteenth Century America*, ed. S. D. Kang (Cambridge: Cambridge University Press, 2012).
Hole, Robert, *Pulpits, Politics and Public Order in Britain 1760–1832* (Cambridge: Cambridge University Press, 1989).
Holmes, D. J., *More Roman than Rome: English Catholicism in the Nineteenth Century* (London: Burns & Oates, 1979).
Livingston, J. C., *Modern Christian Thought: The Enlightenment and the Nineteenth Century* (Upper Saddle River, NJ: Prentice Hall, 1998).
Marsden, G., *Fundamentalism and American Culture* (Oxford: Oxford University Press, 2006).
Moore, J. R., *The Post-Darwinian Controversies* (Cambridge: Cambridge University Press, 1979).
Noll, M., *America's God* (Oxford: Oxford University Press, 2002).
Noll, M., Bebbington, D. W. and Rawlyk, G. A. (eds.), *Evangelicalism, Comparative Studies of Popular Protestantism in North America, the British Isles, and Beyond, 1700–1900* (Oxford: Oxford University Press, 1994).
Pereiro, J., *Ethos and the Oxford Movement: At the Heart of Tractarianism* (Oxford: Oxford University Press, 2008).
Philipps, P. T., *A Kingdom on Earth: Anglo-American Social Christianity 1880–1940* (College Park, PA: Pennsylvania State University Press, 1996).
Raphael, M. L. (ed.), *The Columbia History of Jews and Judaism in America* (New York: Columbia University Press, 2008).

Reardon, B., *Liberalism and Tradition: Aspects of Catholic Thought in Nineteenth-Century France* (Cambridge: Cambridge University Press, 1975).

Religious Thought in the Victorian Age: A Survey from Coleridge to Gore (London: Longman, 1980).

Reuther, R. R., *America, Amerikka: Elect Nation and Imperial Violence* (Oakdale, CT: Equinox, 2007).

Royle, E., *Radical Politics 1790–1900: Religion and Unbelief* (London: Longman, 1971).

Stein, S. J. (ed.), *The Cambridge History of Religions in America*, 3 vols. (Cambridge: Cambridge University Press, 2012).

Stephens, L., *The English Utilitarians* [1900] (New York: Augustus M. Kelley, 1968).

Vidler, A. R., *A Century of Social Catholicism 1820–1920* (London: SPCK, 1964).

Vital, D., *A People Apart: The Jews in Europe 1789–1939* (Oxford: Oxford University Press, 1999).

Ward, W. R., *Theology, Sociology and Politics: The German Protestant Social Conscience 1890–1933* (Berne: Peter Lang, 1979).

Wilson, J. E., *Introduction to Modern Theology: Trajectories in the German Tradition* (London: Westminster John Knox, 2007).

Chapter 4

Hegel, G. W. F., *Elements of the Philosophy of Right*, ed. Allen W. Wood, trans. H. B. Nisbet (Cambridge: Cambridge University Press, 1991).

Encyclopedia of the Philosophical Sciences in Basic Outline, trans. and eds. Klaus Brinkmann and Daniel O. Dahlstrom (Cambridge: Cambridge University Press, 2010).

Lectures on the Philosophy of World History: Introduction: Reason in History, trans. H. B. Nisbet, intro. Duncan Forbes (Cambridge: Cambridge University Press, 1975).

Heine, Heinrich, *On the History of Religion and Philosophy in Germany* [1835], trans. Howard Pollack-Milgate, intro. Terry Pinkard (Cambridge: Cambridge University Press, 2007).

Hoffheimer, Michael H., *Eduard Gans and the Hegelian Philosophy of Law* (Dordrecht: Kluwer, 1995).

Marcuse, Herbert, *Reason and Revolution: Hegel and the Rise of Social Theory* [1941], 2nd edn (New York: Humanities Press, 1954).

Moggach, Douglas (ed.), *The New Hegelians: Politics and Philosophy in the Hegelian School* (Cambridge: Cambridge University Press, 2006).

Moggach, Douglas and Gareth Stedman Jones (eds.), *The 1848 Revolutions and European Political Thought* (Cambridge: Cambridge University Press, 2018).

Pippin, Robert B. and Otfried Höffe (eds.), *Hegel on Ethics and Politics* (Cambridge: Cambridge University Press, 2004).

Riedel, Manfred, *Between Tradition and Revolution: The Hegelian Transformation of Political Philosophy* [1969], trans. Walter Wright (Cambridge: Cambridge University Press, 1984).

Toews, John Edward, *Hegelianism: The Path Toward Dialectical Humanism, 1805–1841* (Cambridge: Cambridge University Press, 1980).

Chapter 5

Abrams, P., ed., *The Origins of British Sociology: 1834–1914* (Chicago: University of Chicago Press, 1968).

Bryant, C. G. A., *Positivism in Social Theory and Research* (Basingstoke: Macmillan, 1985).

Horowitz, A. and T. Maley, eds., *The Barbarism of Reason: Max Weber and the Twilight of Enlightenment* (Toronto, ON: University of Toronto Press, 1994).

Jones, S. S., *Durkheim Reconsidered* (Oxford: Polity, 2001).

Kemple, T., *Intellectual Work and the Spirit of Capitalism* (Basingstoke: Palgrave, 2014).

Levine, D. N., *Visions of the Sociological Tradition* (Chicago: University of Chicago Press, 1995).

Miller, W. W., *Solidarity and the Sacred: A Durkheimian Quest* (Oxford: Berghahn, 2012).

Ross, D., *The Origins of American Social Science* (Cambridge: Cambridge University Press, 1991).

Seidman, S., *Liberalism and the Origins of European Social Theory* (Berkeley: University of California Press, 1983).

Wernick, A., ed., *The Anthem Companion to Auguste Comte* (London: Anthem, 2017).

Chapter 6

Burrow, J. W., *The Crisis of Reason: European Thought: 1848–1914* (New Haven, CT: Yale University Press, 2000).

Den Boer, P., *History as a Profession: The Study of History in France, 1818–1914*, trans. A. Pomerans (Princeton, NJ: Princeton University Press, 1998).

Dyhouse, C., *No Distinction of Sex? Women in British Universities: 1870–1939* (London: University College London Press, 1995).

Fischer, D. H., *Albion's Seed: Four British Folkways in America* (Oxford: Oxford University Press, 1992).

Kadish, A. and K. Tribe, eds., *The Market for Political Economy: The Advent of Economics in British University Culture* (London: Routledge, 1993).

Kelley, D., *Fortunes of History: Historical Inquiry from Herder to Huizinga* (New Haven, CT: Yale University Press, 2003).

Macintyre, S., Maiguashca, J. and Pók, A., eds., *The Oxford History of Historical Writing*, vol. 4: 1800–1945 (Oxford: Oxford University Press, 2011).

McKettrick, D., 'Libraries, Knowledge, and Public Identity', in *The Organisation of Knowledge in Victorian Britain*, ed. Martin Daunton (Oxford: Oxford University Press, 2005), pp. 287–312.

Novick, P., *That Noble Dream: The 'Objectivity Question' and the American Historical Profession* (Cambridge: Cambridge University Press, 1988).

Porter, T., *The Rise of Statistical Thinking, 1820–1900* (Princeton, NJ: Princeton University Press, 1986).

Rüegg, W., ed., *A History of the University in Europe* (Cambridge: Cambridge University Press, 2004).

Slee, P., *Learning and a Liberal Education* (Manchester: Manchester University Press, 1986).

Smith, B., *The Gender of History: Men, Women, and Historical Practice* (Cambridge, MA: Harvard University Press, 2000).

Stephens, W. B., *Education in Britain, 1750–1914* (London: Macmillan, 1997).

Chapter 7

Jürgen Kocka, *Capitalism: A Short History* (Princeton, NJ: Princeton University Press, 2016).

Chapter 8

Abrams, M. H., *The Mirror and the Lamp: Romantic Theory and the Critical Tradition* [1953] (Oxford: Oxford University Press, 1971).

Bell, Matthew, *The German Tradition of Psychology in Literature and Thought, 1700–1840* (Cambridge: Cambridge University Press, 2005).

Brooks III, John I., *The Eclectic Legacy: Academic Philosophy and the Human Sciences in Nineteenth-Century France* (Newark: University of Delaware Press, and London: Associated University Presses, 1998).

Chadwick, Owen, *The Secularization of the European Mind in the Nineteenth Century* (Cambridge: Cambridge University Press, 1975).

Collini, Stefan, *Public Moralists: Political Thought and Intellectual Life in Britain 1850–1930* (Oxford: Clarendon Press, 1991).

Darwin, Charles, *The Descent of Man: Selection in Relation to Sex* [1871], intro. Adrian Desmond and James Moore (London: Penguin Books, 2004).

Ellenberger, Henri, *The Discovery of the Unconscious: The History and Evolution of Dynamic Psychiatry* (London: Allen Lane, Penguin Press, 1970).

Foucault, Michel, *Discipline and Punish: The Birth of the Prison* [1975], trans. Alan Sheridan (London: Allen Lane, 1977).

    The History of Sexuality. Volume I: An Introduction [1976], trans. Robert Hurley (London: Penguin Books, 1981).

    The Order of Things: An Archaeology of the Human Sciences [1966], trans. Alan Sheridan (London: Tavistock, 1970).

Frank, Joseph, *Dostoevsky*, 5 vols. (Princeton, NJ: Princeton University Press, 1976–2002).

Goldstein, Jan, *The Post-Revolutionary Self: Politics and Psyche in France, 1750–1850* (Cambridge, MA: Harvard University Press, 2005).

Huxley, T. H., 'On the Hypothesis that Animals Are Automata and Its History' [1874], in *Method and Results: Essays* (London: Macmillan, 1894), vol. 1. pp. 119–250.

James, William, *The Varieties of Religious Experience: A Study in Human Nature.* [1902] (New York: Penguin Books, 1982).

    'The Will to Believe' [1896] in *Pragmatism and Other Writings*, ed. Giles Gunn (New York: Penguin Books, 2000), pp. 198–218.

Joravsky, David, *Russian Psychology: A Critical History* (Oxford: Basil Blackwell, 1989).

Makari, George, *Revolution in Mind: The Creation of Psychoanalysis* (London: Duckworth, 2008).

Mandelbaum, Maurice, *History, Man, & Reason: A Study in Nineteenth-Century Thought* (Baltimore, MD: Johns Hopkins University Press, 1971).

Pick, Daniel, *Faces of Degeneration: A European Disorder, c.1848–c.1918* (Cambridge: Cambridge University Press, 1989).

Richards, Robert J., *Darwin and the Emergence of Evolutionary Theories of Mind and Behavior* (Chicago: University of Chicago Press, 1987).

Richardson, Alan, *British Romanticism and the Science of Mind* (Cambridge: Cambridge University Press, 2001).

Rose, Nikolas, *Governing the Soul: The Shaping of the Private Self* [1989] 2nd edn (London: Free Association Books, 1999).

The Psychological Complex: Social Regulation and the Psychology of the Individual (London: Routledge & Kegan Paul, 1985).

Schopenhauer, Arthur, *The World as Will and Representation* [1818], trans. E. F. J. Payne, 2 vols. (New York: Dover, 1966).

Sechenov, I. M., 'Reflexes of the Brain' [1863], in *Selected Works* [1935], ed. and trans. A. A. Subkov (Amsterdam: E. J. Bonset, 1968), pp. 263–336.

Seigel, Jerrold, *The Idea of the Self: Thought and Experience in Western Europe since the Seventeenth Century* (Cambridge: Cambridge University Press, 2005).

Shuttleworth, Sally, *Charlotte Brontë and Victorian Psychology* (Cambridge: Cambridge University Press, 1996).

The Mind of the Child: Child Development in Literature, Science, and Medicine, 1840–1900 (Oxford: Oxford University Press, 2010).

Smith, Roger, *Between Mind and Nature: A History of Psychology* (London: Reaktion Books, 2013).

Free Will and the Human Sciences in Britain, 1870–1910 (London: Pickering & Chatto, 2013).

Inhibition: History and Meaning in the Sciences of Mind and Brain (London: Free Association Books and Berkeley: University of California Press, 1992).

Taylor, Charles, *Sources of the Self: The Making of the Modern Identity* (Cambridge: Cambridge University Press, 1989).

Taylor, Jenny Bourne and Sally Shuttleworth, eds., *Embodied Selves: An Anthology of Psychological Texts 1830–1890* (Oxford: Clarendon Press, 1998).

Young, Robert M., *Mind, Brain, and Adaptation in the Nineteenth Century: Cerebral Localization and Its Biological Context from Gall to Ferrier* [1970] (Oxford: Oxford University Press, 1990).

Chapter 9

Burrow, John, *Evolution and Society: A Study in Victorian Social Theory* (Cambridge: Cambridge University Press, 1966).

Claeys, Gregory, *Dystopia: A Natural History* (Oxford: Oxford University Press, 2016).

Imperial Sceptics: British Critics of Empire, 1850–1920 (Cambridge: Cambridge University Press, 2010).

'Malthus and Godwin: Rights, Utility and Productivity', in *New Perspectives on Malthus*, ed. Robert Mayhew (Cambridge: Cambridge University Press, 2016), pp. 52–73.

Marx and Marxism (London: Penguin Books, 2018).

Mill and Paternalism (Cambridge: Cambridge University Press, 2013).

'Wallace and Owenism', in *Natural Selection and Beyond: The Intellectual Legacy of Alfred Russel Wallace*, eds. Charles Smith and George Beccaloni (Oxford: Oxford University Press, 2008), pp. 235–62.

Clark, Linda L., *Social Darwinism in France* (Tuscaloosa, AL: University of Alabama Press, 1984).

Crook, D. P., *Benjamin Kidd: Portrait of a Social Darwinist* (Cambridge: Cambridge University Press, 1984).

Darwinism, War and History (Cambridge: Cambridge University Press, 1994).

Darwin, Charles, *The Descent of Man* (London: John Murray, 1882).

On the Origin of Species by Means of Natural Selection (London: John Murray, 1859).

Dickens, Peter, *Social Darwinism* (Buckingham: Open University Press, 2000).

Francis, Mark, *Herbert Spencer and the Invention of Modern Life* (Chesham: Acumen, 2006).

Hawkins, Mike, *Social Darwinism in European and American Thought 1860–1945* (Cambridge: Cambridge University Press, 1997).

Hochschild, Adam, *King Leopold's Ghost: A Study of Greed, Terror, and Heroism in Colonial Africa* (London: Papermac, 2000).

Hofstadter, Richard, *Social Darwinism in American Thought* (Philadelphia: University of Pennsylvania Press, 1944).

Huxley, T. H., *Ethics and Evolution* (London: Macmillan & Co., 1894).

Irvine, William, *Apes, Angels and Victorians. Darwin, Huxley and Evolution* (New York: McGraw-Hill, 1959).

Jones, Greta, *Social Darwinism and English Thought* (Brighton: Harvester, 1980).

Kelly, Alfred, *The Descent of Darwin: The Popularization of Darwinism in Germany, 1860–1914* (Chapel Hill: University of North Carolina Press, 1981).

Kidd, Benjamin, *Social Evolution* (London: Macmillan, 1894).

Kohn, Marek, *A Reason for Everything. Natural Selection and the English Imagination* (London: Faber & Faber, 2004).

Mackintosh, Robert, *From Comte to Benjamin Kidd: The Appeal to Biology or Evolution for Human Guidance* (London: Macmillan, 1899).

Moore, James R., 'Deconstructing Darwinism: The Politics of Evolution in the 1860s', *Journal of the History of Biology* 24 (1991), 353–408.

The Post-Darwinian Controversies: A Study of the Protestant Struggle to Come to Terms with Darwin in Great Britain and America, 1870–1900 (Cambridge: Cambridge University Press, 1979).

Nicolas, M. P., *From Nietzsche Down to Hitler* (London: William Hodge & Co., 1938).

Olusoga, David and Casper W. Ericsen, *The Kaiser's Holocaust: Germany's Forgotten Genocide* (London: Faber & Faber, 2010).

Pick, Daniel, *Faces of Degeneration: A European Disorder c.1848–c.1918* (Cambridge: Cambridge University Press, 1989).

Pittenger, Mark, *American Socialists and Evolutionary Thought, 1870–1920* (Madison: University of Wisconsin Press, 1993).

Ritchie, David, *Darwinism and Politics* (London: Swan Sonnenschein, 1901).

Rogers, James Allen, 'Darwinism and Social Darwinism', *Journal of the History of Ideas* 33 (1972), 265–80.

Searle, G. R., *The Quest for National Efficiency. A Study in British Politics and Political Thought, 1899–1914* (Oxford: Basil Blackwell, 1971).

Singer, Peter, *A Darwinian Left: Politics, Evolution and Co-operation* (London: Weidenfeld & Nicolson, 1999).

Stack, David, *The First Darwinian Left. Socialism and Darwinism 1859–1914* (Cheltenham: New Clarion Press, 2003).

Stone, Dan, *Breeding Superman: Nietzsche, Race and Eugenics in Edwardian and Interwar Britain* (Liverpool: Liverpool University Press, 2002).

Taylor, M. W., *Men Versus the State: Herbert Spencer and Late Victorian Liberalism* (Oxford: Clarendon Press, 1992).

Weikart, Richard, *Socialist Darwinism: Evolution in German Socialist Thought from Marx to Bernstein* (London: International Scholars Publications, 1999).

Wiltshire, D., *The Social and Political Thought of Herbert Spencer* (Oxford: Oxford University Press, 1978).

Winch, Donald, *Riches and Poverty: An Intellectual History of Political Economy in Britain, 1750–1834* (Cambridge: Cambridge University Press, 1996).

Wealth and Life: Essays on the Intellectual History of Political Economy in Britain, 1848–1914 (Cambridge: Cambridge University Press, 2009).

Chapter 10

Bauer, D. M. and P. Gould, eds., *The Cambridge Companion to Nineteenth-Century American Women's Writing* (Cambridge: Cambridge University Press, 2001).

Burman, S., ed., *Fit Work for Women* (New York: Routledge, 2013).

Cott, N., *The Bonds of Womanhood: "Woman's Sphere" in New England, 1780–1835* (New Haven, CT: Yale University Press, 1997).

Cott, N., and E. Pleck, eds., *A Heritage of Her Own: Toward a New Social History of American Women* (New York: Simon & Schuster, 1979).

Erskine, F., 'The Origin of Species and the Science of Female Inferiority', in *Charles Darwin's The Origin of Species: New Interdisciplinary Essays*, eds. D. Amigoni and J. Wallace (Manchester: Manchester University Press, 1995), pp. 95–121.

Faderman, L., *Surpassing the Love of Men: Romantic Friendship and Love between Women from the Renaissance to the Present* (London: Women's Press, 1985).

Fellman, A. C. and M. Fellman, *Making Sense of Self: Medical Advice Literature in Late Nineteenth-Century America* (Philadelphia: University of Pennsylvania Press, 1981).

Gordon, L., *The Moral Property of Women: A History of Birth Control Politics in America* (Urbana: University of Illinois Press, 2002).

Haller, J. S. and R. M. Haller, *The Physician and Sexuality in Victorian America* (Urbana: University of Illinois Press, 1974).

Hewitt, N., 'Taking the True Woman Hostage', *Journal of Women's History* 14 (2002), 156–62.

Jackson, M., *The Real Facts of Life: Feminism and the Politics of Sexuality c 1850–1940* (London: Taylor & Francis, 1994).

Kerber, L. K., 'The Republican Mother: Women and the Enlightenment: An American Perspective', *American Quarterly* 28 (1976), 187–205.

Lerner, G., 'The Lady and the Mill Girl: Changes in the Status of Women in the Age of Jackson.' *Midcontinent American Studies Journal* 10 (1969), 5–15.

Maines, R., *The Technology of Orgasm: 'Hysteria', the Vibrator, and Women's Sexual Satisfaction* (Baltimore, MD: Johns Hopkins University Press, 1999).

Matthews, G., *'Just a Housewife': The Rise and Fall of Domesticity in America* (Oxford: Oxford University Press, 1987).

The Rise of Public Woman: Woman's Power and Woman's Place in the United States 1630–1970 (Oxford: Oxford University Press, 1992).

McFadden, M., *Golden Cables of Sympathy: The Transatlantic Sources of Nineteenth-Century Feminism* (Lexington: University Press of Kentucky, 1999).

Mosher, C. D., *The Mosher Survey: Sexual Attitudes of 45 Victorian Women*, eds. J. MaHood and K. Wenburg (New York: Arno Press, 1980).

Patterson, M. H., ed., *The American New Woman Revisited: A Reader, 1884–1930* (New Brunswick, NJ: Rutgers University Press, 2008).

Poovey, M., *Uneven Developments: The Ideological Work of Gender in Mid-Victorian England* (Chicago: University of Chicago Press, 1988).

Rendall, J., *The Origins of Modern Feminism: Women in Britain, France, and the United States, 1780–1860* (New York: Palgrave, 1985).

Richardson, A., *Love and Eugenics in the Late Nineteenth Century: Rational Reproduction and the New Woman* (Oxford: Oxford University Press, 2003).

Rosenberg, R., *Beyond Separate Spheres: Intellectual Roots of Modern Feminism* (New Haven, CT: Yale University Press, 1982).

Rowbotham, S., *Women in Movement: Feminism and Social Action* (New York: Routledge, 1992).

Russett, C. E., *Sexual Science: The Victorian Construction of Womanhood* (Cambridge, MA: Harvard University Press, 1989).

Sanchez-Eppler, K., *Touching Liberty: Abolition, Feminism, and the Politics of the Body* (Berkeley: University of California Press, 1993).

Smith-Rosenberg, C., *Disorderly Conduct: Visions of Gender in Victorian America* (New York: Oxford University Press, 1985).

Vicinus, M., ed., *Suffer and Be Still: Women in the Victorian Age* (Bloomington: Indiana University Press, 1972).

Vickery, A., 'Golden Age to Separate Spheres? A Review of the Categories and Chronology of English Women's History', *The Historical Journal* 36 (1993), 383–414.

Wayne, T. K., *Women's Roles in Nineteenth-Century America* (Westport, CT: Greenwood Press, 2007).

Chapter 11

Chakrabarty, Dipesh, *Provincializing Europe: Postcolonial Thought and Historical Difference* (Princeton, NJ: Princeton University Press, 2000).

Fabian, Johannes, *Time and the Other* (New York: Columbia University Press, 1986).

Goldberg, David Theo, *The Racial State* (Oxford: Blackwell, 2002).

Makdisi, Saree, *Making England Western: Occidentalism, Race and Imperial Culture* (Chicago: University of Chicago Press, 2014).

Polanyi, Karl, *The Great Transformation: The Political and Economic Origins of Our Time* [1944] (Boston: Beacon Press, 2001).

Said, Edward, *Orientalism* (New York: Pantheon, 1978).

Stoler, Ann Laura, *Race and the Education of Desire* (Durham, NC: Duke University Press, 1995).

Thompson, E. P., *The Making of the English Working Class* (New York: Vintage, 1966).

Chapter 12

Beaumont, Matthew, ed., *A Concise Companion to Realism* (Chichester: Wiley-Blackwell, 2010).

Beer, Gillian, *Open Fields: Science in Cultural Encounter* (Oxford: Oxford University Press, 1996).

Chadwick, Owen, *The Secularisation of the European Mind in the Nineteenth Century* (Cambridge: Cambridge University Press, 1975).

Chapple, J. A. V., *Science and Literature in the Nineteenth Century* (Basingstoke: Macmillan, 1986).

Christie, John and Shuttleworth, Sally, eds., *Nature Transfigured: Science and Literature 1700–1900* (Manchester: Manchester University Press, 1989).

Curran, Stuart, ed., *The Cambridge Companion to British Romanticism*, 2nd edn (Cambridge: Cambridge University Press, 2010).

Dale, P. A., *In Pursuit of a Scientific Culture: Science, Art and Society in the Victorian Age* (Madison: University of Wisconsin Press, 1989).

Davie, Donald, *The Heyday of Sir Walter Scott* (London: Routledge, 1961).

Heilman, Ann, *New Woman Fiction* (Basingstoke: Macmillan, 2000).

Hemmings, F. W. J., ed., *The Age of Realism* (London: Penguin, 1974).

Honour, Hugh, *Romanticism* (London: Allen Lane, 1979).

Houghton, Walter E., *The Victorian Frame of Mind* (New Haven, CT: Yale University Press, 1985).

Larsen, Timothy, *Crisis of Doubt: Honest Faith in Nineteenth-Century England* (Oxford; Oxford University Press, 2008).

Levine, George, *Realism, Ethics and Secularism: Essays on Victorian Literature and Science* (Cambridge: Cambridge University Press, 2008).

Rossel, S. H., *A History of Scandinavian Literature, 1870–1980* (Minneapolis: University of Minnesota Press, 1982).

Terras, Victor, ed., *Handbook of Russian Literature* (New Haven, CT: Yale University Press, 1985).

Vance, Norman, *Bible and Novel: Narrative Authority and the Death of God* (Oxford: Oxford University Press, 2013).

Wu, Duncan, ed., *A Companion to Romanticism* (Oxford: Blackwell, 1998).

Cambridge Companions to ...

AUTHORS

Edward Albee edited by Stephen J. Bottoms

Margaret Atwood edited by Coral Ann Howells

W. H. Auden edited by Stan Smith

Jane Austen edited by Edward Copeland and Juliet McMaster (second edition)

Balzac edited by Owen Heathcote and Andrew Watts

Beckett edited by John Pilling

Bede edited by Scott DeGregorio

Aphra Behn edited by Derek Hughes and Janet Todd

Walter Benjamin edited by David S. Ferris

William Blake edited by Morris Eaves

Boccaccio edited by Guyda Armstrong, Rhiannon Daniels and Stephen J. Milner

Jorge Luis Borges edited by Edwin Williamson

Brecht edited by Peter Thomson and Glendyr Sacks (second edition)

The Brontës edited by Heather Glen

Bunyan edited by Anne Dunan-Page

Frances Burney edited by Peter Sabor

Byron edited by Drummond Bone

Albert Camus edited by Edward J. Hughes

Willa Cather edited by Marilee Lindemann

Cervantes edited by Anthony J. Cascardi

Chaucer edited by Piero Boitani and Jill Mann (second edition)

Chekhov edited by Vera Gottlieb and Paul Allain

Kate Chopin edited by Janet Beer

Caryl Churchill edited by Elaine Aston and Elin Diamond

Cicero edited by Catherine Steel

Coleridge edited by Lucy Newlyn

Wilkie Collins edited by Jenny Bourne Taylor

Joseph Conrad edited by J. H. Stape

H. D. edited by Nephie J. Christodoulides and Polina Mackay

Dante edited by Rachel Jacoff (second edition)

Daniel Defoe edited by John Richetti

Don DeLillo edited by John N. Duvall

Charles Dickens edited by John O. Jordan

Emily Dickinson edited by Wendy Martin

John Donne edited by Achsah Guibbory

Dostoevskii edited by W. J. Leatherbarrow

Theodore Dreiser edited by Leonard Cassuto and Claire Virginia Eby

John Dryden edited by Steven N. Zwicker

W. E. B. Du Bois edited by Shamoon Zamir

George Eliot edited by George Levine and Nancy Henry (second edition)

T. S. Eliot edited by A. David Moody

Ralph Ellison edited by Ross Posnock

Ralph Waldo Emerson edited by Joel Porte and Saundra Morris

William Faulkner edited by Philip M. Weinstein

Henry Fielding edited by Claude Rawson

F. Scott Fitzgerald edited by Ruth Prigozy

Flaubert edited by Timothy Unwin

E. M. Forster edited by David Bradshaw

Benjamin Franklin edited by Carla Mulford

Brian Friel edited by Anthony Roche

Robert Frost edited by Robert Faggen

Gabriel García Márquez edited by Philip Swanson

Elizabeth Gaskell edited by Jill L. Matus

Edward Gibbon edited by Karen O'Brien and Brian Young

Goethe edited by Lesley Sharpe

Günter Grass edited by Stuart Taberner

Thomas Hardy edited by Dale Kramer

David Hare edited by Richard Boon

Nathaniel Hawthorne edited by Richard Millington

Seamus Heaney edited by Bernard O'Donoghue

Ernest Hemingway edited by Scott Donaldson

Homer edited by Robert Fowler

Horace edited by Stephen Harrison

Ted Hughes edited by Terry Gifford

Ibsen edited by James McFarlane

Henry James edited by Jonathan Freedman

Samuel Johnson edited by Greg Clingham

Ben Jonson edited by Richard Harp and Stanley Stewart

James Joyce edited by Derek Attridge (second edition)

Kafka edited by Julian Preece

Keats edited by Susan J. Wolfson

Rudyard Kipling edited by Howard J. Booth

Lacan edited by Jean-Michel Rabaté